W9-CCV-521

The Civic Mission
in Educational Reform

Education and Society

Gerald A. Dorfman, general editor

Publications in the Education and Society series, a research project of the Hoover Institution on War, Revolution and Peace, address issues of education's role in social, economic, and political affairs. It is hoped that insight into the relationship between inculcated values and behavior and a society's approach to development will contribute to more effective education for the establishment and preservation of justice, freedom, and peace.

The Civic Mission
in Educational Reform

PERSPECTIVES FOR THE PUBLIC
AND THE PROFESSION

R. Freeman Butts

HOOVER INSTITUTION PRESS

Stanford University   Stanford, California

Hoover Press Publication 377

First printing, 1989
95 94 93 92 91 90 89   9 8 7 6 5 4 3 2 1
Simultaneous first paperback printing, 1989
95 94 93 92 91 90 89   9 8 7 6 5 4 3 2 1

Manufactured in the United States of America
Printed on acid-free paper

Library of Congress Cataloging in Publication Data
Butts, R. Freeman (Robert Freeman), 1910–
    The civic mission in educational reform.

    (Education and society)
    (Hoover Press publication ; 377)
    Includes index.
    1. Civics—Study and teaching—United States.
2. Education—United States—Aims and objectives.
3. Public schools—United States—Curricula.   I. Title.
II. Series.
LB1584.B84   1989   370.11'5   88-32015
ISBN 0-8179-8771-1 (alk. paper)
ISBN 0-8179-8772-X (pbk : alk. paper)

*For the late Paul R. Hanna,
long-time friend, colleague,
and sometime sparring partner
without whom this book—
quite literally—would not
have been written*

Contents

Foreword

Paul R. Hanna, the founder of the Hanna Collection on the Role of Education in Twentieth-Century Society and of this Education and Society series, passed away in 1988. It is especially fitting that this volume, which is the last he coedited, is authored by R. Freeman Butts, his good friend and colleague.

"J" Butts (as he is known to his many friends) and Paul Hanna knew each other at Columbia University's Teachers College and at Stanford University. In recent years, they worked together at the Hoover Institution, where Paul was a senior research fellow and "J" a visiting scholar with the Hanna collection.

During these last years Freeman Butts began intensive work to reform the teaching of civic education. Paul Hanna was enthusiastic about these efforts and pleased when they gained a significant place in the debate about the reform of education in this country. Both scholars have believed strongly in the importance of revitalizing the civic mission of education. Paul Hanna was convinced that what happens in the classroom today, as well as in the larger formal and informal educational process, directly affects the course of societal development. Deeply concerned that our schools were not successfully teaching the important shared values that underpin and bolster our democracy, his support for "J" Butts's work fits well into the establishment and continuing growth of the Hanna Collection on the Role of Education in Twentieth-Century

Society. Paul Hanna worked tirelessly to collect the archives of individual leaders and organizations so that scholars like "J" Butts could research and write about the role of education in hopes that the fruits of this work would contribute to the development of a strong, democratic society and a more peaceful and developing world community.

The Hanna collection and its Education and Society series will continue to pursue Paul Hanna's important purpose, as exemplified in this fine study by R. Freeman Butts.

GERALD A. DORFMAN

Preface

In 1980 the Phi Delta Kappa Educational Foundation published *The Revival of Civic Learning,* which I had written as a personal statement at the invitation of Stanley Elam, then editor of *The Kappan.* That slim volume was primarily addressed to the educational profession in the hope that teachers and administrators in the public schools would take more seriously their historic mission to educate oncoming generations for their role as citizens in the American Republic.

In it, I reported briefly on some of my experiences during the late 1970s, which led me to the view that the wounds of Vietnam, Watergate, and campus unrest could not be healed by halfway measures. I argued for a wholesale effort to revitalize teaching and learning, the curriculum, and the governance of schools.

The response to that book was positive but underwhelming—or so it seemed to me. It did attract the attention of a few key educational leaders who encouraged me to keep addressing the theme. In this book I refer gratefully to some of them. Here, I simply mention those who have been most sustaining and encouraging since 1980.

David Mathews, president of the Charles F. Kettering Foundation, has honored me with a Kettering Senior Fellow appointment and thus enabled me to participate actively in organizing the Council for the Advancement of Citizenship, to serve on its board of directors, and to chair its Jennings Randolph Forum. Charles Quigley, executive director of the Law in a Free Society project of the Center for Civic Education, has repeatedly involved me in its work. And Paul Hanna and Gerald Dorfman, fellows of the Hoover Institution of Stanford University, have made it possible for me to continue my research and writing as a visiting scholar at Hoover. They prompted me to write this book for their "Education and Society" series.

This book draws heavily on *The Revival of Civic Learning* and the works I have produced at Stanford since its publication. But the focus has changed in major ways, largely as a result of the remarkable expansion of interest in educational reform that was forecast in the 1980 report of the Rockefeller Foundation Commission on the Humanities and Mortimer Adler's *The Paideia Proposal,* published in 1982. This issue exploded on the public scene with the publication of the report of the National Commission on Excellence in Education in 1983. With a few notable exceptions mentioned in Chapter 1, however, the civic mission of education was muted or even wholly ignored in the many reports and reform efforts that blossomed at national, state, and local levels in the mid- to late 1980s.

So this book is designed to be not so much a personal statement as grist for serious examination by policymakers shaping the role of education in American society. The focus is specifically on education for citizenship in the schools within the broader realm of public policy in education. The audience this time, I hope, will include not only the educational profession but also the many crucial policy leaders who have become convinced that the economic and political future of the United States pivots on its improvement of education. I have no illusions that the book will be read by the president or his cabinet (whoever they may be after 1988), Supreme Court justices, members of Congress, state governors and legislators, or corporate or union managers. But, perhaps, it may come to the attention of some staff members of such leaders and to the hundreds of faculty committees, boards of education, task forces, and textbook writers and publishers grappling with the details of educational content and curriculum.

I do not mean to imply that this is a handbook or curriculum guide. Rather, I have tried to bring together relevant scholarly materials that could give some perspective to those seeking to reform education: those who are disgruntled with public education and who are calling on the family to reassert its prerogatives and exercise its choice in education; those who believe education should be deregulated from federal or state authorities and returned to local, religious, ethnic, or private management; or those who are committed to public education as the prime educational agency in preparation for citizenship but who find that mission uncertain, ambiguous, or in conflict with other educational goals.

The three chapters in Part I provide historical perspective on the changing roles of families, schools, and communities in education for citizenship; on the competing claims of civic cohesion, pluralism, and modernization; and on the diminishing role of civic purpose in public schooling.

Part II discusses the attempts to revitalize the civic mission of education in recent decades, not only in the schools but in the liberal and professional education of all teachers and administrators. Education at all levels should include improved civic learning if genuine reform is to be embedded in the institutions of American education. This calls for the formulation of a viable conception of citizenship that will see the Republic safely into and through its third century.

The public schools can better serve U.S. democracy if they focus on the public and civic values we share as citizens. They cannot bring all citizens into a common fold of religiously based moral values, no matter how broadly defined. The strength of the democratic polity is that common civic values are supported by differing groups—who base those values in their own particular theology, moral law, or natural law without imposing those grounds of belief on others, especially not through the power of government.

I hope this book will be a modest contribution to the long-range process of probing the meaning of American citizenship and thus building an education that will better fulfill its historic civic mission. My well-thumbed Latin dictionary defines *summa* as follows: "the main thing, chief point, principal matter, sum, essence, substance." So in the belief that Miss Ethel Luke of Springfield High School would continue to forgive my halting translation of English into Latin, I hope this may contribute to the nation's latest effort to formulate a *Summa Educationis Pro Civitati*.

R. Freeman Butts

The Dilemmas of Teaching Civic Values in the Schools of a Pluralist Democracy

The Excellence Movement Overlooks Civic Learning

Since the early 1980s the United States has been inundated by public discussion of the plight of American education. A succession of more than 30 reports by high-level national commissions and task forces, diagnosing the schools and prescribing treatment for their improvement, has touched a remarkably responsive chord among the public. These reports loosed many articles and editorials in the press, commentaries on talk shows, and debates in legislatures as well as in academic and professional circles.

The password for educational reform was most often "excellence," a goal that few in the public or the profession would dispute. Excellence was most often defined in fairly simplistic ways the public could easily understand:

- increasing the number of courses required for graduation from high school, especially in science, mathematics, and computer science (at least 40 states)
- prescribing higher standards of student achievement for promotion from grade to grade and admission to college through more rigorous testing and homework (at least 30 states)
- lengthening the school day and school year
- raising teachers' salaries, especially through merit pay or career ladders to attract and hold more able people in the profession

• upgrading the qualifications of teachers by testing their competency and improving their education (at least 30 states).

Using the arguments these reports provided, the legislative hoppers were filled to overflowing. By the middle 1980s nearly all fifty states were involved in educational reform, whether through legislation or state-level commissions. At least thirty-five states had passed comprehensive school-reform legislation. Sponsorship came from all branches of state government—governors' offices, education departments, and state boards of education as well as legislatures—suggesting a broad scope of interest. The president of the College Board, Donald M. Stewart, estimated in 1987 that as many as two or three hundred state-level task forces had been or were developing forty-five different kinds of reform activities.[1] The volume and momentum of this movement gave promise that it might have more impact than those of the past.

Not only was there considerable action at the state and local levels, but education once again became an important domestic issue on the national political agenda. The National Commission on Excellence in Education, appointed by Secretary of Education Terrel Bell in August 1981, issued its report in April 1983. Meanwhile the Reagan administration had persistently sought to reduce the federal role in education by cutting funds and returning to the states much of the responsibility assumed by the federal government in the prior twenty years of federal educational activism. The publicity given the commission's report tended to stress its opening sentences: "Our nation is at risk. Our once unchallenged preeminence in commerce, industry, science, and technological innovation is being overtaken by competitors throughout the world." This alarum, of course, was attention getting and newsworthy, especially given the state of the economy. It tended to overshadow, however, a little-noticed section that appears later in the report;

> Our concern, however, goes well beyond matters such as industry and commerce. It also includes the intellectual, moral, and spiritual strengths of our people which knit together the very fabric of our society . . . A high level of shared education is essential to a free, democratic society and to the fostering of a common culture, especially in a country that prides itself on pluralism and individual freedom.[2]

This mention of the basic civic purposes of public education was emphatically reaffirmed by the commission's chairman, David P. Gardner, president of the University of California, in his keynote address at the commission's third anniversary conference in April 1986. The first unfinished item of business of the educational-reform movement was to reaffirm that the schools exist primarily to foster intellectual competence and informed citizenship in our free society. They do not exist to respond to every social, political, or single-issue group. The schools must restore a sense of purpose and coherence to foster the skills of citizenship rather than provide a cafeteria of fragmented offerings demanded by special interests. Gardner also stated forcefully that it was more urgent than ever for the federal government to reassert its primary responsibility to identify the national interest in education and protect the constitutional and civil rights of students and teachers.[3] These arguments had been all but ignored in most of the intervening public discussions of the commission's proposals.

Much the same thing happened with the publicity surrounding the Twentieth Century Fund Task Force on Federal Elementary and Secondary Education Policy. Its report not only affirmed the national interest in improving the quality and excellence of education but also reaffirmed the necessity of an active federal role:

> That interest can be asserted and dramatized most effectively by the federal government. The federal government, after all, is charged with providing for the security and well-being of our democratic society, which rest largely on a strong and competent system of public education. It is in the best position to focus public attention on the vital importance of quality in our schools and to support its attainment. The federal government should be able to foster excellence in education, serving as a firm but gentle goad to states and local communities without impeding or restricting state and local control of and accountability for the schools.[4]

This task force departed still further from Reagan administration policy when it opposed tuition tax credits and vouchers for use in private schools and called public schools "the nation's most important institution for the shaping of future citizens." It held that "the provision of free public education must continue to be a public responsibility of high priority, while support of nonpublic education should remain a private obligation."[5] President Reagan, however, has continued throughout his tenure to reaffirm his support for prayer in the public schools and tax credits and vouchers for parents who send their children to private schools. This agenda was reinforced after 1985 when William J. Bennett became secretary of education.

In contrast, the report of the Carnegie Foundation for the Advancement of Teaching, written by its president, Ernest L. Boyer, called for recognizing the importance of public education for the country's well-being: "There is a growing national consensus that our future depends on public education . . . It is in the public school that this nation has chosen to pursue enlightened ends for all its people. And this is where the battle for the future of America will be won or lost.[6]

It is not surprising that the reports of the National Task Force on Education for Economic Growth, the Business-Higher Education Forum, the Committee for Economic Development, or the National Science Board Commission should stress science, mathematics, and computer literacy in their efforts to promote greater productivity in jobs and the economy. But it is disheartening when public attention is not focused on a forthright recognition of the basic civic purposes of free, universal, compulsory, and common schooling; namely, to prepare informed, rational, and humane citizens for participation in a democratic republic. Most of the national commission reports made little of this purpose, but even when they did mention it in passing, the public discussion was most often focused elsewhere. The Committee for Economic Development came closer to the mark when it cogently urged the business community and federal government to strengthen massive public education programs aimed especially at the young children of the poor and disadvantaged.[7]

Of the several major reports that appeared in the early 1980s, the civic purpose of education was prominent in only a few: the 1980 report of the Rockefeller Foundation Commission on the *The Humanities in American Life,* Mortimer Adler's *The Paideia Proposal* in 1982, Ernest Boyer's reports for the Carnegie Foundation, and the Twentieth Century Fund report on federal education policy. But the public commentary and discussion did little to make explicit or operational the substantive ideas that would give highest priority to the civic mission of American education.

When the report of the Twentieth Century Fund Task Force was announced, the front-page story of the *New York Times* on May 6, 1983, played up the report's recommendation that federal bilingual-education funds be shifted to teaching English to non-English-speaking children. Little attention was given to the forthright recommendation for a core program for all students, which should include a "knowledge of civics, or what Aristotle called the education of the citizenry in the spirit of the polity." And less attention was given to the civic reasons why the task force stressed the primacy of English:

> Our political democracy rests on our conviction that each citizen should have the capacity to participate fully in our political life; to read newspapers, magazines, and books; to bring a critical intelligence to

television and radio; to be capable of resisting emotional manipulation and of setting events within their historical perspective; to express ideas and opinions about public affairs; and to vote thoughtfully—all activities that call for literacy in English.[8]

Boyer's Carnegie Foundation report went even further, saying that the mastery of reading, speaking, and writing English is the "first and most essential goal of education." It recommended mandatory core curriculum for all high school students, linked English with history (of the United States and world civilization) and civics (government) as the dominant elements of education required for citizenship. By comparison, mathematics and science were viewed as specialist subjects. In these respects Boyer's Carnegie report came closer than several other reports to Mortimer Adler's *The Paideia Proposal,* which called for a common prescribed curriculum.[9]

The lack of attention to the civic purposes of education in the national reports applies as well to most of the widely acclaimed reports by individual educators. A few examples must suffice. John I. Goodlad's eight-year study of more than one thousand classrooms, reported in *A Place Called School,* did recommend that school districts assure the presence in each school of a comprehensive curriculum encompassing academic, citizenship, vocational, and personal goals.[10] The study's main impact on the public discussion, however, has been to show that the most effective schools are those in which extensive dialogue is carried on among the teachers and principals at the local district and building levels regarding curriculum goals. Surveys of parents revealed the civic goal lags far behind the academic, and students voted the social studies at or near the bottom of their interest level. This leaves the civic goal in a kind a limbo, resting on the ideas, vision, and commitment of the principals and teaching staff of particular schools. The effective-schools movement seems to have had little success in defining or refining the civic goal of U.S. education.

Another widely heralded study leaves the matter even more ambiguous. In *Horace's Compromise,* Theodore Sizer does include "civic understanding" along with literacy and numeracy as minimal competences to be expected of all young people:

Civic understanding means a grasp of the basis for consensual democratic government, a respect for its processes, and acceptance of the restraints and obligations incumbent on a citizen. These restraints and obligations are eloquently summarized in the Bill of Rights. One need not go much further: if all American citizens had mastered at the least the complex principles there, this would be a more just society.[11]

Further, he would organize the high school into four areas or large departments: inquiry and expression, mathematics and science, literature and the arts, and philosophy and history. For most high school students the disciplines of geography, economics, and sociology should be the handmaidens of history, but moral and political philosophy should have a special place:

> A political philosophy, essentially that of American constitutionalism, is the bedrock of enlightened democratic citizenship, and adolescence, more than any other stage of life, is filled with a search for values. The study of elementary ethics, for example, not only provides excellent opportunities for learning intellectual skills, but also powerfully engages students' interests.[12]

Sizer's ambiguity regarding civic purpose arises from his overwhelming emphasis on the intellectual goals of education and his fascination with "character" as an inescapable purpose of schools. These seem to have prior claims on his attention. In his DeGarmo Lecture delivered about the time his book came out in 1984, Sizer said, "The overriding central purpose of schooling for adolescents should be to help them to use their minds well. That is, the pre-eminent, if not the exclusive, purpose of high school education is intellectual.[13]

When asked what special role for civic learning he saw for the schools and for teacher education, Sizer replied that he saw none. If schools concentrate on their intellectual and academic tasks, the civic education of citizens will take care of itself. He sought no government role in developing civic virtue. This general view permeated the conclusions of the two succeeding volumes in his overall project, "A Study of High Schools," sponsored by the National Association of Secondary School Principals and the Commission on Educational Issues of the National Association of Independent Schools.[14] It remains to be seen whether the "Coalition of Essential Schools," formed among a dozen public and private schools to try out Sizer's ideas with considerable foundation support, will become as interested in the civic preparation of their students as with their academic and personal goals. Will "reading, writing, and reasoning" take care of citizenship?

Apparently the College Board's "Project Educational Equality" thought so. It defined the goals of high school preparation for college as reading, writing, speaking and listening, mathematical ability, reasoning, and studying. The College Board's recommendations for the six academic subjects to develop these six intellectual skills commendably stress a balance between the humanities and the sciences, but the civic learning required of prospective college students to prepare them for citizenship seemed muted at best. Civic values were entirely absent from the discussion of the social studies.[15]

The stream of books, articles, and reports by individuals places much the same stress on the intellectual and academic ingredients of the "excellence movement" as do the reports of the formal commissions and task forces. With a few notable exceptions to be mentioned later, the explicit goal of citizenship was vague or absent.

A case in point is the Educational Excellence Network, organized in 1982 by Chester E. Finn, Jr., of Vanderbilt University and Diane Ravitch of Teachers College, Columbia University. Its purpose is described in a letter soliciting membership:

> We are pleased to invite you to join the EDUCATIONAL EXCEL-LENCE NETWORK, an informal group of education scholars, policy makers, practitioners and others whose chief interest is in fostering educational excellence, primarily at the elementary/secondary level. We are linked by the belief that schools can be orderly, effective and exhilarating places in which children learn to write clearly, to read critically, and to reason logically; where they absorb the essential teachings of the major academic subjects, sharpen their intellects through rigorous thinking, and accustom themselves to high standards; and where they acquire sound character in an atmosphere that is respectful of individual differences, appreciative of the arts, and attentive to physical health and civic responsibility.

"Civic responsibility" is the last of the stated interests, and it finds relatively little attention among the hundreds of magazine articles, books, and newspaper clippings the group has circulated in the past few years. The network's members numbered more than nine hundred by February 1987, after Finn's appointment as assistant secretary of education and the move of the group's headquarters in June 1985 to Teachers College. There it has continued under the direction of Professor Ravitch. In her view the network's essential prerequisites for school improvement, stated in the newsletter of November 1985, are "a pursuit of higher academic expectations; a strong commitment to a curriculum of liberal arts and sciences for all children; a cheerful, orderly school environment; and well-educated teachers."

The one-hundred or so pages representing thirty to forty articles, that the network sends its members monthly form a remarkable collection of studies, research, and opinions about school improvement. They confirm my own view that the civic purposes of education have received little attention in the public, professional, or academic press. Perusal of the network's reprints from 1984 to 1987 reveals quite a few articles devoted to character education, moral education, and values education, all of which indeed have a bearing on citizenship, but only a handful addressed citizenship explicitly. These include Sidney Hook's "Education in Defense of a Free Society"; excerpts from speeches by William J. Bennett as secretary of education regarding civic virtue and study of the common values of Western civilization; an excerpt from an article by Stephan Thernstrom on "Ethnicity and E Pluribus Unum"; an article by Morris Janowitz on "The Good Citizen: A Threatened Species?" based on his book *The Reconstruction of Patriotism;* an article by Christopher Lasch on the moral and civic elements in excellence; a short piece by E. D. Hirsch, Jr., on "Cultural Literacy"; two articles on civic education in the *Christian Science Monitor*—one by Bob Marquand of the *Monitor* and one by myself; and my article on "A History and Civics Lesson for All of Us."

In addition to the reprints, the network's monthly newsletter mentions reports or books that might interest the newsletter's readers. From 1984 to 1987, these newsletters mention only a few reports or books explicitly aimed at civic education. They are *Teaching About Federal Democracy* (edited by Ellis Katz), published by the Center for the Study of Federalism at Temple University; *Democracy at Risk: The Rising Tide of Political Illiteracy and Ignorance of the Constitution* (by Jerry Combee of Baptist Liberty College), published by the Center for Judicial Studies; and *Civic Learning for Teachers: Capstone for Educational Reform* (edited by Alan Jones), published by Prakken Publications of Ann Arbor, Michigan. (This last work is the report of the seminar held on this topic at the Hoover Institution.) One newsletter also mentioned the bicentennial competition launched by the Center for Civic Education.[16]

It is important to note that the early writings of the leaders of the Educational Excellence Network did not explicitly emphasize the theme of democratic citizenship. One of Ravitch and Finn's joint interests had been the role of the humanities in secondary education. The book of papers that resulted from two conferences sponsored by the National Endowment for the Humanities while William J. Bennett was chairman does not pursue the predominantly civic theme so apparent in the report of the Rockefeller Commission on the Humanities. Amherst's president, Peter R. Pouncey, argues that prospective teachers should study political theory (Plato, Hobbes, Locke, and Marx) as well as language, literature, history, and science. But aside from this, the book as a whole makes few references to the role of the humanities in imparting to all students the "profoundly liberal idea necessary for a free society and a democratic polity."

But in their conclusion editors Finn and Ravitch argue that the phrase "social studies" should be banished from the high school curriculum in favor of chronological history:

> What should be taught and learned is history, and this must consist fundamentally of the history of the United States, the enveloping history of Western civilization, and the parallel history of non-Western civilizations. . . . Properly conceived, history includes the history of ideas, cultural developments, and social, political, and economic movements. It includes the evolution of diverse cultures and the changing relationships among peoples, races, religions, and beliefs. Everything worth learning that is commonly found under the rubric of "social studies" can be taught and learned as history, but only if it is taught and learned in an essentially chronological framework can the student emerge with a sense of how he and his society came to be what they are at the present time. And only with that understanding of the past can the student reasonably hope to know where and how he would like himself and his society to be in the future—or what is entailed in getting there.[17]

I believe in chronological history, having taught history that way for forty years. But I also believe that some types of chronological history are more valuable for developing the knowledge and values of democratic citizenship than others. Much depends on the selection of materials, and even more depends on the scholarship and civic values the teachers display. Finn and Ravitch say little about such matters. And their parting shot about social studies alienates a large and important body of teachers organized under the banner of the National Council for the Social Studies. Many would argue that a blanket condemnation of social studies does not serve the cause of improving the civic knowledge, values, or skills that U.S. youth need to contribute to the democratic ideals America proclaims. Both chronological history and the social studies should be evaluated by these criteria.

The leadership of the Excellence Network seemed to recognize this point when the network joined Freedom House (a national organization that monitors civil liberties around the world) in sponsoring the Education for Democracy project, initiated in 1985 by the American Federation of Teachers. The consequent *Statement of Principles* the AFT issued in May 1987 was signed by 150 leaders, reflecting a wide spectrum of outlooks in public life, the media, and the professions as well as in academic and educational institutions. It focuses directly on elevating the role of schools in the purposeful imparting to students of an informed, reasoned allegiance to the ideals of a free and democratic society.

This statement rests on three convictions:

First, that democracy is the worthiest form of human governance ever conceived.

Second, that we cannot take its survival or its spread—or its perfection in practice—for granted. Indeed, we believe that the great central drama of modern history has been and continues to be the struggle to establish, preserve, and extend democracy—at home and abroad. We know that very much still needs doing to achieve justice and civility in our own society . . .

Third, we are convinced that democracy's survival depends upon our transmitting to each new generation the political vision of liberty and equality that unites us as Americans—and a deep loyalty to the political institutions our founders put together to fulfill that vision.[18]

The statement rejects instruction that smacks of propaganda, "knee-jerk patriotic drill," indoctrination, "pious texts," or censorship. It calls for an "objective and balanced picture of world realities, historical and contemporary" as well as critical thinking based on a solid base of factual knowledge. To these ends, every citizen needs to know the fundamental ideas central to the political vision of the founders and the historical background of their views, how the ideas were turned into political institutions and practices, their weaknesses and challenges to them, and the current condition of the world. The statement adds: "For intelligent citizenship, we need a thoroughgoing grasp of the daily workings of our own society, as well as the societies of our friends, of our adversaries, and of the Third World, where so many live amid poverty and violence, with little freedom and little hope."[19]

The statement concludes with a reaffirmation of the study of history as "the chief subject in education for democracy." But it stops short of the earlier unequivocal condemnation of "social studies" by Finn and Ravitch. Rather, it puts history as the central core and integrative element in social studies, to which are added geography, the humanities, and world studies.

The AFT's statement makes a significant step forward by bringing to public attention the necessity for explicitly stressing civic values in schools. It attracted widespread comment in editorial and op-ed columns, both conservative and liberal. The broad ideological and political spectrum of the signatories helped call the public's attention to one of the basic weaknesses of the educational-reform movement.

But the statement still had a major flaw. It alienated major elements of those in the educational profession who have the primary responsibility for teaching history and the social studies. It refers disparagingly, and out of context, to certain passages in a bulletin of the National Council for the Social Studies on International Human Rights which, the statement claims, expressed views of political and moral neutrality rather than praising the democratic system of the United States and condemning the undemocratic systems of China and the Soviet Union. This aroused suspicions that the framers actually had a hidden conservative agenda, both politically and educationally. As a result, few social studies professionals signed the statement, and several members of the newly organized National Commission on the Social Studies pointedly declined to do so. The longer term significance of the statement was thus jeopardized, and the possibility of forming a national consensus on the basic civic mission of American schools could be lessened. Marshaling a list of prominent names—in which the accident of the alphabet brings together Terrel Bell and William Bennett, Norman Lear and Ernest W. Lefever, and Anthony Podesta and Norman Podhoretz—will not easily convince a major professional body of key teachers, especially if they are unnecessarily alienated at the outset. The search for common ground suffers.

At about the same time the AFT issued the *Statement of Principles,* a widely publicized book found general acclaim. *Cultural Literacy,* by E. D. Hirsch, Jr., English professor at the University of Virginia, might debilitate the effort to promote *civic* literacy in the schools in a quite different way. Admiring the classical secondary school curriculum of the Committee of Ten of 1893 and deploring the Cardinal Principles of Education of 1918 (including its goal of citizenship), Hirsch designates Jean-Jacques Rousseau, John Dewey, and the "romantic progressives" as the culprits who caused the fragmentation of the solid, informative curriculum of a hundred years ago. This was the familiar argument of critics of progressive education in the 1950s. Even worse, according to Hirsch, are the language formalists in schools of education who have stressed the skill of reading over the cultural content that makes literacy possible:

> Literacy requires the early and continued transmission of specific information. Dewey was deeply mistaken to disdain "accumulating information in the form of symbols . . ." Only by accumulating shared symbols, and the shared information that the symbols represent, can we learn to communicate effectively with one another in our national community.[20]

One can agree with the generalization concerning the relationship between symbols and information, but still questionable is whether the list of nearly five thousand items printed alphabetically in the book's appendix pays enough attention to civic symbols that unite us into a national community. The subtitle of the book proclaims *What Every American Needs to Know,* but the appendix is more modest in stating "What Literate Americans Know: A Preliminary List." The list contains geographical names, historical events, famous people, patriotic lore, common phrases, grammatical and rhetorical terms, literary allusions, and a special note on scientific terms. Hirsch admits that anyone with special interests will find faults with the specific list. The list could not form the basis of curriculum reform to strengthen our "national community"; its political, civic, and constitutional symbols and concepts are fairly well buried in the avalanche of bits of "cultural" information.

Hirsch's invocation of America's founders comes in the last paragraph of his book rather than at the beginning, where he pays his respects to the influence of Secretary of Education Bennett, Diane Ravitch, Chester Finn, and others. In that last paragraph he says:

> I hope that in our future debates about the extensive curriculum, the participants will keep clearly in view the high stakes involved in their deliberations: breaking the cycle of illiteracy for deprived children; raising the living standard of families who have been illiterate; making our country more competitive in international markets; achieving greater social justice; enabling all citizens to participate in the political process; bringing us closer to the Ciceronian ideal of universal public discourse—in short, achieving fundamental goals of the Founders at the birth of the republic.[21]

Spreading "cultural literacy," as defined in the seventy pages of Hirsch's list, would not be as useful for strengthening the American democratic community as would the kind of curriculum reform advocated by the AFT *Statement of Principles* or by the reforms I advocate here and elsewhere. The national vocabulary of all U.S. citizens should give greater attention to the civic values and symbols underlying our constitutional order. Hirsch relies too easily on a simplistic history of education and on a general condemnation of schools of education and of the reading textbooks written by educationists. Again, he unnecessarily alienates professional educators by not distinguishing among better or worse schools of education, or indeed the variety of views within schools of education. He does not mention that all the historians of education on whom he relies are professors in schools of education and achieved their advanced degrees through schools of education.

It will be interesting to see what comes from the Cultural Literacy Foundation established by Hirsch to draw up standardized tests of general knowledge and to award a "Good Housekeeping-type seal of approval" to textbooks that aim to improve the cultural literacy of students. The tests would be designed to influence the curriculum in schools but not the methods of teaching. The board of directors of the new foundation includes Hirsch; Diane Ravitch; Ernest L. Boyer; James M. Cooper, dean of education at the University of Virginia; Robert L. Payton, associate director of the White Burkett Miller Center of Public Affairs at Virginia; and Bernard Gifford, dean of education at the University of California at Berkeley.[22]

It will also be interesting to discover what yet another commission on the humanities in elementary and secondary schools will recommend concerning civic values. The chairman of the National Endowment for the Humanities, Lynne V. Cheney, appointed a twenty-seven-member panel in February 1987. It included Professors Hirsch and Ravitch, college and high school teachers and administrators, and such noted historians as Daniel Boorstin and Gordon Wood. Cheney made a point of saying that 1987 would be a good time to assess how well the schools are conveying our country's heritage to the next generation. At about the same time, representatives of five professional subject-matter organizations met to consider ways they could play a greater role in the reform of teacher education and certification. They obviously felt they had been neglected so far. Their organizations constituted the principal affiliations for teachers of English, reading, social studies, mathematics, and science.[23] The fires of reform were still being stoked.

Meanwhile, the June 1987 newsletter of the Educational Excellence Network gave top billing, with grudging and faint praise, to two new publications having clear civic significance for the social studies. One was an evaluation of eighteen textbooks on civics and government sponsored by People for the American Way,[24] and the other a pronouncement on the importance of international studies by a nineteen-member commission on global education sponsored by the Exxon, Ford, and Rockefeller foundations.[25]

The textbook study was undertaken by a six-member panel of political scientists and educators, headed by James D. Carroll of the Brookings Institution and including the executive director of the American Political Science Association, Thomas E. Mann. The report's most important aspect was the fourfold criteria used for evaluation. The panel looked for how well the books covered necessary political material, including controversial issues; how well they engaged the student intellectually and emotionally; and how well they dealt with the interrelationships between the branches of government, between citizens and the government, and between the United States and the international community. But they also looked for how well the books covered the Constitution and its themes: the meaning, interpretation, and application of the Constitution throughout U.S. history, including constitutional principles embodied in the Bill of Rights and challenges to constitutional liberties and freedoms, especially in ways that enabled students to relate them to their own lives. If textbook writers took these criteria seriously, civic education would be well served. These political scientists reversed the role that some of their predecessors played in shaping earlier school textbooks, as pointed out in Chapters 4 and 5.

The global perspectives commission was headed by Clark Kerr, John Goodlad, and Harlan Cleveland, and included a notable roster of leading academics, educators, and public figures. Taken seriously, and without the preconceived antipathy held by many conservatives toward the connotations of the term *globalism,* the study gives much-needed attention to citizenship education in the United States (see Chapter 7).

It is impossible to canvass the literature of educational reform to substantiate statistically the relative neglect of civic learning in the early years of the educational-reform movement. However, if you inspect perhaps the most extensive source on the reform movement up to 1985—*The Great School Debate,* edited by Beatrice Gross and Ronald Gross and containing 64 articles in 544 pages—you can find only implications regarding education for citizenship.[26] The theme does not make itself explicit. The same could be said for another collection of essays, *Challenge to American Schools,* edited by John H. Bunzel and also published in 1985.[27]

Although the same theme is not explicit in the statements of most state governors or state superintendents of schools, you cannot miss it in a book by Bill Honig, California state superintendent of public instruction, called *Last Chance for Our Children.* In his persuasive tract on behalf of what he candidly calls a conservative tradition in education, Honig projects the three main purposes of public education in easily understandable terms: to prepare all youth as workers, as citizens, and as private persons. These are by no means original, but in contrast to much other writing by public officials, Honig keeps the idea of citizenship in the forefront of nearly all his public statements and official efforts.[28]

What follows is one more—and an especially intriguing—example of the muting of the civic theme and the dilemma of civic learning in a pluralistic society. In 1980 the National Academy of Education launched a two-year study of the "Value Assumptions Underlying American Educational Policy and Practice," with funding from the National Endowment for the Humanities and the Lilly Endowment. This project was headed by Stephen K. Bailey, then president of the National Academy and a long-time advocate of civic education while teaching political science at Wesleyan, Princeton, Syracuse, and Harvard. Bailey's early draft of chapters on essential values and the essential curriculum reflected his mature views on the political and social goals of education in relation to the national purpose. Bailey, however, died in March 1982, and the book that was finally finished by the other project staff members, *An Education of Value,* did not appear until 1985. Marvin Lazerson, later to become dean of education at the University of Pennsylvania, became the lead author.[29]

But missing in the book's final form was most of Bailey's vision of the civic values that should be embedded in an essential curriculum. The themes defining the purposes of education became "imaginative expression" and "critical thinking." There was general affirmation of the importance of citizenship, but the book centered on such specific problems as urbanism, tracking, class, race, ethnicism, immigration, vocation, IQ, ability grouping, bureaucratization, and the like. Important as such issues are, they cannot replace a coherent view of citizenship and civic values.

Whatever the reasons for the change of emphasis after Bailey's death, it certainly encapsulates the widespread dilemma illustrated in this chapter. When the project began in 1980, a panel consisting mostly of members of the National Academy was appointed to advise Bailey and his project staff. Bailey had this to say about the panel's first meeting:

> The most interesting struggle within the panel is between those who believe that our major problem is too much *pluribus,* and those who believe we have too much *unum* at too low a level (pop culture, TV, etc.). The main line of the staff's thinking at the moment is that both problems are serious. In the field of education alone there is very little coherence about value priorities (witness the current struggles over desegregation, bilingualism, vouchers, tuition tax credits, vocationalism, sex education, evolution, minimum competencies). And there has certainly been a drop in creativity, standards, and a sense of community in the civic sense. Our main job is to explicate these difficult and tangled areas and then to say something constructive about where we go from here.[30]

Apparently the tug to *pluribus* won in the final publication. Had Bailey lived to see the project through to publication at the time when other major reports were being issued, it might have had a remarkable influence in making the civic mission of education a highly visible priority in the reform movement and in the public and academic discussion of the mid-1980s. As it was, *An Education of Value* received relatively little notice.

There is no way of knowing whether a few more powerful voices on behalf of civic values might have had greater influence on some key proposals for reform made in the 1980s. But at least one other opportunity was lost. *The Nation's Report Card*—the report of a group appointed by Secretary of Education Bennett to study assessment of student achievement—was issued in March 1987. The group's chairman was Lamar Alexander, governor of Tennessee; the vice-chairman and study director was H. Thomas James, former dean of education at Stanford and president emeritus of the Spencer Foundation. One of this groups major recommendations was that the National Assessment of Educational Progress (NAEP) begin including history, geography, and civics along with reading, writing, literacy, mathematics, science, and technology as part of the nation's core curriculum to be measured regularly. The report says:

> We strongly urge that these assessments [history, geography, and civics] move beyond simple measurements of factual knowledge toward the assessment of more complex thinking skills. Achievement in such areas as history and civics, for example, may require not only a command of facts but also an ability to pose and analyze a well-conceived problem, often one of value judgments of some subtlety.[31]

But this is about all the report says about civic values. The group's report does not take much account of the excellent paper it asked James P. Shaver, a noted leader in social studies, to write on the "National Assessment of Values and Attitudes for Social Studies." Shaver argued that the "centering concept" of social studies should be citizenship education. Yet the report studiously avoids the term *social studies* in favor of history, geography, and civics. At least a major principle regarding value judgments as an essential part of civic knowledge in a core curriculum had been asserted.

The second part of *The Nation's Report Card* is a commentary by a panel of the National Academy of Education, chaired by Robert Glaser of the University of Pittsburgh, a former chairman of the academy. The opening paragraph sounds as though the panel might take another step toward making civic learning a fundamental, explicit, and central element in any future national assessment program.

> Schools play a critical role in our society. In forming that educated citizenry necessary for the sustenance and growth of our democratic

charter, schools provide the foundation on which our nation rests. This observation is of longstanding historical merit, although it is now largely ignored in public discussions about schools. Current discourse is dominated by a narrow utilitarian conception of purpose that sees the aims of schooling principally as advancing the ability to compete in the world marketplace. We must be always mindful, however, of the broader purposes that schools serve and the real threat that weak schools pose. Quite simply, no democracy can long survive that does not assure its children an education that allows them to take full advantage of the freedom and opportunities which a democracy offers.[32]

The panel then strongly endorses the expansion of NAEP to include regular assessments of history, civics, and geography along with the other basic skills. But then the report grows less explicit about citizenship education, referring simply to needed but difficult assessments in the "aesthetic and moral aims" of education:

Those personal qualities that we hold dear—resilience and courage in the face of stress, a sense of craft in our work, a commitment to justice and caring in our social relationships, a dedication to advancing the public good in our communal life—are exceedingly difficult to assess. And so, unfortunately, we are apt to measure what we can, and eventually come to value what is measured over what is left unmeasured . . . In neither academic nor popular discourse about schools does one find nowadays much reference to the important human qualities noted above. The language of academic achievement tests has become the primary rhetoric of schooling.[33]

Heartening as was the panel's insistence that "higher-order thinking skills" should be developed in the humanities and social studies as well as in mathematics and science, the test-makers will need to pay close attention when they go about their new business. The Academy panel congratulated NAEP for its emphasis on "functional competencies" when it made a recent literacy assessment, for example, writing a letter to correct a billing error, balancing a checkbook, reading a bus schedule or map, or interpreting an appliance warranty. Important as these competencies are in our modern society, such basic literacy should eventually embrace not only economic literacy and cultural literacy but civic literacy, for example, analyzing a political candidate's qualifications; judging the merits of a ballot initiative; weighing the truth and reliability of testimony in a legislative hearing; or estimating the validity of a court's decision on affirmative action, freedom of expression, or religion in education. When such higher-order intellectual skills are tested in history and civics, schools will begin to achieve the goals of civic education attributed to them in the introductory paragraph of the panel's commentary on *The Nation's Report Card*.

The civic purpose did begin to receive increasing attention by leaders in higher education and in teacher education, and there was a good deal of attention to it in various specific projects and curricular programs at the elementary and secondary level. But these movements were not regarded in public discussions as major elements in the so-called educational-reform movement.

Meanwhile, some reports began to stress the need to reform the teaching profession, if school reform was indeed to make real headway. Most of these paid much valuable attention to improving the status, salaries, and functioning of the organized teaching profession, but made little or no mention of the civic or public purposes of teacher education. This applies to the National Commission for Excellence in Teacher Education,[34] the California Commission on the Teaching Profession,[35] and the report of the Holmes Group of Education Deans.[36]

The call for educational reform reached a high point with the issuance of the report by the Carnegie Forum's Task Force on Teaching as a Profession in May 1986. Especially noteworthy was the proposal to establish a board to set nationwide professional teaching standards and to issue certificates to those who meet the standards.

State governors, legislators, and boards of education debated what this would do to their prerogatives, but, surprisingly, both the National Education Association and the American Federation of Teachers gave their approval—with some qualifications—in 1986. Under the Carnegie Corporation's determined leadership, the idea of national standards could have enormous effect upon the preparation of teachers, the school curriculum, textbooks, and the tests given to students and teachers alike.

The Carnegie Report rightly focused on teachers as the key to educational improvement and repeatedly referred to "what teachers need to know and be able to do." Well enough, but in the long run it is the education of teachers in institutions of higher education that will make or break this bold plan for transforming teaching into the kind of profession that sets its own standards of excellence, as medicine and law now do.

But are the colleges and universities listening? And if they are listening, what are they learning from the Carnegie Report and its predecessors? Mostly, they hear that teachers need a "broad liberal education and thorough grounding in the subjects to be taught" and that the rigorous undergraduate curriculum should not stress professional education courses, but should embrace "a common core of history, government, science, literature, and the arts." Fine, many will say, that's just what we are doing now. So what's new?

What should be new is, first, a clear affirmation that the fundamental purpose of both liberal education and universal schooling is preparation for citizenship in a democratic political community and, second, a spelling out of what that means for the substance and content of "what teachers need to know and be able to do."

Though the Carnegie Report was candidly aimed primarily at the economic role of education, it did recognize its civic role:

> We reject the view that preparation for work should be the only, or even the most important, goal of education. From the first days of the Republic, education has been recognized as the foundation of a democratic society for the nation and the individual alike. A passive electorate that derives much of its knowledge from television is too easily manipulated. School must provide a deeper understanding necessary for a self-governing citizenry.[37]

So there you have a fine statement of the most important goal of American education, but the report never comes back explicitly to that point. If schools are to perform their fundamental civic mission, then the teachers must be prepared to carry it out. "What teachers need to know" must include an understanding of the basic ideas and ideals that undergird a free and democratic society and the education that nourishes it. The substance of this knowledge is not to be decided primarily by state legislatures, Congress, or the U.S. Department of Education, but principally by the academic and professional communities, relying upon the best scholarly knowledge available. It's doubtful that a national board will try to assess such knowledge unless determined efforts are made by all concerned.

Meanwhile, all colleges and universities professing to prepare teachers should mobilize their faculties of arts and sciences, education, and the professions to initiate effective programs of teacher education in which the civic purpose is explicit and prominent. Several proposals along these lines are discussed in Chapter 6. If we are to have national standards for the teaching profession, we need a national vision of the civic mission of American education.

Instead, by the end of the 1980s the country had before it numerous proposals for education reform dealing primarily with academic excellence, asking for higher standards and requirements, and hoping for increased financing. Yet too few influential voices were asking for a serious and sustained re-examination of the historic ideas and values of American citizenship and a reassessment of the role that schools and colleges should play in shaping the civic values and knowledge of American citizens in the coming decades. We still need to identify clearly and cogently the substantive ideas, content, and spirit of educational programs that will lead to the civic discipline and commitments essential if the citizenry is genuinely to realize the common purposes of our constitutional order.

In February 1910, as war loomed, William James's memorable lecture on "The Moral Equivalent of War" was published. In it he pleaded for peaceful means to achieve the historic "martial virtues" of discipline, patriotism, honor, obligation for the public good, and cohesiveness—values primarily promoted for centuries by wars and preparation for war. But war has also been bestial, squalid, and enormously destructive: "the gory nurse that trained societies to cohesiveness."[38]

How are we to achieve the ideal cohesive values of the "martial virtues" through devotion to peaceful causes and to the ideals of justice, freedom, and equality? James answered by proposing "instead of military conscription a conscription of the whole youthful population to form for a certain number of years a part of the army enlisted against Nature . . ."[39] And his examples of public service later found echoes in the Civilian Conservation Corps, the Peace Corps, the Teacher Corps, and VISTA. He argued that as we spark a "civic passion . . . on the ruins of the old morals of military honour, a stable system of morals of civic honour builds itself up . . . The war-function has graspt us so far; but constructive interests may some day seem no less imperative, and impose on the individual a hardly lighter burden."[40]

James concluded his paper on this hopeful note:

> The martial type of character can be bred without war. Strenuous honour and disinterestedness abound elsewhere. Priests and medical men are in a fashion educated to it, and we should all feel some degree of it imperative if we were conscious of our work as an obligatory service to the state . . . The only thing needed henceforward is to inflame the civic temper as past history has inflamed the military temper.[41]

William James died later in 1910, and thus it is idle to speculate what his view would have been if he had lived through two world wars, Korea and Vietnam. This quote is a reminder to the educational profession that the demands for moral values in the schools are not only historically insistent but come from a wide spectrum of political, economic, religious, and ideological points of view. James's call for igniting the moral values of civic virtue is more timely and urgent than ever.

As we encounter the bicentennial of the Constitution and the Bill of Rights, what is missing in our current debates over educational reform is how best to inform as well as inflame the civic temper in American schools. Now is the time for the excellence movement as well as the bicentennial commemoration of the Constitution and the Bill of Rights to give added momentum to a renaissance of civic learning. But we must reckon with three extremely important attendant movements. The best known in the public view is probably the call for education to stress moral, ethical, and religious values. This prompting comes from all sectors of the political spectrum but has been especially fueled by conservative political and religious sectors since the 1970s. Less obvious to the public, perhaps, has been the call for teaching a common core of values in the curriculum of schools and colleges, a core that stresses the values of Western civilization that all students should attain. And least well known to the public is the recrudescence of viewpoints within the academic disciplines urging scholars to stress normative values in the social sciences and the humanities rather than to hew solely to value-neutral, empirical, and behavioral knowledge.

American civic education urgently needs to capitalize on the public's awakened concern for educational reform. But we also need to channel the public's concerns for values into a defensible conception of citizenship. We need a well-reasoned and persuasive theory for the practice of citizenship that can enlist the support of diverse groups whose differing moral, ethical, or religious values could be mobilized on behalf of those common civic values that will serve as the centerpiece of American education. The theme of citizenship could become the binding element in a common core curriculum, resting on solid scholarship and providing a meeting ground for the plurality of beliefs and attitudes held by different groups.

The civic mission of American education can better be served if schools and colleges concentrate on those values we share as democratic citizens rather than stressing those moral or character traits that some individuals share with other individuals who are linked in particular groups based on race, ethnicity, kin, religion, party, class, or life-style. Common character values such as honesty, integrity, and compassion are obviously important for the schools to impart. But the schools' best approach to moral values is through substantive teaching and learning of the civic concepts and values underlying the morality of democracy and democratic citizenship. The risks of talking (or teaching) about values in moralistic religious terms are illustrated by events following a dinner on November 18, 1986, held by the Ethics and Public Policy Center in Washington, D.C. President Reagan said:

> The central issue of our times . . . [is] the issue of ethics in public policy, the issue of our vision of man and the moral order, the issue of values. When we proclaim our faith in God and the dignity of man, our love of freedom and our fidelity to Judeo-Christian values . . . we give hope to every freedom-loving soul that truth is strong and that the hollow shell of totalitarianism may one day crack and let its people go.[42]

The next day, President Reagan was bombarded at a news conference by questions concerning possible secret dealings between Israel and the United States in selling arms to Iran. Later, congressional hearings revealed discrepancies between the ethics of public talk and the ethics of government practice. How are citizens eventually to judge the merits of the policies and the practices of the Iran/contra affair? Surely not by any simple or easy formulas, but in the long run only by careful judgments, informed by a reasoned historical perspective and a meaningful conception of the basic values underlying our constitutional order and the nature of citizenship and leadership in a democratic republic.

The time is ripe for American education to pay more attention to how much agreement can now be reached about the civic values that schools and colleges should be transmitting through serious study. No one expects consensus about outcomes or acceptance of beliefs as a result of such study. Some agreement, however, might emerge about what is worth studying.

Why is it so difficult to inform, let alone inflame, the civic temper in American schools? We must look beyond the blandness that often characterizes the textbooks in history, civics, and social studies and the boredom that afflicts many students. The real reason has something to do with the multiplicity of private agendas, constantly pressing upon the schools through the dissident pluralisms of special-interest groups. Voluntary groups can have a positive impact on democracy when they act as mediating agents between the individual and the state. But some groups harm the educative process and the common civic purpose by seeking to impose their particular values on the schools, each intent on identifying its own values with the public good.

Why is it so difficult "to inflame the civic temper" in American schools? I do not think I can improve on the answer I gave in 1977.

> For two hundred years the American people have struggled with the dilemma of politics and education. They believe that education is

fundamental to the health and vitality of a democratic political community, but they do not believe that schools in a democracy ought to be involved in "political education." We have gone to enormous lengths to provide universal, free, compulsory, common schools in response, at least in part, to the rhetoric that civic education for all is necessary; yet we draw back from the precipice of political indoctrination or inculcation of political ideas.

The horns of the dilemma are clear for all to see; we believe that schools should educate for democratic citizenship, yet "political" education in democratic values is somehow viewed as undemocratic. We believe in education for national unity (especially in times of crisis), but we also believe in pluralistic freedoms of belief and action. We expect the schools, above all the public schools, to serve both causes. The danger is that they will serve neither *Unum* nor *Pluribus* as well as they might.

This danger and this concern have arisen many times before in our history. The urge to promote citizenship education arises most insistently when the threats to national unity seem to be most critical or when severe social changes seem to threaten social and political stability. The threat is viewed with very different perspectives, and the prescriptions for unity lead to quite different conclusions.

No wonder then that professionals and public alike often try to ignore or avoid or suppress the civic role of schooling by stressing the *other* purposes of education in the hope that citizenship will be served indirectly by the prescriptions for academic quality and achievement.

But the need for a better civic education keeps bubbling to the surface in troubled times. It may be seen as a response to foreign threats or to fundamental changes in domestic life marked, for example, by a cynicism or alienation from political institutions that seem to falter or crack, increasing crime and violence in the streets, corruption in quiet places, disruption or faithlessness in family and community life, decline in religious, sexual, and moral virtues, overpowering conformity imposed by the mass media and popular culture, or a pervasive retreat to the privatism and personal ego satisfaction of doing one's own thing. While this list may sound like a description of the present era (and it is), it also has a familiar ring out of a past that has periodically led to calls for the schools to improve their civic role. It all began with the founding of the Republic itself.[43]

Other Clamorous Claims on Educational Reform

Special-interest groups have spoken in many tongues, but since 1980 the most outspoken and clamorous voices have carried three general messages to the schools:

Technological Literacy and Vocational Preparation

Powerful claims are laid on the schools to modernize themselves in science, mathematics, and computers and thus to develop technological literacy among their students so that they may meet the economic challenges of an electronic age. High technology is attractive to business, industry, and labor as well as to computer-savvy high school whiz kids. By 1984 nearly half the states had enacted some kind of computer literacy requirement for schools. But ethical and political questions are unable to compete with enthusiasts who want to make sure that computers are universally available to students for the sake of jobs or profits.

Instead, the media make it seem that the most important reforms center on requiring more courses, especially in science, mathematics, and computer technology. Computer literacy and technological competence somehow seem more important than civic virtue and civic literacy. This is not entirely the fault of the press, which made much of selected parts of the reports. The pervasive parading of electronic enticements for schools tended to color the discussions. Two days before the report of the President's Commission on Excellence in Education was issued in April 1983, the Spring Survey of Education of the *New York Times* proclaimed "New Priority: Technological Literacy." Most of the eighty-page issue was devoted to articles and advertisements about schooling and high technology. On the last two pages were short, plaintive articles on "Leave Some Room for the Liberal Arts" and "Feeling Low about High Technology." The July 27, 1983, issue of *Education Week* carried a sixty-four-page supplement on mathematics and science education. And the National School Boards Association established a Technology Leadership Network, whose report viewed optimistically the role of technological instruction in transforming learning in the schools.[44]

I have mentioned several commission reports designed specifically to stress the economic importance of education in keeping the United States a strong competitor in the global marketplace. Education for international economic competition is especially appealing to politicians as well as business leaders. The heartening side of many of these reports is their concentration on the public schools and the possibility of partnerships in which business would exert its political clout to improve public schools.[45] A Harris poll released in 1986 showed that large majorities of business leaders as well as of the public would be willing to pay higher taxes to improve public education. Some business leaders began to re-emphasize academic excellence and the liberal arts as the best preparation for business leadership. For example, Felix G. Rohatyn argued that business should forget business schools and recruit the best young liberal arts students they can find.[46] But some academics and professional educators warned against the possibility that a closer partnership of business and public schools might mean an effort to infuse the curriculum with a conservative ideology biased in favor of free enterprise and a market economy. The Foundation for Teaching Economics tried to steer a middle course of careful and objective study of "how our economy works."[47]

There was by no means universal agreement that increased stress on academic studies was the only way to strengthen America's economy and prepare all students for life work. As might be expected, the vocational education community responded to some of the major reports with dismay and resistance. A notable example was the report of the National Commission on Secondary Vocational Education entitled "The Unfinished Agenda: The Role of Vocational Education in the High School."[48] The commission was appointed by the National Center for Research in Vocational Education at Ohio State University with funds from the Office of Vocational and Adult Education of the U.S. Department of Education. It is clear that the vocational interests, which have historically been strong in American educational policy and practice, were by no means retiring from the scene.

One of the most provocative and influential attacks on reform efforts that concentrate too exclusively on academic excellence came from Youth and America's Future: The William T. Grant Foundation Commission on Work, Family, and Citizenship. In its interim report on January 1987 the commission criticized much of the reform movement for neglecting the needs of the "forgotten half" of youth who are not college bound and who must go directly from high school to the work world. Schools should not be as standardized and uniform as contemplated by academic-minded reformers. And the federal government cannot retreat from this obligation.[49] Chaired by Harold Howe II of Harvard's Graduate School of Education, the commission includes a distinguished roster of leaders in the academic and business world. The study is directed by Samuel Halperin, one of Washington's most knowledgeable and experienced social researchers.

Another approach to the market view of education is the new interest of corporations in establishing their own private schools for profit—at both the elementary and secondary school levels. The success of post-secondary schools emphasizing undergraduate degrees in computer science and electronics, such as those run by the DeVry schools of Bell and Howell, has led other corporations to consider operating lower schools in competition with the public schools. International Telephone and Telegraph and Encyclopedia Brittanica as well as Bell and Howell have been reported to view proprietary schools as possible investment opportunities, thus combining the entrepreneurial interest of producers with the interest of consumers in an education that will provide direct economic payoff.[50] So we move from the vocational and technical aim of public schools to the consumer aims of private schools. There are shades here of the proprietary schools of the eighteenth century—massively large, with no discernible civic goal.

Consumer Sovereignty and Family Choice

A second message, increasingly proclaimed by conservative political voices, may be summed up in the term "consumer sovereignty." It preaches the evils of government regulation or government monopoly in education, the advantages of private schools over public schools, and the priority of parental rights to seek the educational values they prefer for their children through such means of public funding as vouchers or tuition tax credits. An article in the *National Review* made clear what conservatives should concentrate on in the next ten years:

> There are many things wrong with the schools, from overly powerful teachers' unions to look-say methods of reading instruction. But the thread that links them all is government monopoly. It is this monopoly that forces parents to enroll their children in schools that they know are not as good as they used to be, not nearly as good as local private schools, and often brazenly hostile to the parents' religious and moral convictions.[51]

In this outlook civic learning is not considered an important value when parents make decisions about their children's schooling. Little attention is given to such concepts as justice, civic participation, or public responsibility when compared to the stress placed on the values of the marketplace, educational competition, and parental freedom of choice.

As Robert Nisbet, Albert Schweitzer Professor Emeritus in the Humanities at Columbia University, so perceptively points out, the conservative claims for parental and consumer rights in education are embedded in the conservative philosophy stemming back at least to Edmund Burke. But he says these claims began being revived in the United States as early as the 1950s by such writers and scholars as Lionel Trilling, Russell Kirk, William F. Buckley, Jr., Milton Friedman, and

Nisbet himself.[52] Then in the 1960s came the neoconservatism of Irving Kristol as editor of *The Public Interest* and Norman Podhoretz as editor of *Commentary,* which heightened the attacks on political and social liberalism as the underpinnings for the welfare state and for a positive rather than a limited government. The intellectual foundations for fundamental criticism of public education, not only in practice but in theory, were being laid.

Priority for parental and private control found rooting in Nisbet's succinct definition of conservatism: "Conservatism's greatest strength is its possession by historic right of such values as localism, decentralization, family, neighborhood, mutual aid, and belief in the growth of business on the one hand and of religion on the other." [53]

By the mid-1980s these values of conservatism, bolstered by the election victories of Ronald Reagan, gave added strength to campaigns for vouchers or tax credits, whereby parental choice could genuinely be exerted by all families, poor as well as middle class and rich. Interestingly enough, April 1986 witnessed two major conferences on the related subjects of privatization and choice in education. The Graduate School of Administration at the University of California at Davis conducted a television debate on the resolution "We should move toward privatization, including the schools." The proponents were William F. Buckley, Jr., Milton Friedman, and Thomas Sowell. The opponents were Albert Shanker, president of the American Federation of Teachers; Bill Honig; and Paul Starr, professor of sociology at Princeton. The opponents based much of their argument on the prediction that the basic civic goals of public education would be submerged, if not lost, if schools were privatized with public support. The proponents did not make an argument based on the civic purpose of education, except to say that poor parents would be able to send their children to the kind of better schools that more affluent parents could now afford.

A few weeks later, the University of Virginia School of Education sponsored a symposium entitled "Choice in Education." The participants discussed keeping choice confined to public schools or whether to include private schools through the use of vouchers. The voice of the U.S. Department of Education was unmistakable when Assistant Secretary Chester Finn proposed that states adopt vouchers for all education funds because schools of choice provide better education. He said, "Instead of asking for regulation of private schools, why not deregulate the public schools?"[54] One assumes that Finn reflected Secretary Bennett's views.

In general, during the past two decades few advocates of choice have paid much attention to the common civic purposes of education. It was not evident in 1979 in California when John E. Coons of the University of California at Berkeley Boalt Hall School of Law circulated petitions to amend the state constitution to make vouchers legal. Little or no argument regarding education for citizenship appeared in proposals for vouchers or tax credits in several states. It was not apparent in President Reagan's 1987 budget "Agenda for the Future" or in the Department of Education's The Equity and Choice Act (TEACH) proposal. This plan called for applying the voucher principle to the remedial education of disadvantaged youth so they could attend private schools but it found such rough going in Congress that it was withdrawn in June 1986.

However, Secretary Bennett was talking about citizenship education in his February 1986 speech to the National Association of Secondary School Principals. In that speech he referred approvingly to *The American Citizen Handbook* published by the National Education Association (NEA) in 1941. Secretary Bennett's emphasis upon citizenship education deserves applause, but it's doubtful if "choice" is the road that will lead to that education.

In his first policy statement as secretary of education, delivered at the National Press Club in Washington in March 1985, Bennett announced his priorities for American education to be the three Cs: character, content, and choice. By *character* he identified such qualities as "thoughtfulness, kindness, honesty, respect for the law, knowing right from wrong, respect for parents and teachers, diligence, self-sacrifice, hard work, fairness, self-discipline, and love of country." *Content* should stress a common core of history and literature central to American and Western civilization. *Choice* includes parental rights to choose a private or religious education with the aid of public vouchers or tuition tax credits.

For over a decade, I have also been proposing what amounts to a set of three Cs as priorities for American education: civism, civitas, and civility. *Civism* is the primary purpose for universal, free, common schooling; that is, developing among all students the virtues of good citizenship and especially a sense of personal obligation for the public good, what many founders called "civic virtue." The basic knowledge and content of study should focus on *civitas;* that is, the substantive concepts and core principles underlying our democratic constitutional order. *Civility* is the behavior befitting a democratic citizen, not only informed but committed and competent to participate in public affairs.

It was gratifying to see Bennett's report on elementary education, issued in late 1986, give a great deal of attention to civic literacy, along with historical literacy and geographic literacy, as chief goals of the social studies:

> What . . . is the goal of American elementary education? I believe its highest purposes are to prepare children well for further education and to lay the groundwork for their own eventual entry into the community of responsible adults and democratic citizens. In our time, in this land, democratic citizenship requires an array of knowledge and skills: a common language through which we all can communicate; an understanding of our civilization and its institutions; knowledge of our national symbols; a grasp of America's unique cultural pluralism; and respect for the values and precepts that enable people from different backgrounds to live together as Americans.[55]

The trouble was, however, that Bennett's bona fides with many in the academic community and educational profession had so deteriorated by 1987 that his publication *What Works* was called an expression of a conservative political philosophy rather than a consensus of scholarly research.[56] A survey of one hundred leaders of education, government, and labor in twenty-four states revealed that most agreed that the Reagan administration's school-reform agenda could not be achieved with constantly lowered federal support.[57] It was labeled "a half-trying approach."[58] And Clifton R. Wharton, Jr., summed up a major view among college educators in a speech at Colgate University:

> Why does Mr. Bennett alarm seasoned educators? For two reasons: first, because he and his supporters have been programmatically attempting to recast today's education in the inflexible mold of yesterday's. And second, because they have been attempting to employ the rallying cry of "excellence" to make a systematic retreat from the equal-opportunity goals that were among the noblest accomplishments of an entire generation.[59]

Meanwhile, efforts were continued to work out ways to combine the goals of common citizenship with practices of parental choice and consumer sovereignty. One solution proposed in late 1986 by the National Governors' Association called for increased choice among public schools. Under the leadership of Governor Lamar Alexander of Tennessee, the NGA set up seven task forces to forge a five-year agenda for U.S. education. One task force concentrated on parent involvement and choice under the chairmanship of Richard D. Lamm of Colorado. The governors decided not to recommend that public support for choice be extended to private and religious schools, as earlier proposed by Joe Nathan, the NGA coordinator.[60] The overall governors' reports had much to say about the readiness of young children for school, school facilities, professional leadership, educational technology, the teaching process, college quality, and teacher education, but relatively little to say concerning the civic goals of education.[61] The subject of family choice in relation to state support and to state regulation is taken up again in Chapter 4.

Traditional Moral and Religious Values

A third group puts the teaching of traditional values as a top priority for public as well as private schooling. These proposals are often couched in terms of "those traditional moral and religious values that made our nation great." For example, Mel Gabler and Norma Gabler in Texas have long aggressively advocated restoring to the public school curriculum and to textbooks the basic Judeo-Christian "values upon which our nation was founded." For years, they have attacked those textbooks they claim undermine such values as "monogamous families, anti-homosexuality, anti-abortion, American patriotism, morality, conservative views, teaching of honesty, obeying laws, changing bad laws through a legal process, etc."[62]

When teachers or administrators in the public schools are faced with arguments like these or those of the Moral Majority (now merged into the Liberty Foundation), the Eagle Forum, the Christian Broadcasting Network, the National Association of Christian Educators, Scientific Creationists, the American Coalition for Traditional Values, or Citizens for Excellence in Education, the tendency is to become defensive, to plead academic freedom, or to try to ignore the whole thing. Ignoring the problem has become more difficult, however, since representatives of People for the American Way first challenged the Gablers at hearings of the Texas Textbook Committee and insisted upon defending textbooks criticized by the Gablers. Those influential hearings became more of an arena for two-way debate and discussion than simply a unilateral critique by those objecting to the values expressed in some textbooks.

Indeed, in the mid-1980s the efforts both of traditional religious groups and of liberal civil rights groups have snowballed around matters of curriculum, textbooks, teaching and learning, censorship, and freedom of religion and scholarship. A considerable literature of advocacy, court litigation, and scholarship appeared during that time. One example is the May 1987 special issue of *Educational Leadership,* which is devoted to "Religion in the Public Schools." The several articles and their supporting references reveal the intensity and seriousness of the confrontations.[63]

Meanwhile, at least four surveys of textbooks complained about the way textbooks treat religion in American history and government.[64]

The four surveys agreed that texts are woefully lacking in the extent and quality of their treatment. A traditionalist view of the remedy is that texts should give a positive picture of the valuable role Christianity has played in Western and American civilization.[65] A liberal view is that texts should highlight the positive role that religious freedom and separation of church and state have played in American history.[66]

But disputes over textbook content are not simply pedagogical questions or curricular matters to be decided at district or state school board meetings. They arrived on the national stage in the early 1980s partly, at least, because fundamentalist and evangelical Christian groups joined the coalition of conservative forces that won Ronald Reagan such resounding electoral and popular support. The extraordinary vitality—and possible dangers—are documented more fully than anywhere else in a compilation of papers edited by Richard John Neuhaus and Michael Cromartie, *Piety and Politics.*[67] Robert Nisbet has noted, however, "the dark side of ideological triumph" in the conservative victories since 1980 and reminded readers that Edmund Burke feared the "political theologians" and "theological politicians" almost as much as he feared the Jacobins of the French Revolution.[68]

Nisbet speaks of the "conservative renaissance" that fundamentalist Christian groups joined. However, their political role, as it applies to public schooling, is more accurately called a "conservative counterreformation"—an effort to combat and banish religious and secular views that do not agree with their views of Christianity. The parent in the eastern Tennessee federal district court on July 14, 1986, put the view as clearly as could be. Since Jesus Christ was the only means of revelation, "We cannot be tolerant of religious views on the basis of accepting other religions as equal to our own."[69] In this view, the favorite terms often used by Jefferson and Madison, the "equal rights of conscience," do not apply in the schools of eastern Tennessee, according to this parent and presumably to her sponsoring organization, Concerned Women for America, founded by Beverly LeHaye, wife of the television evangelist Tim LeHaye.

Beverly LeHaye has made the views of Concerned Women for America explicit on many occasions by calling for "a renaissance of the biblical values of our founding fathers":

> Adherents to the Judeo-Christian tradition are motivated to act in accordance with the eternal and immutable laws of the Bible. True Christians . . . understand that the answers to the political, economic, cultural, and moral problems of the world are clearly addressed in Scripture . . .

> Concerned Women for America hopes to educate Americans on the
> pernicious philosophy and effects of Secular Humanism. We would
> like to see Secular Humanism thrown out of the government schools
> and biblical morality restored. Meanwhile, CWA will continue to
> defend the rights of parents and children to opt out of classes offensive
> to their beliefs.[70]

Throughout our history, the relations of politics, religion, and
education have been controversial. Few will deny, however, that the
presidential campaigns of 1980 and 1984 witnessed a heightened role of
religious issues in American politics, perhaps unprecedented since the
1920s. They played a prominent part in the executive, legislative, and
judicial arenas during the first half of the 1980s, and they promise to
continue to do so for the foreseeable future. People for the American
Way has been documenting the rapid increase of efforts to censor
textbooks, citing 133 incidents in forty-four states in 1986 alone.[71]

The reciprocal relationships of religion and politics require thoughtful consideration of their portent for citizenship in American life. This
effort requires careful analysis of the historical and constitutional backgrounds of these relationships and their implications for the future
welfare both of religion and of the political process. At the heart of the
manifold issues of religion and politics is the interpretation of that part
of the First Amendment which states that "Congress shall make no law
respecting an establishment of religion, or prohibiting the free exercise
thereof."

Ronald Reagan set the tone for this issue in two campaign speeches
he made in Dallas just four years apart. On August 22, 1980, candidate
Reagan said:

> When I hear the First Amendment used as a reason to keep traditional
> moral values away from policy-making, I am shocked. The First
> Amendment was written not to protect the people and their laws from
> religious values, but to protect those values from government tyranny.
> But over the last two decades the Federal Government seems to have
> forgotten both 'that old time religion' and that old time Constitution.[72]

On August 23, 1984, President Reagan said: "The truth is, politics and
morality are inseparable. And as morality's foundation is religion,
religion and politics are necessarily related." [73]

These speeches provoked a rash of heated arguments regarding the
proper relationship between politics and religion, and once the campaigning was over the historical meaning of the First Amendment for
the role of religion in educational policies affecting public and private

schools remained a burning issue. During the first half of the 1980s, conflicts over religion and education reached a high point in American politics, erupting in political campaigns, state legislatures, the courts, the press, and numerous local school districts.

Since May 1982, when President Reagan advocated adopting a constitutional amendment to permit organized prayer in public schools, Congress has been bitterly divided over repeated efforts to pass legislation that sought to amend the Constitution or strip the Supreme Court and the federal courts of jurisdiction in deciding cases of school prayer in the public schools. Similar controversies have arisen over efforts of the Reagan administration to promote tuition tax credits and vouchers that would give public financial aid to parents who send their children to private religious schools.

This contest over "traditional values" and public education has been fueled especially since 1984, not only by powerful voices from President Reagan in the White House itself but also by the Justice Department, led by Attorney General Edwin Meese III; the Department of Education under Secretary Bennett; the Senate Judiciary Committee, which under Republican control was led by Senators Strom Thurmond and Orrin Hatch; and from a divided Supreme Court itself (to be noted later).

The complexities and details of this contest cannot be followed here, but it was symbolized in the summer and fall of 1986 when Christian parents in Tennessee and Alabama brought suit in federal courts for relief from a public school curriculum whose textbooks they claimed violated their religious beliefs because of the "secular humanist" values being purveyed in the books.

In October 1986 Federal Judge Thomas G. Hull in the Tennessee Eastern District decided that the children of fundamentalist Christian families need not be required to study the Holt, Rinehart and Winston readers because they were offensive to their conscientiously held religious beliefs:

> The plaintiffs believe that, after reading the entire Holt series, a child might adopt the views of a feminist, a humanist, a pacifist, an anti-Christian, a vegetarian, or an advocate of a "one-world government."
>
> Plaintiffs sincerely believe that the repetitive affirmation of these philosophical viewpoints is repulsive to the Christian faith—so repulsive that they must not allow their children to be exposed to the Holt series. This is their religious belief. They have drawn a line, and it is not for us to say that the line [they] drew was an unreasonable one.[74]

The judge conceded that the state has a compelling interest in providing public schools for citizenship education, but

The Court must decide whether the state can achieve literacy and good citizenship for all students without forcing them to read the Holt series.

It seems obvious that this question must be answered in the affirmative . . . The Court must also find that no compelling state interest justifies the burden on the plaintiffs and that the state's interests can be served by less restrictive means.[75]

Among those means were letting students opt out of the school district's reading program whenever offensive books were being studied and receiving instruction by parents at home, so long as the children meet standardized testing requirements. Although the judge declared this to be a narrow case applying only to the families bringing the suit, it was widely agreed that appeals to higher courts would ensue and that a rash of similar cases could break out in many parts of the country. In fact, a three-judge panel of the United States Court of Appeals for the Sixth Circuit unanimously reversed Judge Hull in August 1987. The parents appealed to the full court of appeals in October with the aid of the National Legal Foundation, founded by Pat Robertson; but the Supreme Court in February 1988 refused to hear the appeal, letting stand the ruling against Judge Hull.

Another case involved fundamentalist Christian parents and Federal Judge Brevard Hand in Mobile, Alabama. His sympathies for the parents had already been expressed in his earlier decision allowing prayer in the public schools, a decision overturned by the Supreme Court. In this case, the parents asked that books that teach secular humanism be removed from the Mobile schools curriculum on the grounds that secular humanism is actually a religion and thus must be banned along with Christianity, Islam, and Judaism. Concerned Women for America aided the parents; People for the American Way opposed.

On March 4, 1987, Judge Hand decided for the parents, agreeing that forty-six textbooks approved by the Alabama State Board of Education should be removed from the schools or that certain parts of some of the books be removed. His list included seven home economics books, nine history books, and thirty elementary school social studies books. The publishers included Ginn; McGraw-Hill; Scott, Foresman; Macmillan; Holt, Rinehart and Winston; Harcourt Brace Jovanovich; Houghton Mifflin; and Rand McNally among others.[76]

Judge Hand proclaimed that the case was not a matter of censorship by narrow-minded proreligionists who deemed the books undesirable, improper, or immoral. It was simply a matter of prohibiting the religious beliefs of secular humanism from being taught in violation of the establishment clause of the First Amendment. Judge Hand accepted testimony that secular humanism was a belief system, that it involved statements based on a faith assumption that amounted to a religion, and that it therefore must be prohibited. In addition, the systematic omission of references to the role of the Christian religion in the history books amounted to indoctrination of irreligious beliefs and thus discrimination against religion, also prohibited by the First Amendment. However, the Court of Appeals for the Eleventh Circuit reversed Hand's decision,[77] and the parents decided not to appeal to the Supreme Court.

If these two cases had been upheld, it might have meant the ultimate elevation of parental choice and the virtual disappearance of an academic or professional role in formulating the curriculum for civic education in public schools. If parents can opt out of what academics and professionals propose and public authorities approve, or if courts can throw out what academics and professionals propose and public authorities approve, what standards of excellence or achievement can be expected? From what source comes a common core of studies or of civic values? One can argue, as many have done, that some or all of the textbooks in these cases reflected shoddy scholarship and deserved to be thrown out. But that was not the basis on which they were attacked.

Even the question of scholarship is not fully settled, despite the Supreme Court's 7–2 decision on June 19, 1987, striking down Louisiana's law requiring equal time for the teaching of creationist science whenever evolution is taught in the schools. Justice William J. Brennan's decision called the law an effort to bring religious doctrines into the schools under the heading of a sham creation science. But Chief Justice Rehnquist and Justice Antonin Scalia dissented, and who knows how persuasive they may be for Justice Anthony Kennedy, the newest appointee, and perhaps for some of the others?[78]

These cases, as in so many other instances, involved such organizations as the American Civil Liberties Union and People for the American Way on one side and such organizations as Concerned Women for America and the National Legal Foundation (established by television evangelist Pat Robertson) on the other. They involve complex constitutional questions about religion, education, and the First and Fourteenth Amendments, but they also involve complex questions of public policy for educators, legislators, parents, and school officials. How will the schools and textbook publishers respond when both sides profess belief in and commitment to basic American values? And it was not a simple confrontation of religionists versus secularists, nor of moralists versus value-free neutralists, as many Protestant fundamentalists would portray it. Secular educators are deeply concerned about moral values and character development in public elementary and secondary schools.[79]

Although spokesmen for America's mainline churches are usually not as shrill as fundamentalists or evangelicals, their views are firmly on the side of keeping the government and the public schools properly secular as well as moral. Excellent scholarly examples of these views are contained in the Public Education Policy Studies of the United Ministries in Education, published in conjunction with the Education in Society unit of the National Council of Churches of Christ in the USA.

Particularly appropriate here is the monograph "Secular Humanism and the Public Schools" by James E. Wood, Jr., who is Simon and Ethel Bunn Professor of Church-State Studies at Baylor University. Wood points out that in 1980 the Washington office of the National Council of Churches sent all Senate members a letter stating, "The National Council of Churches, representing 32 major Protestant and Orthodox communions in this country, believe that the religious experience of children is not the business of either the government or the public schools . . . [but is] rather a responsibility and sacred trust of the family and the church."[80]

Citing copious references, Wood presents a forceful case against the religious right's efforts to "Christianize" the government and the public schools, as he claims Tim LeHaye, Pat Robertson, and Jimmy Swaggert would do if they could:

> Significantly, the strongest support for the Supreme Court's rulings outlawing state-sponsored prayers in the public schools has come from the major religious denominations of America, both Christian and Jewish. Any suggestion that the Supreme Court "took God out of the public schools" is without any real theological meaning or historical verification. God is not some object the Supreme Court (or any court) can move around at will . . . The very charge that the Court "took God out of the public schools" is viewed by many of America's mainline churches as both theologically meaningless and offensive.[81]

Reaffirming that the American government is properly secular and that the secular is not an enemy of religion but is an ally of religious liberty, Wood applies the same argument to public education:

> In rediscovering the meaning and significance of the secular state, so also there needs to be a rediscovery and recommitment to the public school as a secular institution. In so doing, the distinct raison d'etre of the public schools as institutions of learning for those of all faiths and of no faith, is fulfilled and thereby their *public* character is maintained. Schools which seek neither to advance religion, nor to ignore, nor to denigrate its role in American and world history. Recent efforts aimed

at the Christianization of the public schools should be seen as both a threat to religious liberty as well as to public education. To be sure, there are those engaged in the battle over "secular humanism" in the public schools who are quick to affirm that their goal is but the inculcation of "Judeo-Christian" values in public education. But to Jews, "Judeo-Christian" is an American political invention that is generally, as Martin Marty has observed, but a code word for "Christian." Even "Judeo-Christian," however, does not begin to take account of the religious pluralism of America with its multitudes of Muslims, Buddhists, Hindus, and adherents of other faiths—to say nothing of more than 80 million Americans without any religious affiliation or identity.[82]

Public schools and public educators have been thus caught in the crossfire between the contending forces of excellence, parental choice, and traditional moral and religious values. No wonder that many administrators and teachers prefer to try to ignore all sides and rally around still another set of three Cs like those proposed by former California Governor Jerry Brown in 1982: computing, calculating, and communication through technology. These three Cs remind us that achieving either citizenship or character values is made more difficult by persisting cultural pluralisms of race, religion, language, and ethnicity and by pervasive changes in industrial and urban society, the economy and workplace, the family, and the whole paraphernalia of technology and modernization. There are no easy, simplistic answers to educational reform.

What's Missing: A Conception of Citizenship

We should try to frame the public debate so that the diverse and contesting claims upon the schools are judged by their contribution to the prime purpose of universal education: preparation for citizenship in our pluralist democracy. We should try to develop an intellectual framework about civic values through which citizens may better judge the policies put forward by business or labor groups, political parties, religious, or other special-interest groups. The primary focus of schools should be on the civic values that pertain to the public life of the political community, which all citizens need to know about and share, rather than on the private values of religious belief or personal life-styles. Individuals and groups should be free to choose their values and beliefs but should not impose them on others, especially not by legislation or government regulation.

In a perceptive essay on trends in articles published from 1965 to 1985 in the conservative magazine *The Public Interest,* associate editor Marc Lilla makes an interesting point. The early articles stressed general reflections on topics such as the "twilight of authority" (Nisbet) or "post-industrial society" (Daniel Bell). These gave way to specialized research studies, especially in economics, devoted to matters of consumerism in the welfare state. These articles generally attacked "public consumerism" (entitlements to public assistance programs) and defended private consumerism regulated only by the free market.

However, what was missing, according to Lilla, was a stream of thought that treats "the welfare state as a question of citizenship, and particular programs as efforts at civic inclusion, and not simply as providing social needs and wants. It has a *civic,* as distinct from merely *public,* understanding of the modern welfare state." Lilla refers to the classic restatement of this view by T. H. Marshall in 1949 on "Social Class and Citizenship," which Lilla sums up as follows:

> The end of the welfare state and the educational system then becomes, not the provision of needs and wants simply, but the creation of a nation of citizens. And, in contrast to the public-household language [Daniel Bell] of consumers, management, consensus, economic equality, and negotiation, the "civic" tradition (as we might call it) speaks of citizens, guaranteed minimums, rights, and duties.[83]

Lilla goes on to argue that *The Public Interest* has been almost silent regarding citizenship and the welfare state. Although one might disagree with many of his conclusions concerning the outcomes of welfare state programs over the past fifty years, it is interesting that he finds so significant the civic appeals of the New Deal and Great Society:

> All developed welfare states mix "public" and "civic" elements in rhetoric and practice, and in this the American case has been no different. Both types of thought have been articulated in this century. But the one tradition to which American society as a whole has been most responsive is, I think, the civic. The Progressives spoke the language of rational management and social needs, and only acquired an elite following, while the New Deal was tremendously popular— one might say "populist"—because Franklin Delano Roosevelt spoke *to* citizens, *about* citizens. He spoke of "one-third of a nation"—*nation,* not society or family—implying that one-third of all Americans were less than full citizens because they were ill-clothed, ill-housed, and ill-fed. However mixed the political motives of its designers, or the actual shape of its programs, the New Deal succeeded in capturing the

American imagination because it promised to be a great act of civic inclusion.

Similarly, the civil rights movement of the 1950s and 1960s acquired moral legitimacy in the public eye when it made the case for equality in civic terms (and lost much of it with the social language of redistribution and affirmative action). The extension of the New Deal agenda to the Great Society was also secured on the civic grounds that blacks were less than citizens in the public realms of schooling, voting, and public services, and in the social realms of employment and housing. John F. Kennedy and Lyndon Johnson understood this, and were our last presidents comfortable speaking of the public interest as the civic interest of its citizens.[84]

The civic dimensions of American life today constitute a profitable line of inquiry, especially as related to public education.[85] If, in fact, conservatives could join liberals in reaffirming the civic mission of public education, the whole educational-reform movement could take on a new and vibrant life. If, however, conservatives continue to ignore or downplay or attack *civitas* as an enemy of the people or at least as an evil burden to be got off their backs, education will be lost as a civic property in what Lilla aptly calls "an age of public affluence and civic squalor."

The educational profession should reaffirm the priority of its historic mandate to educate for citizenship first by promoting the most careful scholarly study of the basic historic concepts, principles, and values underlying the constitutional order (about which there has been controversy since the Constitutional Convention of 1787) and second by giving fair treatment to conflicting views as revealed in current controversies over the role of government and the meaning of constitutional principles for today. Such study must rest upon the best scholarship available in history and the humanities, in political and social science, and in law and jurisprudence.

Succeeding chapters spell out the values on which our institutions of self-government presumably rest: first those ideas that promote cohesion and unity in a democratic political community (justice, equality, rightful authority, civic participation, significant truth, and personal obligation for the public good); and second those ideas that promote pluralism and individualism in a democratic political community (freedom, diversity, privacy, due process, property rights, and international human rights). There is tension, sometimes conflict, between these sets of ideas. But schools should try to promote a realistic understanding of their meaning—in the past and in the present, in theory and in practice.

It will be obvious that these are normative concepts, each with extensive histories of scholarly analysis and controversial interpretation in history, the humanities, the law and jurisprudence, and the social sciences. But they are also the very stuff of practical political life and public affairs, and of school life itself. Schools should confront these ideas directly and explicitly as appropriate to the age and capacity of students.

These concepts are not couched in the terms of personal moral qualities or character (persistence, tact, courage, and so on) that some parents might prefer, nor are they the traditional family-life values some religious groups might wish. However, these ideas do appear in the highest reaches of political discourse and jurisprudence, the ordinary language of governance in schools and communities, the media, political campaigns, court proceedings, hearings, and indeed in the language of the streets. They require nothing less than a lifetime of study and first-hand experience if they are to become more than mere symbols or empty mouthings.

Such efforts in the schools should include not only the curriculum, textbooks, and formal teaching in the classroom but also the whole range of learning experiences taught by the governance and environment of the school itself. This is often called by educators the "hidden curriculum." It involves the whole context of social interaction among teachers, students, administrators, parents, government, and community agencies.

One advantage of the term *civic learning* over the more common *civic education* is that the former embraces the multiple meanings of the word *learning*. It conveys the importance of knowledge and scholarship, as historians do when they refer to the classical "revival of learning" in the pre-Renaissance and Renaissance periods of European civilization, or as scholars do when they speak of universities as custodians of the "world of learning." In this sense, *learning* refers to a corpus of knowledge that informs, stimulates, and challenges the highest reaches of the intellectual, moral, and creative talents of humankind. And civic learning receives sustenance from philosophy, history, literature, and the humanities as well as the social sciences and law. One need only mention the course of ideas about citizenship from Aristotle and Cicero through Machiavelli, Hobbes, Locke, Montesquieu, and Rousseau to Hamilton, Madison, and Jefferson.

But *learning* also embraces the whole range of experiences whereby individuals not only acquire knowledge and intellectual skills but also the values, commitments, and motivations that affect their learning abilities and achievement at different ages and stages of their development and in the different contexts of family and group life. Psychologists speak of affective learning as well as cognitive learning; social scientists speak of socialization; anthropologists speak of enculturation.

The point here is to emphasize that an efficacious program of civic learning must take hold of the students and involve them where they are, if it is to lead them to any kind of reasonable understanding and commitment to the cohesive as well as pluralistic values of democratic political community. The program must recognize the total range of students to be served; their different cultural backgrounds; their socio-economic statuses; their racial, ethnic, and sexual identities; and their particular learning styles.

The National Assessment of Educational Progress in 1983 made it clear that there are regional and community differences of achievement on tests of political knowledge.[86] Students in the Northeast and Midwest typically performed above the national average; the Southeast below, and the West at about the average. The suburban regions around the large urban centers performed above the national average, the big cities below average. The affluent sections of urban areas performed above the average, while disadvantaged sections of urban areas performed below it. Although there is little difference between the sexes, the higher education level of parents proved to be an advantage to their children. Taken at face value, such a finding should mean that the longer current students stay in school, the better chances their children will have of doing well on such tests. Staunching the flow of dropouts is enormously important.

Although these test scores show the influence of social class and family background on achievement in school, evidence from political socialization studies shows that schooling in civic education has more influence on the political motivation and knowledge of lower-class children than it does on middle-class children.[87]

Therefore, civic learning for youths not college bound is even more important than it is for the more affluent children of middle-class and professional families, who are more likely to attend college. There, they have the chance to acquire more political knowledge and participation skills. But civic learning is most important to the "unincorporated" youth—the disadvantaged minorities, the blacks, and other ethnic groups—who historically have been blocked from access to the mainstream of American political and social life.

This is all the more reason why youths should not be separated into special ability tracks for civic education or into segregated private or public schools. It is important for pluralistic groups to learn about and from each other through study and participation together. Schools should be training grounds for acquiring the sense of community that will hold the political system together. At a time when black and Hispanic leaders as well as the major national commissions are calling for strengthened public schools, the majorities should not pull away into separate schools. Political efficacy should be shared as widely as possible, if the democratic system is to work. Benjamin Hooks, of the National Association for the Advancement of Colored People, has said that the goal for every minority youth is a "high school diploma in one hand and a voter registration card in the other." If so, the task of the schools is to be sure that the diploma and the voter registration card rest on the best political knowledge and skill.

Opinion polls regularly show that students and adults know more about how to participate in government than they understand about the basic concepts of limited government, separation of powers, the Bill of Rights, due process, and the rule of law. For example, a test given high school seniors in 1983 by the Wisconsin Department of Public Instruction found that the students knew more about ways to participate in government (78 percent) than they understood about such concepts as limited government, checks and balances, and separation of powers (59 percent). They also scored low on questions dealing with the Bill of Rights, due process, and the rule of law.[88] The study also found that one-third of the students had not taken any course in government, political science, civics, or comparative politics. We need to stress both the knowledge and the experience of civic learning.

There is no easy road to educational reform. The best first step is for the academic community and the educational profession to reaffirm their commitment to the public purposes of schooling and to the civic goals of universal education as the foundation of a free and flourishing democratic society. And they must try to convince the public that education is primarily a civic good rather than primarily a means to private fulfillment or personal preferment.

In the clash of optimistic hopes and pessimistic fears over what the high-technology age will do to us, more is at risk than the nation's economic or military prowess. The very meaning of our lexicon of democratic values is at risk. This is, above all, the brooding legacy of Orwell's *1984*. With the onset of an information technology that even Orwell could scarcely imagine, how will we surmount the threat of the "Principles of Newspeak?"

In the appendix to *1984* we are instructed as follows:

> The word *free* still existed in Newspeak, but it could only be used in such statements as "This dog is free from lice" or "This field is free from weeds." It could not be used in its old sense of "politically free"

or "intellectually free," since political and intellectual freedom no longer existed even as concepts, and were therefore of necessity nameless . . . As we have already seen in the case of the word *free,* words which had once borne a heretical meaning were sometimes retained for the sake of convenience, but only with the undesirable meanings purged out of them. Countless other words such as *honor, justice, morality, internationalism, democracy, science,* and *religion,* had simply ceased to exist. A few blanket words covered them, and, in covering them, abolished them. A person growing up with Newspeak as his sole language would no more know that *equal* had once had the secondary meaning of "politically equal" or that *free* had once meant "intellectually free," than, for instance, a person who had never heard of chess would be aware of the secondary meanings attached to *queen* and *rook*.[89]

How will we prevent this from happening? There is a special obligation on the teaching profession to keep alive for each generation the civic meaning of our historic democratic concepts. Jefferson said the people themselves are the only "safe depositories" and guardians of their liberty, but if the teachers are not adequately prepared "to inform the discretion of the people by education," one should fear for the future of the Republic.

There are some signs that the educational establishment may be awakening to the civic purposes of liberal and professional education, but this is not enough.

In the best of times civic education is no easy task. It is doubly difficult and important now, when so many citizens have lost confidence in the integrity, authority, and efficacy of public officials and governmental institutions, and when so many young people believe that our institutions do not practice what we preach or what our schools teach. This is a formidable task, involving not just the social studies teachers but the whole of the institution and profession of education. The increase of youthful crime and violence calls for long-range civic efforts as well as short-term security measures.

We well know that didactic moral instruction and formal expressions of patriotism through pledges of allegiance, loyalty oaths, or flag salutes have lost their appeal among many academics. We well know, too, the danger of attempts to use the schools for self-serving patriotism, manipulative propaganda, or partisan politicization by special-interest groups in the community. Yet somehow the schools must promote a strengthened sense of the importance of civic morality and political integrity—a revitalized civism devoted to the political virtues of constitutional self-government that have sustained us at our best, that we have ignored or desecrated at our worst.

In renewing a sense of political community, civic education should help build social cohesion without resorting to coercion, without succumbing to witch-hunts against the deviant, without silencing the unorthodox, and without dwelling on an ethnocentric preoccupation with American society to the neglect of the interdependence of the peoples of the world.

If the teaching profession of two million to three million people took seriously the authority of the enduring ideals and moral commitments of our historic political community at its best, as embodied in the constitutional regime and especially in the Bill of Rights, our schools and colleges *could* mobilize the majority of people on behalf of putting into practice our professed democratic ideals.

But it will take the joint efforts of state and federal authorities, the civic-minded wings of the legal profession, the scholarly and public service professions, the political parties, labor, business, the media, civil rights and civil liberties organizations, women's and ethnic groups, and, not least, students themselves. They should urge schools to revitalize their civic purpose, including the freedom of teachers to deal in a scholarly way with the controversies surrounding the constitutional order and the public policy.

In a desirably pluralistic society, civic education must honor cultural *pluribus,* but it must also strengthen political *unum.* Somehow, civic education must promote and protect the right of all people to hold a diversity of beliefs. But it must also develop a commitment to actions that uphold the common bonds of a free government as the surest guarantee of the very holding of a pluralism of beliefs. It must, in Jefferson's words, render "the people the safe, as they are the ultimate guardians of their own liberty." The road to civic learning in a pluralist democracy cannot be built on computer sovereignty, consumer sovereignty, or family sovereignty. It must be built on citizen sovereignty.

We've heard from Paideia, Clio, excellence, competitiveness, "content, character, and choice." Now, let's hear it for civitas. Amy Gutmann, professor of politics at Princeton, allocates, as I do, the authority for cultivating "common democratic values among all children" (in private as well as public schools) to the democratic ideal itself:

> "Political education"—the cultivation of the virtues, knowledge, and skills necessary for political participation—has moral primacy over other purposes of public education in a democratic society. Political education prepares citizens to participate in consciously reproducing

their society, and conscious reproduction is the ideal not only of democratic education but also of democratic politics . . . The most devastating criticism we can level at primary [and secondary] schools, therefore, is not that they fail to give equally talented children an equal chance to earn the same income or to pursue professional occupations but that they fail to give all (educable) children an education adequate to take advantage of their political status as citizens.[90]

All I can add is a secular amen.

Perspectives on the Roles of Families, Schools, and Communities in Education for Citizenship

Introduction

In view of the momentum of the educational-reform efforts of the 1980s in face of the divergent claims long made upon the public schools, a relevant historical perspective becomes necessary. This is especially true if we are to take seriously our oft-repeated claims that universal education is a fundamental requirement to sustain and nourish a self-governing democratic republic. Such perspective is always desirable for long-range planning, but it becomes even more timely because of the fifth anniversary (in April 1988) of the report of the Commission on Excellence in Education.

To mark the occasion, Secretary of Education William J. Bennett issued his report entitled *American Education: Making It Work*, to President Reagan and the American people. Although he found some progress toward the goals of the commission's 1983 report, he believed that improvement was not good enough and not fast enough, especially in strengthening the academic curriculum content and in toughening the disciplines of achievement and hard work. Bennett leveled much of the blame for the slow progress at the obstructionism of the educational establishment and teachers unions.

As might be predicted, Bennett's report elicited quick and sharp criticism from several responsible leaders in the teaching profession and in universities, including some who had generally been in favor of his views as well as those who had long been opposed.[1] They jointly called his evaluations hasty and premature and said Bennett was expecting too much too soon and blaming everyone except his own administration, whose requests for federal support for education had moved persistently downward during his tenure.

Whatever the merits of these conflicting judgments, Bennett's recipe for future reform included five ingredients: strengthening content, ensuring equal intellectual opportunity, establishing an ethos of achievement, recruiting and rewarding good teachers and principals, and instituting accountability throughout the educational system. He held fast to his demands for a common core curriculum, commended the AFT's Education for Democracy Project and the California Framework's stress on history as the core of social studies, and lauded the textbook studies of the Educational Excellence Network and the Council for Basic Education. But there was little mention of citizenship as a basic goal of universal education, except as he referred to the teaching of history and civics, as had been the case in earlier reports.

Under the heading of "an ethos of achievement," Bennett stressed the teaching of basic moral principles, such as honesty, courage, and other consensus values; of establishing order and discipline in schools; and of encouraging good work habits. He made no particular mention of specific citizenship values beyond respect for law and patriotism. In the training of teachers, he applauded alternative recruitment plans that did not require formal courses in schools of education. And accountability would be enhanced by increasing parental choice among schools. He did not specifically include choice of private schooling supported by vouchers or tax credits. Because of resistance by Congress and the profession, these issues were apparently left for another time.

In preparation for his report, Bennett had invited a number of people to meet with him in one-day seminars during October and November 1987. These seminars also looked toward research priorities for the Department of Education during 1988 and 1989. They were devoted to content, governance, productivity, education of the disadvantaged, the state of teaching, and, of special interest here, "school, family, community." Although this book was not available to this last seminar, it may still be useful in highlighting the role of education for democratic citizenship as the reform movement and federal research roll on. A longer view of civic education is needed as we judge the persisting proposals for a core curriculum, for character and moral education, for more parental choice, and for more partnership among families, schools, and communities.

The purpose of Part I is to provide a brief historical perspective on the changing interrelationships of families, schools, and communities as they have affected education for citizenship in American society. The subject is so complex and ambiguous and the relevant scholarship so recent, so vast, and sometimes so contradictory that this relatively short discussion obviously cannot be a definitive analysis. It is rather a historical essay that tries to identify some of the most persistent and controversial issues that have beset the relationships among these major educative institutions in the past. This section will highlight educational issues to be kept in mind as new national policies are formed.

Generalizations that apply to all parts of the country over extended periods are difficult, if not impossible, to make. This is true not only because of the complexities and vast differences among schools, communities, and households at different periods but also because the *history* of each of these institutions has been rapidly changing in the past decade or two. What was fairly commonly accepted a few years ago about the history of public schooling, of rural and urban communities, and of families has undergone considerable scrutiny and reassessment by revisionist historians of various ideological and historiographical persuasions.

There has been such an outpouring of scholarly and polemical literature on these subjects that it would be easy for this part to be swallowed up in the revisionist debates. Rather, this section refers readers to references containing additional information. The assumption is that most readers are more interested in the policy questions the history may illuminate than in debates of historiographical scholarship. But ideological differences among historians and social scientists make a difference in what they emphasize in the past and in what they consider relevant to the present.

My own conceptual framework should therefore come under critical scrutiny. It has been set forth in a number of articles and books published since 1973, in which I have tried to take account of the several revisionist approaches to educational, intellectual, and social history.[2] I continue to view public education as an essential outcome and contributor to the interplay among three persistent themes in American civilization: (1) the cohesive value claims underlying a democratic political community that has proclaimed public goals and constitutional ideals of justice, equality, authority, consent, and personal obligation for the public good; (2) the pluralist value claims and loyalties to freedom, diversity, privacy, and due process that have sought to preserve identity and coherence to families and communities based on religion, language, culture, property, race, ethnicity, or locality; and (3) the long-term modernizing trends, appearing first in Western societies, that have accelerated much of the world toward national centralization, popular participation, industrialization, urbanization, and secularization of knowledge and life-styles.

The interaction of these often divergent trends, especially the twin drives to cultural pluralism and to political cohesion, has resulted in chronic conflicts and cleavages over the control and practices of education. To single out any one of these factors, such as industrial urbanization, class conflict, or social stratification, to explain what happened to education at any particular time or place is to miss the complicated and subtle interplay of these several ingredients.

The terms *family, school,* and *community* should often be used in the plural, for the variety is almost limitless, and variations change from period to period. Of the three terms, *school* seems to be in least need of precise definition. In the vocabulary of educators and the public alike, *community* usually refers primarily to the local setting in which formal schools exist and function. But there is a vast sociological literature on the meaning of community, ranging from geographic neighborhoods and local political or administrative entities to the ethnic, racial, class, or ideological consciousness that binds people into some sort of feeling of collective identity. The term is used to point to national and world-wide collectivities as well as to the people living in particular localities. Common usage primarily focuses on the local community rather than on regional, state, national, or world community. Nevertheless, a broader meaning will allow for discussion not only of the rural or urban, the agrarian or industrial character of communities but also of the major groupings that influence education in the schools: professional, political, bureaucratic, special interest, public interest, partisan, religious, ethnic, linguistic, and racial.

A definition of *community* that enables me to make useful historical points is that of J. W. Getzels of the University of Chicago. Note that he uses the plural:

> One may think of communities as groups of people conscious of a collective identity characterized by common cognitive and affective norms and values, and may order the variety of communities from those where the collective identity is most dependent on a particular geographic locality to those where it is least dependent, although of course such ordering is approximate and the categories will overlap. Thus, one may be a member simultaneously of a local community (e.g., a particular neighborhood), an administrative community (e.g., a particular school district), an instrumental community (e.g., a particular professional group), an ethnic community (e.g., a particular national or racial group), an ideological community (e.g., a particular

religious or sociopolitical group stretching beyond the local, administrative, instrumental, or ethnic communities).

The character of education offered by the school and the education acquired by the child are a function of the communities in which the school and the child are imbedded.[3]

A similar complexity now surrounds the term *family*. For a long time, sociology and anthropology have been the principal scholarly custodians of the family, but there has been a remarkable burst of interest by historians in the family during the past few years.[4] And much of the traditional view of the family developed by scholars before the 1960s is now being questioned by revisionist anthropologists, psychologists, and sociologists.[5] This is another example of the way present crises prompt new looks at the past. As David Angus of the University of Michigan has put it, the current debate about the family in both public and scholarly circles reflects four possible views of the family:

- The family is *not* in decline and that is a good thing.
- The family *is* in decline and that is a bad thing.
- The family *is* in decline, and that is a good thing, because it is an anachronism in modern life.
- The family is *not* in decline, and that is a bad thing, because it is a barrier to equality for women.[6]

To these four views might be added a fifth: the American family is undergoing a fundamental redefinition.

There is a growing literature on nontraditional families in America: families with one parent, multiple step-siblings of divorced parents who have remarried, shared parenting in a communal setting, and so on.[7] Both the literature on the nontraditional family and the demographic facts underlying it may support Paul Bohannon's contention that "the family is the most adaptable of all human institutions, changing with every social demand."[8]

These conflicting views illustrate significant changes in scholarship on the family in recent decades. Up to the 1950s it was largely assumed that urban industrial societies would force the traditional nuclear family into decline because its customary functions were eroding. In the 1950s this alarmist view was being softened by a renewed confidence in the stability of the family, just as there was a conservative re-emphasis on consensus in political and economic affairs during the Eisenhower years. But in the late 1960s the theory turned toward finding physical and emotional conflict, disharmony, antagonism, and even violence and child abuse to be more persistently characteristic of family life than the earlier consensual theories had admitted. Another recent tendency is to find ethnic and racial strength and value in the immigrant, poor, and minority family life that persisted and held out against the depredations of majority discrimination and modernization. Because the family is constantly being rediscovered, much depends upon one's view as to whether the family is here to stay, whether the school is here to stay, or indeed whether the democratic political community is here to stay.

So that there is some semblance of order to the historical perspective, Part I is divided into three chapters dealing with quite unequal periods of time in American history. Chapter 2 deals with the two hundred years during which the disparate colonies of the eastern seaboard moved toward independent nationhood (1620s to the 1820s). This will take us from the transplanting of European-type families, schools, and communities to the creation of a more politically unified and independent republic, accompanied by new visions for the civic purposes of schools as well as for the functions of community and family life.

Chapter 3 discusses the tensions of change and growth during the one hundred years from the 1820s to the 1920s, during which time schools, communities, and families had to cope with the enormous problems of education for citizenship imposed by the accelerating pace of modernizing and pluralistic changes. These changes affected cities, industry, government, the professions, and bureaucracy. Other problems were created by massive immigration, with its attendant pluralism and diversity of ethnic, religious, and linguistic groups. Above all, there was the unrequited promise of freedom, equality, and justice for blacks, American Indians, Asians, Hispanics, and other minority groups, as well as for the major majority group, women.

Chapter 4 deals with the most recent fifty years of our history, from the 1930s to the 1980s. The pace of change quickened, and the crises for civic education and public education seemed to recur more often and with greater intensity. This feeling arises partly because it is true and partly because many adults have been personally involved for much of that time. The closeness of the problems makes them seem more acute. But it also requires the taking of a longer view so that we can gain a surer sense of the course we have come, be more alert for the shoals and currents that may lie ahead, and be ready with safer moorings if the storms grow still more intense, as we chart our future course.

At a time when powerful voices are preaching that parental choice should be aided by public funds at the same time that government services should be reduced in favor of privatization, it is more important than ever to try to achieve a balanced view of the route we have come in the effort to prepare youth for citizenship. This requires a new look at the course we have run in the interrelationships among families, schools, and communities.

CHAPTER 2

The Approach to Nationhood (1620s–1820s)

During the first two hundred years in which Europeans were becoming Americans, two basic trends can be discerned in the interrelationships among families, schools, and communities that fundamentally shaped the ideas and practices of an emerging citizenship.

First, the relatively more congruent and cooperative relationships between schools and fairly homogeneous families and communities (for example, New England towns, Puritan churches, English Protestant families) gave way to a larger number of relatively more incongruent, competing, and conflicting communities (heterogeneous religious and ethnic groups, settlements moving away from the eastern seaboard, growth of cities, expanding middle-class and capitalist enterprises, incipient factory systems of production, and commercial distribution of goods). This trend weakened the hold of the closely knit homogeneous communities that had set up town or public schools in New England under the predominantly Puritan political/religious authority of government and led to private schools initiated and controlled by pluralistic communities of different religious, linguistic, ethnic, and cultural origins. The seventeenth-century linkage of school and family in a homogeneous political community gave way to an increasing variety and pluralism of communities in the eighteenth century.

Second, a society made up of relatively localized geographic units—relatively self-contained, even autonomous "island communities" operating under a variety of political authorities and colonial jurisdictions (Dutch, French, Spanish, and Swedish as well as English)—moved toward a relatively more extended and extensive entity, seeking a common political community that would embrace the thirteen colonies recently become thirteen independent states as well as the new states to the West. As the erstwhile colonies sought greater unity and a new common political nationhood based on a democratic republican ideology, a new civic role for schools was envisioned to compete with the traditional religious, ethnic, and pluralistic roles of schooling.

The second trend, signalized by the formation of the new Republic in the late eighteenth century, led many of the founders to propose a new civic role for public schools based upon the democratic value claims of the republican political community they were seeking to form and thus to achieve a common cohesive political unity. For some, the ideal was the establishment of public schools devoted to the public purposes of the new Republic to replace schools that perforce were devoted to the special purposes of particular communities or families (whether for homogeneous groups of children in separate church-related schools, for middle-class children in private academies, or for working-class youth in proprietary schools that promised to get them jobs in commerce and business).

Proliferation of Pluralist Communities

The formation of the new Republic is the continental divide of American history. Before that time, the prime purposes of schools were mostly determined by religious, ethnic, family, and private interests. After that time, a new formulation came forward: that public schools devoted to the public purposes of the overall political community of the new Republic should replace the private schools that had been devoted to the private purposes of particular communities. To be sure, the civic ideal was not put fully into practice (and perhaps never has been). But from the time of the writing of the Declaration of Independence, the state constitutions, the United States Constitution, and the Bill of Rights, some of the major rivers and streams of education began to flow in a different direction across the American landscape.

This chapter points to some of the high spots in the history and gives a few examples as illustrations. Readers who wish to explore the history of American education in detail are referred to the most comprehensive treatment and accompanying bibliographies on the subject, by Lawrence A. Cremin, whose three volumes stress the educative func-

tions carried on by families, schools, and communities and the configurations they produced.[1] My own writings rest on a somewhat different
conceptual framework concerning the interaction of schools and a
variety of communities, especially their political aspects; they spell out
in considerable detail the basic interpretation upon which this and later
chapters rest.[2]

Homogeneous Seventeenth-Century Communities

Cremin correctly points out that the family was the most important
educative agency in the earliest days of the English colonies in America.
This was inevitable in a day when the instruments of political authority
were scarcely organized and newly settled. But it was also true that the
English colonists brought with them the ideas and traditions of schooling of an England that was experiencing between 1550 and 1650 an
unprecedented educational revolution sparked by the English Renaissance and Reformation. Attention to education was part of the increasing religious and political authority being exerted first by the Crown
under Henry VIII and Elizabeth and then by Parliament under the
Puritan Commonwealth. Royal injunctions by Henry VIII and Edward
VI urged the newly Anglicized clergy to see to it that parents educated
their children in the Anglican doctrines (at least partly as a means of
strengthening the Church of England against Roman Catholicism). And
the Statutes of Artificers (1563) and Poor Law of 1601 under Elizabeth
relied heavily on governmental authority to see that householders educated children and apprentices in work and doctrine as remedies for
vagrancy, delinquency, pauperism, alienation from the land, and unemployment.

Meanwhile, there was a vast proliferation of primary schools to
teach literacy, mostly, of course, for the benefit of male children. These
schools were located in homes, churches, and eventually in school-
houses. This proliferation was stimulated by the religious impetus of
the Reformation, by a resurgent mercantile economy and growth of an
aggressive merchant class, and by an effervescence of humanistic, literary, and cultural life that inspired much of Elizabethan England. The
"educational revolution" in turn gave further impetus to the English
Renaissance.

So the Puritans who came to America because of their persecutions
by Archbishop Laud in the 1630s were well acquainted with the interplay
of governmental authority and family authority in the religious, moral,
and vocational education of their children. And those who came both

before and after the establishment of the Puritan Commonwealth in 1649 were ready to enlist such congruence between community and family on behalf of Puritan religious orthodoxy mixed with civil authority. It is important to remember that the New England colonies were settled mainly by groups of families bound together by religious and civic ties. This made more likely the establishment of towns as fairly close-knit communities that took collective action to establish schools as soon as the exigencies of survival in the strange land were surmounted.

This type of public collective action was strikingly different from the southern colonies, where the earliest settlers were predominantly single males recruited by the London Company to work on the plantations. Even as late as 1695, three-fourths of the people in Virginia and Maryland were indentured servants. And when free families, lured by tobacco, did settle in the South, they were likely to be dispersed in relatively isolated farmsteads. This means that the southern household—made up of the nuclear family, other relatives, servants, and eventually slaves—was a more important setting for education than schools. This was also true for a much longer time in the South than in New England.

In contrast, the New England towns as early as the 1630s began to establish schools and transfer much of the task of teaching literacy from parents to teachers. Cremin estimates that after 1650 the New England households had largely transferred the teaching of the catechism to the churches and the teaching of reading to the schools. Within a decade of their founding, seven of twenty-two New England towns took civil action to establish schools, and by the 1640s the colonial legislatures of Massachusetts and Connecticut were taking colonywide action to promote the establishment of town schools.

Many towns on their own volition had used their authority to empower civil officials (selectmen) to see to it that parents exercised their responsibility to have their children educated; and the colonial governments in turn tried to see to it that reluctant or indifferent towns did their duty. Families whose parents were reasonably well educated in England before their arrival were likely to respond affirmatively. It is estimated that the proportion of men in the New England colonies in the 1640s who had had a university education may have been higher than in any other society in the world up to that time (perhaps as many as one for every forty or fifty families). These colonies may not have been "born free," but they were largely born "well educated." By the end of the seventeenth century about thirty New England towns had made some public provision for establishing schools.

By the end of the seventeenth century, the colonial legislatures of

Massachusetts, Connecticut, and New Hampshire had exerted civil control over schooling and family in several ways. The colonial governments (later to become state governments) assumed the authority to tell town officials that they had the power and the duty to require parents to provide an education for their children (either by themselves or by specially designated teachers). This amounted to legal compulsory instruction of children by parents, masters, or teachers. In its law of 1642 the colonial government of Massachusetts specified the minimum essentials to be taught: reading in English, knowledge of the capital laws—a kind of civics, the approved catechism, and apprenticeship to a trade. A Connecticut law of 1650 gave the town selectmen authority to "have a vigilant eye over their brethren and neighbors" to see that they obeyed the law and to enforce the laws by fines if necessary.

Colonial governments then moved to require the towns to appoint teachers or establish schools to which parents could send their children. Presumably, some parents and some towns had not responded positively enough to suit the colonial legislators. The Massachusetts law of 1647 required towns of fifty families or more to appoint an elementary teacher and towns of 100 families or more to appoint in addition a teacher of Latin grammar—knowledge of which was required for admission to Harvard College. The colonial governments also authorized the towns to use public tax funds to support the teachers of the town schools.

Community participation in schooling was high in the relatively homogeneous and congruous New England towns. Teachers were subject to direct and close supervision of selectmen, town meetings, clergymen, and parents themselves. Teachers of town schools were appointed at town meetings or by selectmen with approval of the town minister. Selectmen and ministers examined the progress of pupils by periodically visiting the schools and by testing the children orally to see if the instructors were teaching and pupils were learning the basics of the three Rs and of the catechism. Teachers were licensed by civil authorities to assure their religious orthodoxy and good moral character. Accountability of teachers to the community and parents was pervasive and comprehensive.

This kind of close linkage among school, community, and home was possible so long as the families and communities were relatively homogeneous and closely knit in religion, language, ethnic background, and proximity. It was also somewhat characteristic of early communities in New Netherlands while the Dutch were still in control. It was this pattern of community control by towns that was to face considerable difficulties as early as the eighteenth century, and increasingly thereafter, as many different kinds of cultural groups began migrating to the American colonies in large numbers.

The colonial legislatures in the South assumed the same legal authority as those in New England to legislate on educational and school matters, but they chose not to require the establishment of schools in the manner of the New England town schools. For one thing, the dispersed settlements and plantations made this less feasible. In addition, class differences meant that those families who could afford the cost should pay for private tutors or should pay tuition to parish priests or to the few endowed schools. The colonial governments in the South confined themselves to legislation to care for the poor and orphaned children of the lower and indentured classes or for poor parents who could not take responsibility for educating their own children. An act of 1636 in Virginia required that an orphan be bound out to another householder but educated at the social level of his natural parents. In these respects Virginia was following the precedence of the Church of England and the English poor laws, acting primarily to protect society from a possible vagabond and potentially dangerous class. "Free" education thus acquired a social stigma in the South that it did not get in New England, where free education was perfectly proper for self-respecting citizens if provided for all at public expense.

Heterogeneous Eighteenth-Century Communities

Significant changes took place in families, schools, and communities during the eighteenth century before the Revolutionary War. But the most difficult one to tie down is the family.[3] The usual interpretation is that the traditional bonds of the strict, patriarchal, and authoritarian New England family began to loosen in the eighteenth century as the orthodox Calvinist hold upon families began to give way to more liberal and humane views of the relations of parents and children. Such views stemmed from more liberal religious views as well as from the secular deism of the Enlightenment. One or two examples will illustrate the extremes.

There was supposedly little change from the 1640s—when John Cotton, Boston's famous Puritan minister, proposed as part of the colony's laws that rebellious children who continued in riot and drunkenness or who cursed or struck their parents should be put to death—to the 1690s, when Cotton Mather issued his stern warnings to parents and children. The extreme Calvinist tradition remained strong in the manuals of advice that orthodox Puritan ministers were fond of writing. A particularly vivid example is Mather's *A Family Well-Ordered,* published in 1699. It consists of two parts, one addressed to parents and one to children. In the first part parents are warned, and threatened with dire consequences if they do not constantly "charge their children vehemently" to repent their sins and seek salvation through prayer, obedience, and strict behavior. Parents must vigilantly watch over all their children's activities, and those of their friends and associates, rebuking and restraining all evil inclinations and relying, of course, on the use of the rod when necessary.

To the children, Mather's instructions were also vividly clear. Awful consequences would be visited upon the undutiful or disobedient child, who would not only die an untimely death by hanging or suicide or being eaten by vultures but would suffer eternal damnation in the utter darkness of hell. However, the dutiful child, who is reverent, obedient, and offers recompense to his parents in their old age, will receive singular blessings, favor on his enterprises, and prosperity and happiness. And the duties must be paid not only to one's natural parents but to ecclesiastical parents (ministers), political parents (magistrates), and scholastic parents (teachers).

Mather included a long section addressed to servants, enjoining them to pay the same respect and observe the same duties to their masters as children owe their parents. The whole advice is that good order in the family will produce a well-ordered society, whereas lack of discipline in the family will produce a chaotic society. You can infer from the extreme tone of Mather's manual that the traditional views of predestination and orthodoxy were already weakening among many New England families who were becoming restless with the established theocracy. Otherwise, he would not have had to be so vehement and irascible.

Despite these harsh admonitions to parents, Puritanism contained seeds of greater freedom for children and young people. Recent scholarship on the colonial family has challenged the notion that colonial children lived as miniature adults. Church membership was to be undertaken through the rational decision of each individual. The "age of reason," which certainly occurred no earlier than the teens, was generally seen to come at the conclusion of one's youth—often in the late twenties. Ross Beales argues that "in colonial New England, childhood was not succeeded by 'miniature adulthood' but by 'youth,' a lengthy transitional period preceding adult status."[4] Youth was an important period for education in both practical and religious or civic matters. Through apprenticeship in the first case and youth associations in the other, much education was undertaken outside the immediate family.

It is clear that by the 1770s a much more gentle, humane, and kindly view of children and their relation to parents was being expressed openly in print, especially by non-Puritan preachers and teachers. Quakers John Woolman and Anthony Benezet, the Anglican Samuel Johnson, and the Mennonite Christopher Dock were among those who argued for patient attention to the tender nature of children; for sympathetic regard for their different spirits, inclinations, and behaviors; and especially for the use of love, kindness, and inspiration as motivations superior to fear and harsh punishment. And all these writers were talking especially about education by teachers in the schools as well as parent-child relationships in the home.

In characterizing eighteenth-century education, Cremin makes the important point that by midcentury the teaching for literacy had moved largely into the schools from the households, where educated parents had played such a large role in seventeenth century America. He argues persuasively that technical competence for "inert" literacy can be learned almost anywhere, but the "liberating" literacy that leads to broader realms of ideas and knowledge was more likely to be generated, say, in the town schools of New England than in the backwood households of South Carolina or in the closed-in sectarian church communities of rural Pennsylvania. Cremin says there was "a difference in probability, deriving from the historic relationship of schools to learning and to the traditional academic mechanisms for refining, extending, correcting and communicating knowledge."[5]

This points to one of the basic and distinctive roles of schools compared with all the other forms of education that households and communities might perform. But notice that it is not a simplistic function that can be summed up in the phrase "back to the basics."

It is difficult to say how much headway the liberalized views of family and school pedagogy had gained by the 1770s. But it is clear that the Puritan monopoly over communities, schools, and families was weakening in the New England colonies and that more diverse varieties of religious groups were gaining strength in the middle and southern colonies. Scotch-Irish Presbyterians, English Quakers, Baptists, and Methodists, and German Lutherans, Moravians, and Mennonites were bringing their distinctive religious and cultural traditions, often settling in groups of homogenous communities. They infused the colonies with a religious and cultural pluralism that soon launched attacks upon the established Puritan churches of New England and the established Church of England in the South.

Establishments of religion had long meant that the civil government should be closely allied with the churches, legitimately requiring everyone to attend church, outlawing public worship of all but the orthodox doctrines, and taxing all property holders to support the established clergy. The dissenting religious groups fought these aspects of the established churches, objecting to the doctrinal requirements and to the religious taxes. They gradually won freedom for their own forms of religious worship and freedom from the religious taxes. The separation of church and state thus became one of the victories of religious pluralism and was eventually embodied in the several state constitutions and the First Amendment of the federal Constitution.[6]

The other side of religious pluralism was a decline in the idea that schooling could be public in access, public in management, and public in support. All these early ingredients of public education in New England towns were weakened in the middle decades of the eighteenth century. Freedom of religious worship was taken to mean freedom of religious groups to conduct their own schools primarily for families of a common religious persuasion. The idea that families of different religious beliefs should be linked in loyalty to common schools was still in the future. Because the variety of religious and ethnic groups was greatest in Pennsylvania and New York, the variety of schools was greatest there also. Not only were religious schools established to carry on the particular religious teachings of a particular church, but Germans, Dutch, French, Swedes, and Danes also wanted schools taught in their own languages.

By the mid-eighteenth century this aspect of cultural pluralism was beginning to cause considerable anxiety among English-speaking colonists, who were beginning to think of themselves as Americans. Benjamin Franklin's concern over the German speakers and their homogeneous (or "clannish") communities in Pennsylvania and the subsequent efforts to Anglicize their schools were but the beginnings of a long and bitter history of conflict over language policy in schools. If local schools are to be closely linked to the local community and if families and the local community are homogeneous in their linguistic and religious loyalties, why should not the local schools teach the language and the religion of the local community and its families? Local governments and colonial legislatures, influenced by the growing political power of various religious groups, began to ask, Why not indeed? They began to allow and then to authorize religious and charitable groups to build, maintain, conduct, and support their own schools with little governmental oversight. Thus was diluted the civic sense of community, which had originally prompted the New England colonies to authorize and establish their version of a religiously oriented public education.

The congruent communities were not only loosened by religious diversity but they also lost geographic compactness as members moved into the outlying sections of the towns or moved further westward to organize new settlements away from the seaboard. A distinct sense of localism developed in the outlying districts among families who soon wanted their own schools and not simply a traveling teacher from the central town. Thus a tradition of decentralization of school control grew up, a movement recognized and authorized, for example, by a Massachusetts law of 1789. This further weakened the civic solidarity that had marked earlier generations. It was, in a way, a remote forerunner of later persistent demands for community control. The backwoods farmer parents could not see the value of supporting Latin grammar schools or much book learning of any kind when their primary goal was to have their children work on the family farm.

After 1750 a growing number of market towns took on a vigorous urban growth that prepared the way for the industrialization of communities on the coast and on the rivers of New England. In these communities and those of the middle colonies, not only was religious diversity heightened but the earlier economic functions of the family began to be transferred from farming homesteads to commercial enterprises. And the training for this vigorous new economic life began to be transferred from households to private schools that offered to teach almost anything that anyone wanted to learn. Entrepreneurial, private, alternative teachers who offered practical, scientific, relevant studies taught in English for those who could pay the fees gained great popularity over the staid Latin grammar schools that led mainly to the colleges and to the ministry.

Cremin cites some interesting figures to show the expansion of entrepreneurial schooling in the eighteenth century, especially in New York City and Philadelphia. He found that in the period 1638–1688 there were 11 parochial and town schoolmasters and 16 private schoolmasters who could be identified by name in New York City. During the eighteenth century (1689–1783) he found a modest increase to 27 parochial and town schoolmasters, whereas the number of private schoolmasters had jumped to 206.[7] This was a tribute to the desires of young artisans and shopkeepers to improve themselves and to the skill of the entrepreneurs in advertising and delivering on their promises to aid in the economic and personal advancement of a rapidly growing clientele.

As the merchant and middle classes grew in affluence, status, and political power along with the substantial property owners in all sections of the country, legislatures were persuaded to grant charters to groups of businessmen, landowners, and professionals to form themselves into educational corporations, a practice borrowed from the merchant capitalism of the day. The private boards of trustees (thus chartered and tax-exempt) could obtain property, build buildings, hire teachers, select students, and generally conduct their own schools, eventually to be known as academies, much as they saw fit and catering to parents who could pay the fees for residential schooling.

Thus by the middle of the eighteenth century the idea of a common public purpose for education in a commonwealth based upon an established religion was giving way to a variety of schools whose purposes were primarily private, whether for particular religious, cultural, ethnic, or vocational purposes, as envisioned by parents and leaders of the different groups or communities. The idea of public support for free town schools available to all in the community and possibly supported in part by tax funds was giving way to at least two separate types of private schools: free schools supported by religious or charitable organizations primarily for poor children whose parents could not afford to pay for schooling; and tuition-type schools intended for those children whose parents could provide tuition for them to attend schools of their choice. In place of public schools for a public purpose, the trend was toward private schools for private purposes, whether for homogeneous groups of children in separate church-related schools, for predominantly middle-class children in academies, or for heterogeneous clienteles in proprietary schools whose practical studies focused upon self-help, self-improvement, or jobs in commerce or business. This was the situation just before the Revolutionary period: alternative schools galore, education by choice for those who could pay for it.

The founders of the new nation faced several hard questions concerning the role of schools in American society. If they believed in the separation of church and state (and most did), they could not go back to the public schools of the closed, corporate Congregational New England towns. If they wanted to build a cohesive republican political community that would embrace and foster a pluralism of religious, economic, and local interests (and most did), could they be satisfied with the disparate, diverse, and contentious models of private education of competing churches, businesses, and private voluntary associations? Could they achieve political *unum* in the light of this educational *pluribus*? We face much the same questions today.

The Rise of a Civic Ideal for Schooling

In the half century from the Declaration of Independence in 1776 to the deaths of Thomas Jefferson and John Adams on July 4, 1826, the conception of the school's role in American society began to change radically. New forces affecting families and the economic and social bases of communities entered into this change in ideas about education, but none was potentially more momentous than the political revolution itself. As a phase of redefining the very meaning of political community and consequently the required meaning of citizenship in the Republic, some founders began to redefine the major purposes of education primarily in political terms: preparing the people for the common duties of republican citizenship required a common education whose first and basic priority is building and maintaining a cohesive political community devoted to the civic ideals of liberty, equality, popular consent, and personal obligation for the public good. These founders had no hesitation in viewing the common school in political terms rather than as a stepping stone to higher education, academic excellence for its own sake, individual self-fulfillment, or preparation for a job.

Most founders were concerned with more than achieving independence from Britain. Along with many clergymen they were concerned with the growing vice, corruption, and personal self-seeking that were accompanying the rise of a mercantile spirit. Thus some founders proposed a new kind of education, a public education that would be free, universal, common to all, and conducted by governmental authorities on behalf of all. They sought to transform education as part of the larger political transformation—to make it public where it had been private; to make it uniformly republican where it had been ideologically or culturally pluralistic; to make it serve liberty and equality where it had fostered elitism or special privilege; and to make it serve the public good where it had been a badge of personal preferment.

Some of the most thoughtful and prophetic political and intellectual leaders of the later decades of the eighteenth century were thinking and writing about the reforms of education that would be necessary to complete the republican revolution that had only begun with the war for independence.[8] They range from Thomas Jefferson and Benjamin Rush at one end of the political spectrum to Noah Webster, John Adams, and George Washington at the other. All agreed that the core of such an education should be literacy in the English language and inculcation of republican virtues. They differed about the role of religion in a civic education.

What would have happened to the mid-eighteenth century idea of religiously motivated private education if the American Revolution had not transpired is a matter of historical speculation. Possibly it would have maintained itself longer than it did, and the American experience would then have paralleled more closely the slower and more tortuous developments in England itself. But the Revolution did come along to begin a reversal of attitudes. Its major historical significance for education is that it redefined the meaning of political community in such a way that within two decades (1) a new republican political system was designed and established, (2) a new conception of republican citizenship was formulated to fit the new political system, and (3) a new conception of a politically motivated public education was proposed to undergird the new Republic and bind together the heterogeneous population into a viable political community.

An earlier generation of American historians attributed the root causes of the American Revolution to social and economic forces. But today the general tendency of historians is to find that the changes that the revolutionaries sought were above all *political* reforms, not a fundamental overturning of social classes, nor a radical redistribution of the economic sources of wealth or production. In the last quarter of the eighteenth century there were indeed changes in social organization that tended to blur the inherited lines of class superiority and inferiority, but there was no overwhelming tide of egalitarianism that swept away traditional forms of property or wealth. And there was no inherited or entrenched feudalism to be swept away, as in France and other parts of Europe.

The American Revolution had moral, religious, and military ingredients, to be sure, but as Bernard Bailyn, Gordon S. Wood, Edmund Morgan, Robert R. Palmer, and many other historians have argued, the Revolution was above all political. The original flash point in the 1770s and the sustained reformation of institutions in the 1780s and 1790s coalesced around the political. And, as so often happens, the igniting points were conditions or events that mobilized people to act suddenly and decisively. What Americans acted against were abuses of power and of privilege. What they formulated to take their place were the goals of liberty, equality, and the public good.

These not only became ideological and passionate rallying cries for insurrection and war but also became the political principles that were debated, defined, and eventually designed into the political community, the constitutional order, and the governments of the independent states and eventually of the new nation. These political remedies for the real and fancied political abuses go to the heart of the new conceptions of citizenship and of public education that came out of the Revolution. Together, they helped define the process of political and educational modernization that distinguished the United States from the other modernizing nations of the West.

Though the meanings of *liberty* and *equality* are enormously complex and do not hold still for long, especially in a revolutionary era,

there was a consistent thread in English and American Whig republicanism, as Gordon S. Wood so thoroughly documents in his *Creation of the
American Republic.*⁹ Liberty was not so much conceived as the private
right of individuals to act in freedom from any governmental control,
rather it was seen as the right of the people collectively to exercise
political consent and to exert political power free from the restrictions
of a royal power or officialdom that did not represent them and free
from a governmental authority in which they did not participate. The
people were viewed principally as a homogeneous body, represented in
England in the House of Commons and in America in the elected
assemblies, both arrayed against the overweening power of the Crown
or nobility.

So participation by the people in the elective and the governing
process was the essence of republican liberty. When American spokesmen in the 1770s argued for a public education devoted to liberty, they
most often meant education for elective self-government based upon
consent of the people in contrast to rule by a monarch, nobility, or
external authorities. Seldom were the arguments for a public education
couched in terms that education ought to promote the civil liberties of
private individuals or of minority groups as against governmental
agencies or local majorities even in a republican state. The notion grew,
although slowly, that "education for liberty" might mean preparation
to exercise and protect the basic freedoms of religion, press, assembly,
due process, and the other guarantees formally stated in early state
constitutions and then in the Bill of Rights.

Equality was to do away with the special privileges of the ruling
elites whose snobbishness, arrogance, pretentions, and contempt for
"the people" so infuriated the middle classes, the yeomen, the professionals, and the artisans of the American towns and countryside. Again,
equality was an elusive term. Then, as now, it sometimes meant that all
people should have an equal chance or opportunity to develop their
talents and not be handicapped by inherited status of family, property,
or class. Sometimes it seemed to imply that a rough equality of
condition would be desirable, but seldom was there great stress on
economic leveling. It was more often a determination that political
equality was the desideratum, for it was widely believed that there were
bound to be natural intellectual differences as well as social distinctions
based upon ability.

The important thing was to keep the avenues of mobility open so
that differences of property, wealth, or status would not harden into
political hierarchies and privileges, as they had in the ancient regimes of
Europe. Rewards were to be made upon the basis of achievement and

merit in a society in which equality of opportunity was kept open through the political process and especially through public educational systems, where all would have the opportunity to make the most of their natural talents. So, for two hundred years the creed of equality and the creed of public education have gone together, each bound to the other with extraordinary fidelity despite major blind spots.

Like the creed of equality, the creed of public education has often been charged with being merely rhetoric, and the search for alternatives has been prolonged and pervasive. But over and over again, the idea of public education, born in the Revolution, has been called upon to help promote equality—social, economic, and political—while alternatives to public education, whether charitable, philanthropic, entrepreneurial, or religious, have persistently had to face the charge that they promoted inequality. And most of the time, advocates for alternatives to public education have often affirmed sanctions for social hierarchy that tended to downgrade the aspirations of the poorer classes.

The third republican ingredient in overcoming the abuses of power and privilege personified by British officialdom was the need for developing civic virtue among the people so that they would promote the public good. Pleas for devotion to the public good rang throughout the revolutionary period. Few doubted that a republican form of government required the individual to sacrifice personal interests to the greater good of the community. Indeed the ideal of a commonwealth, a democratic corporate society in which the common good was the chief end of government, could only be solidly built upon the foundation of the public commitments and sense of community achieved by the citizens of the commonwealth, the people. The need to develop self-sacrifice, loyalty, patriotism, and moral regeneration was therefore one of the most important instruments for achieving the Revolution and in building a secure Republic. Nothing less than creating "a new kind of person" could do; for a monarchy can be based on the inculcation of obedience or fear or the exercise of punishment through force, but a Republic must be based on the individual's willingness to put the public good above private desires. And how better to promote the common weal than through a common education and to promote the public good through public schools?

Education and Constitution Making

The most exciting and engrossing political activity following the Declaration of Independence was the making of the new state constitutions. By mid-1777 ten states had produced new constitutions proclaiming their independent republican status. Massachusetts embarrassedly could not agree on a constitution until 1780; Connecticut and Rhode Island felt satisfied that a revision of their charters took the British Crown and Parliament out of their future; and Vermont's uncertain status was finally settled only with its admission to the Union in 1791. Of the first fourteen states, seven had specific provisions for education in their early constitutions: Pennsylvania (1776), North Carolina (1776), Georgia (1777), Vermont (1777), Massachusetts (1780), New Hampshire (revision of 1784), and Delaware (revision of 1792).

Interestingly enough, the most radically republican and the most forthright on the separation of church and state were also the first to include provisions for education. Pennsylvania's constitution of 1776 is generally recognized to be the most radical and populist of the early state constitutions. It included the following provision:

> A school or schools shall be established in every county by the legislature, for the convenient instruction of youth, with such salaries to the masters, paid by the public, as may enable them to instruct youth at low prices; and all useful learning shall be duly encouraged and promoted in one or more universities.
>
> Laws for the encouragement of virtue, and prevention of vice and immorality, shall be made and constantly kept in force.[10]

Similar provisions for public schooling were incorporated in the politically radical and religiously liberal constitutions of North Carolina (1776) and Georgia (1777) and in the constitution first proposed for Vermont (1777).

Just why Virginia did not include education in its first constitution is not clear. But it soon became a matter of public debate in perhaps the most spectacular failure of a state to enact a public school law. This was the case possibly because the radical and conservative forces were so evenly matched or because Thomas Jefferson's legislative proposal itself was so fully spelled out on republican and secular principles as to give the political and religious conservatives the jitters that liberty and equality were being carried too far. Jefferson was convinced that the Virginia constitution of 1776 had not gone nearly far enough in reforming the aristocratic institutions and class distinction inherited from British rule. Thus, in 1779, he proposed bills for the elimination of primogeniture and entail, for religious freedom, and for public education, all viewed as agencies for regaining and regenerating the liberty, equality, and civic virtue that he believed the Revolution was designed to achieve.

Jefferson saw more keenly than anyone up to his time that public

schools aimed at serving the whole citizenry must be under governmental direction and be free from religious, sectarian, or private control.
He also saw that such an education under public control must extend
from the lowest to the highest levels and must include a comprehensive
system of elementary schools and secondary schools capped by a state
university. Others had been concerned to achieve direct governmental
control of one or more levels of schools, but Jefferson saw the need for
a complete system of public education.

Probably more illuminating than the organizational details of Jefferson's proposals was his rationale for public education as the wellspring
of the public good. Note how the ideas and sentiments of the Declaration of Independence resound through Section I of his "Bill for the
More General Diffusion of Knowledge," introduced into the Virginia
legislature in 1779:

> Whereas it appeareth that however certain forms of government are
> better calculated than others to protect individuals in the free exercise
> of their natural rights, and are at the same time themselves better
> guarded against degeneracy, yet experience hath shown that even under
> the best forms those intrusted with power have, in time and by slow
> operations, perverted it into tyranny; and it is believed that the most
> effectual means of preventing this would be to illuminate, as far as
> practicable, the minds of the people at large, and more especially to
> give them knowledge of those facts which history exhibiteth, that,
> possessed thereby of the experience of other ages and countries, they
> may be enabled to know ambition under all its shapes, and prompt to
> exert their natural powers to defeat its purpose. And whereas it is
> generally true that the people will be happiest whose laws are best and
> are best administered, in proportion as those who form and administer
> them are wise and honest; whence it becomes expedient for promoting
> the publick happiness, that those persons whom nature has endowed
> with genius and virtue should be rendered by liberal education worthy
> to receive and able to guard the sacred deposit of the rights and liberties
> of their fellow-citizens, and that they should be called to that charge
> without regard to wealth, birth, or other accidental condition or
> circumstance; but the indigence of the greater number disabling them
> from so educating, at their own expence, those of their children whom
> nature hath fitly formed and disposed to become useful instruments
> for the public, it is better that such be sought for and educated at the
> common expense of all, than that the happiness of all should be
> confined to the weak or wicked.[11]

The second wave of state constitution making, culminating in the
Massachusetts Constitution of 1780, may be regarded as more conser-

vative than the radical constitutions of 1776–1777 in that the powers of the elected popular assembly were to be balanced by an upper house of the legislature, where men of "wisdom and learning" or of wealth and property would counteract the more egalitarian leanings of the ordinary people.

The point here is that both conservatives and radicals agreed that the state should promote public education on behalf of liberty, equality, and the public good, despite their differences over the precise meaning of those terms when it came to questions of representation, separation of powers, checks and balances, bicameralism, the role of the state in religion, and other matters of republican constitution making.

The Massachusetts Constitution of 1780, formulated largely by John Adams, put it this way, and New Hampshire followed suit in its revision of 1784:

> Wisdom and knowledge, as well as virtue, diffused generally among the body of the people, being necessary for the preservation of their rights and liberties; and as these depend on spreading the opportunities and advantages of education in the various parts of the country, and among the different orders of the people, it shall be the duty of legislatures and magistrates, in all future periods of this common-wealth, to cherish the interests of literature and the sciences, and all seminaries of them; especially the university of Cambridge, public schools and grammar schools in the towns.[12]

Throughout the first decade of this complex, fluid, and sometimes baffling process of working out a new republican political system, public education was often, although not always, seen as a critical factor. It was seen as a nurturer of the public good in the making of a new political community, as a constituent part of the new constitutional order of the independent states, and as indispensable for a citizenry that would elect the governing authorities and that would participate in the actual functioning of government. To specify education as an integral element of the fundamental law of so many state constitutions while the war was being fought in the 1770s was a considerable achievement—a recognition of the political importance of education long before the practice of public education was being widely adopted in the mid-nineteenth century. The Revolutionary era set the pattern for the prominent role that public education came to play in the constitutions of virtually every state as the Union expanded from thirteen to fifty states.

In contrast to the engrossing process of state constitution making that absorbed the creative political energies of the 1770s, the problem of creating a national political community and a national constitutional order attracted relatively little attention until the mid-1780s. From 1774 onward the Continental Congress did spark a cohesiveness necessary to fight and win the war and did draw up and adopt the Articles of Confederation in 1777 (although they were not ratified by all the states until 1781).

Most historians agree that one of the most significant actions the Continental Congress took under the Articles of Confederation was forming policies to handle public lands eventually ceded to the federal government by the several states that had claims to western land. The policies for disposing of the land and governing the territories were formulated by two congressional committees, both of which were originally chaired by Thomas Jefferson, and both ordinances as eventually adopted contained significant provisions for public education.

The first ordinance, the Land Ordinance of 1785, provided for the survey of the public lands into rectangular townships six miles square, each consisting of thirty-six sections of 640 acres each; the sixteenth section (in the middle of each district) was to be reserved "for the maintenance of public schools within the said township" when the lands were sold. This was a notable step in the direction of public support for public schools, one in general line with policies long adopted in New England and conforming to Jefferson's own bill of 1779 for public education in Virginia.

In 1787, the Congress adopted the Northwest Ordinance, which created the governmental machinery for not less than three states and not more than five states in the territory north of the Ohio and east of the Mississippi. Whenever any such proposed state had 60,000 free inhabitants, it was to be admitted to the Union "on an equal footing with the original states."

In what amounted to a kind of bill of rights, the ordinance set forth six articles to guarantee permanently a republican constitutional order for the new states as they were added to the Union: the free exercise of religion; the rights of habeas corpus; trial by jury; proportional representation of the people in the legislature; judicial proceedings, no cruel or unusual punishment, no deprivation of liberty or property except by due process; and no slavery or involuntary servitude (except that fugitive slaves from one of the original states shall be lawfully reclaimed).

Article III contains two sentences: one is the deservedly famous and well-remembered provision about schools, and the other is the equally deserved but often forgotten provision about good faith with the Indians:

> Religion, morality, and knowledge being necessary to good government and the happiness of mankind, schools and the means of educa-

tion shall forever be encouraged. The utmost good faith shall always be observed towards the Indians; their lands and property shall never be taken from them without their consent; and in their property, rights and liberty they never shall be invaded or disturbed, unless in just and lawful wars authorized by Congress; but laws founded in justice and humanity shall, from time to time, be made for preventing wrongs being done to them and for preserving peace and friendship with them.[13]

In one bold and hasty stroke, the federal government set down the rules for applying to the new states of the old Northwest Territory the principles of liberty, equality, and the public good that infused the republican state constitutions of the 1770s and early 1780s. The old conception that new territories acquired by established governments should be treated as colonies for the good of the latter was abrogated. New states were to be equals of the old. Indeed, the new states of this particular region were *not* to be slave states, and they were to promote public education as well as the civil rights and civil liberties that a republican government ought to protect among Indians as well as white citizens. One could argue that the whole business was immoral and illegal as far as the Indians were concerned. But given the subsequent history of two hundred years, the principles stated by the Northwest Ordinance were still far in advance of the actual practices of unfair dealings with Indians.

It is sometimes argued that the linking of religion with morality and knowledge in the Northwest Ordinance indicates that the founders favored the teaching of religion in the public schools. It is, however, just as plausible to argue that the term *religion* was inserted because it was assumed in Massachusetts, Connecticut, and New Hampshire that the states should promote religion. In 1787 all three had "establishments of religion." And thus such a phrase would be an inducement for New Englanders to settle and take up the land in the Northwest Territory. It was the aggressive political tactics of the Ohio Land Company, principally by General Rufus Putnam and the Reverend Manassah Cutler, that persuaded the Continental Congress to adopt such wording in 1787 while Jefferson was in Paris. This clearly was not in Jefferson's original proposals for the territory, which his committee drew up in 1784. The Ohio Land Company even hastily convinced Congress in the summer of 1787 to set aside the twenty-ninth section of land for religion along with the sixteenth section for public schools, a provision Jefferson would surely not have approved had he still been in the Congress.

The provision for using the sale of land "for religious purposes" was soon eliminated, but the high-sounding phrase linking religion, morality, and knowledge remained, along with the antislavery provisions promoted by such notables as Rufus King and Nathan Dane, as inducements for migration and settlement by sober, pious, law-abiding, and liberty-loving New Englanders. The sale of land under the Northwest Ordinance reflected an early example of the mixing of high civic ideals for the public good along with a down-to-earth wheeling and dealing for financial, private, and special interests. But perhaps this was an inevitable part of the political process requiring the arts of negotiation and compromise, along with the longer range vision of the fundamental goals of republican self-government.

Despite the prominent place given public education in the land ordinances of the Continental Congress, the subject of education received surprisingly little attention in the reported deliberations of the Constitutional Convention in Philadelphia and subsequently no explicit mention in the Constitution at all. The reasons for this are still unclear, and much painstaking research may never lead to fully supportable conclusions. So far, the lack of evidence still requires that generalizations be based upon inference rather than on substantive proof.

My own conclusions go something like this. By the summer of 1787 it had been pretty well decided that if any government was to take major responsibility for the control and support of education it was to be the state governments. After all, the several states by now had had a full decade of independent existence and experience in running their internal affairs, having delegated to Congress under the Articles of Confederation only limited and often ill-defined powers to deal solely with external and foreign affairs. As we have seen, roughly half of the original states provided for education in their state constitutions, and virtually all had passed some laws concerning education. The passage of the Northwest Ordinance in July 1787 by the Continental Congress in New York at the very time that the Constitutional Convention was deliberating in Philadelphia may well have meant to delegates that there was nothing to debate further: education was a matter for the states to promote under encouragement and indeed with the aid of proceeds from the sale of public lands, both provided by the central government.

Jefferson had made it clear that public, common school education and university-level education should be up to the states, rather than private or charity groups. And he surely would not have condoned a national system of education controlled by a not-yet firmly constituted federal government. In a letter to George Washington in 1785 he said: "It is an axiom in my mind that our liberty can never be safe but in the hands of the people themselves, and that too of the people with a certain degree of instruction. This it is the business of the state to effect, and on a general plan.[14]

We have seen, however, that Jefferson saw a positive role for the federal government in promoting public education in the states through the largess of public lands provided by the Land Ordinance of 1785. David Tyack and Thomas James have recently reminded us how important that federal support became in the development of public education in the old as well as in the new states.[15]

Some framers, especially those of strong nationalistic leanings, undoubtedly thought that the new federal government would inherently have implied powers to deal with education, even as the Continental Congress had done. Others believed that state or local governments should have power over education. Still others undoubtedly believed that education should be left to private groups, churches, or charitable groups. No doubt still others believed there were more urgent problems than education for the convention to deal with.

The place of education in the new political order was discussed and debated more fully outside the convention in Philadelphia and the state ratifying conventions than inside. At the Philadelphia convention and at the subsequent state conventions, the debates centered on reconciling the confrontation of interests represented by Federalists and Antifederalists. Until these were worked out, the role of education would remain uncertain even in theory.

The Constitutional Convention basically decided to try Madison's middle ground between a strongly centralized and consolidated nation and a loose collection of individual, independent sovereign states. As a result, it was going to be difficult to define precisely what role education ought to have in a compromise federal political system, one whose allocation of powers and functions was still largely to be worked out. If Hamilton's or Jay's strongly centralized national government had clearly won, it might have been easy to design a centralized national system of education. Or if the Convention had adopted the New Jersey plan to tinker with the Articles of Confederation but leave the states fundamentally alone—as Patrick Henry, Sam Adams, and others wished—the authority for education would clearly have remained exclusively in state or private hands.

But these extreme alternatives did not win. Out of the clash of Federalist and Antifederalist views came a new constitutional order that created a new federal government but did not automatically or immediately create a new or unified political community. The problem, therefore, that was bequeathed to education was how to help develop the social cohesion and sense of community required of a republican nation while the educational systems remained in state, private, or religious hands. The convention debates were so engrossed in the

Federalist-Antifederalist opposition and in the political process of winning an argument or reconciling differences that education was either ignored or postponed until the more basic question of union or disunion was settled.

A New Education for a New Republic

Meanwhile, however, public men and educators began redefining what the role of education for citizenship should be in the new Republic. There were differences of opinion, of course, but also much ambiguity and much uncertainty. Many Federalists who might have been expected to argue for a centralized national education system were so aristocratic in temper that they were not enthusiastic about making education universally and equally available to the lowly as well as to the well placed. So they did not argue for federally controlled public education. Some Antifederalists were not convinced that a bookish academic education was essential for politically wise decisions to be made. On the other hand, most Antifederalists who were likely to favor universal common education as a means of inculcating republican virtues surely did not want such an education to be centrally directed by a new and feared national government. Thus, proposals for a federally promoted system of education were relatively few, although several did come along within the decade following adoption of the Constitution. Whatever the views regarding the control or organization of education, most proposals did agree that somehow a new public education should be developed that would instill the republican values of liberty, equality, and the public good. On these matters, there was an increasing consensus among Federalists and Antifederalists alike before the Constitution was adopted, and among Federalists and Republicans after it was adopted. But just how to give effect to the ideals of a new civic role for education continued to be a matter for intense public debate.

The problem facing the Revolutionary generation was not so much the cultural assimilation of massive groups of foreigners as it was of welding into a cohesive, national whole the politically diverse regional, sectional, and state factions that had joined together to fight and win the Revolutionary War. To this end, the dominant view was that education should stress the common values of a republican government and a democratic society. In different ways the stress was thus put upon uniform, homogeneous, thoroughgoing systems of education devoted to the republican purposes of public liberty, public equality, and the public good.

All this required a public education whose prime purpose would be the continuous building and strengthening of the cohesive democratic republicanism that had its considerable beginning during the first decade of the Republic, but was being eroded and threatened during the second decade. The new nation established by the Constitution needed this social cohesion even more than did the independent states proclaimed by the Declaration of Independence and the Articles of Confederation. The motto *e pluribus unum* was the prime goal to be achieved by education in the hearts and minds of the new Americans even more than it was a factual statement describing the actual establishment of one nation out of many independent states. *Unum* permeated the dominant mood of the major proposals for education in the new Republic, though *pluribus* continued to describe the reality of educational practice to the end of the nation's first half century in the 1820s.

In the hectic days of growing crisis and disenchantment with the Articles of Confederation which led to the calling of the Constitutional Convention and the Constitution's subsequent adoption, two major statements on education published by prominent Americans reflected the urgency of rekindling a common sense of public virtue among Americans in all stations of life. The first was by Benjamin Rush, all-round patriot, signer of the Declaration of Independence, educator, physician, and liberal reformer.

His stress throughout was to "tie the state together by one system of education." He did not propose national control of education through a central government, but his general essay in 1786 certainly stressed the need for the kind of education in the states that would produce the common sentiments necessary for achieving a truly national political community. In direct opposition to Jefferson, Rush believed that republican education must be founded on religion, and specifically on the Christian religion, for "a Christian cannot fail of being a republican." His argument was clear: without religion there can be no virtue; without virtue there can be no liberty; and liberty is the object of republican government.

> NEXT to the duty which young men owe to their Creator, I wish to see a SUPREME REGARD TO THEIR COUNTRY inculcated . . . Let our pupil be taught that he does not belong to himself, but that he is public property. Let him be taught to love his family, but let him be taught at the same time that he must forsake and even forget them when the welfare of his country requires it.
>
> He must watch for the state as if its liberties depended upon his vigilance alone, but he must do this in such a manner as not to defraud his creditors or neglect his family. He must love private life, but he must decline no station, however public or responsible it may be, when

called to it by the suffrages of his fellow citizens. He must love popularity, but he must despise it when set in competition with the dictates of his judgment or the real interest of his country . . . He must love family honor, but he must be taught that neither the rank nor antiquity of his ancestors can command respect without personal merit. He must avoid neutrality in all questions that divide the state, but he must shun the rage and acrimony of party spirit . . .

While we inculcate these republican duties upon our pupil, we must not neglect at the same time to inspire him with republican principles. He must be taught that there can be no durable liberty but in a republic and that government . . . is of a progressive nature . . .

From the observations that have been made it is plain that I consider it as possible to convert men into republican machines. This must be done if we expect them to perform their parts properly in the great machine of the government of the state.[16]

Much less a reformer of social causes than Rush, but even more a reformer of language and culture, Noah Webster wrote a series of essays on education at roughly the same time (1787–88) and with a surprisingly similar ring to his calls for public virtue and liberty as the goals of education.

Our constitutions of civil government are not yet firmly established; our national character is not yet formed; and it is an object of vast magnitude that systems of education should be adopted and pursued which may not only diffuse a knowledge of the sciences but may implant in the minds of the American youth the principles of virtue and of liberty and inspire them with just and liberal ideas of government and with an inviolable attachment to their own country.[17]

In this earlier and more liberal essay, Webster opposed the use of the Bible in schools, but in his later spellers he frankly embraced not only specific Christian moral virtues but a frankly Federalist political catechism.

Meanwhile, a proposal was published that went well beyond Rush and Webster in its greater stress on equality than on liberty and public virtue. At the age of 30, Robert Coram had become an ardent Antifederalist editor and publisher in Wilmington, Delaware. In a political essay of 1791, Coram came at the problem of education from a long and involved analysis of the relation of property to government. In an emotional and passionate attack on Sir William Blackstone's theory of the origin of private property, Coram adhered to a philosophy of natural rights in which he rejected the notion that property had to be vested in individuals if agriculture and civilization were to prosper. He pointed out that American Indians pursued agriculture but still held land in common and enjoyed the fruits of their labor. Thus it is labor that constitutes the right to property, not the natural right of possession. Landed property is the result of arbitrary acts of government, which in turn divest propertyless men of their rights to citizenship.

So the vast majority of men have been cheated out of their right to the soil, and this unequal distribution of land is the parent of most disorders besetting governments. This truth offers a foundation upon which to build a system of equal education; that is, a state that obliges citizens to give up their natural liberty and common right to property must protect them in their civil liberties so that they can acquire the means to obtain some property. That means is knowledge, which can alone enable citizens to support themselves. So schools should be provided equally to all in order that all citizens may acquire the knowledge necessary for their sustenance. And such schooling should be free and compulsory; it cannot be left to the accident of wealth nor to the whims or indifference of parents:

> Education, then, ought to be secured by government to every class of citizens, to every child in the state . . .
> Education should not be left to the caprice or negligence of parents, to chance, or confined to the children of wealthy citizens; it is a shame, a scandal to civilized society, that part only of the citizens should be sent to college and universities to learn to cheat the rest of their liberties.[18]

Throughout Coram's essay there is deep concern for the poor and for the inequities between rural and urban communities. He saw that if the miserable rural schools for the farmers' children were not improved and made more comparable with town schools, the urban mercantile classes, with their greater ability to provide education for their children, would always control the government. He believed, therefore, that schools should be public, not private, available everywhere, free to all, and supported by public taxes. The best protector against inequality was an equal education.

While Coram's Republican Antifederalism led him to stress equality in education as diffused by a general system of elementary schools throughout the nation, the Federalist view under the new Constitution was more likely to stress the public good: the need to achieve a sense of community that transcended regional rivalries, which had reasserted themselves after the war's conclusion. This had been one of the prime arguments of the Federalist advocates for a stronger and more centralized national government in the first place.

In the forefront of advocates for this unifying view of education was George Washington. With regard to elementary or secondary education, he spoke only vaguely of the value of "wide diffusion of knowledge." But he returned many times to the theme that a national university under the auspices of the federal government would bring together the future leaders of the nation for a common education in science and literature at the advanced levels. In his first annual message to Congress in January 1790, Washington urged Congress to patronize and promote science and literature:

> Knowledge is in every country the surest basis of public happiness. In one in which the measures of government receive their impression so immediately from the sense of the Community as in ours it is proportionately essential. To the security of a free Constitution it contributes in various ways: By convincing those who are intrusted with the public administration, that every valuable end of Government is best answered by the enlightened confidence of the people; and by teaching the people themselves to know and to value their own rights; to discern and provide against invasions of them; to distinguish between oppression and the necessary exercise of lawful authority; between burthens proceeding from a disregard to their convenience and those resulting from the inevitable exigencies of Society; to discriminate the spirit of Liberty from that of licentiousness, cherishing the first, avoiding the last, and uniting a speedy, but temperate vigilance against encroachments with an inviolable respect to the Laws.[19]

Even though Washington stated his public beliefs about schooling only in the most general terms of "institutions for the general diffusion of knowledge," a band of intellectuals probed much more deeply and explicitly into the "best system of liberal education adapted to the genius of the government of the United States." This was the topic for an essay contest conducted by the American Philosophical Society (whose president was Thomas Jefferson) in the year Washington retired as president of the United States. Not surprisingly, the two essay winners were Jeffersonian in their advocacy of thoroughgoing systems of public education, but scarcely Jeffersonian in their proposals that there should be a national system of education under federal auspices and control.

The two contest winners wrote the longest and the most detailed plans that appeared during the two revolutionary decades. They were also the most radical in their proposals for a national system of education; and therefore they were probably the least influential, for the idea of federal control of education never did overcome the state and local loyalties and the private and religious values of most Americans. But the logic of their views at the end of the 1790s was impeccable. If state systems of public education were the proper accompaniments of the coming to independence of the American states, and if those states after a decade of separate independence saw the necessity of a stronger federal union, then there should be a federal system of education to support the new national political community, of which the new federal government was the embodiment. So argued the two Samuels who shared the prize, though neither turned out to be a very good prophet.

The younger of the two was Samuel Harrison Smith, graduate of the College of Philadelphia (University of Pennsylvania) at age 15 in 1787 and only 25 when he won the prize in 1797. For many years he was editor of the *National Intelligencer,* a pro-Jefferson newspaper in Philadelphia. After a long discussion of the close connection between virtue, wisdom, and happiness as the goals of education, Smith arrived at a stunning proposal for a national system of public, compulsory education:

> It is the duty of a nation to superintend and even to coerce the education of children and . . . high considerations of expediency not only justify but dictate the establishment of a system which shall place under a control, independent of and superior to parental authority, the education of children . . .
>
> Guided by these principles it is proposed:
>
> I. That the period of education be from 5 to 18.
> II. That every male child, without exception, be educated.
> III. That the instructor in every district be directed to attend to the faithful execution of this injunction. That it be made punishable by law in a parent to neglect offering his child to the preceptor for instruction.
> IV. That every parent who wishes to deviate in the education of his children from the established system be made responsible for devoting to the education of his children as much time as the established system prescribes.
> V. That a fund be raised from the citizens in the ratio of their property.
> VI. That the system be composed of primary schools, of colleges, and of a *University.*[20]

Smith proposed that a fourteen-member national board of literature and science be established to administer and superintend the national system of education from top to bottom, including the selection of textbooks for all schools and colleges. In the first instance, the board was to be established by law (presumably by Congress) and thereafter to be chosen by the professors in the university and approved by the colleges. The professional interlocking of the whole system could be further enhanced by an appointment process whereby university professors appointed college professors and college professors appointed school teachers.

In talking about linking universities and schools and raising the prestige and qualifications of teachers by the efforts of a national professional board of educators, Smith was two hundred years ahead of the Carnegie Task Force on the Teaching Profession. He was also quite unrealistic in expecting parents to accede readily to compulsory education or states to be willing to agree to national standards of curriculum, textbooks, or teacher qualifications.

The other winner, Samuel Knox, was more modest in his rhetoric and respectful of address to his readers, as befitted one who had recently come to America when he wrote his long essay. A graduate of the University of Glasgow and a Presbyterian minister, Knox undoubtedly was influenced by the Scottish experience with a national system of schools. But, remarkably, he seemed to stress all three of the major American revolutionary goals: the public good, civil liberty, and equality. And as latecomers are often superpatriotic, so was Knox an extreme American nationalist in proposing a centralized system of public schools throughout the country, what he called "an entire, general, uniform, national plan" of public education from bottom to top.

In contrast to Rush and the later Webster, Knox made a great point of divorcing religion from public education to allow the pursuit of science and literature free from religious bigotry and prejudice. No public funds should go to the support of religious teachers. In his essay published in 1799, Knox obviously was one of the first to sense the eventual significance of the First Amendment for public education:

> It is a happy circumstance peculiarly favorable to a uniform plan of public education that this country hath excluded ecclesiastical from civil policy and emancipated the human mind from the tyranny of church authority and church establishments. It is in consequence of this principle of our happy civil constitution that theology, as far as the study of it is connected with particular forms of faith, ought to be excluded from a liberal system of national instruction especially where there exist so many various denominations among the professors of the Christian religion.[21]

As might be expected of a Presbyterian minister, Knox made much of the need for a well-disciplined school. Because indulgent parents pampered their children too much, he considered public education in a school under the authority of a teacher preferable to private tutoring at home. He favored "preserving submission to the well directed discipline and progressive improvement of academical instruction."

For Knox, it was educational excellence, yes; parental choice, no. And to assure some equality of opportunity and diversity of background in the teaching profession, he proposed what today sounds quite novel: that a number of boys from poor families be selected and sent to college and university at public expense, provided they became teachers. Knox's plan for national organization went so far beyond the practice of the day that it stood little chance of realization. It did have the vision, however, that what he and others were pleased to call a "uniform plan" could "be productive of not only harmony and sentiments, unity of taste and manners, but also the patriotic principles of genuine federalism amongst the scattered and variegated citizens of this extensive republic."[22]

This constant reference to uniformity, the size of the country, and its diversity of population reflected the kinds of problems facing the newly independent country trying to achieve a sense of community and national identity in the late eighteenth century. Similar problems faced the newly independent states of Asia and Africa in the late twentieth century. The search for community in the face of diversity is an enormous burden to load upon education at any time. America also might have had even better luck than it did if it had responded more positively to some of the plans and dreams of its Revolutionary reformers.

In the half century from Jefferson's Declaration of Independence in 1776 and his bill for public education in 1779 to his death in 1826, the grand hopes for civic education through systems of public schools were only uncertainly realized on the state and local levels and scarcely at all on the national level. The goal of *unum* in education was still far in the future; the practice of *pluribus* remained the predominant reality, as it had been in the later colonial period. But one cannot study this period without noticing growing momentum for using the instrument of the new state governments to promote education, especially for elementary schooling and for higher education. These efforts were uneven in different parts of the country and even in different sections of the states. They were sporadic in effect, often originating with the passage of laws, ordinances, or resolutions, but with indifferent results or long delays in practice. They often were directed at specific groups: the poor at the bottom or the privileged at the top. And the governmental efforts were often closely intertwined with private, philanthropic, or religious efforts. But momentum on behalf of the common school did grow in the mid-nineteenth century, especially in New England and New York. This momentum swept most of the country in the following hundred years.

In general, this restless searching for the civic role of public education in American society was part of the broader movement toward nationhood and modernization that began in the last quarter of the eighteenth century and continued unabated in the nineteenth and early twentieth centuries. National independence spurred a reassessment of the role education ought to play in an independent republic and promulgated ideas that continued to reappear for nearly two hundred years in public statements, legislation, and countless actions of local boards of education. These ideas eventually filtered into general attitudes and beliefs, formless and indefinite though they might be when it came to actual practice.

The principal educational problem as seen by the Revolutionary era leaders was how to instill the idea that a pluralist "we" were really Americans and how to achieve in the midst of great diversity a sense of national identity. They began the search for an educational underpinning for democratic republican political institutions. They began to formulate the idea that free, universal, compulsory, common schooling was indeed the necessary underpinning. In recent years, however, massive assaults have been launched against the idea and practice of public education. We not only need to reassess the idea but to work doubly hard to perfect it.

Resurgent Pluralisms in Schools, Families, Communities

Despite the formulation of a new civic purpose for public schools to promote democratic virtues under state auspices, the idea was eclipsed in the early decades of the nineteenth century by two major movements that diminished the civic role of schools. One was the intense religious revivalism that dominated the lives of many families; the other was the modernization of the economy in the form of a massive movement of families to the cities and the shift of the workplace from households to factories for children and women as well as men. Religion and work overshadowed the civic goal of republican citizenship as the prime purposes of education.

A majority of Americans apparently still believed that the new constitutional order of the young Republic could be supported and maintained by educational systems that remained largely in private or religious hands, despite the early efforts of the fledgling states. Voluntary and philanthropic associations grew up in the early nineteenth century in many cities to encourage the giving of money for the establishment of free schools and charity schools designed primarily for poor children. This was dramatically evident in New York City. The Free School Society was founded in 1805 to seek money through private donation and subscription for charity schools for the poor, but it soon turned to city and state governments for public financial aid, which it received over a period of years. Eventually, it argued that public schools attended in common by rich and poor alike would be more likely to provide the schooling that was the right of all free people—and that full public funding was necessary.[23] The society thus became a transition agency between private support and control of schools to full public support and control. The stronger the pluralist religious, ethnic, and private segments were, as in New York City and Pennsylvania, the longer it took for the idea of public schooling to win popular support in the nineteenth century.

The major blind spot in the new civic ideal for public education was, however, the education of black children—whether of freedmen or slaves.[24] The revolutionary fervor of the 1770s and 1780s prompted attempts to establish schools for blacks and even mixed schools in some northern states. But as the antislavery momentum waned between 1790 and 1810, separate schools for blacks became common in the North, and few or no schools for blacks remained the custom in the South. This does not mean that there was no education for blacks. The historical evidence now points to a remarkable persistence in black families and churches of a determined desire for education, which was surreptitiously conducted by blacks themselves and by some white teachers in the South, and more openly by voluntary and religious groups both black and white in the North. But the new civic ideal of a common, universal, free public education for all did not mean *all* for most of two hundred years.

As with black children, a concern for the education of the children of American Indians arose from religious and philanthropic motives rather than civic. Leading Quakers, like William Penn, John Woolman, and Anthony Benezet, were not only promoting a more gentle approach to the education of white children but also for black and Indian children. The Anglican Society for the Promotion of the Gospel in Foreign Parts urged its missionaries to give special attention to Indian children in the effort to Christianize them; and teaching Indian youth was an original purpose for founding the Anglican College of William and Mary and

Congregational Dartmouth College. Native American children also became an early target of federal legislation. In 1819 Congress passed the so-called Civilizing Act, designed to change the life patterns of New England Indians, making their communities more harmonious with those of the white population. This act appropriated $10,000 to hire teachers for Indian children to be instructed in the virtues of hard work and Christianity.[25] It was to be another century before the citizenship of Indians was finally clarified and efforts made to prepare Indians for citizenship rather than simply to be assimilated to a modernizing white American society.

The education of females also constituted a major weakness in the new civic ideals for public education in a democratic nation, although this issue was addressed more often and more successfully than that of education for blacks or Indians. In her study of women's roles and experiences in the American Revolution, Mary Beth Norton points out how that event led to fundamental changes in the beliefs and practices surrounding the education of females:

> In the new republic . . . the importance of female education was repeatedly emphasized. The American's vision of the ideal woman— an independent thinker and patriot, a virtuous wife, competent household manager, and knowledgeable mother—required formal instruction in a way that the earlier paragon, the notable housewife, did not. Moreover, Americans' wartime experiences convinced them that women needed broader training to prepare them for unforeseen contingencies.[26]

By the late eighteenth century, public elementary education was opening wider for girls. Private girls' academies also grew up alongside those established earlier for boys. Linda Kerber observes that sometime between 1780 and 1850—she estimates 1830 as the most probable date— the "literacy gap" between American men and women was closed because of the rise in public education.[27] Although women were not to become full participants in the political system until the twentieth century, their role as mothers of citizens required that they too become infused with civic virtue.

As the eighteenth century came to a close and the nineteenth century opened, the civic ideal for education, which the Revolution and constitution making had generated, began to be eclipsed by two other significant developments in community and family life already briefly mentioned. The religious revivals of the early decades were so widespread and engrossing for so many young as well as older people that the period has been called the Second Great Awakening and even the

Protestant Counterreformation. It is often regarded as a conservative reaction of Protestant clergy aimed at recapturing some of the moral authority that had shifted away from them during the height of the revolutionary cause, with its stress upon natural rights, civic humanism, and humanitarianism stemming from the European and American Enlightenment.

In any case, as fervent revivalism swept the country, the Methodists and Baptists displayed remarkable organizational ability in forming active religious societies in nearly all sections of the country. Since they had also been active in the movements to disestablish Congregational and Episcopal churches from their preferred legal status (a process that was not entirely completed in Massachusetts until 1833 and Connecticut in 1818), these newly successful proponents of an age of voluntarism could not go back on the idea of separation of church and state. But they were successful in reaffirming the belief that the United States was not only a Christian nation but really a Protestant one. And thus they believed that the moral tone of all schools, public and private, should conform to Protestant morality and religion. The Jeffersonian stress on republican civism in the schools was either soft-pedaled or fused with a Protestant and Federalist moralism in the schools.

Even more diverting from the civic ideal of personal obligation for the public good, however, was the upswing in economic modernization attendant upon the growth of cities and early industrialization that marked the late eighteenth and early nineteenth centuries. These hit many families with extraordinary force. The conventional view of many historians and social scientists has long been that this complicated and pervasive modernization process produced profound changes in family life. The traditional family had been the basic economic unit in agrarian societies as well as the principal social unit for the procreation and education of children, producing most goods and services, giving vocational training, caring for the sick and elderly, and even rehabilitating the delinquent or the criminal. This functional view of the family thus asserted that modernization forced the family to give up its educative functions to the schools, the workplace moved from households to the factories, vocational education moved from apprenticeship in the household to schools and industries, care of the sick to hospitals, care of the poor to almshouses, orphans to orphanages, and the deviant to asylums or prisons.

Recent scholarship has tended to revise this traditional view of the decline or disruption of the family in response to modernization. But there can be no doubt that strains, tensions, and changes occurred that fundamentally affected family life and schooling, especially of the poorer segments of society. Robert Wells, for example, argues that the decline in birth rate, which has so often been considered as an outcome of urbanization and industrialization, in fact began before these processes had really taken off. He argues that the attitudinal shift of modernization preceded the social and economic manifestation of that process, even beginning in the early colonial period.[28]

There is, however, no doubt that changes in workplace for children and women were brought about by the factory system and the movement of families from farming communities to urban communities with the onset of industrialization in the late eighteenth century. The growth of the cotton and wool industries in the New England towns of the 1760s led to the transitional development of household workshops for cording and fulling of yarn while spinning was still done at home. Because women and children had long worked at these operations at home, it seemed only natural to transfer them to the household workshops and then eventually to the full-fledged factories that began to appear in the 1790s. It is estimated that by 1816 the cotton mills of southern New England employed a labor force that was made up of 90 percent women, children, and boys under seventeen. Fifty percent or more of the entire labor force were children.[29]

Whether the industries housed whole families together in compact company towns or whether they set up boarding houses for young girls, the changes were great. Many families ceased to be independent and autonomous economic units. The factory required a discipline of work habits, punctuality, and specialization of task that was far different from the work of field or farm in a rural household and different from learning all the elements of a trade as an apprentice. The factory had no obligation to teach a whole trade, give a general education, or look after the worker's manners and morals, and there was little or no protection against abuse. The child worker was now the subject of dual masters— the father's authority at home and the foreman's authority at the factory: in the factory room, family members became part of a crowd, each repeating a specific function and being disciplined by a foreman.[30]

It is true that some enthusiastic advocates of promoting America's "infant" industries, especially with expensive government subsidy or protection and with inexpensive child labor, put a good face on children in the factory. The American Society for the Encouragement of Domestic Manufacturers in 1817 extolled factories as "seats of health, cheerfulness and learning" that provided instruction to promote order, cleanliness, and the exercise of civil duties. And the *Niles Weekly Register* in 1817 reported a cotton mill in Baltimore where the "little work-people" would learn to read and write handsomely.[31] Some company owners turned to the English practice of Sunday schools to teach reading and the Bible to the child laborers. But social reformers were not satisfied by such assurances and increasingly turned to the government to require factory employers to provide some education for their child employees. Enforcement was usually so lax that it took nearly a century of advocacy and legal effort before child labor laws came to have much effect. Modern advocates of the educative advantages of the workplace will not find that history very edifying or encouraging.

Some eager industrialists justified child labor on grounds that work was good for everyone as a road to salvation, and especially good for the poor and idle who would otherwise be threats to the good order of society. The lot of the dependent child was not always happy even under the more personal arrangements that antedated the factory system. The custom had been to bind out poor children by indenture into the care of families who would be reimbursed by public authorities at public expense until the child was old enough to be apprenticed.

This sounds much better than the picture painted of impersonal, even cruel, almshouses or orphanages, but remember that thrifty New Englanders developed an ingenious system whereby dependent children were auctioned off to the lowest bidders to save tax money. Binding out poor children to avaricious or merely penurious farmers, sea captains, tradesmen, or artisans could often amount to involuntary servitude under the fiction of apprenticeship. Similar provisions were made for delinquent children until the states and cities eventually were persuaded to build institutions that, it was hoped, would give better care to the unfortunate under public auspices than under private, even though more personal, auspices. Abuses under both systems eventually led to efforts to reform the schools and other educative agencies that were deeply affected by the era of massive modernization to come.

There is a good deal of debate among historians about the loosening of family ties in the early years of the Republic. Some argue that a greater democracy in family relations with less arbitrary authority by an autocratic father and more active participation by the younger "citizens" of the family reflected the growing democracy in political and social relations in the wider society. Others argue that this view reflects an uncritical assumption that liberalized family ties were a sign of progress.[32] Still others argue that the opening decades of the nineteenth century witnessed a complex transformation in social and family values that elevated romantic personal affection and private sentiments above the eighteenth-century devotion to self-restraint and public obligation,[33] or that public life itself changed in character as the emergence of political parties required professional politicians in place of amateur public servants imbued with civic virtue.[34]

Whatever the merits of this debate, there seems to be good evidence that older children or youth were finding outlets for participation that had not been available earlier. They left the farms, flooded into the cities, and exercised a wide range of vocational, intellectual, and personal choices. Youths were moving from a position of considerable dependence upon parents and family for jobs and life-style to positions of greater independence, or at least semidependence characterized by greater freedom and new responsibilities. Older youths joined and even organized all sorts of voluntary institutions connected with churches, volunteer fire and military companies, social clubs, and self-improvement societies. They were especially active in the religious revivals of the Great Awakening and in the conversion experiences and missionary enthusiasm that marked this period in schools, colleges, and in the new overseas missions. All this, Joseph Kett observes, led not only to an evangelical idealism but also sometimes to neurotic disorientation.[35]

From the early colonies through the first decades of the Republic, religious diversity and linguistic pluralism were major elements in the tensions between families, schools, and communities. As religious pluralism increased, schools became a focal point for maintaining religious and linguistic identity. Eventually, the competing claims of different religions for political authority were countered, though not squelched, by the need for political unity and by the constitutional principle of separation between church and state. The Revolution and the formation of the Republic, combined with the beginnings of modernization, began to push education out of the family and religious circles and into the public realm, in which an increasing proportion of young people could be exposed to the civic principles upon which the nation was founded. But the tensions grew still more acute during the nineteenth and early twentieth centuries.

CHAPTER 3

The Tensions of Complex Nationhood: Pluralism and Modernization (1820s–1920s)

As we look at the hundred years between the 1820s and 1920s to discern the major interrelationships between schools, communities, and families, two generalizations stand out: (1) schools, in comparison with families and communities, played an increasingly prominent and powerful role in preparing for citizenship in American society; and (2) schools, along with families and communities, were forced to adapt themselves in complex ways to the onrush of economic and secular modernization and to the enormous diversities and bewildering pluralisms generated by successive tides of immigration. These trends recurrently challenged the hopes of reformers that the civic ideals of the Republic might somehow survive the clamor and conflict aroused by the confrontations between modernization and pluralism. Chapter 2 describes the basic ingredients of that democratic faith in liberty, equality, popular consent, and obligation of the individual for the public good. Here now, a discussion of two other major forces that shaped the goals and forms of American citizenship: modernization and pluralism.

Modernization is a shorthand term to refer to three or four characteristics that have come together with enormous power over the past three or four centuries, first in Western Europe, then pre-eminently in the United States between 1820 and 1920. They are now fundamentally affecting the societies of Eastern Europe, Asia, Africa, and Latin America. The usual characteristics associated with the transformation from a traditional to a modern society are identified by such terms as the following: (1) urbanization (the shift from a predominantly rural to a citified society); (2) industrialization (the shift from agriculture and other primary means of production to commerce and machine production in factory and city); (3) the centralizing and mobilizing power of the national state in relation to other institutions of society (requiring highly organized and differentiated bureaucracies, including large-scale educational systems); and (4) the secularization of knowledge (symbolized by scientific, empirical, and rational methods of inquiry and research and their application to practical social as well as material problems).[1]

What complicated the modernization as well as the democratic process in the United States was the arrival of vast varieties of peoples bringing with them an almost infinite diversity of religious beliefs, ethnic backgrounds, and traditional cultures—far more than in any other country attempting to modernize in the nineteenth century. A useful term for this phenomenon is *pluralism,* or *plurality.* Michael Kammen in his penetrating analysis of the origins of American civilization defines a plural society as "a polity containing distinct cleavages amongst diverse population groups."[2] He usefully distinguishes between "stable pluralism" and "unstable pluralism":

> Stable pluralism requires a strong *underpinning* of legitimacy. A plural society is best insured by the rule of law—law made within the framework of an explicit constitution by elected representatives, executed by a partially autonomous administrative staff [bureaucracy], and adjudicated by an independent judiciary. Insofar as all these were created in 1787 and achieved in 1789, those dates do distinguish a genuine watershed in American history.[3]

Kammen also refers to "unstable pluralism," which might come to threaten the very authority of the polity because of conflicts among religious, racial, or regional groups, each forming its own political party, schools, and ideology. Thus a stable pluralism can become one of the glories of a free society, but unstable pluralism can become a divisive threat to the survival of democratic institutions. This bipolarity of attitude toward pluralism created persistent tensions among schools, communities, and families throughout the century of massive modernization.

Another significant interpretation of the role of pluralism is that of Robert H. Wiebe in his analysis of "segments" in American life:

> What segmentation denotes is a configuration of small social units—primary circles of identity, values, associations, and goals—that have

sufficient authority to dominate the terms of their most important relationships with the world outside. Some of these units have been kinship networks. Others, notably in the twentieth century, have been occupational groups, and even more in this century have been various blends of family, locality, occupation, and ethnic affiliation. The standard segments during the eighteenth and nineteenth centuries were communities, constructed around a marketing or an administrative center perhaps, or an intense religious belief, or simply a plot of land to preserve against a stream of strangers. All of these communities shared two distinguishing attributes: a membership able to visualize their social unit as a self-contained system and recognize each other's places within its scheme; and a set of indigenous institutions capable of managing the normal, everyday affairs of its members.[4]

Thus the basic unit of eighteenth-century society was, as Wiebe put it, "the family in a community" interconnected in the many ways we have seen. In the nineteenth century, however, the segments that had centered largely upon geographic localities increasingly became many sets of parallel endeavors in which particular groups sought their own economic opportunities without too much interference from outside. America became a series of "island communities" divided according to distinctive religious, ethnic, or racial identities and based upon the assumption that a properly ordered society would comprise countless, isolated lanes where Americans, singly and in groups, dashed like rows of racers toward their goals.[5]

How was this segmented society to be kept from becoming fragmented into an unstable pluralism? Wiebe replies by pointing to the internalizing of some basic values that the island community families held in common—"kernels of truth"—derived from the Bible, the founding fathers, Adam Smith, or Horace Mann. More recently, other scholars have come to call this common set of values a "Christian capitalism";[6] a "Protestant moral consensus";[7] a "common Victorian culture predominantly British-American, evangelical Protestant, and bourgeois";[8] or Yankee moralistic republicanism joined with an elitist entrepreneurial nationalism to form a WASP America.[9] What all this means is that the mainstream of American historical scholarship, which in the past stressed economic or geographic forces as the basic dynamics in political history, has given way to a much greater stress recently on "cultural politics," or the interrelationships and conflicts between modernization and pluralism.[10] This trend in historiography illuminates the linkages—or lack of them—between schools, communities, and homes.

We can no longer be content with a straight chronological political history of successive eras in American history: the Jacksonian Age, Civil

War and Reconstruction, the Gilded Age, the Progressive Era. There was too much continuity in those one hundred years. Nor can we be content with a strictly "class conflict" interpretation of politics or modernization. There was too much complexity in the pluralistic pressures and demands made upon schools, communities, and families. In fact, there was a constantly shifting axis or polarity of such demands, which may be summed up as dual efforts: to achieve greater *coherence* in the educational system when it seemed to be too loose and chaotic; and, conversely, efforts to attain more *differentiation* when the system seemed to be too rigid and oppressive. Educators, parents, and community groups were constantly attracted to one or the other of these poles, and sometimes to both at the same time. It is remarkable that the schools were able to surmount these twin drives and retain any semblance of distinctive civic purpose.

In the conflicts and controversies arising from these fundamental currents, the civic ideals of the Republic were often submerged by the confrontations between modernization and pluralism or were co-opted by one or the other. On one hand, schools were importuned to adapt to an aggressive capitalist, industrialized, business-oriented, urban society (more work discipline, more efficiency, more standardization, more bureaucracy). On the other hand, they were looked upon as prime agents for assimilating and Americanizing the immigrant diversities so that a "stable pluralism" could be the underpinnings of a common political legitimacy and not become an "unstable pluralism" that would threaten the survival of the polity. The idea of public education for public purposes under public control supported by public funds came to be viewed as a prime means to achieve civic cohesion and prevent a segmented society from becoming fragmented into an unstable pluralism. A growing consensus, despite much opposition, accepted public education as a chief article of faith in the American creed: a belief in free, universal, common, compulsory, secular schooling.

If we take the century as a whole, the arguments for modernization of American society through public schools were winning acceptance in the general public, especially when modernization through business enterprise was portrayed as the truly democratic and American way of life. Public control and funding of schools surpassed private sources; states gained in authority over local districts, often at the expense of parental involvement. Some educational professionals were willing, if not eager, to ape the management efficiency of business and industry; others were more concerned for the welfare of children, the poor, and the minorities in the many reform movements that arose periodically to give special attention to the child laborers, handicapped, delinquent, disease-ridden, and dependent. By and large, such reform movements often originated among voluntary, philanthropic, or charitable organizations involving widespread citizen participation, but they then often led to government action and funding. The most successful of such efforts on the national level was vocational education through public schools.

An intermediate step, allocating public funds to private agencies, was often tried. The trend, however, in elementary and secondary schooling was to deny public funds to private schools, especially on the grounds of religious freedom and separation of church and state. Here, the religious pluralism of the nation had a major effect. Politically, Protestant groups closed ranks to deny tax funds to Catholic schools; and, for their pains, deliberate sectarian Protestant religious instruction in public schools gradually lessened or disappeared. This is one of the most crucial and persistent arenas of controversy in American educational history. Less and less could one speak of "the community" as of one piece religiously—or ethnically.

The most bitter battles between communities were fought in the most pluralistic localities, especially in the big cities where the diversity of immigrants was the greatest. Some immigrant groups opposed or were indifferent to the public schools; others viewed them and used them as the principal means of access to a new, and better, life. The greatest failures of the ideal of public education before the 1920s had to do with enforced segregated schooling for blacks, Indians, Mexican-Americans, and Asians, whether by law or by the discriminative practices of predominant members of local communities. In both cases, this kind of linkage between school and community served to deny in practice the civic ideals of the democratic political community envisioned in the early Republic.

Schooling in Modernizing Communities

We have seen how the original Revolutionary idea of a basically civic role for schooling was declining in the early decades of the nineteenth century in the face of growing privatism and pluralism. By the 1830s and 1840s, however, booming modernization and surging immigration led a remarkable series of educational reformers to revive and promote the civic purposes of free, universal, and common schooling. They employed much of the rhetoric of the founders on behalf of the cohesive values of a democratic republican society. But they added the urgent need to prepare citizens for the burgeoning city and factory life of modernization and the necessity for assimilating the growing flood of immigrants to ward off what they feared might otherwise become an unstable pluralism.

Thus from 1820 to 1870, the political process in most states and in thousands of cities and towns led to the building of the first tier of a complete system of public education: elementary schools for younger children. From 1870 to 1920, a second tier was built to accommodate a large proportion of older children in the public high schools. As a result of this century of public discussion, agitation, organization of political parties and voluntary groups, lobbying, conflict, and propaganda, the outlines of the idea of American public education were drawn and built into institutional form. One of the chief articles of faith in the American creed became a belief in free, universal, common, compulsory, secular schooling. Taken together, these six terms summed up the general idea of American public education by the mid-twentieth century.

Free meant that all children could go to public schools without paying fees, rate bills, or tuition. Schools were free of the stigma of charity for poor children and could become effectively free only when they were tax supported, publicly controlled, and open to all.

Universal meant that all children could and should go to school regularly. At first, three or four years of primary schooling were deemed to be sufficient for a largely rural and homogeneous populace; later, it came to be agreed that virtually all older children should go to or through high school in a largely urban, pluralistic, modernizing nation.

Common meant that it was good for the children, the families, and the communities that children from the whole range of social, cultural, economic, and political backgrounds go to school together. Common schooling, it was argued, amid the pluralisms of religious, ethnic, and socioeconomic classes would help achieve a durable political community based upon freedom, equality, justice, and personal obligation for the common good.

Compulsory schooling was eventually resorted to first as a defense against the exploitation of child labor by getting the children out of factories and into schools and second as a means of protecting the society against the neglect, indifference, or avarice of parents who did not wish to send their children to school.

Schooling itself was increasingly looked upon as a desirable and essential means of socializing the young, preparing them for life in urban, industrial, modernizing communities, and giving them a way to acquire the knowledge, values, and skills required of citizens in demo-cratic political communities.

Finally, if public schools were to be characterized by public access, public control, and public support in a pluralistic society in which religious freedom and separation of church and state were part of the constitutional order, the public schools could not be based upon institutional religion; they must be *secular*—free of religious devotional practices and doctrine. The converse was that public funds should not go to private religious schools. All six elements of the idea of public education were hammered out in the course of a century of great conflict and controversy. None were more inflammatory than the confrontations between religious-ethnic-political pluralisms.

As the common school system was built, all three of our basic themes were present in various proportions at different times. But by and large the modernization theme, often relying on the democratic civic ideal as argument, took precedence over the pluralistic theme from the 1820s to 1920s. This involved two major subthemes: one had to do with public funding by government taxation rather than relying upon private sources, and the other concerned the exercise of state authority on behalf of public schools rather than reliance upon the localism of districts or the segmented pluralism of voluntary groups. There was recurrent resistance to the growth of public funding and state authority in education, but the overall trend was clear. In the second round of state constitution making, which took place from the mid-1840s to the mid-1850s, virtually every state embedded into its fundamental law a recognition of public education as essential for maintaining a republican form of government and obligated its legislature to establish free, public, or common schools to that end.

For much of these hundred years, the actual role of the state was fairly ineffective. But by the end of the Progressive Era in the 1920s, the state systems had become more "thorough and efficient" in response to pressures for building large-scale organizations in education to cope with the enormous increases in school enrollments at the secondary as well as at the elementary level. This was part of an overall trend toward bureaucratization taking place in city and state governments as well as in commerce, business, and industry generally.[11]

The cities, especially, were inundated by massive numbers of students throughout most of the century. David Tyack points out that in 1850 in Chicago 21 teachers had to deal with 1,900 pupils; in 1860 there were 123 teachers to deal with 14,000 pupils in the city schools. With a ratio of one teacher to some 100 pupils, it was no wonder that something had to be done—hiring more and better-trained teachers, paying them more, grading pupils by age or achievement, and using graded curriculum materials. But by the beginning of the twentieth century, the cry arose that the schools were too routinized, too much in lockstep, and too uniform in content. Some critics called for the schools to become more humane, more concerned with individual differences, and more open to free and creative expression for children.

Meanwhile, other public reformers argued that large school systems with thousands of students and hundreds of teachers could not be run efficiently by the kind of organization that had been inherited from rural agrarian days when public participation meant that lay citizens literally ran the public schools. In the 1850s, Boston had 190 part-time lay trustees who supervised the primary schools in their respective districts, hired teachers, fixed their salaries, levied taxes, built schools, selected textbooks, and supervised the curriculum. Similarly, Philadelphia in 1860 had twenty-four wards whose board members did the same for the ninety-two schools in the city.

It seemed increasingly clear that a professional staff of administrators was needed to deal with board members on one side and teachers on the other. This was one response to the failure of voluntary efforts to cope adequately with city modernization. Private water and sewage systems, voluntary fire and police companies, philanthropic and family efforts could no longer meet the needs of the booming cities. To cope, urbanized populations turned to municipal governments to build organized, consistent, regular, reliable, and specialized efforts. This meant that a professional bureaucracy was needed, as modernizing communities all over the world were finding out. But it also meant less direct participation by interested members of the public or by parents in the day-to-day management of the schools. Both benefits and costs were involved in the transition.

This process has posed one of the most difficult tensions in the theory and practice of education since the 1820s. In theory, the public should have a predominant voice in determining the policies of the schools in a democratic society. But what if the public wants the schools to promote authoritarianism rather than liberty, inequality rather than equality, injustice rather than justice, and obligation to private interest rather than to the public interest? And who is to define which is which? It was in the process of trying to find their way through such questions that the public and educational reformers of the Progressive Era arrived at their proposals for increased reliance upon democratic and professional reforms in government and education.

Appalled by what they believed to be the excesses of private industry and laissez-faire capitalism in the single-minded pursuit of an inhumane exploitative modernization, Progressive Era reformers turned to government agencies to try to regulate corporate monopolies, protect ordinary citizens, and promote the social welfare of the unfortunate and underprivileged. Middle-class liberals of the cities took the lead in much of the Progressive Era reform movements to improve conditions in prisons, cities, factories, and schools after the earlier, more radical populist protests among laborers and farmers had failed by the 1890s. After the election of McKinley over Bryan in 1896, populism declined, Jim Crow revived, reform movements for women's suffrage and temperance fell off, and anti-Catholic, anti-immigrant, anti-Semitic movements of Protestant nativism were on the rise. At the turn of the twentieth century, an impending sense of crisis gave rise to Progressivism, which turned as part of the remedy to the reform of public schools as well as to the reform of many other sectors of society.

Robert Wiebe illuminates this movement by noting that it reflected a growing vitality among professional groups in a number of fields, in the productive occupations, such as organized business, organized labor, and organized farmers, as well as in such new service occupations as medicine, law, social work, education, journalism, and public administration.[12] Both types of professionals recognized the need for new modes or structures of organization to cope with rampant modernization. The business-oriented Progressives looked toward agencies of "social control" and "social efficiency." The welfare-oriented Progressives looked to "social service." The result was a two-pronged attack on the crime, corruption, ugliness, and poverty that accompanied the industrialization and urbanization of the day. In the factory, this meant scientific management; in the government, it meant civil-service reform; in the school systems, it meant centralized boards of control and the elevation of professional administrators; in the classrooms, it meant uniform texts and tests. These all added up to a greater role for the expert, the professional, and for the efficiency and economy of operation dear to the hearts of business-oriented progressives.

On the other hand, the welfare-oriented progressives pushed hard for government sponsorship and support of social services related to families, children, and education.[13] And much of this represented community participation by individuals and voluntary groups of many kinds who urged or demanded that government provide special facilities for children formerly consigned to familial care. Most often, the philanthropic or charitable agencies would take the lead, soon find that private voluntary efforts were woefully inadequate, then turn to government for public funds to help the private agencies, and finally demand that the government itself build, manage, and support the enterprises.

This was a long process that began in the mid-nineteenth century. By the mid-1850s, the public almshouses and orphanages that had resulted from the "poor law" ideology of the eighteenth century were vigorously criticized as examples of apathy and wretched management; and legislatures were persuaded to give public money to private agencies that would serve particular religious or ethnic groups. The idea grew that dependent children would be better off in foster homes than in institutions, but minority ethnic groups and Roman Catholics often continued to prefer institutional care. In any case, as the century wore on, Progressive reformers worked harder for state patronage and protection of children who were not properly cared for, whether by neglect, sheer poverty, abuse, or conditions of disease or defect. In this respect, state authority was enhanced and parental authority diminished.

It was not until after the Civil War that the federal government became involved in welfare activities aimed at children other than the children of Native Americans. Barbara Finkelstein analyzes federal legislation for children as belonging to three categories established during the latter half of the nineteenth century and the first decades of the twentieth century. She classes legislation such as the Civilizing Act of 1819 as "child-saving," with its aim of removing children from what were perceived as detrimental family influences. Following the Civil War, widows and children of Union Army veterans were guaranteed financial support, the first cases of "family-saving" efforts, evoked when families were considered to be suffering unduly from forces beyond their control. The educational efforts of the Freedmen's Bureau, aimed at black parents and children and predicated on the belief that black family structure had been destroyed under slavery, were the first cases of "family tutoring" legislative strategies.[14]

The advocates of public responsibility and governmental regulation usually came from liberal-minded middle-class professionals, and resistance came from ethnic, religious, or working-class groups who wanted to maintain parental control over the lives, schooling, and work of their children. Nevertheless, state subsidies for pensions to poor mothers to keep their children at home were increased, and at the same time state after state passed extensive laws to exercise greater public supervision over both the institutions for child care and the placing of dependent children in foster homes.

With regard to delinquent children, there was a rapid expansion of state institutions (reform schools) in the mid-nineteenth century to parallel the privately run "houses of refuge" for children. After the Civil War, the states became much more active in establishing public nurseries for very young poor children and "industrial" schools for older youths in the hope of preventing delinquency, not just punishing it. Eventually, juvenile centers were established in the belief that youths needed special treatment different from adults and that delinquency was largely a physical, mental, or cultural disease and should be treated as such.

The reform movements also included increasing attention to the health of children and care for special handicaps of deafness, blindness, and feeblemindedness. Special schools for handicapped children were established early in the nineteenth century, special hospitals for children appeared in the 1850s, and the whole public health movement gained headway in the late nineteenth and early twentieth centuries as the sources of disease were traced to sanitation, bacteria in milk, and virus contagion. By the 1890s, public schools were drawn into the public health effort to help discover and control contagious diseases by use of examinations and vaccination and by the hiring of school nurses. One of the most important signs of growing governmental concern was the establishment of the Children's Bureau in 1912; this finally acknowledged a federal responsibility for promoting the health and welfare of children.

However, the greatest example of mobilized community participation in reform efforts affecting education was undoubtedly the series of public campaigns in the Progressive Era to outlaw child labor by state and federal government action. In the middle decades of the nineteenth century the public reformers were not necessarily opposed on principle to children working; after all, work was a socially useful and even beneficial enterprise for children. What they objected to was the work in factories and mines that prevented so many children from getting any schooling at all or any training for a trade.

The earliest child labor laws were simply designed to see to it that if children were to work in factories or mines they must also have some schooling, either beforehand or concurrently. The first such law was passed in Massachusetts in 1836 but was hard to enforce. It was not until 1842 that Massachusetts and Connecticut passed laws prohibiting children under age 12 from working more than ten hours a day. Even this was difficult to enforce among reluctant employers eager for profits or among reluctant poor parents who needed the added income for support of the family. Horace Mann estimated that even with this modest effort to control child labor some 40 percent of children in the working class received no schooling at all.

After the Civil War, however, public opinion was increasingly aroused not only by the exploitation of children but by reports of the miserable working conditions in the factories and mines, which left youths stunted both mentally and physically. It is estimated that in 1870 about one child in eight was at work. In the 1870s, fourteen states enacted child labor laws; in the 1880s, another ten. Even so, by 1900 about one child in six was at work. One-third of all workers in southern mills were children. The campaign now focused on the general welfare of children, not simply to see that working children received some education.

Between 1902 and 1909, forty-three states passed legislation restricting child labor as a result of massive public protest movements organized by all sorts of citizens' groups, especially under the auspices of the National Child Labor Committee, headed by Felix Adler and supported actively by such social work leaders as Florence Kelley, Lillian Wald, and Jane Addams. The committee was even able to convince Congress to pass the Keating-Owen bill in 1916, only to have it declared unconstitutional by the Supreme Court in 1918.[15] Subsequently, the effort to achieve a constitutional amendment was defeated by a resurgent conservatism and pluralism in the mid-1920s. The principal recourse thus became compulsory school attendance laws; if children were in school, they could not be in factories.

As Florence Kelley said, the best child labor law was a compulsory education law, and it was clear that much of the motivation for compulsory attendance laws flowed from the same source of humanitarian and progressive social reforms from which the movement for the abolition of child labor sprang. But it was, of course, not that simple. Compulsory attendance at school was not only a response to the industrial and urban modernization of the United States. It was also a response to the new pluralism accompanying massive immigration. Sometimes this response took the form of a virulent nativism that feared that invading foreign elements would overwhelm the traditional American institutions; sometimes it was a more generous and cosmopolitan belief that immigrants should be assimilated into American citizenship with empathetic respect for their cultural traditions.

In general, the Americanization motive was a more powerful political device in the hands of many citizens' groups and patriotic organizations than was the democratic cosmopolitanism of progressive reformers, especially just before and after World War I. Both motives favored a feeling that the common bonds of national cohesion could and should be strengthened by making sure that all children attended school, preferably in common public schools. In the 1870s, fourteen states enacted compulsory attendance laws; in the 1880s another ten states. By 1918, all states had some sort of school attendance law. From the 1850s to 1890s, enforcement was loose or nonexistent, and much blame was leveled at indifferent parents. By the end of the 1920s, the laws were being enforced much more effectively through a network of rules, attendance records, and truant officers. By 1920 more than 85 percent of those required to attend school were actually doing so; thirty-one states required attendance to age 16; eight states, mostly in the South, required attendance to age 14, and the others to 17 or 18.

Underlying the public campaigns and legislative battles that accompanied the drive to compulsory attendance was a not-so-subtle change in what was regarded as the civic role for schools. Whereas the Revolutionary Era arguments on behalf of liberty, equality, and personal obligation for the public good were echoed by the common school reformers of the pre-Civil War period, the tone changed significantly in the following fifty years. Public pressures on the schools took a much more nationalistic tone. What had been a spirit of invoking the values of a grand and free country now became a shrill exaltation of a great and powerful nation. Manifest destiny, the Spanish-American War, and World War I all led to exaltation of the United States as a superior nation made up of superior people. The obverse was the necessity to be sure that alien immigrants exhibited outward signs of their loyalty to American institutions both governmental and economic. So pledges of allegiance, salutes to the flag, loyalty oaths, required teaching of English, and prohibition of the teaching of foreign languages in the schools became the rage among many voluntary citizen groups.

Infused throughout these patriotic value commitments was the explicit belief that the free-enterprise system of a capitalist economy, self-regulated and free of government controls, was the surest foundation for the American way of life. Schools were importuned at every turn to praise the laissez-faire philosophy and eschew radical doctrines that might threaten or hold back the burgeoning modernization of the economy under the leadership of the business and industrial systems. Many educators found no problem with this kind of public "participation" in schools; others were girding for resistance to such community "intervention."

Schooling in Pluralizing Communities

It is difficult to chart the course of a century's tension between the drives for national cohesion and the resurgent impulses to segmental pluralism. By 1830 the Revolutionary fervor for an overall national political community was losing ground to the particularist tendencies to elevate the interest of different local communities, states, or regions. Weibe puts it this way: "Around 1850 . . . was the culmination of a process of hardening, multiplying segmentation."[16] The growing immigration in the early decades of the nineteenth century contributed to this process. The immigrants were largely from Ireland and Germany, and mostly Roman Catholic, thus raising the level of religious pluralism in what had been up to that time largely a Protestant land. Protestant revivalism thus attacked not only the secular strains of the Revolutionary ideals but also the seemingly more serious Roman Catholic virus. No wonder that a counteracting virulent nativist movement sprouted in the 1840s and 1850s. The earlier rivalry among the Protestant sects, a rivalry that had contributed to the separation of church and state, now led to a closing of Protestant ranks in the face of the greater enemy.

Before the Civil War, the persistent ambivalence about pluralism was put to a more severe test than ever before. One voice counseled: America is the land of liberty and opportunity; the immigrants are welcome and their differences should be honored. Besides, we need their cheap labor for rapid economic modernization. But another voice warned: they are so different, so poor, so uneducated that they threaten our free institutions and our very way of life. School reformers of the period argued that the best solution was to educate the immigrants in public common schools where early comers and newcomers could learn together to become good American citizens. But many newcomers, especially Catholic leaders, argued that public schools were really Protestant and English-oriented schools and thus violated their religious and cultural traditions. They wanted their own schools, and they wanted public funds to support them.

Typical of the contrast of views in the 1840s in Massachusetts were those of Orestes Brownson and Horace Mann. Brownson stated the Catholic case for local, community, and family control of schools:

> The selection of teachers, the choice of studies and of books to be read or studied, all that pertains to the methods of teaching and the matters to be taught or learned are best left to the school district . . . The more exclusively the whole matter of the school is brought under the control of families specially interested in it the more efficient will the school be . . . Government is not in this country, and cannot be, the educator of the people. In education, as in religion, we must rely mainly on the voluntary system.[17]

Horace Mann, the epitome of the common school reformer, argued to the contrary that a republican government must indeed be the surest "educator of the people" on behalf of liberty, equality, and the public good:

> I believe in . . . the duty of every government to see that the means of . . . education are provided for all . . . Under a republican government,

it seems clear that the minimum of this education can never be less than such as is sufficient to qualify each citizen for the civil and social duties he will be called to discharge . . .

The society of which we necessarily constitute a part must be preserved; and, in order to preserve it, we must not look merely to what one individual or family needs, but to what the whole community needs; not merely to what one generation needs, but to the wants of a succession of generations.[18]

These statements are classic examples of a long-lasting confrontation of views: the role of schools in promoting cohesive civic ideals on behalf of the larger political community by the positive action of government against the role of the schools in promoting pluralistic values based upon voluntary, family, and local community action. In the decades before the Civil War, heated conflicts took place in many cities and states over such views as these. The most heated were in Massachusetts and in New York. Most of Mann's battles in Massachusetts were with fundamentalist Protestant groups who wanted the public schools to teach Protestant doctrine as local religious groups viewed it; if this could not be done, then the state ought to provide religious groups with the funds to run their own sectarian schools. Mann could not agree to either solution and gradually developed a view that amounted to a nondenominational Christian consensus upon which he hoped all could agree.

Roman Catholics, however, could not agree with nondenominationalism. Arguing that this would inevitably be Protestantism, they carried on an aggressive political campaign in New York to gain public funds for their parochial schools.[19] They were not successful in extracting public monies, but the net result was that public funds were denied private Protestant schools as well as Catholic. Thus the public schools were strengthened by taxation, but they were also eventually divested of much of their religious teachings and devotional practices. The trend in public education was increasingly away from nondenominational Christian teaching toward less specific religious instruction, that is, toward secularism. Conflict among pluralistic religious groups brought this result, but the predominance of Protestant majorities in much of the country also brought legal prohibition against the allocation of tax funds to private and parochial schools. By 1850, positions were hardening, and several state constitutions as well as laws and court decisions separated sectarian schools from public funds. The issue even came to a head in the effort of the Republican Party under President Grant to amend the U.S. Constitution to this effect. The Blaine Amendment was easily passed in the House but was defeated in the Senate in 1876 with many senators abstaining.

In a perverse way, this was an indication that the worst excesses of the anti-Catholic and antiradical nativism of the 1850s had subsided somewhat in what John Higham calls the "Age of Confidence."[20] For a decade or two after the Civil War, there was an increasing confidence that newcomers could be assimilated in America in a generous and cosmopolitan acceptance of different cultural traditions. German was taught in the public schools of Cincinnati, St. Louis, and other cities. San Francisco established "cosmopolitan schools," which were taught in French and German as well as English. But in the 1880s the complexion of the problem began to change again radically.

For the next fifty years, the flood tide of immigration brought millions of newcomers to the United States, approximately tripling the number that had come in the prior fifty years (nine million from 1826 to 1876 and twenty-seven million from 1876 to 1926). Even more important was the fact that most newcomers were coming from the less modern and more agricultural countries of central, eastern, and southern Europe, the three largest groups being Italians, east European Jews, and Poles. The new variety of ethnic stocks, languages, and cultural and family traditions led to renewed nativist movements and to new fanciful and real fears about the ability of the nation, especially in large cities, to assimilate such massive numbers who had come in such a short time.

Demands for instant Americanization echoed in all quarters of the country. These ranged from cruel racist calls for the immigrants to change and adapt or go back where they came from to more reasonable and generous efforts to help the immigrants cope with their new surroundings and still maintain respect for their cultural traditions. By and large, the humanitarian voices of progressive social workers and educators of the 1890s were drowned out by the nativist clamor of the early 1900s. On the national level, Congress passed the Johnson-Reed Act of 1924, which for the first time in U.S. history restricted immigration according to annual national quotas. Not surprisingly, these were worked out to favor the peoples of western and northern Europe over those from eastern and southern Europe.

This marked a high point in federal legislative attacks on pluralism, but it was part of the nativism that had spread across the country before and after World War I under assiduous stroking by such patriotic citizens' groups as the Daughters of the American Revolution, the Sons of the American Revolution, and the American Legion. German was outlawed from the public schools in many states, and between 1917 and 1921 some thirty states passed laws requiring that all instruction in public schools be given in English. These laws were clearly aimed at religious and ethnic groups conducting their schools in "foreign" languages.

The 1920s, however, were definitely a transition period. For just as the state legislatures and Congress were defining Americanism largely in Anglo-American terms, the Supreme Court began to define pluralism as an integral part of American constitutional law. Two landmark cases were decided in the 1920s. In *Meyer* v. *Nebraska* (1923) the court ruled that laws in Iowa, Nebraska, and Ohio prohibiting the teaching of any subject in any school in any language except English and prohibiting the teaching of foreign languages in elementary schools were unconstitutional.[21] The court agreed that the states could compel attendance at *some* school and make general regulations for *all* schools, including teaching in English. But states could not, under the due process clause of the Fourteenth Amendment, unreasonably interfere with the rights of parents to seek the kind of education they desired for their children.

In *Pierce* v. *Society of Sisters* (1925) the court ruled further that Oregon could not require parents to send their children to a public school, because that also unreasonably restricted the liberty of parents to guide the education of their children—a liberty again protected by the Fourteenth Amendment.[22] These two cases stand as charters of liberty for parents in the education of their children while at the same time affirming the authority of the state to regulate all schools, require attendance at some school, and see to it that teachers be of "good moral character and patriotic disposition" and that studies "plainly essential to good citizenship" be taught. Civic ideals and parental pluralism must somehow live together in public and private schools alike.

In the mid-1920s the early doctrines of cultural pluralism began to be formulated with considerable clarity. This view had a background in the earlier Progressive educational views of such reformers as Jane Addams and John Dewey. Both stressed the necessity for the public schools to respect and cultivate the cultural traditions and languages of various ethnic groups. But Horace M. Kallen is usually considered to be the father of cultural pluralism as a social philosophy.[23] He argued that America should be viewed as a "democracy of nationalities," each cooperating in the common political commonwealth, but each seeking cultural self-realization by developing its own emotional, aesthetic, and intellectual life.

Kallen pointedly argued that the common basis for such political community should be laid for all children in the public schools. He opposed the creation of separate schools for different religious or ethnic groups, the introduction of religious teachings into the public schools, and the granting of public funds for religious or private schools. In the 1920s, Kallen represented a broad consensus among liberal Protestants and Jews who expected the public schools to serve the common civic ideals fundamental to the democratic political community, and to respect the cherished values and ideals of the many culturally pluralistic communities. As it happened, many public schools were more likely to reflect the more conservative majority views of mainstream Protestant America. These views consisted of an amalgam of civic and moral conformism along with a fairly unbending insistence upon assimilation or at best an inattention to the values of ethnic differences.

This "inattention" has been interpreted by some recent historians to mean that the public schools were deliberately cruel in their concerted efforts to wipe out all trace of ethnic differences among immigrant children on behalf of imposing middle-class American values of speech, dress, cleanliness, punctuality, discipline, and obedience.[24] There is undoubtedly some truth in this picture. But the weight of historical judgment, both in the past and in the present, is that the public schools proved to be an enormous aid to those immigrant groups that were able and willing to take advantage of them—aids to adjustment to mainstream American society and to improved economic status for the children and grandchildren of the immigrant parents.[25]

It is true that some immigrant groups did oppose compulsory attendance laws and the compulsion to learn English, but it is also true that going to public school was a central and key element in the dreams that attracted millions to the new life in America. The response of immigrant groups was often conditioned by the traditional cultures that they brought with them, and thus the attitudes toward education in general and the public schools in particular varied greatly.

For example, Timothy Smith's studies show that the attendance of children of foreign parentage was as high as that of children of native-born parents, and that ethnic associations and the press urged public school attendance upon newcomers as a means of coping with an industrial (modern) way of life and becoming good citizens.[26] David Cohen reports that immigrant groups (Germans and Jews) from the more urbanized parts of Europe did better in school than those from more rural sectors (southern Italians and Poles).[27] Olneck and Lazerson find that children from groups that came from northern and western Europe stayed in school longer than those from eastern and southern Europe.[28] And Stephan Thernstrom reports a good deal more economic mobility among immigrant males in Boston following 1880 than he had earlier reported for Newburyport, especially among those who attended public rather than parochial schools.[29]

Despite the overall contribution of schooling to the assimilative process by which American society coped with modernization and still maintained a reasonably stable pluralism, it is true that newcomers generally were handicapped and at a disadvantage compared with those who had arrived earlier and had already begun "to make it." In addition, other groups were even more handicapped than the European immigrants. The special disadvantages of slavery for blacks, of reservation life for Indians, of exclusion for Asians, and of pervasive de facto segregation for Mexican-Americans underline the glaring exceptions to the generalizations made so far about European immigrants. For them, it scarcely makes sense to speak of a "linkage" between school, community, and home in view of the segregation or separation imposed by the majority communities upon these minority communities.

Before the Civil War, schooling for black slaves in the South was minimal. What there was went on informally in the households of whites who ignored or deliberately violated the legal prohibition against educating slaves. Meanwhile, slavery was gradually abolished in northern states, but most northern communities established separate schools for black children either by custom or by law, where any schools were provided at all. Similarly, philanthropic and religious groups normally conducted separate schools for black children. But the effort to admit black children to the common public schools (and thus make the schools genuinely common) did gradually gain some headway in several towns in Massachusetts in the 1840s and 1850s.

However, the movement received a major setback when Boston insisted on assigning black children to separate black schools, and the Massachusetts Supreme Court upheld the practice of "separate but equal" facilities in *Roberts* v. *Boston* (1849). Thus, despite Charles Sumner's eloquent arguments that separate schooling could not be a consistent part of a *common* school system, the doctrine of "separate but equal" was legally approved in Massachusetts until the legislature prohibited segregated schools in 1855. But the doctrine lived on in state and federal constitutional law, bulwarked by the Supreme Court in *Plessy* v. *Ferguson* (1896), until finally banished, at least in constitutional law, by the *Brown* decision of 1954.

After the Civil War, the northern states moved more or less rapidly to do away with school segregation laws; eighteen had done so by 1880. Needless to say, they were not able to overcome entirely the customs of local communities (especially in the urban centers) whose school boards seldom had black members. The major battleground over schooling for blacks shifted to the southern states and to the federal government for a decade or so after the Civil War. Under "gentle" Reconstruction from

1865 to 1867, the southern states moved quickly to pass the Black Codes that imposed legal segregation upon many aspects of life, including schools, if and when public schools were to be established for blacks at all. During the Civil War, several religious and missionary societies from the North sent teachers for black schools to sections of the South under the Union Army's control. After the war these efforts were redoubled, and the federal government's Freedmen's Bureau established several thousand schools for blacks.

Then came the "harsh" Reconstruction by the Radical Republicans in Congress, beginning with the Civil Rights Act (1866), the Reconstruction Act (1867), the Fourteenth Amendment (1868), the Fifteenth Amendment (1870), and, in effect, ending with the Civil Rights Act (1875), which was later declared unconstitutional. Throughout this decade of impassioned debate on the question of federal authority versus states' rights, no subject was more bitterly discussed than whether the central government could require states to integrate their public schools. Bill after bill was proposed, ranging from offering federal aid to those states that would establish "mixed schools" to proposals for a full-scale national system of schools to be erected in those states that refused to integrate their schools. In 1872 Sumner argued basically the theme of equality:

> How impossible it is for a separate school to be the equivalent of the common school . . . The separate school wants the first requisite of the common school, inasmuch as it is not open equally to all . . . Such a school is not republican in character . . . How precious the example which teaches that all are equal in rights. But this can be only where all co-mingle in the common schools as in common citizenship.[30]

Sumner's argument was to no avail. The momentum went out of the Radical Republican drive, and no federal education bills were passed. During the 1880s and 1890s all the former Confederate states reinstated strong Black Codes that enforced segregated schools by constitution or by legislation. Because of the congressional political process, it was clear that pluralistic localism was stronger than cohesive nationalism in the realm of equality of education. Decisions on segregated schools were to be left to the majority communities in the states. This was one of the most striking confrontations of different communities in American history, aside from the Civil War itself. The Supreme Court put its seal of approval upon the "separate but equal" doctrine in *Plessy* v. *Ferguson* in 1896.[31]

In practice, however, it became clear that black schools were becoming *un*equal as well as separate. In 1870, expenditures of southern states were approximately in the proportion of three dollars for a white child to two dollars for a black child; by 1930 the proportion was seven dollars for whites to two dollars for blacks. Black school terms were shorter, attendance lower, teachers' salaries and qualifications lower, buildings and facilities inferior.

The clash of communities over the education and schooling of American Indian children had both parallels and differences with that of blacks. After the Indians were finally defeated in their wars with the federal government by 1890, they were largely confined to reservations for which the federal government took responsibility. Whereas the federal government eventually found its hands tied by the states with regard to the education of blacks, it maintained direct authority over the Indians, with no communities in between, except for the delegation of schooling to missionary societies (ignoring the principle of separation of church and state) for much of the period from the 1870s to the 1920s. In the 1800s federal government day schools were established on the reservations, and several private boarding schools were established off the reservations with support from the Bureau of Indian Affairs.

In all cases, the major goal of the schooling seemed to be to assimilate the Indians as quickly and as thoroughly as possible to the "American" language and customs by stripping the children of their traditional tribal and family culture. The Indian community itself did not have much to say about the whole process until the 1920s. A new consciousness of pride and identity was symbolized by the organization in 1911 of the Society of American Indians, whose professional leadership and commitment to achieving greater freedom and equality through democratic political processes and education somewhat paralleled the founding of the National Association for the Advancement of Colored People two years earlier.

After the Snyder Act in 1924 conferred citizenship upon all Indians, proposals for educational reform began to gain attention. As part of a whole reassessment of the federal government's Indian policies, a major report, drawn up in 1928 under the direction of Lewis Meriam and the Brookings Institution, argued that the "alien" white curriculum should be drastically modified by indigenous materials suitable to Indian life and conducted in community-centered schools. It was not, however, until the New Deal that genuine reform of Indian education began to accompany new policies of self-government for tribes and renewed respect for the pluralism of Indian cultures.

Although the historical conditions were much different for Mexican-American communities, the actions of the Anglo-Americans who began to pour into the Southwest after the Mexican War ended in 1848 often rivaled that of other colonial victors. They treated the Spanish-speakers as the conquered, depriving them of land and property rights, were reluctant to grant them political rights, and were disdainful of their Spanish language and culture as well as their general lack of modern skills. Though the state governments of the Southwest did not go the full route to legal segregation of schools, the practices were scarcely distinguishable in many places: separate schools or at least separate classes, less money, and poorer buildings, facilities, and teachers.

In some cases, the Anglos who did bring their public school ideas with them and who tried to encourage the Mexican-Americans to come to school found often a reluctance or an indifference to the idea of schooling on the part of families of peasant or peon background who saw little value in the book learning, especially in English. The poor parents often identified schooling only with the upper-class clergy or the landed aristocrats in Mexico and saw little benefit for their children in an Anglo schooling that might undermine the traditional ties of family and church. In the large and crowded barrios to which the Chicanos were attracted or confined, many found that learning English was scarcely necessary. Spanish was the predominant language of daily life for almost everyone; there was no babble of many different tongues as in New York or Chicago. Far from the metropolitan centers of the East and North, the educational plight of Mexican-Americans did not come to the consciousness and conscience of the national community until the 1940s. It took still longer for historians and other scholars to focus attention on Chicano education.[32]

Pluralist Families in Modernizing Communities

Thus far, the stress has been on the variety of communities and their often conflicting demands upon the schools as they sought to cope with the industrial and political trends of the period. Directly involved in all this group pluralism, although often implicitly, was the role of individual families and their responses to the changes. Successive strains and tensions affected families differently, depending upon their economic status, modes of work, and the whole inherited network of relationships between parents and children. These relationships were shaped by the ethnic background, religious ties, language loyalty, and sense of identity with wider kinship or nationality origins. All these factors had a share in molding the attitudes of families toward modernization and schooling.

It is tempting to argue that before the Civil War there was a fairly high degree of consonance between families and the public schools and that the dissonance and alienation grew only after the Civil War. There is some truth in this observation, especially as it applied to fairly homogeneous village or rural communities that had been relatively untouched by modernization or pluralities before the war. It was, however, not so true in the diversifying large cities, where dissonance seemed to be characteristic, notably in New York, both before and after the Civil War. There was considerable consonance between white, Protestant, middle-class families and the schools they dominated, whether public or private, but there was a persistent dissonance between some families of the new minorities and the public schools. However, more ethnic groups eventually began to send their children to public schools for longer periods.

David Hogan's study of working-class groups in Chicago between 1880 and 1930 shows that different groups responded differently to the problems of modern factory life and schooling.[33] All immigrant groups had difficulty giving up children's wages for schooling, and thus many poor families opposed child labor restrictions. At first, the children's wages were needed to survive; later, they were needed to help the parents buy their own home, which loomed large in their cultural traditions. Still later they sent children to school for longer periods so that the children's earnings would be increased. In a sense, poor immigrant families faced a tension between survival and schooling. Because the Slavic families in Chicago put such a high premium upon home ownership, they delayed extended schooling for their children until the economic security of home ownership was achieved. And many Slavic families, especially the Poles, felt an intense sense of ethnic and religious identity that made Catholic parochial schools especially attractive to them wherever possible. When not possible, they wanted Polish rather than German taught in the public schools. The vitality of the ethnic community was more important to many of them than the Americanization and secular intent of the public school.

Jewish immigrants had a quite different set of attitudes toward schooling. A prime example is Mary Antin's triumphant remembrance of her entrance to the public schools of Boston in 1894—the first day of school was the "apex of my civic pride and personal contentment."[34] It was a common desire among many Jewish parents that their children should quickly take on American ways, but Mary Antin also noted the prospect of a sad process of disintegration of home life. She observed that boundless liberty for children might result in "that laxity of domestic organization, that inversion of normal relations which makes for friction, and which sometimes ends in breaking up a family that was formerly united and happy."[35]

Alan Wieder's interview study points to the changes in attitudes of successive generations of Jewish immigrants.[36] The first generation looked upon the public schools as the essential ingredient in achieving the freedom and equality promised by the New World. It was invested with virtually a spiritual quality. So parents insisted that their children attend school, stay in school, work hard, and thus be able to get ahead. Among the second generation, many of whom had done well, the attitude toward the public school no longer had the character of a spiritual ideal, but it was viewed respectfully, pragmatically, and then essentially as a passport to college, the professions, and even possibly to the suburbs. The closely knit Jewish community and family were loosening in the early decades of the twentieth century.

In fact, the general weight of social science scholarship up to the early 1970s was that the families of all ethnic groups were disintegrating at an alarming rate during the nineteenth century. David Angus, building upon the work of Talcott Parsons but not always adhering to its implications, summarizes the scenario of the family's decline in the face of industrial modernization as follows:

> During the 19th century the family became nucleated and mobile. One by one its "functions" were "assigned" to other emerging agencies and with the loss of these functions went the capacity of the family to regulate and control the lives of its members. What the family lost the individual partially gained as concepts of individual rights and bureaucratically defined justice began to prevail. These changes to the family were particularly marked in the cities where poverty, overcrowding, disease and other assorted ills destroyed family life altogether for some groups. By the mid-twentieth century the family was thought to have no function beyond bedding and boarding the young until they could be spun out to form new pairs. By the 'seventies, marriage itself was thought to be obsolete and most children were presumed to be unwanted.[37]

Now this picture may be a straw man—or straw family—as Angus says, but it had great influence and directly affected the development of family welfare policies from the New Deal to the Great Society. But, as scholars are wont to do when a point of view becomes too popular, many historians and social scientists began to punch holes in the easy overgeneralizations, revise some of the basic postulates, or at least point to major exceptions. This revisionism began in the late 1960s and continued in the 1970s.[38] In effect, many new studies have pointed to the adaptability, durability, and strength of the family in coping with social change.

For example, some families survived by sending daughters out to work as domestics (Irish and German in Buffalo, New York); others took in lodgers and boarders to compensate for loss of income when children left home (in northeastern cities); women from southern Italy living in Buffalo did begin to work and earn added income, but they worked at home or took part-time jobs that did not upset the patriarchal traditions of a male-dominated family. In general, many of the studies found considerable continuity and persistence in the peasant views of cooperation and fatalism that immigrants brought from the premodern societies to industrializing America.[39]

Especially important was the revision of the image of poor black family life under slavery and emancipation down to the 1920s. An increasingly popular view of the 1960s was that slavery had virtually destroyed the black family or at least had left it broken, passive, pathological, or unstable, with a high proportion of absent fathers, and that the poor black family had not been able to recover from the deprivation and degradation of slavery. This was the burden of Daniel Patrick Moynihan's report in 1965.[40] Within the past decade many studies of the black family in both the North and the South have disputed the Moynihan generalizations.[41]

The most impressive of the studies is by Herbert G. Gutman, professor of history at the City University of New York.[42] His massive documentation shows that the vast majority of black families persisted remarkably well under slavery. Immediately after the Civil War, between three-fourths and five-sixths of former slave households consisted of a married couple of two parents and their children, and an even higher proportion was maintained in the South and in the migrations to northern cities in the early twentieth century. He attributes this durability to the values that slaves and freedmen put upon family life and legal marriages, and the passing on of black cultural traditions from one generation to the next. There is indeed great disorganization among black families today, but Gutman argues that it is a result not of slavery or its aftermath but of the failures of the economic and social system since the Great Depression of the 1930s.

Despite the exaggerations that may have been used in describing the historical changes that tended to disrupt the family in the era of disorienting industrialization and urbanization, it is probably wise to resist an opposite extreme that tends to venerate the achievements and durabilty of ethnic families in maintaining traditional pluralisms of all kinds. Angus sums it up well: "The main idea . . . is that recent scholarship has shown the family in America to be far more resilient in the face of massive societal change than we thought only a few years ago."[43] But, he concludes:

The filiopietism which has been emerging over the past few years tends to exaggerate the strength of the immigrant or working-class family and its autonomy as an institution. For the time being, we are without a single comprehensive theory of the family that can take account of the seemingly endless variety of family forms which family historians are discovering . . . From 1880 to 1930, the American family resisted the social currents swirling around it. It did not succumb, neither did it triumph. It did, however, survive, and for better or worse it is surviving still.[44]

Generalizations for new federal policy are difficult to formulate on the basis of such historical variety, but at least we should be wary of easy or simple conclusions. What can be said, however, about this period is that by its end there was a vastly larger proportion of children attending schools for a longer period than there was at its beginning. This necessarily meant, as Joseph Kett has pointed out, that they spent less time at work and that schooling not only kept them from employment but separated them from the adult world and classified them with others of their own age group. It meant, too, that families were no longer as important in gaining children their eventual jobs as were the schooling and the credentials that were earned as prerequisites to the specialized and technological jobs that now prevailed over unskilled employment.[45] As a result, peer culture began to conflict with parental or family culture, but age grading and systematization of schooling were compatible with industrialization, urbanization, and immigration.

On top of the greater hold of the school upon the time and energies of the young, a new psychology announced the discovery of adolescence as a special stage of physical and emotional development, which required special attention by schools and nonschool educators.[46] G. Stanley Hall and his followers are given much credit for the invention of the idea of adolescence, and child development psychologists like Arnold Gesell at Yale began to stress the importance of freedom for children to grow and develop naturally with spontaneity, grace, initiative, and creativity. All this looked in the direction of greater stress upon individual differences among children and special care in teaching and cultivating their unique talents.

While such views were gaining headway among some middle-class parents and private progressive schools, other parents were more attracted to sponsoring youth organizations that would more positively direct young people toward desirable moral, religious, and civic goals (for example, Boy and Girl Scouts, YMCA, YWCA). Kett makes much of the point that these organizations were age graded, as were the schools, and that they employed new professional workers as well as volunteers from among interested parents.

Perhaps the most successful example of large-scale national mobilization of special-interest groups to effect changes in schooling during this period came in connection with the drive for vocational education.[47] And it was the most obvious and direct curriculum response to modernization—but for many different reasons. The National Association of Manufacturers wanted education to train workers for industry. The American Federation of Labor, somewhat reluctantly, joined in to support the idea of federal funds for vocational education to enable workers to get better jobs. Social workers and some educators wanted vocational studies that would make schooling more vital, practical, and interesting to those youth who wanted and needed early jobs.

A great debate took place over whether such schools should be run by industry (the National Association of Manufacturers said yes; the American Federation of Labor said no); and whether vocational education should be run by public authorities in a separate system from the regular public schools (business-oriented professionals and social-efficiency vocationalists said yes; welfare-oriented professionals and social-reform educators said no). The result was a compromise, and funds from the Smith-Hughes Act of 1917 poured federal money into the public education system for support of differentiated courses in the comprehensive high schools, which helped them to become the predominant type of secondary school. Separate vocational schools did not win the day, as they had done in most European countries.

Once again, a variety of communities proved to be successful in putting monumental new burdens upon public schools.[48] Vocational education has had powerful lobbyists in state and federal government circles who have been persuasive with their arguments that it has helped make the United States strong in agriculture, industry, and defense. Others have argued that it has had the effect of channeling working-class youth into the lower paid occupations and has "tracked" them away from colleges, the professions, and the managerial careers in society.[49] Thus vocational education has been blamed for maintaining and hardening social class distinctions to the greater disadvantage of already disadvantaged minority ethnic and racial groups. There is truth in both views.

In the long run, however, the effort to embrace vocational studies along with academic studies in a comprehensive high school system rather than relegating them to separate vocational schools in a dual-track system was one more achievement on behalf of free, universal, common public schools, an effort that proved to be a major characteristic of a distinctively American system of education. At its best, the comprehensive high school enhanced the civic education available to a wide cross section of pluralist groups it served. But at its worst, the civic mission got lost in the shuffle of cross purposes of a modernizing and pluralizing society.

The debate over vocational schooling illustrated the monumental new burdens being placed on the public schools between the 1820s and 1920s, but it also reflected the growing tensions in educational policy between the goals of civism, pluralism, and modernism. For some ethnic communities, the desire to maintain their cultural, linguistic, and religious traditions conflicted with the equally strong desire that their children reap the advantages of American life, which depended in turn on education to be an American. Some segments of the white, native-born population feared the growing diversity and pluralism of the nation and sought countermeasures in the form of schooling dedicated to uniform, national ideals, or at least a channeling of newcomers into courses more likely to lead to lower-level jobs and social status.

Throughout these hundred years, and for long thereafter, certain ethnic communities were at the same time excluded or discouraged from participation in common schooling. What had once been a pluralism largely of one dimension—religion—became a multidimensional pluralism of race, ethnicity, language, social class, and religion. This growing pluralism, in conjunction with massive modernization, placed education in the cross fire of contending claims. The triumph of comprehensive over dual-track schools represented one step toward realizing the goal of common schooling on behalf of democratic citizenship. But there were many more obstacles on the way, and the steps to be taken were not at all clear.

Civics Caught Between Unum and Pluribus (1820s–1870s)

In the mid-nineteenth century, the political values inculcated by the civic education programs of the schools did not change substantially from those celebrated in the Republic's first fifty years. In the textbooks of the day, their rosy hues if anything became even more golden. To the resplendent values of liberty, equality, patriotism, and a benevolent Christian morality were now added the middle-class virtues (especially of New England) of hard work, honesty and integrity, the rewards of property and even riches for individual effort, and obedience to legitimate authority. Ruth Elson sums up hundreds of textbooks this way:

> Unlike many modern schoolbooks, those of the nineteenth century made no pretense of neutrality. While they evade issues seriously

controverted in their day, they take a firm and unanimous stand on matters of basic belief. The value judgment is their stock in trade: love of country, love of God, duty to parents, the necessity to develop habits of thrift, honesty, and hard work in order to accumulate property, the certainty of progress, the perfection of the United States. These are not to be questioned. Nor in this whole century of great external change is there any deviation from these basic values. In pedagogical arrangements the school book of the 1890s was vastly different from that of the 1790s, but the continuum of values was uninterrupted. Neither the Civil War nor the 1890s provided a water-shed of basic values.[50]

Of all the political values the textbooks extolled, liberty was pre-eminent. Whenever they attempted to explain why children should love their country above all else, the idea of liberty took first place. This was undoubtedly of prime importance in promoting unity in an increasingly diverse and pluralistic society. Yet the loyalty to liberty was more in affective terms of feeling than in analytical terms of knowledge. Elson puts it this way:

> All books agree that the American nation politically expressed is the apostle of liberty, a liberty personified, apostrophized, sung to, set up in God-like glory, but rarely defined. To discover what liberty means in these books is a murky problem. The child reader could be certain that it was glorious, it is American, it is to be revered, and it deserves his primary loyalty. But for the child to find out from these books what this liberty is would be astonishing.[51]

As the Civil War approached, the textbooks began to speak of the dangers of disunion and, being mostly northern in origin, began to become more outspoken about the evils of slavery. Still, in the antebellum period, the South continued to use northern textbooks. Even after the Civil War, textbooks published in the South never did equal the quality of northern texts. In fact, the Confederate books that were written and published revealed political attitudes not much different from those that continued to flow from the North to the South, except on the subject of slavery. After the Civil War, a common custom was for southern teachers simply to excise the northern discussion of the Civil War and Reconstruction by pinning the pages together so young readers would presumably skip them in favor of the truth delivered by the teacher. To make up these gaps, the southern books and teachers could easily expand on the southern heroes in the Revolutionary War, with Washington brooking no competition.

According to Elson, the predominant political tone of nineteenth century textbooks was Federalist and conservative:

> Although schoolbook authors consider themselves guardians of liberty, they can be more accurately described as guardians of tradition. On social questions the tenor of the books is consistently conservative. The United States is always identified with freedom, but this freedom is best identified as that established in 1783 after separation from Great Britain. The nineteenth-century child was taught to worship past achievements of America and to believe in the inevitable spread of the American system throughout the world. But contemporary problems are conspicuously absent, and reform movements which would have profound social or political effects are either ignored or derided. While Jeffersonian and Jacksonian democracy agitated the adult world, the child was taught the necessity of class distinctions. Nor are Jefferson and Jackson ever ranked as heroes; . . . in the schools Hamilton and Daniel Webster governed the minds of the children.[52]

Although the textbook writers seemed to have no compunctions about taking sides for patriotic virtue, Republican devotion to liberty, or Federalist devotion to property, the school people in the 1830s and 1840s began to face the difficulties posed by pluralism in the burgeoning modernization of the new nation.

None was more eloquent than Horace Mann on what he candidly called "political education." Summing up his conclusion in 1848 on twelve years as secretary of the state board of education in Massachusetts, Mann began with the assumptions of the founders that citizens of a republic must "understand something of the true nature of the government under which they live." He spelled out the civic program in terms that will sound familiar to all teachers of civics since that time:

> The constitution of the United States and of our own State, should be made a study in our Public Schools. The partition of the powers of government into the three co-ordinate branches,—legislative, judicial, and executive,—with the duties appropriately devolving upon each; the mode of electing or of appointing all officers, with the reason on which it was founded; and, especially, the duty of every citizen, in a government of laws, to appeal to the courts for redress, in all cases of alleged wrong, instead of undertaking to vindicate his own rights by his own arm, and, in a government where the people are the acknowledged sources of power, the duty of changing laws and rulers by an appeal to the ballot, and not by rebellion, should be taught to all the children until they are fully understood.[53]

The distinction between the basic ideal values of the political community and the actual operation of the system began to be apparent even to the educators. Caught in the swirl of contesting forces in Massachusetts occasioned by the immigration of Roman Catholic Irish and Germans and by the changes in urban life attendant upon the industrial factory system, Mann knew all too well that "if the tempest of political strife were to be let loose upon our Common Schools, they would be overwhelmed with sudden ruin." He recognized that many would object to any study of political matters in the schools because the Constitution was subject to different readings. He saw the dangers of political partisanship in the appointment of teachers on the basis of their political fitness in the eyes of the local school committee or of the majority in the community:

> Who shall moderate the fury of these conflicting elements, when they rage against each other; and who shall save the dearest interests of the children from being consumed in the fierce combustion? If parents find that their children are indoctrinated into what they call political heresies, will they not withdraw them from the school; and, if they withdraw them from the school, will they not resist all appropriations to support a school from which they derive no benefit?[54]

Mann could not admit that the public schools should avoid political education altogether, nor could he risk the destruction of the public schools by urging them to become "theatres for party politics." His solution was similar to that which he proposed for religious controversies: schools should teach the common elements that all agreed to but should skip over the controversial:

> Surely, between these extremes, there must be a medium not difficult to be found. And is not this the middle course, which all sensible and judicious men, all patriots, and all genuine republicans, must approve?—namely that those articles in the creed of republicanism, which are accepted by all, believed in by all, and which form the common basis of our political faith, shall be taught to all. But when the teacher, in the course of his lessons or lectures on the fundamental law, arrives at a controverted text, he is either to read it without comment or remark; or, at most, he is only to say that the passage is the subject of disputation, and that the schoolroom is neither the tribunal to adjudicate, nor the forum to discuss it.[55]

Thus would Mann stress the transcendent values of the political community but avoid indoctrination and pass over controversial ideas about the constitutional order and omit critical judgments about the actual operation of the system. Political knowledge should concentrate on the formal structure of governmental institutions, but the skills of participation should be delegated, along with the controversial, to the nonschool agencies of party, press, and caucus of adults.

Mann was so intent upon getting common schools established for an ever wider range of the potential school population that he would not risk the failure of the common school idea in order to bring political controversy into the schools. Thus it came about that the emerging public schools were largely satisfied with civic programs that initiated the poor, the foreigner, and the working-class children into the political community by literacy in English, didactic moral injunctions, patriotic readers and histories, and lessons that stressed recitations on the structural forms of the constitutional order. But Mann's emphasis on a "common core of civic values," taught without mention of controversial issues, had its problems then, just as it does today.

Upon the centennial celebration of the Revolution in 1876, the children of the "unincorporated" were still largely blocked from the public schools and thus from the civic education offered by the nation's schools. The Reconstruction reforms had visualized extension of public school systems to the southern states, but these efforts were largely dissipated by the 1870s. And northern states were slow to admit blacks to common schools, often preferring to establish separate schools for white and black. These failures of the educational system to put into practice the stated values of the political community helped widen the gap between ideal and reality. Millions of immigrants were being incorporated into citizenship by civic education despite the patronizing and often hostile ethnic image the textbooks portrayed of Irish and immigrants from southern Europe, but millions of members of racial minorities born in the United States were still beyond the pale of white citizenship education. In the face of mounting cultural pluralisms, the goal of civic education began to embrace rapid assimilation to a stridently nationalistic Americanism along with embracing an ideal of progressive humanitarian reform.

The Civics of Aggressive Modernization and Progressive Reform (1870s–1920s)

In the fifty years straddling the turn of the twentieth century, the character of civic education programs began to undergo much more searching examination than they had for the nation's first one hundred years. Although the picture of basic values constituting the political community did not change radically, there were three significant alterations in emphasis in the schools in response to the rapid social transformations of a half century of modernization. First, the earlier stress on love of a grand, free country became a more shrill and passionate devotion to a great and powerful nation. The doctrines of Manifest Destiny, winning the West, building an empire overseas, and making the world safe for democracy led to exaltation of the United States as the superior nation of the world, a nation imbued with the mission to lead all the rest and thus deserving, nay demanding, a loyalty to "my country, right or wrong." All this led to an increasingly nationalistic and strident tone to civic education.

Not only did the Spanish-American War and World War I stimulate a militaristic fervor and chauvinistic flavor to civic education, but the massive immigration that characterized almost the whole period added a second aspect: the demand for instant Americanization of immigrants. To many conservatives and liberals alike, immigrants posed a basic threat to the commitments of the democratic political community, to the stability of the constitutional order, and to the functioning of governing authorities. These critics could point to ghettos, crime in the streets, bloody strikes in the factories, corruption in government, and the spreading of socialist, communist, and revolutionary doctrines by radical groups.

This lurking fear of the alien and foreign was fueled by the millions of immigrants who poured in from southern and eastern Europe and Asia. While civic textbooks might attribute this influx to the search for liberty and equality, the civic education programs of settlement houses, patriotic organizations, and nativist associations began to turn more to Americanization programs that not only stressed didactic praise of the historic values but also demanded outward signs of loyalty from the new citizens as well as the old. Stress upon the public pledge of allegiance, salutes to the flag, loyalty oaths, patriotic songs and marching, required instruction in English, and attacks on teaching foreign languages in the schools were added to the more traditional and prosaic textbook instruction.

A third shift in emphasis in the political value commitments was a more prominent role given to the image of the self-made men, the self-reliant individuals who had shifted from pioneering in the West to pioneering in the development of the industrial, urban, business system that was modernizing America so rapidly and thrusting her producing and consuming capacity ahead of that of all other nations. The political side of this image was, of course, that it had all happened under the auspices of a free-enterprise system apart from government controls.

But liberal reactions to the social and political results of an aggressive industrial, capitalistic order led to the Progressive Era movements dedicated to popular political reforms in the electoral systems and civil service; to social reforms in the cities, prisons, sweat shops, child labor; and to movements for women's rights, temperance, and the rest. Underlying the progressive reforms was a belief in the collective efforts of government to control rampant business enterprise, protect the rights of the people, and bring about good government through honest and efficient civil service, rational bureaucracies, and regulatory agencies.

These conflicting political values began to reveal themselves in different approaches to civic education as educators responded in different ways to the ebullient modernization of America's polity and economy. They faced the problem of what to do about the massive increases in school enrollments brought about by a growing consensus that education was a prime means to get ahead in American society, aided and abetted by compulsory attendance laws aimed at abolishing the evil of child labor and achieving the goal of assimilation through Americanization. The problems were especially acute at the secondary school level, where the schools tried to cope with a majority that was not college bound.

One response of the academically minded educators in the 1880s and 1890s was to expand the study of history (thereby reducing the emphasis on study of civil government) by introducing more rigorous scholarly knowledge into the history texts and courses. In the early 1890s the Madison Conference on History, Civil Government, and Political Economy made proposals that became a part of the overall re-examination of the entire secondary school curriculum undertaken by the Committee of Ten of the National Education Association, whose report was published in 1893.

The main assumption of the Committee of Ten, headed by President Charles W. Eliot of Harvard, was that all courses in high school should provide the same strong mental discipline for the non-college-bound majority as for the college-bound minority. The teaching of history was thus not primarily to develop good citizenship and love of country but also to teach high school students to think like historians. Echoes of this view are found in the excellence movement of the 1980s.[56]

For two to three decades the academic orientation of the Committee of Ten dominated curriculum thinking and curriculum making in the civic education programs of the secondary schools. In history, the emphasis was on the use of primary sources to develop in pupils a historic sense and to train them in the search for historical materials, the weighing of evidence, and the drawing of conclusions. In the effort to get children to think like historians, the flamboyant nationalistic and patriotic history of the previous century would be counteracted. In 1899 a Committee of Seven of the American Historical Association urged the use of primary sources as supplementary to the textbook. *History Teachers Magazine* (founded in 1909) and the work of Henry Johnson at Teachers College, Columbia University, both contributed to the new movement to stress historical problem solving and reasoned judgment in a laboratory or workshop setting.

On the other hand, a Progressive response in the early 1900s was an upsurge in the study of civil government as new ideas about civic education began to appear among scholars in the new social sciences of political science, economics, and sociology. In 1916 a committee of the American Political Science Association, reflecting the Progressive reform movements, argued that the standard courses in civil government should be shaken up. Instead of starting with the study of the U.S. Constitution and a description of the formal and structural organization of government and then proceeding to a similar study of state constitutions and governments, the procedure should be reversed. The committee endorsed the study of "community civics," assuming that political affairs nearest to home were the most interesting and important and thus should be considered first. The Progressive-inspired Municipal League promoted this idea.

Another, but far less popular, response was the effort by progressive educators and social settlement workers of a liberal humanitarian persuasion to urge that civic education not simply view the ethnic heritage of immigrants as an ancestral bondage that should be quickly and thoroughly removed by assimilation; instead, that heritage should be honored and used as a generous and sympathetic process of Americanization. Jane Addams and John Dewey thus criticized the public schools for insisting upon a one-way Anglo conformity that denationalized immigrant children too rapidly and blatantly.

In the long run, however, the rising movement to make citizenship education the special province of the social studies was even more influential, for it came to pervade the elementary as well as the secondary school. This movement took place under the auspices of the National Education Association's Commission on the Reorganization of Secondary Education, whose final report, *Cardinal Principles of Secondary Education*, was published in 1918. From 1913 to 1916 the Committee on Social Studies prepared its report for the overall commission. Again reflecting the Progressive views of reform, the committee brought citizenship to the forefront of the social responsibility of the secondary school more explicitly than this had ever before been stated. In a preliminary statement in 1913, the committee's chairman, a sociologist, revealed the social reform intent to make civics much more than a study of government:

> Good citizenship should be the aim of social studies in the high school. While the administration and instruction throughout the school should contribute to the social welfare of the community, it is maintained that social studies have direct responsibility in this field. Facts, conditions, theories, and activities that do not contribute rather directly to the appreciation of methods of human betterment have no claim. Under the test the old civics, almost exclusively a study of Government machinery, must give way to the new civics, a study of all manner of social efforts to improve mankind. It is not so important that the pupil know how the President is elected as that he shall understand the duties of the health officer in his community. The time formerly spent in the effort to understand the process of passing a law over the President's veto is now to be more profitably used in the observation of the vocational resources of the community. In line with this emphasis the committee recommends that social studies in the high school shall include such topics as the following: Community health, housing and homes, public recreation, good roads, community education, poverty and the care of the poor, crime and reform, family income, savings banks and life insurance, human rights versus property rights, impulsive action of mobs, the selfish conservatism of tradition, and public utilities.[57]

In the committee's final report the term *social studies* was used to include not only history, civics, and government but also concepts from sociology and economics, which related directly to the organization of society and man as a member of social groups. History still held a major place in the course proposals for grades 7 to 12, but a "problems approach" was to infuse the whole program. Civics was proposed for the junior high school years as well as a new course in "problems of democracy" for the twelfth grade, all to enable students to "acquire the social spirit."

Hazel Hertzberg summarizes the influence of the committee's report this way:

> Instruction in the social studies should be organized around concrete problems of vital importance to society and of immediate interest to the pupil rather than on the basis of the formal social sciences. . . . The

social studies should contribute directly to the "social efficiency" of the student, helping him "to participate effectively in the promotion of social well-being" in the groups of which he is a member, from his own community to the "world community" . . . The skills to be learned by pupils were those of good citizens participating in the building of an invigorated society, not those of historians carefully interpreting evidence, developing criticism, and arriving at synthesis . . .

The Report of the Committee on Social Studies had a significant impact on the direction of educational reform. It represented many of the deepest, most pervasive, and most characteristic viewpoints of the Progressive period. No doubt it would have been exceedingly influential in any case, but the circumstances that it was issued just before American entry into World War I created a climate favorable to its concern with personal and social immediacy and utility and what is today referred to as "relevance."[58]

The committee's final report had a great effect on making citizenship one of the cardinal goals of education, especially of the social studies. And although it tended to reduce emphasis upon abstract academic material in favor of live problems, it also tended to reduce the relative importance of political concerns in civic education in favor of greater emphasis on social, economic, and practical personal problems. Note the withdrawal from "constitutional questions" in the pursuit of good citizenship:

While all subjects should contribute to good citizenship, the social studies—geography, history, civics and economics—should have this as their dominant aim. Too frequently, however, does mere information, conventional in value and remote in its bearing, make up the content of the social studies. History should so treat the growth of institutions that their present value may be appreciated. Geography should show the interdependence of men while it shows their common dependence on nature. Civics should concern itself less with constitutional questions and remote governmental functions and should direct attention to social agencies close at hand and to the informal activities of daily life that regard and seek the common good. Such agencies as child welfare organizations and consumers' leagues afford specific opportunities for the expression of civic qualities by the older pupils.[59]

Despite the retreat from "remote governmental functions," the skills of civic participation began to be touched upon as social studies teachers were attracted to progressive education's new stress on projects, units, and activities in the classroom to promote the habits and outlooks appropriate to democratic behavior. The autonomy of the professional teacher, so widely proclaimed in the 1980s as essential to the improvement of the teaching profession, was even hinted at. The *Cardinal Principles* found valuable

> the assignment of projects and problems to groups of pupils for cooperative solution and the socialized recitation whereby the class as a whole develops a sense of collective responsibility. Both of these devices give training in collective thinking. Moreover, the democratic organization and administration of the school itself, as well as the cooperative relations of pupil and teacher, pupil and pupil, and teacher and teacher, are indispensible.[60]

Although this approval of the study of problems and "socialized recitation" in classrooms may seem to be a modest and familiar proposal to modern teachers, it by no means swept the profession off its feet. Teachers lectured, and students took notes, asked questions, memorized passages for recitation, wrote essays, and took exams—all these continued to be the prime methods used in history and civics classrooms. And venturing out into the community was still more radical, especially if a zealous civics teacher actually ran up against local business, religious, or patriotic organizations. In this case, the study of "remote governmental functions" could actually be conducted more freely than treading on local political toes.

But at least the idea of participation could now take its place alongside the inculcation of values and political knowledge as the main ingredients of a civic program in the schools. And the way was being prepared for distinguishing and comparing the stated values of the political community with the actual operation of the governmental authorities by the stress upon critical thinking, scholarly sources of knowledge, and first-hand study of the actual functioning of government, at least at the municipal level of community civics.

Above all, it was recognized that the high schools had to deal with a very different kind of population from that of the secondary schools of the nation's first hundred years—that is, the non-college-oriented students. Assimilation of vast numbers of foreign immigrants, both youthful and adult, nearly engulfed the schools and exhausted their energies. Teaching English and the rudimentary structure of government was the easiest way. For all the protestations of progressive educators, of the national committees, and of the teachers of teachers, the courses in American history, civics, and civil government, which were engrossing to countless thousands of adult immigrants seeking citizenship, were boring to millions of high school students. These students found they went through expanding cycles of social studies, second only to English and physical education in total time allotments of the usual curriculum. They studied "communities" in the third and fourth grades, civics in the ninth and twelfth grades, American history in the fifth, eighth, and eleventh grades, with geography, state history, and European or world history sandwiched in, probably in the seventh and tenth grades.

So the fifty-year period following the 1920s was given over to all kinds of attempts to reform and break out of the social studies cycles on behalf of a better civic education, and even more belatedly to incorporate at last the minority and disadvantaged groups in society that had long been "outsiders" to the mainstream of American political and educational life.

But what shall we think about these first two hundred years? The Revolutionary War ideal of education as a means of regenerating a sense of political community should continue to be a prime goal for the education of each new generation of would-be Americans. The sense of community I have in mind is a commitment to the basic values of constitutional government as denoted by such concepts as freedom, equality, popular consent, and personal obligation for the public good. These values were promulgated by the Republic's founders in the Revolutionary Era and were embodied in the Declaration of Independence, the Constitution, and the Bill of Rights. The Republic's welfare rests on an educated citizenry, as the founders argued. The prime purpose, the highest priority, for a genuinely public education is the political goal of empowering the whole population to exercise the rights and cope with the responsibilities of a genuinely democratic citizenship.

But we also should learn from history that society and government and thus the nature of citizenship have changed drastically in the past two hundred years. So we cannot be content with the prescriptions for a civic curriculum produced in the late nineteenth or early twentieth centuries. Simple literacy in the three Rs for elementary school white boys is obviously not enough. Simple history as proposed by Jefferson or the elements of civil government as proposed by Washington are not enough. Vague preachments on the glories of liberty, as described by Ruth Elson, are not enough. Textbooks should not be left to the socially or politically conservative authors. Didactic appeals to the moral, spiritual, or political virtues are not enough, and partisan indoctrination of particular economic or ideological platforms is not appropriate.

Yet, somehow, the schools have a responsibility for doing all they can to teach the values, knowledge, and participation skills required of a modern democratic citizenry. Such ingredients should not be left to the political parties, the newspapers, the ministers, or the coffee houses, as they were in the Revolutionary period; nor to modern business or labor, special-interest groups or media commentators.

In re-examining the stated purposes used to justify the development and spread of the common public school in the mid-nineteenth century, I believe that the citizenship argument is still valid. The highest priority for a genuinely public school is to serve the public purposes of a democratic political community. Those in favor of "excellence" or "back to the basics" should be reminded that citizenship is the basic purpose for universal literacy. If the fundamental purposes of schooling are to be confined to preparing for a job or developing individual talents, these might well be achieved in private schools that select students for particular destinies. But the faith of the common school reformers, as of the founders, that the civic tasks can best be performed by public schools that are characterized primarily by a public purpose, public control, public support, public access, and public commitment to civic unity was soundly based.

It is obvious that the public school reformers of the early nineteenth century did not fully achieve these goals. Horace Mann was on the right track when he argued for the necessity of what he candidly called "political education." But he fell short of what is needed (then as well as now). Although he stressed the understanding of the constitutional regime and knowledge about civil government, he backed away from the discussion of controversial political or constitutional questions in the schoolroom. He thus helped establish the tradition that the schools are not legitimate forums in which to discuss politically sensitive matters. This was a difficult issue for Mann, but he concluded that it was better to have neutral public schools than to have none, a denouement he feared would come about if the schools became "theatres for party politics." We can and must find a way to surmount Mann's difficulties.

A second thing we should learn from the mid-nineteenth century is that at least two lines of thought influenced the civic role of public education with regard to the assimilation of the immigrants who began to come in large numbers before the Civil War. It is undoubtedly true that a growing nativism from the 1830s to the 1850s sometimes gave to the public school movement an anti-Catholic, antiradical, and Anglo superiority tone. But we should also remember with John Higham that there was another more democratic and more cosmopolitan point of view displayed by some public school proponents who argued that the schools should be a humane assimilative force. In the 1860s and 1870s ethnic rivalries declined, nativism was muted, modernization welcomed enormous new pools of manpower, a Christian belief in the brotherhood of man was still alive and well. All these influences flowed into what Higham calls the Age of Confidence, that is, confidence in the country's capacity to accept great diversity and pluralism as a basic characteristic of the democratic political community. And the public schools could contribute to this cosmoplitan view of assimilation. Bilingual public schools in several states during the nineteenth century exemplified this faith.

The main lesson we should learn from the Gilded Age and Progressive Era is that there were two major pressures upon the schools to prescribe their citizenship education. The first and most influential through most of this period emanated from the business-oriented and nationalistic nativism associated with a burgeoning modernization movement. The three significant changes in civic education already noted reflect these pushes to conformity: (1) the shrill and passionate patriotism owed to a great and powerful nation that was exercising its Manifest Destiny, winning the West, building an empire, and making the world safe for democracy; (2) the demand for instant Americanization of the millions of immigrants who flooded into the United States from the 1880s to the 1920s; and (3) the glorification of the self-made man, who labored (and prospered) on behalf of free enterprise unhampered by a limited government. It is not difficult to see these trends illustrated in textbooks on American history and civil government.

For much of the period these elements of the modernization mood dominated the civic education in the schools as they did much of American public life. They overshadowed the value claims of the historic democratic political community and of the newly arrived and varied pluralistic communities. Often, some business-oriented or economy-minded progressives joined in these views on behalf of social control.

But, as Robert Wiebe points out, there was a second strain among the new middle-class professionals who were welfare-oriented or social-service progressives. Their concern was the use of liberal government on behalf of social reform (in prisons, sweatshops, child labor, and temperance) as well as political reform (civil service, electoral innovations, women's suffrage, and compulsory attendance on behalf of universal education). This stream of Progressive endeavor resulted in a number of efforts to reform citizenship education in the schools. These included the stiffening of history teaching by basing it on primary sources and thus combating the chauvinism of the rampant nativism; the effort to develop a community civics to replace a sterile approach to constitutional structures; and the new civics embodied in the social studies movement and in the Seven Cardinal Principles. Some welfare-oriented progressives even tried to reorient the Americanization process so that assimilation would be accomplished generously and sympathet-ically with respect for immigrant cultures and traditions. Thus was cultural pluralism born.

I hope we are done with the excesses of the nativistic and superpa-triotic conformity that marked the aggressive modernization period. We could learn a good deal from the effort to stress reasoned problem solving on behalf of "all manner of social efforts to improve mankind." I hope that schools can take seriously the problems approach to social, economic, and political issues. But one result of this period's reform movements in civic education was a reduction of the political concerns of history, civics, and social studies. There has been a withdrawal from the study of the basic ideas of the constitutional regime and the political community. The general civic education curriculum seldom dealt with the fundamental concepts and meaning of liberty, equality, justice, and obligation for the public good. Still less often did the practices of schools reflect these ideas in their governance or activities. I continue to hope that we can learn these lessons from our longer history, but first we must reckon with the more recent trends of the past fifty years.

Diminishing the Civic Purposes of Public Schooling (1930s–1980s)

For a large part of the past fifty years the American people have looked to an activist government as a powerful force for economic and social welfare, especially during the New Deal, Fair Deal, New Frontier, and Great Society. But from the mid-1960s to the present we have entered an era of decline in confidence in public institutions. This political and moral malaise has affected education and has led to increasing doubts about the very idea of public education and its historical reliance upon systems of free, universal, common, secular, compulsory schooling.

In this chapter we return to the theme with which our history began, the continuing search for the role that public education should play in building a sense of community among all Americans. This comes down to two questions: what kind of authority should be the basis for the nation's common undertakings and what kind of education can best serve to legitimize, maintain, and improve that national civic community? We seen how the Republic's founders rejected military power, religious sanction, and the inherited prerogatives of kinship or hierarchical social class as the basis for the authority of the new American community. They proclaimed instead that the democratic political community was to be the binding element of social cohesion and that this political community was to be based upon such basic values as liberty, equality, and justice. And the most appropriate kind of education for achieving and preserving the democratic political community was public education permeated by a public purpose rather than private education devoted to military, religious, ethnic, or social class preferments.

I have tried to indicate how successive efforts to reform public education have been pulled and hauled by the divergent forces seeking cohesion on one side and differentiation on the other. This tug of war may be described as the tension between the public and the private, as Robert Wiebe does; or between inclusiveness and exclusiveness, as Nathan Glazer does; or between integrationists and pluralists, as John Higham does. But all three agree that significant changes occurred in the 1960s.

Historian Wiebe argues that the 1960s revealed a national style that was sectarian, not pragmatic, a style that looked for boundaries that divided people, not common ground that bound them together. Thus a major casualty was the dream of moderation, accommodation, and cohesion.[1] Sociologist Glazer points to the ideal of inclusiveness that welcomed immigrants and their differences of national style. This ideal seemed to be winning—up to the 1880s and 1890s, when the exclusiveness of the nativist attacks on foreigners gained ascendancy and set up obstacles to free immigration in the 1920s. He argues that the exclusive mentality was beginning to be dismantled in the 1930s and increasingly so in the 1960s until, he might have said, a startling new ethnic exclusiveness set in.[2] Historian Higham describes vividly the persistent dilemma posed on one hand by integrationists who stressed the equality of individuals, majority rule, the elimination of cultural boundaries, a unifying ideology and cohesion around the American creed of the past or the visions of a Great Society in the future; and, on the other hand, by pluralists who sought to maintain cultural boundaries, who looked to the little communities of the past, who found cohesion in the heritage of distinctive memories, and who stressed the equality of groups and their minority rights.[3]

Any one of these interpretations would be a useful basis for analyzing the search for community in the last half of the twentieth century. But there is danger that the values and virtues of community might be seen as wholly on one side, on the side of the public, of inclusiveness, or of integration. Such an assumption would be far too simplistic to explain a complex and often ambiguous history. Almost all people seek some sort of community or communities to which they can feel attached and at home. The questions here are what sort of community should provide the authority for public education and to what sort of community should the goals of public education most appropriately lend legitimacy? It is clear from the history of public schooling that public education once had powerful moral as well as legal authority behind it. Until almost yesterday the public school was a well-fixed article in the American public creed, commanding powerful moral authority as a national unifier, liberator, and equalizer.

At various times the public school has drawn upon the political authority of the ideals of the nation's founders, the religious authority of nondenominational Protestantism, the moral virtues and work ethic of middle-class ideology, the academic authority of literacy and of knowledge in an education-oriented society, the cohesive authority of assimilator and Americanizer in an immigrant-flooded society, and the socializing authority as agent of progressive reform in a rapidly modernizing and industrializing society. But for a decade or more in the 1960s and 1970s, the erosion of the legitimacy of some of the major institutions in American society began to affect the "deauthorization" of the public school as well; that is, its moral authority to act as a guide or leader in social affairs has been seriously questioned and weakened. At the end of the nation's two hundredth year, the value of public education was being attacked from several quarters, and the American people were engaged in searching anew for the legitimate authority for public education in the future.

The question has become, what sort of community can most appropriately give legitimacy to the goals of education in general and to public education in particular? There are two principal replies: one says that authority should rest with a number of pluralistic communities; the other says the authority should reside in the overall political or civic community. In oversimplified but useful terms the two general approaches may be identified as pluralism and civism.

Pluralism seeks moral authority and legitimacy for education in the many diverse communities that serve to bind individuals and groups together on the basis of religion, race, ethnicity, language, culture, social class, or local cohesion and unity. Pluralists see such positive values in diversity and variety of associations that they consider them to be the essence of community around which education and schooling should cluster. Some pluralists are exceedingly critical of public education for being so conformist in outlook and practice, recommending that public schools should emphasize ethnic studies, multicultural studies, bilingual studies, and in general reflect the enormous diversity of American communities. Other pluralists see no special authority in public education at all, viewing it as no more legitimate or authoritative than private schools or any number of other educative agencies, such as the family, churches, and voluntary associations of all kinds. Still others view public education as positively illegitimate because of its historic connection with an exploitative, capitalist, corporate liberal state.

By contrast, civism seeks the principal authority and legitimacy for public education in the democratic political community. Though not found often in current usage, the word *civism* is a perfectly good English word, simply meaning "good citizenship." It is found in Webster's unabridged dictionary (second and third editions), the *Oxford English Dictionary,* and even the *American College Dictionary. Civism* is taken from the French *civisme* (taken in turn from the Latin *civis,* meaning citizen). The French term was coined to refer to the devotion or well-affected disposition toward the new nation they established in their own Revolution of 1789. In English, *civism* refers generally to the "citizen principle" as envisioned in the ancient Greek and Roman republics, especially concerning the tradition of self-sacrifice for the public good. It came by extension to mean in general "the principles of good citizenship" in a republic. It connotes the need for building a sense of cohesion that will bind citizens together into a viable political community. It includes "the virtues and sentiments of a good citizen."

Civism argues that public education has a special responsibility and legitimacy for being a positive force in promoting the civic values, civic knowledge, and civic skills of participation required for maintaining and improving the democratic political community and for strengthening the freedom, equality, justice, and popular consent promised by the Declaration of Independence, the Constitution, and the Bill of Rights. These values, which themselves provide protection for the diversity of plural associations, must be held in common by all the pluralities, or else privatism, contention, and conflict might threaten the welfare of any but the most powerful groups in the society.

Pluralism and Privatization

Despite the origins of the term "cultural pluralism" in the early twentieth century, it did not gain widespread professional or popular usage until it had sudden rebirth in the 1960s, when it became exceedingly popular in the hands of a number of different critics as well as friends of public education. Only three examples can be mentioned here. They represent the new ethnicity, a neoconservative as well as a New Left political philosophy, and a variety of critics in educational policy who espoused pluralism both from within and outside the educational establishment.

Heartened by the success of blacks in the civil rights movement of the 1960s but frustrated by the feelings that similar forms of discrimination continued to apply to the descendants of white immigrants, a new and sometimes fierce pride in ethnic traditions appeared in both the professional and popular literature and reappeared as a lively political force in the elections of the 1960s and 1970s. Books and articles by Michael Novak, then on the staff of the Rockefeller Foundation, Nathan Glazer and Daniel Patrick Moynihan at Harvard, and Reverend Andrew Greeley, director of the Center for the Study of Pluralism at the University of Chicago, became well known.[4]

In 1974 Father Greeley became the editor of a scholarly quarterly called *Ethnicity,* whose purpose was described as "a new journal devoted to the empirical and theoretical study of ethnic diversity and integration . . . concerned with understanding both the persistence of ethnic consciousness and the interaction of ethnic groups within a society. It will place special emphasis on elucidating the basic belief systems and cosmologies of ethnic groups."

The new ethnicity was defined by Michael Novak as

a movement of self-knowledge on the part of members of the third and fourth generation of southern and eastern European immigrants in the United States. In a broader sense, the new ethnicity includes a renewed self-consciousness on the part of other generations and other ethnic groups: the Irish, the Norwegians and Swedes, the Germans, the Chinese and Japanese, and others . . .

The new ethnicity entails: first, a growing sense of discomfort with the sense of identity one is *supposed* to have—universalist, "melted," "like everyone else"; then a growing appreciation for the potential wisdom of one's own gut reactions (especially on moral matters) and their historical roots; a growing self-confidence and social power; a sense of being discriminated against, condescended to, or carelessly misapprehended; a growing disaffection regarding those to whom one had always been taught to defer; and a sense of injustice regarding the response of liberal spokesmen to conflicts between various ethnic groups, especially between "legitimate" minorities and "illegitimate" ones. There is, in a word, an inner conflict between one's felt personal power and one's ascribed public power; a sense of outraged truth, justice, and equity.[5]

Novak argued for the introduction of ethnic studies into the public school curriculum:

With even modest adjustments in courses in history, literature, and the social sciences, material can be introduced that illuminates inherited patterns of family life, values, and preferences. The purpose for introducing multicultural materials is neither chauvinistic nor propagandistic but realistic. Education ought to illuminate what is happening in the self of each child. What about the child of mixed marriage, the child of *no* ethnic heritage—the child of the melting pot? So much in the present curriculum already supports such a child that the only possible shock to arise from multicultural materials would appear to be a beneficial one: not all others in America are like him (her), and that diversity, as well as homogenization, has a place in America.[6]

From views and sentiments like those of Novak, the demand rose for ethnic heritage studies and multicultural studies in the public schools.

But another approach arising from the new ethnicity was the argument that ethnic schools would be better than common public schools. Andrew Greeley implied this when he argued that an "ethnic miracle" had been achieved by some of the immigrant groups in rising out of poverty, hatred, and discrimination by their own efforts and in spite of the public schools. In fact their own parochial schools helped Irish Catholics, Italians, and Poles achieve financial success and middle-class status in a matter of a few decades from their arrival in the United States. He argued that the public high school did not assist in this process, because the immigrants' financial success came *before* they began to flock to schools. It was their family life, hard work, ambition, courage, work ethic, and sacrifice. They were given no favors and no help, but they were given personal freedom and the chance to turn their hard work into economic progress. Greeley also argued that Catholic students in parochial schools were more tolerant and less racist than those Catholics who attended public schools.

The goal for social policy in all this was that public funds should aid ethnic schools, which have been so important in the "ethnic miracle" of the past:

> One might take it as a tentative hypothesis that the school is a rather poor institution for facilitating the upward mobility of minority groups—until they first acquire some kind of rough income parity. The native American faith that equality of education produces equality of income seems to have been stood on its head in the case of the ethnics. For them, better income meant more effective education.
>
> Nor did the public schools play the critical "Americanization" role that such educators as Dr. James B. Conant expected them to play in the 1940s and 1950s. Even taking into account parents' education and income, the most successful of the ethnics—educationally, occupationally, and economically—went to parochial schools, and they did so at a time when the schools were even more crowded than they are today,

staffed by even less adequately trained teachers, and administered by an even smaller educational bureaucracy than the very small one that somehow manages to keep the parochial schools going today. Again: a social hint: Maybe what matters about schools for a minority group is, as my colleague Professor William McCready has remarked, that they are "our" schools (whoever "we" may be).[7]

A second fountainhead for the new pluralism sprang from a variety of analyses in the fields of moral and political philosophy. These analyses raised fundamental questions concerning the future of public education and more broadly the whole range of institutions that make up liberal democratic government in America.

It seemed clear that during the early 1970s there was a growing conservative reaction against the educational and social reform efforts of the 1960s. One could cite the more obvious political and economic policies of the Nixon, Ford, and Reagan presidencies designed to withdraw from or roll back the social, humanitarian policies of the New Frontier/Great Society programs; the efforts to cut back federal financial support for welfare and education; the retreat from judicial desegregation and the exploitation of the busing issue; and the efforts to "restore" religion to the public schools. But even more significant in the long run was the resurgence of a neoconservative stance in the intellectual and academic community. This fashioned a new and persuasive element in the climate in which educational debates took place. One could cite Robert Nisbet of Columbia in historical sociology, Robert Nozick of Harvard in political philosophy, Milton Friedman of Chicago (and later the Hoover Institution) in economics, Harvard's Nathan Glazer in education and social structure, and the Heritage Foundation, whose policy proposals were influential in providing a rationale for much of the "Reagan revolution."

Theirs was a call for the reassertion of the values of private freedoms, individual rights, the free-market mechanism, the minimal state, the free play of voluntary groups, mutual aid associations, and reinforcement of pluralistic ethnic and social groupings of all kinds. There was also an attack upon the overweening welfare state, the inquisitional and repressive measures of the regulatory bureaucracies, and in general a disenchantment with the liberal welfare state and its policies. Neoconservatism added its voice to the efforts to reform the public schools by the use of vouchers and tax credits, free schools, alternative schools, or other measures. The aim of these efforts was to loosen the alleged monolithic monopoly of public schools and their authoritarian, bureaucratic machines that imposed welfare state values through compulsory education.

One example of the new conservatism, a most elegant and persuasive one, was that by Robert Nisbet. By the mid-1970s the evidence of "citizen unrest, citizen indifference, citizen alienation, and citizen hostility to government" was overwhelming, as Nisbet put it. The political community is at bay in the face of new challenges to governmental despotism personified in military dominance, huge regulatory agencies, innumerable laws of Congress, and the like. It is more than just rhetoric to speak of the "twilight of the governmental authority" of the liberal democratic state in the face of the upthrust of ethnic nationalism and fundamentalist religion, of the retreat to the communes, and of the unrestrained activities of multinational corporations. But the question is, How shall authority be restored?[8]

Nisbet's prescriptions for restoring authority were to recover the central values of social and cultural pluralism rather than political cohesion, and to revive the prestige of the private as contrasted with the public. In brief terms, Nisbet defined four central values of pluralism. First, pluralism preserves the functional autonomy of major social institutions (avoiding intrusion of the state into the spheres of school, university, family, and religion); second, it decentralizes power into as many hands as possible; third, it recognizes that hierarchy and stratification of function and role are unavoidable, honorable, and are to be preserved from intrusion by the arbitrary power of regulatory agencies in the "name of a vain and vapid equality"; and, fourth, it relies as much as possible upon informal custom, folkway, spontaneous tradition—sanctioned habits of mind—rather than formal law, ordinance, or administrative regulation.

Thus Nisbet argued for the renascence in education of kinship, localism, and voluntary association. Though he did not focus on public education, he clearly used it as an example in all of his major points. For example, regarding kinship Nisbet says it was a great mistake of the democratic dogma to think that political institutions like the public school could do better than the family in education. On localism, he says the opposition to busing springs from pride of attachment to neighborhood rather than from racism. Regarding voluntary association Nisbet argues that the prime agents of human accomplishment are the intimate, free, relevant, and spontaneous associations of self-help and mutual aid, the best illustration of such laissez-faire phenomena being Milton Friedman's proposal for educational vouchers.[9]

In other words, private schools under the auspices of churches, labor unions, cooperatives, neighborhoods, and families have been notably less expensive and more efficient than public schools. Nisbet says: "From what labyrinths of bureaucracy we would be saved in the grim worlds of social workers and educational administrators had there been instituted in the beginning a system [of education] whereby a natural, already existing social group—the household—would be the means of distributing public funds for welfare and for education."[10]

In the concluding paragraphs of *Twilight of Authority,* Nisbet argues that it all comes down to the way we conceive the nature of citizenship. And he clearly prefers the medieval version, in which the essence of citizenship was the urban man's freedom from the exactions of obedience to the feudal countryside while still bound by the loyalties and obligations of kinship, occupation, and religion. In early modern times, citizenship was fastened to the national state by ties of a broader patriotism that were vastly stronger than the smaller patriotisms. For a time, the citizen in the United States was bounded by a hierarchy of local, state, and regional authorities. But the Civil War and World War I largely overcame the loyalties of locality and region in the tides of war fervor, totalitarian enthusiasms, and melting pot assimilation. Today we see the twilight of this centralized conception of citizenship. Nisbet says: "If there is to be a citizenship in the useful and creative sense of that word, it must have its footings in the groups, associations, and localities in which we actually spend our lives—not in the abstract and now bankrupt ideal of *patrie,* as conceived by the Jacobins and their descendants." [11]

If the signposts of the future are the upthrusts of ethnicity, localism, regionalism, religion, and kinship, remember that this is exactly what we had in the late eighteenth century, when the framers of the American commonwealth sought to overcome those very pluralistic elements in the founding of a political community and a constitutional order whose motto became *E Pluribus Unum.* And Nisbet's notions of private education based upon these same elements of traditional pluralism were exactly the characteristics of the schools and colleges of the colonial period, schools that some founders and their successors sought to replace by their proposals for a public education that would be universal, free, common, and eventually secular and compulsory.

So conservative intellectuals joined radicals in questioning the unifying value of public education. For more than a decade the major attacks on the public schools for being authoritarian, bureaucratic machines imposing the wrong values upon helpless minorities through compulsory education came from the radical sector of the academic and professional community rather than from the conservative. These attacks came from romantic critics like Paul Goodman, Edgar Friedenberg, Jonathan Kozol, Herbert Kohl, and Ivan Illich as well as from radical revisionists in the history of education like Michael B. Katz,

Clarence Karier, Paul Violas, Joel Spring, and Marvin Lazerson, and
from radical social scientists like Christopher Jencks, Samuel Bowles,
and Herbert Gintis.[12]

In the introduction to their *Roots of Crisis,* Karier, Violas, and Spring
asserted their value orientation as follows:

> If one believes this society is not constructed to embrace the dignity of
> man but rather to foster a dehumanizing quest for status, power, and
> wealth, then the liberal historians fail to explain how we got where we
> believe we are . . . If one starts with the assumption that this society is
> in fact racist, fundamentally materialistic, and institutionally structured
> to protect vested interests, the past takes on vastly different meanings.
> The authors of these essays write from such a conception of the
> present, which shapes their own view of the past.[13]

The radical view of the public schools as instruments of capitalist
oppression on behalf of the privileged upper classes ranges from the
anarchist libertarian view of Joel Spring and the romantics—who said
the public schools were hopeless and might as well be abolished in order
for the freedom of stateless anarchy to prevail—to the more "neutral"
views of Katz, who said the schools should be stripped of their value
teaching and reduced to the three Rs so that they could not do too much
damage with their racist, materialistic, exploitative, capitalistic, class-
biased teachings. The remedy of both spokesmen was to return to
small, informal groups, abolish compulsory attendance, root out bureaucracy, and give power to teachers, students, and citizens of the
community rather than to administrators. The neoradical remedies
paralleled closely Nisbet's neoconservative views.

At a symposium on the history of education and its meaning for the
education of citizens, held by Research for Better Schools in Philadelphia
in 1978, three radical revisionist historians of education argued for
"value-neutral" public schools. Clarence Karier of the University of
Illinois read the history as the steady victory of the totalitarian state over
individual freedom and said the schools have always been a party to this
victory of the state. Thus the schools should not teach loyalty to the
government or the Constitution. So he was pessimistic about the role
of schooling in citizenship education. Marvin Lazerson, then of the
University of British Columbia and now dean of education at the
University of Pennsylvania, found that citizenship education has not
permitted root differences among cultural groups to be thought of as
legitimate differences; so he too was pessimistic that citizenship education can be reconceptualized unless the state itself is reconceptualized. I
take this to mean that the historic liberal state must be "reconceptual-

ized" along socialistic lines. And Michael Katz of the University of Pennsylvania found the essence of our history to be a conflict of social classes: the schools always on the side of the upper classes, imposing their middle-class values upon a reluctant lower class. So the schools should be value neutral and simply teach the basic academic skills. He was not in favor of deliberate programs of civic or moral education, because they are bound to be used to maintain the present exploitative, class-based status quo.[14]

Though his views may not spring from the same philosophic underpinnings as either the socialist, anarchist, or neoconservative views, still another support for pluralism came from a widely acclaimed libertarian political philosopher in the mid-1970s. Robert Nozick of Harvard attacked the radical anarchist and Marxian approaches as well as the liberal welfare state in his defense of the inviolability of individual rights and the desirability of autonomous voluntary associations operating in the framework of a minimal state. Nozick's view sums up the essence of an individualistic utopia:

> Our main conclusions about the state are that a minimal state limited to the narrow functions of protection against force, theft, fraud, enforcement of contracts, and so on, is justified; that any more extensive state will violate persons' rights not to be forced to do certain things, and is unjustified; and that the minimal state is inspiring as well as right. Two noteworthy implications are that the state may not use its coercive apparatus for the purpose of getting some citizens to aid others, or in order to prohibit activities to people for their *own* good or protection.[15]

Although Nozick does not deal explicitly with education, it is clear that his views of the minimal state would not include public education. Since individuals have an absolute entitlement to the property that they have properly acquired, no just claim can be levied upon the natural right to property for reasons of civic obligation, charity, or benevolence. So taxation would not be permissible for the support of public education; compulsory education would not be permissible, because it uses the coercive power of the state to get citizens to aid the children of others, even if education were deemed to be for the good of all. Only a private education voluntarily promoted by individuals or by voluntary communities would seem to be justified in Nozick's utopia.

Nozick's libertarian search for community thus leads to a variety of voluntary communities, which would be unlimited in the minimal state. People would have full freedom to contract themselves into any kind of community they wish, even into communities that would deny any further freedom:

> This is merely another way of pointing out that in a free society people may contract into various restrictions which the government may not impose upon them. Though the framework is libertarian and laissez-faire, *individual communities within it need not be,* and perhaps no community within it will choose to be so. Thus, the characteristics of the framework need not pervade the individual communities.[16]

Thus parents apparently would have unlimited right to treat children as they wish, to refuse them medical care or schooling, and the state would be indifferent. Or a person could contract himself into an authoritarian community that would not permit him to opt out of the contract, while the nation itself would be required to permit the person to opt out of *its* requirements. Why this difference? Nozick answers:

> The difference seems to me to reside in the difference between a face-to-face community and a nation. In a nation one knows that there are nonconforming individuals, but one need not be directly confronted by these individuals or by the fact of their nonconformity. Even if one finds it offensive that others do not conform, even if the knowledge that there exist nonconformists rankles and makes one very unhappy, this does not constitute being harmed by the others or having one's rights violated. Whereas in a face-to-face community one cannot avoid being directly confronted with what one finds to be offensive. How one lives in one's immediate environment is affected.[17]

Nozick's search for community thus leads to a vast pluralism of communities of the widest variety, coexisting under the framework of a minimal state. Nozick does not seem to face the question as to what would hold all the smaller communities together or whether they would have enough in common to form any kind of state or larger political community at all. He assumes that the political community is simply to provide an arena for the conflicts between the wants and preferences of individuals or groups and that it has no role in judging the moral value of such wants or preferences. And thus obviously the political community has no right to promote an education that would attempt to influence the formation of such wants and preferences or to achieve civic values stressing equality and personal obligation for the public good along with liberty.

One particularly interesting policy position regarding pluralism in education was that taken by Theodore R. Sizer, dean of the Harvard

Graduate School of Education from 1964 to 1972 and more recently chairman of education at Brown University. He argued in 1976 for a pluralism of educational institutions as the best solution for the future. He acknowledged that he had been particularly influenced by Lawrence A. Cremin's *Public Education,* David T. Tyack's *One Best System,* Nathan Glazer's *Affirmative Discrimination,* and Glazer and Moynihan's *Ethnicity.*

Sizer's policy proposals were threefold. The first: do not simply reassert that the public schools are the one best system.

> The sooner those responsible for public education recognize that nonpublic schools, the so-called deschooling movement, the alternative education movement, and the advocates of neighborhood community schools all in their several ways represent a new reality in American educational politics, so much the better for the children. It is no surprise that efforts at a national unified teachers union have lost momentum and the political interest for increased federal involvement in the "improvement" of education has slowed. Disaggregation is a policy with new adherents. One need only look at the growing edge of the curricula of teacher training institutions to see the interest in alternatives and in the special educational needs of special groups, increasingly ethnic as well as racial groups. The *common* school, the single institution built around a common American creed, never was and clearly never will be.[18]

A second pluralistic injunction from Sizer rested on Cremin's argument that schools can play only a limited part in the education of children. In fact, he goes so far as to acknowledge that Cremin's message on ecology and configurations will serve to bury the public school:

> *The times are ready for a new kind of pluralism in schooling,* a pluralism which relates the schools with other institutions in carefully contrived and thoughtfully constructed ways. Cremin's "Public Education" drives the final nail in the coffin of the late-nineteenth century nativist creation of a "one best system." The sooner that the educational establishment at large recognizes this, the better (again) for the children.[19]

Sizer was apparently not worried about the segregative aspects of alternative schools. He believed that the "thread of nationhood" and social cohesion would be adequately served by the much more powerful mass media. He was apparently willing to leave the common thread to media commentators.

His third proposal was that youngsters could divide their time between different kinds of schools—ethnic, community, regional, even "national" schools. So his final message was that there should be multiple opportunities for all children and parents to choose among complementary institutions, that is, a "smorgasbord of schools":

> *As a matter of public policy, education should move toward institutional pluralism.* It should recognize the non-school influences within the configurations of education for youth, and it should seriously and openly recognize that there are *many* "best systems"—schools—for the intentional education of youths. Each youth should attend several.
>
> What we need is a smorgasbord of schools, all of high quality (that is, accredited and all open and accessible to those who would choose among them). The smorgasbord metaphor takes full account of the importance of group consciousness found in American society and accommodates to it in ways that are not abrasive and harmful, but rather which serve to make this a constructively pluralistic nation, one that takes account of group needs and identities within a larger American culture. Diversity in schooling need not be divisive; schools can collaborate, not only compete; schools can be complementary, not only alternative to one another. We must lay to rest the bugbear that a diverse system is necessarily a corrosively segregated and unequal system. Fresh, open, undefensive thinking is needed among schoolmen. And fresh metaphors, like the smorgasbord.[20]

One wonders if a smorgasbord of schools is that much different from "the shopping mall high school" that Sizer's colleagues found to be so inadequate in 1985.[21] *Alternatives* became one of the most popular terms in the educational lexicon of the 1960s and 1970s. Vernon Smith, Robert Barr, and Daniel Burke compiled a useful summary of meanings and practices up to 1976.[22] At that time, alternatives ranged from full-fledged efforts based on a well-thought-out rationale like that of the Parkway Program in Philadelphia to almost any kind of improvisation that would take disruptive youths off the hands of embattled and harassed public school administrators.

But by the late 1980s the call for alternatives had been reinforced by the increasing political claims of parental choice as a part of the larger movement toward privatization sparked by the Reagan administration.[23] The President's Commission on Privatization, headed by David F. Linowes, professor of political economy and public policy at the University of Illinois, proposed that certain major government activities be turned over to private effort. Financial help to increase parental choice in education was included along with the sale of Amtrak, electrical utilities, and Navy petroleum reserves to private ownership and the transfer of air regulation, prisons, and postal services to private hands. Whether the commission's recommendations would give a major impetus to the use of public funds for private education through vouchers or tuition tax credits was still unclear at the time its report was issued in March 1988.

Belief that the highest priority among the goals of education is to promote a public sense of civic community and personal obligation for the public good was not a major theme in pluralism or privatization by the 1980s. Questioning and doubts about the authority of the government in the realm of education led to a decline, especially since the late 1960s, in the sense of legitimacy concerning public institutions in general and public education in particular. This decline in confidence threw doubt upon the fundamental purpose of public education: its contribution to achieving a sense of cohesive civic values, which includes a profound respect for individual freedoms.

It was in the midst of a widespread political and moral malaise of the late 1960s that the long-held belief in public education began to be called into question by those who proclaimed the values of a diminished rather than activist government and the desirability of pluralism, privatism, and parentalism in education. Until recently one of the chief articles of faith in the American public creed was a belief in the values of free, universal, compulsory, secular, common schooling. Put together, the six words of that phrase defined public education. By the 1980s every word in that phrase was under critical, sometimes bitter, attack. Let me run through the list again.

Not long ago *free* simply meant that children could go to public school without paying rate bills, fees, or tuition. Today, it is being argued that free education should include private and parochial schools, which means that public funds should be distributed to all parents through vouchers, tax credits, or scholarships so that they may choose any kind of school they wish: private, parochial, or proprietary. And, of course, "free schools" have come to mean to some people any kind of school not under public control. The recent free school movement was often fueled by anti-public-school motives.

Universal meant that all children should go to school, preferably on a regular, full-time basis. First, it applied to a minimum number of years for younger children, and then it came to mean that virtually all young people should attend high school. But in the 1970s we heard that high school was unsuitable or unnecessary for large numbers of youth, or simply that they did not want to be there. So they should be encouraged to stop in or stop out, or indeed it might even be better for some of them to drop out to go to work or engage in some other kind of more constructive activity than simply going to school. By the 1980s dropouts had become a serious concern again, with as many as one-third or more students not finishing high school.

Compulsory was widely believed to mean, and still is by the vast majority of the public, that for the sake of the child and of the society the state should require children to attend school, and should not leave it to chance, neglect, indifference, or avarice. But compulsory attendance requirements have come under increasing fire since the early 1970s, almost as much from certain educators as from the public at large. Some argue that the high school should no longer be simply a custodial institution for youth beyond age fourteen, because they can learn by that time all they need to get a job, from which they can probably learn more than from school. Besides, if the youths who disrupt schools were doing something else, the schools could get on with their proper academic work.

Common? A hundred years of effort led to the belief that it was good for children of all social, cultural, and economic levels to go to school together. It was believed this common education worked for justice, equality, and unity. Today common schools are being downgraded as we hear that homogeneous, separate schools are more natural and desirable places for the children of different ethnic, racial, religious, linguistic, or cultural groups. The rationalization ranges from a sophisticated argument on behalf of a philosophy of cultural pluralism or privatization to the euphemism for ethnicity involved in the "neighborhood school" or to a blatant or latent racism involved in the term "forced busing."

Secular? Its meaning was arrived at as a result of persistent battles among religious communities who finally decided that common schooling could not be achieved if any particular religious tenets were taught. The failure of efforts to define religious beliefs common to all churches led to schools that did not teach religion at all, thus becoming secular. But in recent years, the term has been turned into a pejorative connotation of irreligion or antireligion by fundamentalist activists. Secular humanism continues to agitate some portion of the population who feel that moral education cannot take place unless grounded on religious values, particularly their own religious values. Recurrent efforts are made to require prayers or some other kind of religious observance in public schools. These efforts reached climactic proportions in the presidential election years of 1980 and 1984.

Schooling? Throughout the world for more than three hundred years, the school has been increasingly looked upon as a prime agent for socializing the young into the knowledge, values, and skills needed for adult life in a modern society. In fact, the more modern the society, the more it has relied upon formal schooling in place of the informal agencies of education characteristic of traditional societies. Lately we heard from social scientists that schooling is not all that important for cognitive achievement or economic income in comparison with families, social class, occupation, or pure luck. Although the "deschooling" movement seems to have lost its momentum of a few years ago, the trend toward playing down the values of schooling, especially of public schooling, has increased in favor of the other agencies of society, including home schooling, which presumably can do a better job of education than the school can—or does.

Meanwhile, it is instructive to remember the most intriguing "innovations" in the schools during the 1960s and 1970s. These included, for example, behavioral objectives, competency tests, accountability, personalized learning, individualized teaching, open classrooms, team teaching, inquiry learning, community schools, career education, educational parks, back to the basics, sensitivity training, value clarification, sex education, drug education, consumer education, year-round schools, national assessment, multicultural education, bilingual education, black studies, women's studies, ethnic studies, joy in the classroom, and, above all, alternatives to all of the above. Many of these were either initiated by, or caught the fancy of, critics and groups outside the schools and were pressed upon teachers and school administrators. Few of these sought to counteract the decline in the sense of political community; many were responsive to the growth of privatism. And the urge to privatization of public functions snowballed during the Reagan years even to the intrusion of private entrepreneurs into foreign affairs, as revealed by the Iran-Contra hearings.

The so-called innovations in schools often resulted from linkages between community agencies and the schools. David Tyack gives an excellent historical survey of the way many campaigns, begun outside the schools, have persuaded boards of education, legislatures, and school administrators to undertake the delivery of additional social services in the schools during the late nineteenth century and early twentieth centuries.[24] He points to dental, medical, and nursing services, social workers, vaccinations, health and physical education programs, playgrounds and recreation programs, extracurricular and student government activities, lunches and dietician services, driver education, thrift and savings education, temperance and tobacco education, vocational education and vocational guidance, summer schools, psychological counseling, mental testing, care for the mentally retarded and physically handicapped, programs for gifted children, continuation schools and life-adjustment education. Tyack makes the significant point that many of these "innovations" have become permanent, especially those that were promoted by, and continued to have the backing of, community groups.

Then, in the late 1970s, the public's general dissatisfaction concerning public schools received great publicity: youth and adult functional illiteracy (as many as one in five persons), test scores that have declined since 1970, incompetent teachers holding on to tenure, desegregation of schools before neighborhoods were desegregated, too many electives, grade inflation, social (or automatic) promotion, high absenteeism, and, yes, too much television and too poor programs. Because of such criticisms, the most popular linkage between school and community has been a widespread call for a move "back to the basics" (by which is usually meant the three Rs) and the imposition of minimum competency tests for teachers and students alike. These were reinforced by the outgrowth of the excellence movement of the 1980s.

They illustrate, however, that educational politics has been formulated through a political process marked by the activities of special-interest groups, often in response to perceived social ills as well as to particular categorical educational deficiencies. This history cannot possibly be detailed here, but it is well to recall three issues that have diminished the civic mission of American education.

Parental Rights vs. Compulsory Education

One of the most troublesome issues to beset American education in the past fifty years is the scope and limits of the rights of parents, children, and voluntary groups in relation to the authority and rights of the teaching profession and of the public as organized in state and federal government. The clash of these interests has been no easy lineup of rights and wrongs, but rather of the clash of rights, each legitimately contesting for priority in certain circumstances. The contest often arose between the rights of parents to guide the direction of their children's education according to their religious beliefs and the authority of the state and the academic freedom of the profession to guide the education of children on behalf of preparation for citizenship and the public good.

This long-debated and long-fought issue rose again in the 1920s, as an aftermath of World War I. In the 1920s state laws were passed to prohibit the teaching of foreign languages to elementary school children and to require all children to attend public schools. The two principal cases, *Meyer* v. *Nebraska* and *Pierce* v. *Society of Sisters,* exerted the authority of the federal courts to tell the states what they could and could not do under the Fourteenth Amendment.

States could indeed make reasonable regulations for all schools, including basic instruction in English and in good citizenship, and states could compel all children to attend some school. But the states' efforts to require parents to send children only to a public school were an unconstitutional interference with the parents' rights to direct their children's education. This included the right to send their children to a private religious school as long as such a school met reasonable state standards regarding curriculum and teacher qualifications, and as long as the school was not inherently harmful to the child or the state. This important federal policy has served as a charter of liberty for private schools and for parents' freedom to patronize them.

By the early 1920s, there was widespread agreement—in legislation, judicial review, and public opinion—that the state has a legitimate authority to require all parents and guardians to see that the children under their control receive a certain amount of schooling in state-approved institutions. The age limits in most states are from seven to sixteen, with some states extending it to eighteen and with a wide latitude for exemptions. All states now have some sort of compulsory attendance law.

In the half century following World War I, most of the issues were raised by two cases in the early 1920s, by two cases in the early 1940s, and by one case in the early 1970s. All the cases occurred in postwar periods, and all had religious overtones.

Between 1917 and 1921 some thirty states passed laws requiring all instruction in the public schools to be given in English. This was obviously a reflection of the patriotic fervor against Germany engendered by World War I and by a heightening of nativistic nationalism regarding the massive foreign immigration of prior decades. In 1919, Nebraska passed a law prohibiting the teaching of foreign languages to children who had not completed the eighth grade and requiring that all subjects be taught in English in public or private schools. In 1923 the Supreme Court ruled in *Meyer* v. *Nebraska* on cases brought from Iowa, Nebraska, and Ohio that the law was unconstitutional under the due process clause of the Fourteenth Amendment. The court ruled that the Fourteenth Amendment protects the liberty of teachers to make contracts to engage in the common occupations of life (Meyer was a teacher of German in a Lutheran school) and the liberty of parents to educate their children as they see fit (by sending them to private and religious schools). The court also ruled that the state has the power to compel the attendance of children at some school and to make reasonable regulations for all schools, including the giving of instruction in English, and that it can prescribe a curriculum for institutions that it supports. But a state cannot reasonably interfere with the liberty of parents to seek the kind of education they desire for their children:

> The American people have always regarded education and the acquisition of knowledge as matters of supreme importance . . . Corresponding to the right of control it is the natural duty of the parent to give his children education suitable to their station in life, and nearly all the states, including Nebraska, enforce this obligation by compulsory laws.
>
> Practically, education of the young is only possible in schools conducted by specially qualified persons who devote themselves thereto. The calling always has been regarded as useful and honorable, essential, indeed to the public welfare.[25]

Meyer was an early attempt by the Supreme Court to define the line between the rights of parents to freedom of choice and the authority of the state to promote the public welfare. The court soon had another occasion to be even more precise. In 1922, Oregon passed a compulsory attendance law requiring, with certain exceptions, that all normal children between eight and sixteen must attend a *public* school, or that any who attend a private school must obtain the permission of and be examined by the county superintendent of schools. Fearful that the law would seriously harm or destroy parochial schools, a Roman Catholic teaching order brought suit to have the law declared unconstitutional, which the Supreme court unanimously did in *Pierce* v. *Society of Sisters* in 1925.

Those who favored the law argued that the requirements of citizenship justified the state's use of its authority to see that all potential citizens be given appropriate preparation for their responsibilities; that the increase in juvenile delinquency had followed upon an increase in enrollments in nonpublic schools; that attendance at a common school would tend to prevent religious hostility and prejudice; and that instruction in American government and institutions for immigrant children could best be given in public schools, where children of all classes and creeds were being taught together.

In its *Pierce* ruling, the Supreme Court became still more explicit regarding the balance between the rights of parents and the authority of the state:

> No question is raised concerning the power of the State reasonably to regulate all schools, to inspect, supervise and examine them, their

teachers and pupils; to require that all children of proper age attend some school, that teachers shall be of good moral character and patriotic disposition, that certain studies plainly essential to good citizenship must be taught, and that nothing be taught which is manifestly inimical to the public welfare . . .

Under the doctrine of *Meyer* v. *Nebraska* . . . we think it entirely plain that the Act of 1922 unreasonably interferes with the liberty of parents and guardians to direct the upbringing and education of children under their control. As often heretofore pointed out, rights guaranteed by the Constitution may not be abridged by legislation which has no reasonable relation to some purpose within the competency of the State. The fundamental theory of liberty upon which all governments in this Union repose excludes any general power of the State to standardize its children by forcing them to accept instruction from public teachers only. The child is not the mere creature of the State; those who nurture him and direct his destiny have the right, coupled with the high duty, to recognize and prepare him for additional obligations.[26]

Both *Meyer* and *Pierce* were decided under the due process clause of the Fourteenth Amendment: to wit, no state shall deprive any person of life, liberty, or property without due process of law. The liberty of parents to guide the education of their children is a constitutional right, but one always hedged about by the legitimate authority of the state to legislate reasonably upon matters essential to its welfare and within its competency, such as education for citizenship.

It was in these two school cases of the 1920s that a conservative Supreme Court began to give a broad substantive meaning to the concept of "liberty" as a right protected by the Fourteenth Amendment against infringement by state action. In *Meyer* and *Pierce*, "liberty" was taken to mean that the states could not deprive parents of their constitutional right to choose to send their children to a private school, even though the framers of the Fourteenth Amendment may not have had that particular liberty in mind.

In his confirmation hearings before the Senate Judiciary Committee in 1987, Judge Robert H. Bork argued that the Supreme Court was faulty in giving such a broad substantive meaning to "liberty," even though that interpretation had since become settled constitutional law. If the Supreme Court should now restrict its meaning of liberty along the lines of Judge Bork's reasoning, it could undercut much of the current demand for parental choice, a move that would surely, and ironically, outrage conservatives.

As *Meyer* and *Pierce* were debated in the aftermath of World War I passions, so two more cases were heard and decided in the heat of World War II. In the 1940s, a second general principle of freedom for parents had to do with the freedom of religious belief protected by the First Amendment versus a public profession of loyalty in the schools as a sign of the cohesive ties of a democratic political community. In 1940 the issue in *Minersville* v. *Gobitis* was a ruling by the board of education in Minersville, Pennsylvania, that all teachers and students take part in a daily pledge of allegiance and salute to the flag. This was objected to by parents who were Jehovah's Witnesses on the grounds that the require- ment violated their rights to free exercise of religion under the First Amendment. Their religious belief based upon a literal version of Exodus (chapter 20, verses 4 and 5) prohibits worship of any "image," which they consider the flag to be. Although this case dealt with a compulsory flag salute and not directly with compulsory attendance at school, it raised in Justice Felix Frankfurter's words "the conflicting claims of liberty and authority . . . [W]hen the liberty invoked is liberty of conscience, and the authority is authority to safeguard the nation's fellowship, judicial conscience is put to its severest test."

The majority opinion, written by Frankfurter, upheld the rules as a legitimate exercise of state authority. One of the key points Frankfurter made is the following:

> The ultimate foundation of a free society is the binding tie of cohesive sentiment. Such a sentiment is fostered by all those agencies of the mind and spirit which may serve to gather up the traditions of a people, transmit them from generation to generation, and thereby create that continuity of a treasured common life which constitutes a civilization . . .
>
> A society which is dedicated to the preservation of these ultimate values of civilization may in self-protection utilize the educational process for inculcating those almost unconscious feelings which bind men together in a comprehending loyalty, whatever may be the lesser differences and difficulties. That is to say, the process may be utilized so long as men's right to believe as they please, to win others to their way of belief, and their right to assemble in their chosen places of worship for the devotional ceremonies of their faith, are fully re- spected.[27]

Because the flag "summarizes" these values, Frankfurter held that legislatures and boards of education should be permitted by the courts to compel a pledge of allegiance to the flag. The lone dissenter was Justice Harlan Fiske Stone. In his dissent, Stone held that it is the function of the courts to try to arrive at a reasonable accommodation between the interests of liberty and the interests of government. His sense of accommodation was that the state should not try to coerce affirmation of belief contrary to religious conviction but should try to achieve feelings of cohesion by requiring study and instruction in civil liberties:

> So here, even if we believe that such compulsions will contribute to national unity, there are other ways to teach loyalty and patriotism, which are the sources of national unity, than by compelling the pupil to affirm that which he does not believe and by commanding a form of affirmance which violates his religious convictions. Without recourse to such compulsion the state is free to compel attendance at school and require teaching by instruction and study of all in our history and in the structure and organization of our government, including the guaranties of civil liberty which tend to inspire patriotism and love of country.[28]

In 1941 Stone became chief justice. In 1943 his *Gobitis* dissent became, in effect, the court's ruling as it reversed the *Gobitis* decision in *West Virginia State Board of Education* v. *Barnette*.[29] The 6–3 decision was written by Justice Robert Jackson and now supported by three liberal justices who had changed their opinion: Hugo Black, Frank Murphy, and William O. Douglas. In essence the argument was that the First Amendment prohibited the states from compelling students to declare a belief contrary to their religious convictions, but that the schools could require the study and teaching of history and government, which are "plainly essential to good citizenship." This would come about by persuasion and example but not by imposition of any ideological discipline nor by a compulsion that "invades the sphere of intellect and spirit." Such study is a proper and necessary means of maintaining political cohesion, loyalty, and patriotism.

The earlier sporadic questioning of various aspects of compulsory education by minority religious groups, which began in the 1920s, became a flood tide of doubt about the very idea itself during the 1970s. In its September 1972 issue the *Phi Delta Kappan* reported Gallup poll findings that 73 percent of the public favored compulsory attendance at high school, whereas only 56 percent of professional educators agreed. More of the public would require attendance of students seventeen and eighteen years old than would the educators.

The early 1970s were watershed years as the Vietnam War gradually wound down. In May 1972 the U.S. Supreme Court upheld the Wisconsin Supreme Court decision of 1971 that Old Order Amish parents were not required to obey Wisconsin's compulsory attendance laws by sending the children to school to age sixteen. The reasoning in *Wisconsin v. Yoder* was that the First Amendment protected the free exercise of a parents' religious views. In this case, those views hold that an elementary education is sufficient to prepare their children for the separated rural and traditional way of life commanded by their religious beliefs and that a high school education in modern and secular values would be detrimental to the Amish community's way of life as demanded by their religious convictions. The U.S. Supreme Court held that the Amish religious beliefs had been genuinely and conscientiously held for centuries and thus took precedence over the undoubted right of the state to require school attendance to age sixteen.

Chief Justice Burger conceded that

> there is no doubt as to the power of a State having a high responsibility for education of its citizens, to impose reasonable regulations for the control and duration of basic education. Providing public schools ranks at the very apex of the function of a State. Yet even this paramount responsibility was, in *Pierce*, made to yield to the right of parents to provide equivalent education in a privately operated system . . . so long as they, in the words of *Pierce*, "prepare [them] for additional obligations."[30]

The court's opinion was that the state's interest in universal compulsory education beyond elementary school was not of such magnitude nor compelling enough to overbalance the Amish legitimate claims to the free exercise of religion. The state's public interest and paramount responsibility for universal education had to give way to the private religious freedom of the parents.

In other words, the court accepted the notion that the requirements for citizenship education in the modern world can be satisfied by an elementary school education that normally ends at age fourteen. Here is an issue that needs serious analysis. The court apparently did not believe that one or two years of further schooling would make that much difference in preparing Amish children for good citizenship and accepted Amish arguments that those extra years would do irreparable damage to their way of life. However, Justice Douglas went so far as to argue that while the parents' rights had been served by the decision, the children themselves should have had more to say about whether they wished to go to high school. In a partial dissent, Douglas argued that the rights and freedoms of the children had not been protected by the court's decision and warned that the children's future may have been jeopardized and unduly restricted:

It is the future of the student, not the future of the parents, that is imperilled by today's decision. If a parent keeps his child out of school beyond the grade school, then the child will be forever barred from entry into the new and amazing world of diversity that we have today. The child may decide that that is the preferred course, or he may rebel. It is the student's judgment, not his parents', that is essential if we are to give full meaning to what we have said about the Bill of Rights and of the right of students to be masters of their own destiny. If he is harnessed to the Amish way of life by those in authority over him and if his education is truncated, his entire life may be stunted and deformed. The child, therefore, should be given an opportunity to be heard before the State gives the exemption which we honor today.[31]

These words on behalf of children's rights breathe much of the spirit that motivated the arguments of a century and a half in favor of compulsory attendance at school—a compulsion on behalf of students that could enable them to achieve more freedom than may be provided to them by upholding the parents' rights to the free exercise of their religion. Advocates of children's rights were inclined to agree with Douglas.

Major arguments for and against compulsory education followed the *Yoder* decision. Robert M. Hutchins wrote a powerful article called "The Schools Must Stay" in which he argued that the essential purpose of universal, free compulsory education is to form independent, self-governing members of a self-governing community. And he, like the Amish, appealed to the First Amendment, but he stressed the free speech clause rather than the religious freedom clause:

The basic commitment is that of the First Amendment which lays it down that Congress shall make no law abridging the freedom of speech. This provision means that every American is encouraged to express himself on public questions—or on any other subject. The notion is that of a self-governing community of self-governing citizens locked in argument. This was the kind of community the founders wanted. They could not hope to have one of this kind without an educated people. They had to have citizens who could think, and think for themselves.

Is this a sufficient basis for a political community? I think it is when combined with universal citizenship and universal suffrage. Does it justify compulsory schooling in institutions supported and controlled by the state? I think it does.

Every child must be given the chance to become the kind of citizen the First Amendment demands. The obligation is too important to be left to parents. The community must compel them to allow their

children to have this opportunity either by offering the education itself
or through institutions it approves.[32]

Hutchins is persuasive on this point, and I so argued in *The Nation*
in 1973 and at a major conference on compulsory education in 1975.[33]
My own disposition concerning compulsory attendance goes something
like this: the term *compulsory education* has acquired an unfortunate
authoritarian connotation. We are not likely to give it up easily, but I
hope that we could redefine the phrase to stress the *obligation* involved
rather than simply the coercive nature of *compulsion*. I like the term
obligatory education. Obligation carries a moral as well as a legal tie that
binds a person to a group or to a course of action. Obligation is virtually
a synonym for a sense of duty: what in general one ought to do or that
which is required of a good citizen. The sense of obligation carries a
more immediate or specific reference than duty. Thus the general duty
of a citizen includes, among other things, the specific obligation to
pursue a course of study to prepare for that citizenship.

Obligatory education is therefore at least a threefold mutual duty
devolving upon parents, youths, and the state. The civic obligation of
the state is to provide educational opportunity freely, universally,
equally, and commonly among the whole people. The civic obligation
of parents is to see that their children attend school with the prime
purpose of becoming good citizens. The civic obligation of youth, who
are now recognized as people with legal rights under the Constitution,
is to pursue courses of study that will lead to good citizenship. This
three-way mutual educational obligation requires schooling in citizenship until at least eighteen years of age. Not even the brightest fourteen-
year-olds can acquire the range of values, depth of knowledge, skills of
participation required of citizenship in today's world. There should be
no gap between the legal age of adulthood and the citizenship schooling
aimed at the public good. Lowering or abolishing compulsory attendance would return us to the dual systems we have been trying to
escape—one system for those academically inclined and another system
for those of lesser academic inclination or desire.

Choice: Deregulate Private Schools
But Give Them Public Support

Another significant consequence of *Yoder* was that the whole question
of the very legitimacy of public education was opened up. Arguments
began to be advanced not only that compulsory attendance laws should

have lower age requirements but that they should be abolished altogether as unconstitutional and that all education be privatized. Stephen Arons of the University of Massachusetts expressed one example that appealed to extreme libertarians. He argued that *all* beliefs and values, not simply religious beliefs, are protected by the First Amendment; that all education inevitably inculcates beliefs and values; and that public schools necessarily shape values on behalf of the government. Therefore, public schools will necessarily violate the beliefs and values of some parents and children, and thus public schools are unconstitutional and should be separated from the state. The only schools that are genuinely constitutional are those that conform to the beliefs and values of the parents who send their children to them. So private schools should be free of state regulation, compulsory attendance laws should be reduced or abolished, and public educational institutions done away with.[34]

That such arguments are not just the utopian theorizing of academic-minded lawyers and philosophers is illustrated by a growing number of court cases brought by fundamentalist Christian groups to prevent state governments from enforcing any minimum standards upon their schools. These groups claim that such enforcement violates their right to the free exercise of religion. They have won some cases and lost others. But with thousands of such schools having sprung up in recent years, the issue is far from settled.

A harbinger of what was to come in the Reagan administration was a conference held on May 9, 1975, when the Heritage Foundation posed the question, "Public Education: Freedom or Compulsion?" In the brochure announcing the conference the foundation made it clear where it stood:

> What is the role of government in education? . . .
>
> Prompted by recent outbreaks of protest against the public schools, the Conference will focus on the complaints of parents and educators around the country, and will discuss the merits and demerits of proposed, and occasionally practiced, alternatives to compulsory public schooling.
>
> It seems essential to find viable alternative means of educating America's youth: the diversity and freedom so cherished by this nation cannot long endure when many compulsory education systems, against which there is no recourse, continue to fail to meet the minimum requirement of the communities which support them.

In her letter of April 11, 1975, to educators announcing the conference, Connaught Marshner, education director of the Heritage Foundation, made the agenda quite explicit: "Why should compulsory attendance laws be a sacred cow? Parents who can't afford private schools should have some freedom of choice in their children's education: how best to give this freedom is a main concern of the Conference. The voucher system, the basic alternative school, the home-education program, and others, will be examined."

From the mid-1970s to the mid-1980s the philosophy of pluralism sometimes was diverted by extremists into a plea for complete privatization of education: leave education to parents, churches, and all sorts of private agencies—but with two major provisos: (1) remove state regulations in order to give maximum freedom for religious, social, and cultural diversity, but (2) give public funds to support all such efforts, if not by direct aid to the schools themselves, then by vouchers or tuition tax credits to enable parents to send their children to schools of their choice.[35]

My view is that states may reasonably regulate all schools (as Meyer and Pierce agree) to achieve the best possible balance between the democratic goals of political and civic cohesion and the goals of religious, intellectual, and cultural freedom. In the course of two hundred years, a set of constitutional and policy agreements has been worked out to achieve these goals, including the following:

The welfare of the Republic rests upon an educated citizenry, and thus universal education of all children and youth is plainly essential for preparation for good citizenship. The promotion of citizenship education of all children has come to be recognized as a major purpose within the competency and obligation of the states to undertake, as virtually all state constitutional and statutory law now testifies.

Inasmuch as attendance of all children at school in order to acquire a basic citizenship education is not only within the states' competency to require but also their responsibility to promote, compulsory attendance is clearly a power within the states' legislative purpose to exert. Thus education for citizenship is a primary goal of all schools, and parents have an obligation to see that their children are educated for citizenship by sending them to some school for some specific period of time, and under reasonable public regulation.

In the past century and a half most Americans came to believe that the best guarantors of an educated citizenry were state systems of free, universal, common schools that were public in purpose, public in access, public in control, and public in support. But in order to safeguard religious conscience in an increasingly pluralistic society, the predominant view came to be that public schools should not promote religious belief or practice but should leave religious instruction and devotionals to families, religious institutions, and private schools. Public schools should be basically secular, as the First Amendment requires government itself to be. So we come to the question, What authority for citizenship education should secular governments have over religious and other private schools?

Parents have the right to meet their obligations for educating their children for citizenship by sending them to private schools if they wish. But one of the primary goals of those private schools must be education for citizenship, as it is for public schools. Thus the states' regulations for public schools in the realm of citizenship education should also apply reasonably to private schools. In addition, private schools are free to teach particular religious, moral, or spiritual values, or special ethnic, social, or cultural traditions. In general, the particularities of belief, values, and outlook of private schools are protected by the First and Fourteenth Amendments. But on matters so vital to the constitutional order as positive education for good citizenship, the states' responsibility and authority for the public good cannot leave them indifferent to the quality of education for citizenship provided in private schools.

This is not to say that all present regulations of private schools by all the states are reasonable and justifiable; nor are they all coercive and unjustifiable. The goal is to arrive at fair and reasonable arrangements whereby both private and public schools are expected to perform their obligation to prepare successive generations to become informed, rational, and humane citizens, enabled to participate effectively in the democratic political community. State regulations to this end should be applied evenhandedly to both public and private schools.

I like the phrase the Twentieth Century Fund report used to define the federal government's role in fostering educational excellence in the states and local communities. I paraphrase for our problem here: state regulation should be a "firm but gentle goad" to private schools to live up to excellence in civic education for their students.

This is by no means an easy solution when it comes to questions of curriculum, textbooks, and qualifications and certification of teachers. But the emphasis on civic education gives us a key to simplifying and rationalizing state regulations in general as well as reconciling the authority of the state to promote the public good along with the private rights of parents to guide the education of their children. A clue can even be found in the long, tangled, and complicated history of court litigation on the matter. A few reminders from history have been given in the preceding pages. *Meyer* and *Pierce* guaranteed parents the liberty to guide their children's education, but this right was at the same time hedged by the legitimate authority of the state to legislate and regulate reasonably upon studies "plainly essential to good citizenship." Chief

Justice Stone made a useful distinction between efforts to coerce affirmation of belief contrary to religious conviction (which public schools could not do) and requiring all students to study "our history and structure and organization of government, including our guaranties of civil liberty which tend to inspire patriotism and love of country" (which both private and public schools should do).

The distinction between requiring *study* and compelling *belief* holds good for private schools as well as for public schools. Private schools may indeed try to compel or impose religious beliefs, but they still must require study of those subjects "plainly essential to good citizenship." Such studies include not only the basics of the three Rs but the basics of English, history, civics, and government. State regulations may ascertain that such instruction and study in private schools are equivalent to that required of public schools. This is a reasonable condition of their accepting students to fulfill the states' compulsory attendance laws.

Note the idea of equivalence between public and private schools and note furthermore that Chief Justice Burger in *Yoder* emphasized that parents could exercise their freedom to guide the religious and moral education of their children so long as they provide equivalent education in a privately operated system and "prepare [them] for additional obligations," which must be read to include the elements of good citizenship. Neither parents nor private schools are exempt on the basis of their religious convictions from the obligation to provide their children with an education for good citizenship. Civic education is clearly "an additional obligation."

In the years since *Yoder* (1972) the clamor has grown to reconsider, revise, or even do away with some of the policy and constitutional agreements discussed here. Some lawyers are trying to interpret the First Amendment to mean that *any* state regulation of private schools is an unconstitutional invasion of private belief and values, whether religious, social, or intellectual. Others propose lowering, loosening, or doing away with compulsory attendance laws. Still others propose abolishing the public school system as an unconstitutional infringement of the private rights and beliefs of parents and private schools.

These appeals to parental or family sovereignty, consumer sovereignty, or religious sovereignty are often coupled with proposals for using public funds to support these private sovereignties by vouchers, tuition tax credits, or tax exemption. I, of course, oppose such proposals. To deregulate private schools and then to support them with tax monies would make for doubly bad policy and bad constitutional law.

In recent years Christian Fundamentalist schools have begun to rely upon the ideas of parental and religious sovereignty to argue against state regulation on the grounds that their schools are integral parts of their religious ministries and therefore should not be subject to any state authority because that would amount to unconstitutional licensing of their ministries. The rapid growth of such schools in the past decade has led to increased litigation in the courts and much debate in state legislatures, but, as James Carper reports, no consistent guidance has resulted from a dozen state courts in the early 1980s. Several state courts, notably in Vermont, Ohio, New Hampshire, Kentucky, and Maine, have ruled that their state regulations have violated the religious convictions of the parents and schools and thus decided in favor of some forms of deregulation. To the contrary, cases in Michigan, Hawaii, North Dakota, Massachusetts, and Iowa have reaffirmed the states' right to impose reasonable regulations on private schools to guarantee the quality of a basic education for all children in all schools.[36]

Any definition of "basics" must include the obligation for all children to acquire an effective preparation for participation in the democratic political process and for self-reliant citizenship. This is a proper and compelling interest of the state in assuring that private schools perform their secular civic function. This principle of equivalence does not necessarily mean that private schools must conform to every specification or minimum standard mandated for public schools, but it does require an equivalence when it comes to "studies plainly essential to good citizenship." This equivalence should apply to curriculum guidelines and qualifications of teachers insofar as state regulation for public schools is exerted on these matters.

This is not to say that all present practices of all states in these regards should be defended. But there are some models that might be carefully considered, as, for example, the *History/Social Science Frameworks* adopted by the California State Board of Education in 1981 and 1987 and the *Social Studies Syllabuses* issued by the New York State Education Department in 1987.

But, above all, I agree with Ernest Boyer in his recent Carnegie Foundation report on *The High School* when he says, "We believe that today America has the best opportunity it will have in this century to improve the schools." The Carnegie recommendations for a core of studies that includes English, history, civics, and government and that are required of *all* students are echoed in the reports of the Twentieth Century Fund, the Commission on Excellence in Education, and the *Paideia Proposal*. The Carnegie report goes still further and spells out in some detail the academic foundations necessary for the "schooling of teachers" as well as the need for teachers to study the history and current issues facing public education.

Insofar as such proposals for core programs will also improve the qualifications of those teachers who will conduct the studies plainly essential for good citizenship and insofar as they are good for public schools, such recommendations should also apply reasonably to teachers in private schools. All teachers who are delegated to prepare the youth for citizenship should have solid grounding in the best scholarship available in English, history, and other humanities and in the political and social sciences. Only in this way can they be prepared to deal accurately and adequately with the historic concepts and values under-lying our constitutional order and give fair treatment to the controversial issues that continue to agitate Americans over questions of justice, freedom, equality, privacy, authority, due process, and the rights and responsibilities of citizenship.

The summer 1983 issue of *Daedalus* was devoted to an analysis of the arts and the humanities as taught in public, private, and parochial schools. Stephen Graubard, the editor and historian, wrote that the present crisis in education applies to private as well as to public schools: "It is not only the public schools that have entered a time of massive decline . . . The simple fact is that the schools of the country are substantially class-ridden . . . While the system is defended as an expression of freedom—with parents being invited to choose whatever they think to be best for their children—the conditions that prevail today make a mockery of that pretended choice."[37]

Graubard concludes his analysis of the history and social studies classes he observed in both private and public schools with a call for a desperately needed intellectual debate on "how can we revive our schools, *all* our schools?" Such an intellectual debate on the rationale for improving both private and public schools should indeed take place throughout the nation, and the civic purposes of both private and public schools should be given a prominent place.

To that end, a reassessment of the role of state regulations for public as well as private schools is crucial. It should be informed by the best academic scholarship that can be mobilized from the fields of the humanities, law, and the social sciences, by the expertise of the educa-tional profession, and by the deliberative and reasoned judgment of constituted public authorities and of the independent sector. Constitu-tional principles as well as sound public policy are necessarily involved. It is therefore proper that the results of such debates should be formu-lated into state regulations that are reasonable for both public and private schools and thus productive of an improved citizenship educa-tion for all American children and youth.

As the 1970s ended and the 1980s opened, a particularly formidable alliance between privatism in politics and pluralism in schooling began to be forged around the voucher idea. Not surprisingly, the movement gained headway in California on the heels of the property tax reform measure Proposition 13 and the momentum to cut taxes, reduce government expenditures, and limit the role of government services. The ideological framework was supplied by John E. Coons and Stephen D. Sugarman, professors of law at the University of California at Berkeley.[38] The political instrument was an initiative to be voted on by Californians in June 1980 to amend the state constitution to provide public funds for parental choice through vouchers.

The basic argument went as follows: parents and families should be the primary authorities in guiding the education of children. These "private sovereigns" are more likely to know best and care most for the welfare of their children, and to provide effective care for the children's interests. Therefore, the family or familylike clusters should have priority in educational decisions over the "public sovereigns" of children—teachers, social workers, juvenile courts, and other professionals. The power of educational choice should thus be kept as close as possible to the individuals whose interests are at stake. To enlarge parental control over the education of children, *all* children should be eligible to receive scholarships provided by public funds to enable them to attend any certified school of their parents' choice, whether public, private, parochial, or profit-making.

Recall for a moment Jefferson's proposal of 1779 that Virginia amend its constitution of 1776 to "come in aid of the public education." Now let's compare Jefferson's basic civic purposes for public education with the Coons proposal two hundred years later. The latter sought to amend the constitution of a state that had indeed established by its constitution and its code of laws "a system of general instruction," which reached every description of its citizens from the richest to the poorest, to an extent that Jefferson could not have imagined.

In 1979, Coons circulated petitions to amend California's constitution as follows:

> It is the purpose of the people hereby to enlarge parental control over the education of children; to make every elementary and secondary pupil eligible for a scholarship redeemable in certified schools; to improve the variety, quality, and efficiency of education; to assure that spending for a child's education in common schools may not be a function of wealth; to empower families, regardless of income, to choose among common schools on an equal basis; to assure that thereby the state aids no institution, religious or secular; to protect freedom of religion but aid no religion; to eliminate discrimination

and segregation by race; to protect pupils from unfair discipline or dismissal; and to control spending by limits and competition.

The initiative then would have redefined the meaning of common schools in California as follows:

> There shall be three classes of common schools for grades kindergarten through twelve, namely, public schools, public scholarship schools, and private scholarship schools. Public schools are those publicly owned, funded, and administered and not certified to redeem scholarships. Public scholarship schools are those organized by the authority of public school districts or public institutions of higher learning and which are certified hereunder to redeem scholarships. [These must be non-profit corporations.] Private scholarship schools are those privately organized and certified hereunder to redeem scholarships. [These could be non-profit or profit-making corporations.][39]

Although the purposes of the proposition stressed the values of freedom of religion and elimination of racial segregation in schooling, there was no mention of the civic purposes of education or the preparation of citizens for participation in a common democratic political community. The whole emphasis was on fulfilling the private wants and desires of parents with regard to the education of their own children. This proposal sought to reverse the two-hundred-year effort to surmount the potential divisiveness of the many segments in America through genuinely common public schools. It sought to solidify the differences and the diversities of a pluralistic society by embedding public support for differences in the state constitution. It did not recognize the validity or legitimacy of the state's concern to promote the values and ideals of a democratic political community through the agencies of common public schooling.

Fortunately, the petitioners failed to get enough signatures to place their initiative on the ballot. Nowhere in the proposed purpose was there a hint of Jefferson's basic purpose to prepare citizens for self-government. We may well amend the form or structure of "a system of general instruction," as Jefferson expected we would, but he would not have approved a principle of "choice" that virtually ignores the underlying civic purposes of universal, free, common, secular education. And few advocates of choice have paid much attention to the common civic purposes of education during the past two decades.[40] It was not in the proposals for vouchers for tax credits in several of the states or in the legislation passed in Minnesota and Iowa. It was not in President Reagan's 1987 budget "Agenda for the Future" nor in the Department of Education's bill, The Equity and Choice Act (TEACH), a voucher proposal to aid poor parents to send their children to private schools, which was withdrawn in June 1986 in the face of congressional opposition.

The campaign for aid to private schools increased during the Reagan administration, but it took a somewhat different turn. The effort increasingly highlighted the rights of the family and softpedaled the religious issue, possibly to circumvent the constitutional test of the separation of church and state, which continued to block the administration's efforts to inject prayer in the public schools.

The political campaigns for public aid to families for the educational costs of private education, campaigns that took place on the state and federal levels, were expressed in an increasingly sophisticated theoretical scholarship centering upon the use of vouchers. Interestingly enough, the advocates ranged across the political spectrum—from Hoover Institution economist Milton Friedman on the right to Harvard sociologist Christopher Jencks on the left. The most elaborately argued position was that of Coons and Sugarman. Their *Education by Choice* carried a foreword by James S. Coleman and an endorsement on the dust jacket by Rev. Andrew M. Greeley, director of the Center for the Study of American Pluralism, who proclaimed: "If the oppressive, monopolistic bureaucracy of the public schools is ever to be broken . . . then Coons and Sugarman will deserve a lot of credit."

The appeals to freedom of parents, to family control, to middle-class interests, to private enterprise and competition in education, and to the limitation of governmental institutions made the voucher idea a formidable proposition, which, if adopted, could become a historic turning point in American education.

By mid-1987 the idea and practice of parental choice were still the subject of lively debate. A good example was the special section in the June 1987 issue of the *Phi Delta Kappan*. Joe Nathan, who directed the National Governors Association task force on choice, reported that at least fifteen states have taken some formal action to increase the variety of schools from which families could select. Most states so far have limited the choice to public schools, but a few help support private, nonsectarian programs. He argues that such choice has helped to reduce the number of dropouts, increase student achievement, improve parental involvement and satisfaction, encourage racial and economic integration, provide extra challenge for students dissatisfied with the conventional programs, and raise the morale of educators who were allowed to create distinctive programs. Aside from the mention of increased integration, the civic purpose of choice was not apparent.[41]

An interesting contrast with Nathan's views was the article by Deborah Meier, principal of a new high school in East Harlem of New York City and recipient of a prestigious MacArthur Foundation Fellowship. She frankly extolled the values of the progressive education tradition of building a democratic community of teachers, parents, and students, harking back to John Dewey as "our mentor." Choice is a factor in the heavily black and Hispanic school, but she has managed to keep a much higher proportion of whites than are represented in the particular district.

In light of the usual emphasis of the excellence movement for stricter discipline, achievement, and traditional values, it is refreshing to hear such a meritorious school leader say that it is time for progressive education to tackle the high school again and demonstrate the values of democratic practice as students and teachers together take greater responsibility for their education. However, aside from complaints about the required courses and standardized examinations imposed by the regents, Meier did not say much about the role of the curriculum in developing citizenship in her school.[42]

The most pointed article on the educational policy of choice was by Mary Anne Raywid, long an eloquent advocate of alternatives and choice in education. She is exceedingly forthright in distinguishing choice for parents within the public school framework, which she advocates, and the use of vouchers to enable parents to use public funds for private schooling, which she opposes. And she does this for the good reason that education ought to be viewed primarily as a public good that benefits the community and not solely as a private benefit for individuals.

She argues persuasively that viewing competition among schools as an analogy to the competition among sellers in an economic marketplace is a misguided analogy. The better analogy for the principle of choice is the system of checks and balances of democratic governance in which all the major parties to educational authority play a part: the various levels of government as well as the educators, school boards, parents, and students. Although Raywid does not deal explicitly with matters of curriculum content that might provide a common core of civic knowledge, values, or skills for students in different kinds of alternative schools chosen by parents, she sets the proper framework within which discussion ought to take place and possible agreements sought. Her article and the references she cites are must reading for those considering choice and vouchers.[43]

It also provides a countervailing argument for those like James S. Coleman, who argue that private high schools (and especially Catholic high schools) promote substantially more learning than public high schools and that public schools should therefore emulate private schools. But even advocates of that view such as John E. Chubb and Terry M. Moe in their Brookings Institution study found that: "In terms of general goals, public schools place significantly greater emphasis on basic literacy, citizenship, good work habits, and specific occupational skills, while private schools—regardless of type—are more oriented toward academic excellence, personal growth and fulfillment, and human relations skills."[44]

Although Chubb and Moe argue that effective control over schools should be transferred from government to the market, they say that government should "still set minimum requirements," but these requirements are undefined.

Not only has the public policy of vouchers been debated but the social science findings favoring private school student achievement have been severely criticized by a whole series of social scientists from the time of Coleman's earlier studies. For a summary of those debates, see the article by Lee M. Wolfle entitled "Enduring Cognitive Effects of Public and Private Schools" in the May 1987 *Educational Researcher*. Wolfle pointed to several studies that reanalyzed the data Coleman and his colleagues used to generalize about the superiority of private over public schools. They all found far less influence by the private schools than Coleman claimed. Wolfle summarized his own studies by saying that the short-term effects found by Coleman do not endure. According to Wolfle, "When it comes to estimating the longer-term direct effects of Catholic schooling, it seems to be that Catholic school students do no better than public school students in vocabulary and do worse in mathematics."[45]

While the social scientists quarrel over the meaning of their data, those who argue for the priority of parental rights in education must reckon with what has been undeniably happening to parents and family life in the past two decades.

Weakened Traditional Family Values

These criticisms of public education raise some of the most fundamental political issues concerning the goals of education in the United States. But those questions are also philosophical, intellectual, and moral. Above all, what agitates parents most and leads them to state year after year that discipline is the primary problem in public schools is exemplified by the ominous increase during the past decades in petty crime, major crime, violence, vandalism, drinking, drug use, and premarital pregnancies among teenagers.

The decline in traditional family values was documented as early as the 1974 Yankelovich survey of youth (ages sixteen to twenty-five) called *The New Morality*. This revolution in the values held by American youth resulted from the startling changes arising among college students around 1967. By the 1980s this revolution had spread to the entire generation of youth, according to Yankelovich's 1981 survey. The 1974 Yankelovich survey pointed to radical changes in three types of values:

1. Moral norms: greater freedom in sexual mores; a lessening of automatic obedience to and respect for the established authority of the law, police, and government; a lessening of the church and organized religion as a source of guidance for moral behavior; and a decline in traditional concepts of patriotism and automatic allegiance to the idea of "my country right or wrong."

2. Social values: relaxing of traditional attitudes toward the work ethic, marriage, family, and the role of money in defining success.

3. Personal values: heightening of concern for self-fulfillment and a greater preoccupation with self and privatism at the expense of sacrificing one's self for family, employer, or community.[46]

In his 1981 work, Yankelovich places these values in a wider context of "the search for self-fulfillment," which he considers a candidate for being an American cultural revolution. Although this search is a response to changing socioeconomic conditions, Yankelovich stresses the force that values exert over future social change. In contemporary America, individual autonomy and self-fulfillment weigh heavily as normative forces.[47]

Because so much of the educational-reform movement stresses the linkages between parents and schools, perhaps this is an appropriate place to suggest that not only should the role of schools be carefully reassessed, but also the trends in family life. If families are to be given greatly expanded control in the schooling of their children, what of the future of the family? It is apparent that several long-term trends of family disruption have accelerated in the 1970s and 1980s. Chief among these are the rapid increase in the number of mothers who work, the rapid increase in the number of single-parent households, early sexual behavior and births to unwed females, and child neglect and abuse.

More than half of all mothers with children under six and nearly 70 percent of women with school-age children work outside the home as well as in it. The percent of all full-time workers who are women is above 50 percent. As the divorce rate climbs sharply, more than half of all school-age children will spend part of their school years in single-parent homes. Bureau of Census figures showed that 26 percent of all children under 18 were living with one parent in 1985, up from 15 percent in 1970. In *All One System,* Harold Hodgkinson estimates that of every one hundred children born today, only 40 percent will reach age eighteen in a "normal" family with both parents living together; 60 percent will be born out of wedlock or to parents who divorce, or separate, or die before the child reaches eighteen. Over 90 percent of single-parent families are headed by women, and approximately half of the female-headed families with school-age children are living in poverty (nearly 70 percent of black children living in poverty are in single-parent households headed by black women).

Senator Daniel Patrick Moynihan returned to the subject of family and poverty in his 1985 Godkin Lectures at Harvard, affirming that the problems of family disorganization are as pervasive among whites as among blacks.[48] The threat to the ideal of "the traditional family" is further highlighted by the fact that the number of unmarried couples under 25 living together increased manyfold from 1970 to 1984, that teenage pregnancy has increased dramatically, that the teenage birth rate is twice that of any other Western nation, and that teenage drug use is the highest of any industrialized nation.[49]

Many conservatives believe that subsidies to families to guarantee a minimum annual income—which was the major recommendation of the 1977 report of the Carnegie Council on Children, written by Kenneth Keniston—may further encourage divorces between parents who would have assurance of independent incomes.[50] This seemed to be a major point of the Reagan administration's panel on the family, chaired by Gary Bauer, formerly undersecretary of education and later domestic policy adviser to the president. Issued in November 1986, the panel's report blamed two decades of liberal policies for fraying the fabric of family life, bringing increased illegitimate birth, teenage pregnancy, drug abuse, crime, divorce, sexually transmitted disease, and poverty. It praised the Reagan administration for its efforts to reduce these trends through a pro-family agenda consisting of more restraint, self-sacrifice, and self-discipline in families; more discipline, religion, and character education in the schools; and less government involvement in family life. The report was praised by conservatives at the Free Congress Foundation and Family Research Council, and criticized by liberals, headed by Senators Moynihan and Kennedy.[51]

Following up on the Bauer panel's recommendations, President

Reagan issued an executive order on September 3, 1987, ordering all
federal policies to be assessed for their impact on the family and whether
they strengthened or weakened the rights of parents in educating and
raising their children.

Meanwhile, momentum grew for mounting a more coordinated
and ambitious role for the federal government regarding youths. The
William T. Grant Foundation Commission on Work, Family, and Citizenship had begun to issue a series of reports in the summer of 1987
documenting the disorder and lack of a coherent policy in the federal
efforts on behalf of youth.[52] And a series of bills introduced in Congress
would enormously expand the provision of day-care centers for young
children, including use of the schools. At the end of 1987, Anne C.
Lewis described several such bills, with emphasis upon the following:

> The most ambitious bill . . . is the Act for Better Child-Care Services,
> introduced with bipartisan sponsorship in November. States would
> distribute the funds, and schools would certainly be potential child-
> care providers. In addition, the bill sets aside 10% of its funds to make
> Head Start and Chapter 1 programs in elementary schools into full-
> day, full-year programs.
>
> What is unique about this bill is its whopping price tag of $2.5
> billion annually. In view of the federal deficit and other priorities in
> Congress, asking for so much new money seems more than presump-
> tuous—it seems to be folly. But as Helen Blank, an expert on child
> care with the Children's Defense Fund, said, "We have to have a large
> federal role in child care because we have a disaster on our hands."
>
> The other unusual feature of this bill is the breadth of the coalition
> that supports it. As of the end of October, 90 organizations were
> backing the bill—almost four times as many as lobbied for the creation
> of the U.S. Department of Education. Moreover, this coalition in-
> cludes religious, civic, and professional organizations, as well as those
> more directly involved in education. At the same time, in at least 33
> states, Alliances for Better Child-Care have been formed to lobby for
> legislation at the federal level and to push for state programs that will
> improve child care.[53]

The views of the Bauer panel were not simply a matter of liberal
versus conservative political views. They represented deep-seated differences of educational policy between the Reagan administration's view
of the federal role in educational policy and what may fairly be called
the whole range of the education establishment, including public representatives as well as professional teachers and administrators. Another
good example is a 1987 report of the Forum of Educational Organization Leaders, which called upon the federal government, especially

through Secretary Bennett, to join state governments to provide legislative "guarantees" of school services that would enable all public school students who were at risk of dropping out of school to finish high school. These at-risk youngsters now amount to one-third of America's forty million public school students and will increase as a result of race, poverty, single-parent families, or limited English proficiency unless drastic government action is taken.

The range and depth of these views are illustrated by the coalition of eleven organizations involved, representing elementary, secondary, and higher education:

American Association of Colleges for Teacher Education

American Association of School Administrators

American Federation of Teachers

Council of Chief State School Officers

Education Commission of the States

National Association of State Boards of Education

National Association of Elementary School Principals

National Association of Secondary School Principals

National School Boards Association

National Congress of Parents and Teachers

National Education Association[54]

Similar calls for extending help to troubled youths through the school system came from the mental health community as well as from the educational establishment. An excellent example is a study supported in part by the Carnegie Corporation for the work of Perry London of the Harvard Graduate School of Education. He recognizes the crisis among youth concerning drug abuse, pregnancy, abortion, teen-age parenthood, child neglect and abuse, runaways, violence, delinquency, depression, and suicide. But he also links their mental health treatment to education for citizenship. He thus gives a perspective on the meaning of "character" development and the priority of the schools in character formation significantly different from traditional pro-family views. The problems affecting family life, childhood, and youth must be recognized as "psychosocial epidemics" of major proportions whose "damage control" cannot be exerted without the leadership of the schools:

> We must rethink and synthesize both mental health and character education in the schools. In fact, a kind of developmental damage

control . . . has already become, willy nilly, the business of everyone in education. And what was once the secondary responsibility of schools for character education—reinforcing cultural norms that were inculcated elsewhere (especially in the home) and reinforced everywhere in society—has become a burden that other social institutions can no longer carry.

Schools must now lead the battle against the worst psychosocial epidemics that have ever plagued the children of this society. This requires a "paradigm shift" in school mental health—a radical change in the way mental health workers and educators see their mutual obligations and in the way all of society sees the role of schools in the development of citizens.[55]

London goes on to stress how the traditional agents of character education have been weakened by the pluralism, heterogeneity, and fluidity of modern urban life, much as I have tried to do in these historical chapters. But the significance of his approach for civic learning is that he defines character education not only as personal adjustment through mental health intervention—whereby schools help youths achieve integrity, self-control, and self-esteem—but also as "education in *civic virtue* and in the qualities that teach children the forms and rules of citizenship in a just society":

For the common good, a sane society needs to educate its citizens in both civic virtue and personal adjustment. For schools to provide both kinds of services, they need new intramural programs; new research and training in graduate schools of education, psychology, and social work; and new policy perspectives in both the public and private sectors.

Schools need classroom curricula chiefly for teaching the *civic virtue* side of character . . . The issues and duties of citizenship in a democracy, the rules of inter-personal civility, personal integrity as the basis of citizenship, the nature of equity, and the morality of caring for the weak are all largely cognitive and thus largely teachable in the classroom. Despite the ideological and psychological controversy that surrounds those parts of this curriculum called "moral education," citizenship will probably remain a classroom topic.[56]

A drastically different remedy from that of the Bauer panel was also offered by George J. McKenna III, principal of George Washington Preparatory High School in Los Angeles and president of the Council of Black Administrators of the Los Angeles Unified School District. Instead of simply urging families, especially black families, to rehabilitate themselves without government involvement, McKenna argued that effective educational programs can uplift people and change their conditions:

> The public school system is the most powerful of all the institutions in the country, in that it is the only institution that requires by law that citizens participate in its programs, at a time when those citizens are in their most vulnerable condition—childhood. And the primary purpose of this institution is to shape the minds and values of the participants . . .
>
> Schools *can* effectively educate their clients, despite the children's socioeconomic level, and therefore change the direction of society, including such problems as unemployment, drug abuse, gang violence, and premature pregnancy. It is possible to create educational programs that address these issues in an effective manner, rather then wait for conditions in the community to change before we can become successful as educators . . .
>
> The solution to our problems lies within the educational system of our country. Clearly, when we accept full responsibility for the salvation of the people will America be free of miseducated citizens, who place us all in jeopardy.[57]

Every now and then, especially since the 1960s, the concern for what is happening to the family focuses on the rights of children rather than the rights of parents. In his review of Selma Fraiberg's *Every Child's Birthright: In Defense of Mothering*, Kenneth Keniston predicted remarkably well how the debate about families and children would line up in the 1980s:

> One camp interprets family change as a result of a loss of the ancient virtues of parental self-sacrifice and mothering. It calls for the moral reform of the parent so as to restore an image of stay-at-home mothers, bread-winning fathers, and happy but obedient children. Another camp sees economic, racial, and social injustices as the causes of family troubles, and calls for an assertion of the rights of the poor and minority group members.
>
> Still others focus on the absence of special services for troubled individuals: they call for more child guidance clinics, more marriage counselors, more parent education, more compensatory programs and more child abuse prevention. Finally, there are some who take the problems of women as central. To overcome the legacy of sexism, they argue, we need more opportunities for women to find fulfillment in nontraditional roles and more supports, like day care, so that they can escape oppressive bondage to kitchen and crib. As this debate develops, the danger is that the needs of children will, as usual, be forgotten before the claims of other more vocal groups and interests.[58]

Whatever the merits of the widening proposals for dealing with the family and the debates over the merits of day care,[59] the long-term trend seems to be well summed up by Beatrice Paolucci and Stanley P. Wronski of Michigan State University as a revolution in ideas that looks upon the family not so much as a primary biological hereditary grouping, but largely as a voluntary association:

> That revolution spoke for a simple idea: that all authority relationships exercised by human beings over other human beings are merely provisional, limited, and subject to change when they no longer serve the functions for which they originally existed. It was and is a radical idea. More than in centuries past, it appears its time has come. In its social aspect, this idea heralds a profound change in the relation of individuals to the groups to which they belong, especially the family. It means that the ideal relationship is one that is revocable and alterable—a relationship in which individuals can choose for themselves. The elimination of fixed bonds in marriage, the protection of freedom of association, the right to pick up and move, the 18-year-old vote, the easing of abortion laws, the attack on restricted practices in inheritance of property, child advocacy regulation, and the equalization of rights for women are all examples of the manifestation of this value.[60]

Although the family is not a voluntary association in the sense that the unborn child exercises "family by choice," many new family lifestyles are gaining acceptance more widely than ever before. This fact underlines the argument that J. W. Getzels makes when he points to the discontinuities that arise between the traditional roles of the family as "socializer" and the school as "educator."[61] Too often, some schools do not take sufficiently into account the differences among families in their functionally diffuse roles of influencing the child's health, religion, morals, dress, conduct, motivation, and sense of self-identity. Similarly, some families do not sufficiently recognize the school's unique and functionally specific task of preparing the child for future roles in society, government, work, professions, and citizenship.

We have seen how these discontinuities in the past have handicapped certain ethnic and cultural family groups who did not appreciate or welcome the universalistic character of the American public school, and we have seen how the school was often not flexible enough to recognize the differences and the particularistic characteristics of families. The question now is, What should be the relationship between families that are becoming almost infinitely varied in life-style and schools that have had almost infinitely varied tasks imposed upon them? Should the schools try to adjust to any tasks that any families wish them to undertake? Or are there certain distinctive roles for schools that families under present conditions cannot or should not undertake as appropriately as schools can and should? And are there adjustments and flexibilities that schools should exercise while they pursue their essential purposes in a democratic political community?

However these questions are answered, the trend toward freedom seems to have left a residue of concern for children's rights that goes beyond the humanitarian drives for child labor reform and care for dependent and delinquent children in the late nineteenth and early twentieth centuries. Those drives often assumed that caring adults ought to look out for the welfare of children who could not help themselves. In the past decade or so, however, the tone has changed a bit, as the child-advocacy movement stresses the rights of children as legal persons—rights to a secure and stable home, rights to a quality education, rights to freedom from abuse and neglect, and rights to due process both in and out of school—rights that sometimes conflict with the traditional rights of parents.[62]

The Supreme Court began to enshrine such rights in constitutional law in the landmark case of *In Re Gault* in 1967. In the case of a fifteen-year-old boy in Arizona who had been sentenced to an industrial school, the Supreme Court ruled that he must be given in juvenile court the same procedural rights of due process that an adult has: notice of charges, legal counsel, opportunity to confront and cross-examine witnesses, and the like.[63] Following that case, a whole series of cases and laws began to implant children's rights more firmly in constitutional and civil law: for example, peaceable protest in school in *Tinker* v. *Des Moines* (1969); school suspension in *Goss* v. *Lopez* (1975); the Juvenile Justice and Delinquency Act (1974); the Family Educational Rights and Privacy Act (1974); the Education of All Handicapped Children Act (1975); and school spanking in *Ingraham* v. *Wright* (1977). Public-interest groups active in this field of children's advocacy are the Children's Defense Fund of the Washington Research Project, the National Committee for Citizens in Education, and the American Civil Liberties Union. An eloquent spokesman for children is Harold Howe II, senior lecturer at the Harvard Graduate School of Education and former U.S. Commissioner of Education, who argues that the "self-interest of adults is taking center stage, and the interests of children are being shoved into the wings."[64]

However, children's rights advocates were disturbed by the Supreme Court's decision in June 1979 that upheld the constitutionality of state laws that permit parents to commit their minor children to state mental institutions without the procedural rights of due process in a formal adversary-type hearing before the child is admitted. Thirty-six states have such laws. In his opinion for the majority, Chief Justice Burger wrote:

> Our jurisprudence historically has reflected Western civilization concepts of the family as a unit with broad parental authority over minor children . . . That some parents may at times be acting against the interests of their child creates a basis for caution, but is hardly a reason to discard wholesale those pages of human experience that teach that parents generally do act in the child's best interests. The statist notion that governmental power should supersede parental authority in *all* cases because *some* parents abuse and neglect children is repugnant to American tradition.[65]

In one sense, parental freedom has diminished vis-à-vis educators and other professionals to whose care children are entrusted. Between 1960 and 1967 all fifty states enacted legislation requiring that certain professionals report suspected cases of child abuse to the relevant local authority, generally the state child protective service. Although these laws were initially aimed at doctors, nurses, and other health-case workers, teachers have increasingly come under the category of professionals who are obligated to report suspected cases of child abuse. By the late 1970s, the child–protective legislation of forty-one states mandated this reporting by teachers.[66]

One point often neglected in the debate over the private rights of parents versus those of children pits parents against professionals. Parents complain that teachers and textbooks preach immorality, violence, sex, obscene language, antireligious and "secular humanist" beliefs. Teachers complain that parents exert unwarranted censorship by busybodies who seek to stifle the teaching of scientific and scholarly materials that promote critical thinking. Controversies in Kanawha County, West Virginia, and the furor over "Man, A Course of Study" in the 1970s were symptomatic of a vast resurgence of textbook monitoring and censorship in the 1980s.

This phenomenon made it necessary to reassert once again the importance of the public freedom of the teacher and of the profession of teaching in a free society. The phrase "academic freedom" has a ring that identifies it mainly with higher educational institutions and research enterprises. It would be better to call it "education's role in guaranteeing public freedom," which applies to the whole educational system from elementary school to graduate school. The very welfare of the Republic depends upon the freedom of teachers to teach and the freedom of students to learn.

This freedom rests upon the First Amendment and is interpreted not only by professional and intellectual advocates of civil liberties but also by the Supreme Court to mean that public education has a special responsibility to promote freedom of thought as the foundation of the public well-being in the exercise of self-government. This view has been hammered out over the past fifty years. During the 1920s and 1930s teachers got into trouble with their communities because of their personal conduct outside the classroom, involving restrictions of their drinking, smoking, marriage, divorce, and "moral turpitude" in general. In these matters, teachers have come a long way since the 1920s, but the genuine freedom to teach is still at risk.

Based on the school's historical role in American society, its crucial, role is, or should be, its role in building civic community. This is a function that cannot simply be left to the family or the other educative agencies of the community. It rests upon acquiring the basic skills of literacy and numeracy, to be sure, but it also includes study of the ideal values, scholarly knowledge, and skills of participation required of a citizen in a modern, and postmodern, democratic society. Most other institutions have a different primary purpose. Forming citizens is a by-product of their primary purposes of nurturing children, producing or distributing goods, caring for souls, disseminating information, or enriching the culture.

Reinforcing the longer historical perspective on the diminution of the fundamental civic role of schooling set forth here is the research of two careful observers who have studied the Reagan administration's educational policies. David L. Clark and Terry A. Astuto summarize the basic differences between the pre-1980 federal policies and the post-1980 policies as follows:

Pre-1980 Terms	*Post-1980 Terms*
Equity	Excellence; standards of performance
Needs and access	Ability; selectivity; minimum standards
Social and welfare concerns	Economic and productivity concerns
Common school	Parental choice; competition
Regulations, enforcement	Deregulation
Federal interventions	State and local initiatives
Diffusion of innovations	Exhortation; information sharing

Clark and Astuto summarize their argument as of Fall 1986:

> The educational policy preferences of the Reagan administration will
> all show progress over the next 2 years, and the cumulative effect will
> be to modify further the basic federal role in education, to stimulate
> continued growth and independence of the state governments in edu-
> cational policy development, and to foster the substantive interests of
> the administration in competition, increased performance standards,
> traditional values, parental choice, and a focus on the basics in educa-
> tion.[67]

Such analysis and predictions are not encouraging to those who
would enhance the civic mission of American education. I would not
presume to compete with such predictions, but I shall state my views as
clearly as I can. Federal policy in strengthening schooling should emphasize aid to local and state communities to enable them to strengthen
the civic role of their public schools:

- To make public schools genuinely free, not only in the sense of being
  free of charge to students by virtue of strong public financial support,
  but also academically free for critical inquiry on questions of public
  policy; and devoted above all to the pursuit of intellectual freedom
  and the equal rights of liberty symbolized by the Constitution and
  Bill of Rights as the core values of a free society.
- To make public schools genuinely universal, not only in the sense
  that they are accessible and open equally to all and that they reach
  every child, but also make them universal in the literal sense that they
  require study of the other peoples of the earth and the role that
  Americans ought to be playing in an interdependent world.
- To make public schools genuinely common, not only in the sense
  that they should be common meeting grounds for the young of all
  racial, ethnic, religious, and economic backgrounds, but that they
  seek to develop a common sense of community upon which respect
  for legitimate and desirable pluralist values appropriate to a democratically diverse society can be developed. The federal and state
  governments must not act to inhibit, harm, or destroy private
  schools, but neither must they act to support them with public funds
  in such ways as to inhibit, harm, or undermine public schools, whose
  prime role is to extend common civic cohesiveness, a goal that surely
  lies at the heart of all other purposes of government.
- To make public schools genuinely secular so as not to infringe either
  religious freedom or promote "an establishment of religion"; but so
  as to promote the secular civic values of the democratic constitutional
  order. Fair-minded and scholarly study of the role of religion in

history and contemporary society is a legitimate function of public education as well as private education.

• To maintain and strengthen compulsory attendance laws, but to stress even more the idea of obligatory education so that it will come to mean a three-way mutual duty devolving upon parents, children and youth, and the state to see to it that preparation for citizenship is the number one purpose of schooling.

• To make schooling not merely consist of sitting in classrooms, but a reaffirmation of the value of organized, disciplined study under well-trained, committed, and highly qualified teachers deeply versed in the best resources of scholarship and methods of teaching that can be devised. I am skeptical of much that goes under easy or loose meanings of "learning by experience" or "back to the basics." These are not good enough for the preparation of citizens who must live in a modern civilization, cope with the complexities of a post-industrial world, and still achieve the fundamental values of a free, equal, and just democratic society.

As long as five thousand years ago, the human race began to find that informal experience was not good enough for peoples who would live an urban civilized way of life rather than in nomadic, pastoral, or village-farming ways of life. Schooling became ever more necessary for the development of civilization wherever it appeared on the earth. The modern world of the past three hundred to four hundred years requires ever more and better schooling to enable people to cope with the complexities of modernity and the vast expansion of knowledge. And the modern democratic experiment to educate everyone to cope has scarcely begun. Let us not despair of it or weaken it. A redefined and revitalized free, universal, common, secular, obligatory schooling is still its firmest foundation.

My reading of the history thus leads me to be skeptical of a simple or narrow declaration that schools, families, and local communities should be more closely linked. I am skeptical of the simple and unmodified assumption that more involvement, more "partnership," or more control by parents and local community groups over schools are always for the better.[68] Such linkage, such participation, and such control should be judged on the basis of whether or not they contribute to the overall freedom, equality, public sense of justice, and health of the democratic political community.

Freedom of choice by parents? Yes, to the extent that it also contributes to the freedom and rights of children and is consistent with the freedom and rights of teachers and citizens under the First Amendment and of due process under the Fifth Amendment. What is termed immoral by parents may be deemed censorship by teachers.

Local autonomy and support for schools? Yes, to the extent that they also contribute to the equality of opportunity for historically disadvantaged minorities and are consistent with the Fourteenth Amendment and the equal protection of the laws. What is defended as a neighborhood school by some citizens may be regarded as a segregated school by others. What is viewed as affirmative action by some citizens will be seen as reverse discrimination by others.

Greater pluralism in education? Yes, to the extent that it fosters greater freedom and respect for diversity of religious and cultural traditions and increases the common sense of civic community that strengthens the legitimacy and the democratic values of the overall political community and constitutional order.

Recent movements for community participation and citizen education stress the strengthening of our political institutions from the grass roots to the state and federal levels, but I hope they will also stress the crucial importance of enlisting revitalized public schools in this process.

The excellence movement gives signs that it will make public education a high priority, but so far it has not stressed sufficiently the importance of recalling the public schools to their prime civic role in preparing for citizenship in the democratic political community. Unless it does so, the powerful forces of excessive pluralism and privatization may undercut the whole movement.

The "traditional values" that should guide federal educational policies are those that help state and local communities strengthen the civic role of their public schools. As Terrel Bell, sounding very much like Thomas Jefferson and Horace Mann, said to the state governors: "It isn't just being for education that matters. It's to crusade for it."[69]

PART II

What's Needed: A Renaissance of the Civic Mission in American Education

Part I discussed the historical dilemmas, problems, and impediments to improving education for citizenship not simply to recite a litany of bad news but to give a sense of the realities facing citizenship in a pluralist democratic society. Now for the good news—or at least the better news.

As the United States embarks on its third century as a republic, it is clear that the role of education in our national life is being widely discussed and debated. The arguments abound: education should sharpen our competitive edge in the world community; it should re-emphasize the traditional moral and religious values of Western civilization; it should emphasize cultural literacy, intellectual excellence, critical thinking. These are persuasive views, but I argue for a cogent priority underlying all the others.

Part II argues for revitalizing the historic civic mission of American universal education. This means explicit and continuing study of the basic concepts, principles, and values that bind us together in a distinctive political community and constitutional order. The common core of the curriculum throughout school and college years should be the morality of democratic citizenship. For this goal to be realized, scholarly study of civic morality should become the first priority in the liberal and professional education of the teaching profession.

Part II marshals pertinent historical perspectives and contemporary scholarship with which to look to the future of civic education in the schools and in the preparation of teachers. The Commission on the Bicentennial has urged that the Constitution be studied as "a history and civics lesson for all of us," while the 1987 Iran/contra hearings "taught" us civics lessons for which we were ill prepared. How could the schools have better prepared us?

Chapter 5 gives some perspective on present attempts to revitalize citizenship goals in the teaching of the social studies, that phase of the total school curriculum whose civic purpose is almost universally recognized. Just how this should be achieved has long been hotly debated, or, worse, left ambiguous in the minds of teachers and bland or boring to students.

Chapter 6 broadens the perspective to the education of the members of the teaching profession itself, including the liberal as well as professional ingredients in their preparation. This subject has had little attention in the past and, if possible, even less attention in the present reform movements. Yet there are hopeful signs.

Chapter 7 indicates my own efforts to point to a set of civic ideas and values that should become an explicit focus of study throughout the school curriculum and thus embedded in the liberal and professional preparation of teachers and administrators.

The chapters in Part II should be supplemented by a recent publication of mine, *The Morality of Democratic Citizenship* (published in 1988 by the Center for Civic Education, Calabasas, California). It rounds out the discussion of the role of the social studies in civic education by dealing at some length with two recurring calls for mandating the teaching of history and teaching about the U.S. Constitution and Bill of Rights. It also gives a considerably expanded and well-documented discussion of the Twelve Tables of Civism along with the underlying conception of citizenship upon which they are based. In effect, it should be regarded as a companion volume to this book. Together, they argue that the task of reformulating the civic mission of American education requires sustained cooperative efforts by the scholarly community, the educational profession, and the public. To that task they are dedicated. They seek to inform the outlooks of those who make the curriculum, write the textbooks, and teach in the schools as well as those in educational policy-making positions.

CHAPTER 5

Reviving Citizenship Education in the Social Studies (1930s–1980s)

The outpouring of proposals and projects to create more effective civic-education programs during the mid-twentieth century would take volumes to relate. The variations of details run to infinitude, yet there is a repetitiveness and sameness to the lists of goals and objectives set forth by one commission after another. After the brutal realities and disillusionments of Vietnam and Watergate, some of these earlier statements seem blatantly and grimly superpatriotic, and others exude the bland optimism of Pollyanna herself. All that can be done here is suggest the range of political and pedagogical outlooks that seemed to motivate some of the major approaches to civic education through the social studies.

In the wake of World War I, citizenship education programs in the schools, the textbooks, and the teachers themselves were subjected to almost constant campaigns at the hands of conservative patriotic organizations whose views today seem particularly narrow-minded in their antiforeign, antipacifist, anti-immigration, antiradical outlooks. In the 1920s, as we have seen, the American Legion led the campaigns to get Congress and the state legislatures to require civic instruction, flag salutes, military training, and loyalty oaths. The dominant mood of civic eduction in the 1920s was to rally round the flag, extoll the merits and successes, and say nothing derogatory about the greatest country on earth. Of course, other nations were doing the same thing in their programs of civic education, so well documented in the ten volumes produced between 1929 and 1933 under the leadership of Charles E. Merriam, professor of political science at Chicago.[1]

The New Civism

In contrast, the 1930s witnessed a social reformist outlook sparked by the economic depression, the New Deal, and reaction against totalitarianism in the world. In the 1920s the excessively individualistic and pluralistic character of American society led John Dewey, who was becoming America's leading philosopher, to be concerned about recapturing the meaning of the public, just as the nativist drive for assimilation led Horace Kallen to be concerned about revitalizing the meaning of cultural and ethnic pluralism.

In his widely influential book on political philosophy, *The Public and Its Problems,* Dewey was especially concerned about the search for conditions under which the Great Society could become the Great Community. Modern science, technology, and industrialization had created a Great Society characterized by large-scale joint activity and aggregated collective action. But what was needed was a Great Community that would not be simply physical but would be characterized by a communal life that is morally, emotionally, intellectually, and consciously sustained. No amount of merely aggregated collective action of itself constitutes a community. Dewey found the essence of community in the generic social sense of democracy nourished by intelligence and education. This public philosophy of Dewey's is often deliberately or unknowingly overlooked by critics who view him solely as the godfather of an intellectually soft and content-weak progressive education.

The key to realizing consciousness of community is through revivifying and revitalizing an organized, articulate public. His meaning of the public goes something like this: human acts have consequences upon others; perception of these consequences leads to efforts to control action so as to secure some desirable consequences and not others. Consequences of actions are of two kinds: those that affect only the people directly engaged in a transaction are private; those that affect others beyond the people immediately concerned are public. The effort to regulate these outreaching consequences and care for the welfare of others is the realm of the public. Dewey said: "The public consists of all those who are affected by the indirect consequences of transactions to such an extent that it is deemed necessary to have those consequences systematically cared for. Officials are those who look out for and take care of the interests thus affected."[2]

Significantly, Dewey argued that this supervision and regulation of the consequences of actions by individuals and by groups cannot be accomplished by the primary groups themselves. It is just such consequences that call the public into being. The public organized to conduct these affairs through officials is the state. When the association known as the public takes on the task of regulating the conjoint actions of individuals and groups, the public becomes a political state or political community. And among the major characteristics of a state or political community are not only a temporal or geographic location with organized political institutions like legislatures and courts but a special care for children and other dependents who are looked upon as peculiarly its wards. Dewey wrote: "In the degree, then, that a certain measure of instruction and training is deemed to have significant consequences for the social body, rules are laid down affecting the actions of parents in relation to their children, and those who are not parents are taxed—Herbert Spencer to the contrary notwithstanding—to maintain schools."[3]

The significance of a representative democracy is that every citizen-voter and especially every teacher is an "officer of the public," a representative of the public as much as an elected official is. So every citizen has a dual capacity: as a private person and as an officer of the public. The essential meaning of a representative democracy is to organize its affairs that the public good dominates the private interest. Herein lies the significance of public schools in contrast to private schools—to develop the "officer of the public" role of all individuals and to aid them to enhance their political roles on behalf of the public good.

This concern by Dewey for a search for political community strengthened the recurrent calls for "education for democracy" and especially infused the thought of some professors of education at Teachers College, Columbia University. These professors, known as "social frontiersmen" from the 1930s to the 1950s, are exemplified in the works of George S. Counts, John L. Childs, R. Bruce Raup, Harold Rugg, and their associates and students. But the mood of democratic social reform and the search for a community of persuasion went out of style among philosophers of education and among much of the entire educational profession during the 1950s and 1960s. Eventually, however, the experiences of the Vietnam War, the campus unrest with its attendant changes in values, and the constitutional crisis resulting from Watergate pointed in two directions: an increased cynicism and alienation toward political affairs, and a marked revival of concern for deliberate education in the public schools that would help bring closer to realization the historic value claims of the democratic political community, which I have been summing up under the term *civism*. (See chapter 7.)

By the end of the 1920s and the opening of the New Deal, the climate of opinion in politics and education shifted away from the excesses of reactionary eagle-screaming of the early 1920s. Besides, the legislative mandates to teach the Constitution had virtually covered the country. But the tone and temper of many educational leaders began to shift to other more pressing social issues. Never acceding very willingly to the idea that legislatures should control the curriculum of school or college, many educators looked with skepticism on the intentions and motivations of most of the organizations that sought to legislate teaching of the Constitution.

A generally liberal and progressive view of citizenship tended to permeate the writings of one of the most extensive and elaborate professional studies of the school curriculum ever undertaken: the Commission on the Social Studies of the American Historical Association, supported from 1929 to 1934 by the Carnegie Corporation. Seventeen volumes were issued between 1932 and 1937.[4] The dominant tone of the most widely read volumes (such as those by Charles A. Beard, George S. Counts, Jessie H. Newlon, Merle Curti, Bessie L. Pierce, Howard K. Beale, and Charles E. Merriam) was reflected in the *Conclusions and Recommendations of the Commission* (1934): the age of individualism and laissez-faire in economics and government was closing, and a new collectivism requiring social planning and governmental regulation was emerging. The marshaled arguments sound startlingly familiar today: deprivation in the midst of plenty, inequality in income, spreading unemployment, wasted natural resources, rising crime and violence, subordination of public welfare to private interest, and international struggle for raw materials. A particular curriculum was not promulgated, but it was clear that the commission hoped that this view of political and economic life would guide specific curriculum making for civic education programs. The clear implication was that youth should be taught the values of economic collectivity and interdependence in place of economic laissez-faire while achieving personal and cultural individualism and freedom.

The citizenship theme was strongly expressed from the beginning. As Charles A. Beard approached the task of preparing the first of the commission's volumes, *A Charter for the Social Sciences,* suggestions went to him from three members of the drafting committee—George

Counts, Ernest Horn, and Jesse Newlon, all professors of education. Their suggestions were couched in terms seeking to clarify the historic meaning of American citizenship in light of the economic and political crises of the day:

> We are of the opinion that the general statement might have at least two divisions. The first would present in classic style the American political tradition and the underlying purposes of American society as revealed in great historic documents and in the history of the American people . . .
>
> The second division of the statement . . . would deal more particularly with the contemporary social situation in the United States. It is scarcely helpful, for example, to say that the object of the teaching of the social studies is to prepare for citizenship. Unless some definite content is put into the term *citizenship,* the statement is meaningless . . . If we can issue a report that will challenge the American mind by making positive and unequivocal recommendations of citizenship, it will stand almost unique among the reports of educational committees.[5]

Like-minded proposals were stemming from Counts, Dewey, Harold Rugg, William H. Kilpatrick, John L. Childs, and other social frontiersmen.[6] Counts's *Dare the School Build a New Social Order?* came out in 1932; and as editor of *The Social Frontier* in 1934, Counts specifically endorsed the AHA Commission's *Conclusions and Recommendations* as policy for the new journal. A fresh rereading of their works will reveal how often and how forcefully they came back to the need for clarifying and reinforcing the historic meaning of democratic citizenship as a prime goal of public education.

Naturally, the social frontiersmen set the profession by its ears and elicited vigorous counterattacks. But the major professional organizations generally responded positively, as far as giving renewed attention to civic education was concerned. The National Education Association and the American Association of School Administrators jointly sponsored the Educational Policies Commission in 1935, enlisting Counts along with several more conservative administrators. The pronouncements of the Educational Policies Commission softened the social reconstructionist economic views, but they repeatedly emphasized education for democracy. Charles Beard, then America's leading historian, wrote the first draft of the commission's historical volume on *The Unique Function of Education in American Democracy* in 1937; education for democratic citizenship was the central theme, echoing the views of Counts, Newlon, and others from the earlier AHA commission.[7] Beard made much of the proposals for civic education by Jefferson, Washington, Adams, Rush, and other founders, along with a continuing stress on the need for ethical and moral values of citizenship to be taught in the schools in such way as to transcend partisanship.

When *The Purposes of Education in American Democracy* was produced by the Policies Commission in 1938 (written by William G. Carr, executive secretary), the Seven Cardinal Principles had been reduced to four objectives. But "civic responsibility" was retained as the fourth (in addition to self-realization, human relationships, and economic efficiency). The stated objectives of civic responsibility do not sound particularly daring today. There was little emphasis on liberty, equality, or due process, but there was genuine scope for realistic civic studies if teachers or communities had the stomach for them:

THE OBJECTIVES OF CIVIC RESPONSIBILITY

Social Justice. The educated citizen is sensitive to the disparities of human circumstance.

Social Activity. The educated citizen acts to correct unsatisfactory conditions.

Social Understanding. The educated citizen seeks to understand social structures and social processes.

Critical Judgment. The educated citizen has defenses against propaganda.

Tolerance. The educated citizen respects honest differences of opinion.

Conservation. The educated citizen has a regard for the nation's resources.

Social Applications of Science. The educated citizen measures scientific advance by its contribution to the general welfare.

World Citizenship. The educated citizen is a cooperating member of the world community.

Law Observance. The educated citizen respects the law.

Economic Literacy. The educated citizen is economically literate.

Political Citizenship. The educated citizen accepts his civic duties.

Devotion to Democracy. The educated citizen acts upon an unswerving loyalty to democratic ideals.[8]

The consensual effort to make civic education more realistic while at the same time not embracing the extremes of radical-sounding reconstructionism or reactionary radical-baiting led civic educators to the basic ideals of democracy, à la Horace Mann, and to community activities that would involve students in community participation but not controversy. World War II, which broke into this movement with its emphasis upon mobilizing the schools for the war effort, served to reassert the values of patriotism as the basis for unity.

By the end of the 1930s, however, a few professionals in law and education had begun to look upon the Bill of Rights in a new light as the threat of war in Europe grew and as vigilantism and invasions of civil liberties escalated under the stoking of the House Un-American Activities Committee from 1938 onward. The American Bar Association established a Special Committee on the Bill of Rights in 1938. The new president, Frank J. Hogan, argued that the ABA had long rendered great public service by defending institutions, laws, and ideals important under a free government, but it was now time that the association become vigilant in the defense of the rights and liberties of individuals.

The Carnegie Corporation gave a three-year grant to the committee for the publication of *The Bill of Rights Review*. The initial volume received congratulatory messages from Attorney General Robert H. Jackson, Charles A. Beard, and John W. Davis, among others. After three years the *Review* ceased publication for reasons that I have not discovered—beyond the termination of the Carnegie grants, but a new look had been created. The Special Committee filed a brief of *amicus curiae* in the *Gobitis* flag salute case in 1940, which it lost, but did so again in the *Barnette* case in 1943, which reversed *Gobitis*. But World War II intervened, and an impetus that might have turned to the schools for teaching the Constitution with emphasis on the Bill of Rights was long delayed.

In the 1940s and 1950s both a revival of the reactionary impulses and a renewed liberal impulse gained strength. The American Legion, the Hearst papers, and many other patriotic groups hounded the Rugg social studies texts out of the schools; loyalty oath laws were passed in thirty states by 1952; and the Feinberg Act to ferret Communists out of the schools in New York was passed in 1948, followed by a half a decade of McCarthyism.

On the other side, the Supreme Court began a new interpretation of the First Amendment on religion in the schools (*Everson* in 1947 and *McCollum* in 1948) and a tentative approach to desegregation under the Fourteenth Amendment (in *Sweatt* and *McLaurin* in 1950). The liberal views culminated in *Brown* v. *Board of Education* in 1954 after Earl Warren became chief justice. And President Truman's Commission on Civil Rights forecast in 1947 much of what was to come later.

The upshot of all this is that a few educators' voices began to be raised in favor of teaching about the Constitution in the schools, with special emphasis upon the Bill of Rights. Howard E. Wilson edited in

1941 a bulletin of the National Council for the Social Studies, jointly sponsored by the American Political Science Association, entitled *Teaching the Civil Liberties,* and one of the pamphlets of the *Building America* series published in 1937 at Teachers College dealt with the Constitution in liberal terms. But there was no great demand from public organizations for the schools to launch into such territory, planted as it was with the land mines of World War II, McCarthyism, and the subsequent Cold War of the 1950s. Still, a few schools and a few projects began to surface. One of the best known illustrated the effort to strike a new balance of consensus and accommodation between the earlier approaches to the Constitution that stressed property rights and limited government and the newer stress upon the civil liberties of the Bill of Rights. Again the Carnegie Corporation proved to be a primary catalyst.

In his annual report of 1948 as president of Carnegie, Charles Dollard virtually invited applications for a grant of funds to improve citizenship education:

> the trustees and officers of the Corporation share with others a concern that all the American people have an understanding of the basic principles and practices of a free society, and also that the principles are given more than lip service . . . The Corporation has no easy solutions to propose . . . It will have no part in any program which rests on the assumption that, having achieved Utopia, we should declare a moratorium on honest and responsible self-criticism. What it will welcome is any carefully conceived plan which is designed to give young Americans a fuller understanding of the American tradition and a conviction that what they have inherited is worth transmitting to their children. Such an understanding and conviction widely diffused among people might be our best defense in the hard years ahead.[9]

The long-time dean and president of Teachers College, William F. Russell, with the enthusiastic support of the new president of Columbia University, General Dwight D. Eisenhower, quickly responded to Dollard's invitation, and the Citizenship Education Project (CEP) was established at Teachers College in 1949. For approximately a decade and with a total aid of some two million dollars, the CEP produced extensive materials and resources to help teachers instruct the "Premises of Liberty" that derive from the Constitution, the Declaration of Independence, basic legislation, and major court decisions. The premises were categorized under four headings: the free individual, the free government, the free economy, and the free world. The basic beliefs, social guarantees and responsibilities, civil rights, and civil liberties were spelled out in a useful and dramatic way far beyond the stilted textbooks of the day. And great emphasis was put upon the Constitution, especially upon the civil liberties of the Bill of Rights.

As it tried to tread carefully through the difficult 1950s, CEP proclaimed that it expressed in a noncontroversial fashion the essence of the American way, but that it also aimed to help students deal responsibly with controversy. The Citizenship Education Project at Teachers College made available solid political knowledge, reversing the usual subordination of the political so common in other approaches to civic education. What was probably even more interesting to professional educators, however, was its stress on the skills of participation, which it identified by the neutral term "laboratory practices," perhaps in the hope that it would divert charges that it was dealing with politically controversial issues. Hundreds of laboratory practices detailed how teachers and students could engage together in action-oriented problem-solving in the schools and in the community. Workshops and training programs were conducted across the country for hundreds of schools and thousands of teachers during the 1950s.[10]

Taken seriously, the suggestions could have led to much more than bland good will; for example, studying the local congressional district to see if it provided fair representation of minority groups, making a tax map of the community to see if tax assessments were equitable, getting young people to join political clubs, helping to get voters to register and to cast ballots accurately, providing citizens with nonpartisan political information, informing the community how candidates stand on issues, actually campaigning for candidates of their choice, drafting a real (not a sham) school constitution, and the like. Unfortunately, the CEP had to combat a political neutralism and caution among educators during the McCarthy 1950s. Its funds ran out just before the rise of political activism of the 1960s, and it never was well incorporated into the mainstream of teaching and research at Teachers College.[11]

In the 1950s, education for good citizenship became a rage in many school systems all over the country. Much of this movement aimed to highlight the fact that the schools were not radical and not subversive, but were supporting the basic principles of political democracy and the basic economic values of the free-enterprise system. This was a response to the Cold War crusades against communism in the world and a kind of defense against the onslaughts of McCarthyism at home. The hope was obviously that children could be taught the values of consensus on these matters, reflecting the spirit of accommodation and good will epitomized by the Eisenhower years in the presidency.

One volume admirably reveals these twin drives—a fierce opposition to communism in the world and a hope that good will, cooperative actions, and positive democratic attitudes would strengthen democracy at home. Sprinkled with pictures of smiling, clean, well-dressed groups of white pupils and teachers, the Thirty-second Yearbook of the American Association of School Administrators (AASA), produced by its Commission on Educating for Citizenship, had this to say in 1954:

> At his best, the American citizen has always sought to realize the nation's historic ideals. Now, when communist imperialism threatens all security, he feels a new appreciation for the old ideals as a stable element in a shaky world. The public schools are the means on which the American leans most heavily to make sure that all children carry forward the American heritage. So now, even more urgently than in the past, the citizen demands that the schools educate for citizenship.[12]

In the book's first chapter, entitled "The Threat Is Total," the commission argues that the Russian communist dictatorship threatens our way of life geographically throughout the world, is a political threat to democratic freedoms, and above all "drives directly at our moral and spiritual ideals" and "our religious and ethical standards." So the schools should develop the knowledge, attitudes, problem-solving ability, and the skills of working with others for the general welfare. And the conception of citizenship should not be limited to the political scientists' narrow view of legal relationships to government. Rather, echoing the Cardinal Principles of forty years earlier, the commission opted for a much broader concept of citizenship education that would include "all the mutually helpful social relationships with others which democracy assumes should be characteristic of human life and living." And for the next forty years, the AASA returned repeatedly to citizenship education as a major goal for American schools, not simply in the social studies. In 1987 a useful handbook was heralded in its foreword as "practical counsel for the busy educator who believes that *citizenship* remains one of the Seven Cardinal Principles of education in America."[13]

By thus opening still wider the door of citizenship education to all kinds of social and personal relationships, the AASA commission forecast what often did happen in programs of social studies. Whether adopting some version of the popular core curriculum that mushroomed in the 1950s or sticking to specific courses, "Problems of Democracy" often drifted off to "Problems of Democratic Living," involving the behavior and psychology of adolescents, their personal, marriage, and family problems, vocational interests, and personal values. Just as the social reconstructionists stressed the political and economic side of civic education, so the broad social conception of citizenship often became so broad and so social that it embraced almost all conceivable aspects of a social-studies approach and in the process watered down or neglected the basic political questions of power, influence, and decision making.

This was not true of all citizenship-education proposals or projects in the 1950s. The Twenty-second Yearbook of the National Council for the Social Studies in 1951 listed twenty-four characteristics of the good citizen, reflecting the composite thinking of three hundred public figures and educators. The first thirteen stressed the values of equality, liberty, basic human rights, the law, and other political competencies; the other eleven had to do with economic, family, community, and international matters.[14]

In the 1960s a curious coincidence of forces led to a general relaxing of explicit calls for more and better civic education. Both the new social studies movement and the rise of student unrest and activism undercut patriotism as an argument for civic education. Responding to the successes of the new math and the new science (stimulated by Sputnik) and funded so generously by the National Defense Education Act, the National Science Foundation, and the private foundations, the new social studies took on the patterns of the social science disciplines. They stressed cognitive analysis, systematic acquisition of sequential and organized knowledge, conceptual analysis, inquiry learning, the discovery method, and, in general, an emphasis on thinking like a social scientist. This was reminiscent, as Hazel Hertzberg points out, of the primary sources movement in history teaching of the 1880s to 1900.

The disciplinary approach to knowledge in the social sciences tended not only to belittle "soft," diffuse, and superficial programs of social studies in the schools but also to downgrade explicit citizenship education as a proper goal of the school curriculum. One of the most forthright and explicit statements of this "hard-headed" disciplinary view was made by the executive director of the American Political Science Association and his wife in 1962:

> There is a long-standing tradition according to which secondary-school instruction in political science, or instruction based upon the knowledge political science provides, has as its main objective the making of good citizens. This tradition appears to be based on the belief that instruction in government, politics, the political process, and the important issues of public policy will produce citizens who will discuss, act, and vote rationally and intelligently and that we may thereby achieve a sane and effective democratic society. Without as-

serting that education in the field of government, politics, and public
policy has no role to play in helping form better citizens, we feel
required to state at the outset, in the interests of clarity, that we regard
this tradition and the beliefs upon which it is based as mistaken and
misleading: first because it is based on a distorted conception of how
citizens are made; second because it is based on a distorted conception
of democracy; and, third because it is based on a misconception of
political science.[15]

In other words, citizens are made by the total process of political
socialization outside the schools. Democracy, like all big government,
must rest upon the expert knowledge of specialists, which cannot be
encompassed by the average citizen. And political science is a very
complicated intellectual discipline about political behavior, not a set of
maxims about good citizenship. Caught in the middle by such disciplinary views from one extreme, and the raucous non-negotiable demands
for "relevance now" from militant student activists at the other extreme,
the traditional programs of civic education seemed pale, irresolute, and
outmoded.

It is true that much of the work of the many curriculum-develop-
ment projects of the 1960s was more realistic, more sophisticated, more
analytical and skeptical, and more attuned to the claims for equality of
the unincorporated minorities and their struggles for civil rights than
was the civic education of the 1950s. Yet they did not seem to pay off in
the test results regarding political knowledge and political attitudes to
be discussed shortly. For example, of twenty-six major curriculum
centers and projects on social studies in 1972, only seven or eight seemed
to put special stress on citizenship objectives, especially those with
headquarters at colleges and universities (UCLA, Carnegie-Mellon,
Indiana, and Tufts).[16]

This listing did not include another project that had just recently
closed down. This was the Center for Research and Education in
American Liberties at Columbia University and Teachers College. The
Center began in 1966 at the crest of the wave of the curriculum-reform
movements of the Great Society and at the beginning of the violent
unrest on the college campuses. Its stress on liberty, political values,
knowledge, and skills held great promise, but it succumbed to the
withering of special government funds for curriculum development at
the beginning of the 1970s. The center heralded a growing concern for
law-related civic education, but it was overshadowed during the 1960s
by a massive outpouring of more general, and less politically oriented,
social studies materials. This rapid survey of principal trends in citizen-

ship education brings us to the 1970s and the predicaments of the present.

The Present Predicament of Citizenship Education in the Schools

First, we may note the discouraging results of teaching, whether done according to the old social studies or the new social studies. While the nation and especially the youth were engaging in some of the most extreme political activism in our history during the late 1960s and early 1970s, the result of citizenship education in the schools seemed to leave much to be desired. I can mention only two kinds of evidence: one has to do with nationwide testing of political knowledge and attitudes, the other with surveys of curriculum trends in the social studies and textbooks widely used in the schools.

The most extensive testing program in citizenship and social studies was that of the National Assessment of Educational Progress (NAEP), which reported changes in political knowledge and attitudes of nine year olds, thirteen year olds, and seventeen year olds between 1969 and 1976.[17] The startling result was not that the test scores in general declined, for declining test scores on the College Entrance Examination Board tests had become all too evident. What was impressive, however, was that the test scores on citizenship and social studies declined *more* than those in reading, writing, and science. And the declines for seventeen year olds were by and large greater than those for nine year olds and thirteen year olds.

One could speculate at length about the reasons for the decline and take little encouragement about the nation's future from the level of knowledge revealed by some of the test items. At a time when the United States was facing one of its most serious crises of legitimacy concerning the "structure and function of government," achievement on this section of the test showed the greatest average decline from test scores of thirteen and seventeen year olds between1969 and 1976; and the scores of seventeen year olds, who were eligible to vote in the year following their taking of the test, declined more than did the scores of the thirteen year olds. Less than half the seventeen year olds and less than one-fourth of the thirteen year olds knew that the Senate must approve an appointment to the Supreme Court. This was at a time when one of President Nixon's appointees was turned down by the Senate, and the character of the court was being changed by other appointments. Only two-thirds of the thirteen year olds could even name the Senate as the "other part of the Congress" in addition to the House of Representatives. Most disturbing in this section may have been the fact that less than half of thirteen year olds and only about three-fourths of seventeen year olds could give any word or phrase (let alone a sentence) that could remotely and generously be termed an explanation of the basic concept of democracy.

In the section on political process, similar declines were recorded in the students' understanding of and willingness to participate in the political process. In 1976, less than 20 percent of thirteen year olds and only about a third of seventeen year olds could tell how a presidential candidate was selected, and that was in the year of party nominating conventions. Similarly, low scores and declines characterized the ability of students to name *any* senator or representative from their state.

One could argue that such purely factual items are not a good measure of citizenship, but even if this is granted, it is sobering to learn that so few students could recognize or hold in high esteem some basic constitutional rights. Only a half to two-thirds agreed that it was all right for a person who did not believe in God to hold public office, that a magazine or newspaper had the right to criticize a public official, or that people had the right of peaceable assembly even on unpopular causes. Some comfort could be taken from the fact that the most dramatic increase in scores had to do with the rights of the accused in a criminal case—a tribute that might be divided between television police shows and law-related education programs.

Finally, the items on "respect for others" showed lesser declines than in other topics, and even some improvements on some items. In general, both thirteen year olds and seventeen year olds increased in their understanding of the problems of the poor and in their stated willingness to have people of other races participate in such activities as living in their neighborhoods or voting in elections. This is a tribute, no doubt, to the change in attitudes attendant upon the civil-rights movement and possibly the expansion of teaching about multicultural pluralism. But declines were still marked in matters of constitutional rights of freedom of religion, assembly, expression, and press. While thirteen year olds increased in their replies on understanding the need for law, seventeen year olds declined on that item; and one-third said they would not report to the police if they saw a stranger slashing the tires of a car. At the bottom of the list stood an almost unnoticed item recording the greatest decline of all: only a half of thirteen year olds and two-thirds of seventeen year olds could think of any way in which universal education helps the nation.

The reasons for the decline in achievement are many and complex.

In 1977 those who were asked to consult with NAEP officials in the effort to interpret the results made such observations as the following:

• The assessments spanned a turbulent era in American political history—including the Vietnam War, campus riots, and the erosion of confidence in political institutions culminating in the Watergate scandal—and these events may have influenced student political knowledge and attitudes.

• However, considering all that transpired from 1969 to 1976, it was encouraging that students' valuing of constitutional rights and their respect for others did not decline substantially. The basic beliefs that underlie our constitutional system still appeared to be valued by most students.

• The most encouraging news was in the area of respect for others. Most young people appear to respect the rights of people of other races, to understand the need for laws, and to recognize some of the problems faced by minorities.

• The decline in knowledge about the structure and function of government and the essential concepts underlying democracy was most disappointing and should be the cause for a hard reassessment of the social studies curriculum.

• Students' declining interest in political participation reflects the attitudes of the adult society. The 1970s saw an increasing preoccupation with personal goals, a general disillusionment with the political process, and a trend toward conservatism. It is not surprising that youths should be influenced by these tendencies.

• During the 1970s, declines occurred in funding for the social studies, in consultant support at the state and local levels, and in the extent to which students took courses dealing with political knowledge.

• Teacher training in the social studies is far from uniform across the nation and tends to neglect a basic study of the political and philosophical foundations of civic education. For instance, National Education Association data on social studies certification show that it would be possible to become a secondary social studies teacher with little or no training in government. Typically, social studies teachers major in any one of the social science disciplines and then take courses in education methods. Too often, they are not sufficiently prepared and do not have an opportunity to develop a reasoned political philosophy or competence as citizens.

• The schools espouse the concepts of democracy but often are run as autocratic communities where the students or teachers have

little or no voice in decisions affecting them. The contrast between
the "hidden curriculum" of the schools—implied through teacher
attitudes, administration attitudes, methods of conducting school
affairs—and the concepts taught in the social studies curriculum
affect student attitudes adversely.

• Students appear to do fairly well on topics concentrated upon
by teachers. From 1971 to 1975, a time period roughly correspond-
ing to that covered by the citizenship and social studies assessments, the number of states adopting statewide projects in law-
related approaches to citizenship education increased from 6 to 26,
and the number of active projects jumped from 150 to 400. During
that time the assessment revealed an improvement on many law-
related items. [18]

Whatever the reasons for the declines in test scores as revealed by
the NAEP, the general judgment of scholars in political science and in
social studies was that much of the blame should be shouldered by the
dominant content and quality of the textbooks used in social studies.
The trouble was that the judgers had different academic and political
reasons for their views.

In 1971, the Committee on Pre-Collegiate Education of the American Political Science Association reported on its survey of curriculum
materials and textbooks in elementary and secondary school civics and
government. Its major conclusions were that much of the material:

> • transmits a naive, unrealistic, and romanticized image of
> political life that confuses the ideals of democracy with the realities
> of politics;
> • places undue stress upon historical materials [a customary
> political science view], gives uninspiring and dreary descriptions
> of legal structures and formal institutional aspects of government,
> and fails to transmit adequate knowledge about political behavior
> and processes; and ignores or inadequately treats such traditionally
> important political science concepts as freedom, sovereignty, con-
> sensus, authority, class, compromise, and power, but also such
> newer concepts as role, socialization, culture, system, decision
> making, etc.;
> • reflects an ethnocentric preoccupation with American society
> and fails to transmit to students an adequate knowledge about the
> political systems of other national societies or the international
> system;
> • fails to develop within students a capacity to think about

political phenomena in conceptually sophisticated ways; understanding of, and skill in, the process of social science scientific inquiry; or capacity systematically to analyze political decisions and values;

• fails to develop within students an understanding of the capacities and skills needed to participate effectively and democratically in politics.

• and the socio-political organization of American schools in conjunction with the formal curriculum in civics and government combines to produce a situation where democratic theory has been so divorced from practice that students are skeptical of both and unable to develop an understanding of the skills necessary for meaningful participation in the political life of the society.[19]

Lest these views be taken solely as the supercilious judgments of academic disciplinarians looking down on the lower schools, the general malaise in the social studies field at large was being amply documented, albeit from a somewhat different orientation. For example, Richard E. Gross, professor of education at Stanford, conducted a survey of the changes taking place in the social studies across the nation from 1970 to 1975.[20] With his interest in history, he did not interpret the situation exactly as the political scientists did, but the combined view did not lend encouragement to the civic role of the schools and indeed helped explain some of the reasons for the general decline in political knowledge as measured by the NAEP tests.

Gross found a tendency for secondary schools to follow the lead of many colleges, which had eliminated many required courses, and to permit students to take almost any courses they wanted in grades nine through twelve. U.S. history and U.S. government remained the dominant courses, but enrollments in both markedly declined while enrollments for classes in world history and geography, civics, and problems of democracy declined even more precipitously. It was increasingly difficult for students to acquire a common base of political knowledge. There was no longer anything like the standard curriculum in the social studies that was largely achieved by the Cardinal Principles of 1918. Some of this had to do with loosening of state requirements but even more with the intervention and subsequent popularity of new social science courses, above all, psychology, the fastest growing course, but also economics, sociology, anthropology, ethnic studies, and the like. The popularity of psychology was undoubtedly related to the Yankelovich findings on the rise of interest in privatism, with its strong focus on self.

As for the elementary schools, Gross found teachers backing away from the social studies, especially encouraged by the back to the basics mania and minimum competency testing. To make matters worse, the newer and younger teachers seemed even less interested in social studies than the older ones, and states were becoming more permissive in allowing local districts to interpret the state mandates. But what this led to was a lack of interest in, or even an active movement against, the social studies by grass-roots community groups. Gross comments somewhat pessimistically:

> This is a development which social studies teachers and organizations ought to be able to meet and thrust off if we are properly united, professionally active, and really believe in what we are doing. I am convinced, unfortunately, that a major force in the decline of the social studies is our own lack of conviction and persuasiveness as to the import of the field.[21]

In a study that followed hard on the heels of Gross's, John Jarolimek, professor of education at the University of Washington, Seattle, conducted intensive case studies of the social studies programs in six key areas of the county: Boston; three cities in Ohio; an agricultural center in South Dakota; suburban San Francisco; San Antonio, Texas; and Birmingham, Alabama. His basic finding was the astonishingly great diversity. His conclusion was particularly germane to the civic role of public education:

> It would seem that such diversity and lack of apparent effort to attend to critical elements of the common culture will have serious consequences for citizenship education unless this trend is reversed. Perhaps the only reason there is any similarity in programs at all is because schools everywhere continue to rely heavily on the content and teaching strategies suggested by nationally marketed textbooks.[22]

The importance of the textbook in social studies was re-emphasized by several more surveys in the late 1970s. Three massive studies sponsored by the National Science Foundation were usefully summarized by James P. Shaver, O. L. Davis, Jr., and Suzanne W. Helburn insofar as they apply to the social studies.[23] The findings reinforced the oft-stated proposition that the teacher is the key to what happens to the students in the classroom no matter what a stated curriculum may say; and the textbook is the dominant source of knowledge, tool of instruction, and focus of testing. Whatever uniformity in social studies curriculums there may be across the country is mainly furnished by the publishers' textbooks, which exhibit great uniformity; and the impact of the "New Social Studies" of the 1960s projects turned out to be relatively slight (approximately 10 to 20 percent of teachers reporting that they had used such material).

Of particular interest, however, was the evidence that social studies teachers considered their goals to include not only the teaching of knowledge about history, government, and geography but also to instill in their students positive attitudes about American society. They believed that part of their purpose in preparing students for good citizenship is developing what Shaver calls "emotive commitment" to the basic political values of American democracy. The problem, however, is twofold: those teachers and parents who believe that basic values should be taught do not agree on what those values are; and the academic scholarly community is wary of anything that sounds like indoctrination or inculcation of beliefs. The result has often been that teachers, administrators, and textbooks publishers and writers have tried to avoid the controversial or the seamy side of American history or politics.

The problems surrounding textbook writing, publishing, and adoption have become increasingly more complicated and politicized during the past two decades. Although the full story cannot be told here, a recent volume of *Social Education* provides much useful reference material.[24]

In the 1960s and 1970s social studies and history textbooks began to be criticized for their neglect of blacks, women, ethnic minorities, the disadvantaged, and the handicapped. In the late 1970s and early 1980s the conservative revival began to criticize them for their neglect of traditional religious and family values. And no matter what the ideological point of view of the critic, the note struck in 1979 by Frances FitzGerald gained wide appeal: that too many history textbooks were bland, tedious, "dumbed down," and boring to students and teachers alike.[25]

Within a few months in 1978 and 1979, Michael Novak and Jeane Kirkpatrick blasted a widely used government text for its New Deal bias toward big and activist government;[26] and Jean Anyon criticized seventeen widely used history textbooks for their biases in favor of big business and corporate values to the detriment of the poor and working classes.[27]

In 1986 two quite different studies of history and government textbooks agreed on the surface that the books neglected the role of religion in American life. Paul C. Vitz of New York University attributed the neglect to the preceding decades of liberal political bias against Christian and traditional family values, while O. L. Davis, Jr., of the

University of Texas and his colleagues found authors and publishers too cautious in the face of possible outrage by militant Fundamentalists or militant atheists. They were generally in agreement with Charles C. Haynes's study for Americans United that textbooks neglect the importance of struggles for religious freedom and separation of church and state.[28]

Although Davis and his colleagues were generally encouraged by the improvement in intellectual content in the books they surveyed, Paul Gagnon's study of world history texts found their standards too low when measured by what the texts should be doing to present fully and fairly the basic ideas and practices of democracy in Western and American history.[29] And the results of the latest national assessment of history and literature enabled Diane Ravitch and Chester E. Finn, Jr., to claim the teaching of history and the historical knowledge of students have scarcely improved since the declines of the 1960s and 1970s.[30]

However, it has seldom been noted that the achievement of thirteen year olds and seventeen year olds had already begun to rise between the national assessments of 1976 and 1982, well before the growing mediocrity cited by the National Commission on Excellence in Education in 1983. The clamor for excellence has often rested on a dissatisfaction with the very idea of the conglomerate field known as "social studies" and a belief in the superior values of chronological history. This view was at odds with the approach of the evaluators at the National Assessment of Educational Progress while it was being administered by the Education Commission of the States in Denver (this was before the NAEP moved to the Educational Testing Service at Princeton).

This difference was clearly evident in the NAEP's regular assessment during the year 1981–82, when for the first time citizenship and social studies were treated as a unified area with a single set of learning objectives. To make matters worse in the eyes of excellence reformers, the learning objectives stressed the skills necessary to acquire and use information and the skills necessary to communicate with others, including the ability to identify and examine one's personal values and interact effectively with others. Another objective being tested was the students' "understanding of a wider network of human relationships," the relationships among societies, and their treatment of human rights. Only last did the assessment reach "students' understanding of the development of the United States, including its history, governmental structure, economic and legal systems and political processes."[31]

This 1982 assessment has been roundly criticized by Secretary of Education Bennett, Assistant Secretary of State Elliott Abrams, the Excellence Network, and the AFT *Statement of Principles* of 1987. Particular objection was made to one of its questions concerning the meaning of freedom in China and in the United States: Ming argued that there was freedom in China because people did not go hungry and had free medical care. Maria argued that there was no freedom in China because there is only one political party and no freedom of the press. The test's "best" answer was simply that the two girls differed in their opinions about freedom. This answer was taken by critics to mean that American students were being taught a moral relativism rather than learning positive values about American democracy, which embraces freedom while Chinese Communism does not.

One can take exception to a single question out of a total of ninety or more, but still acknowledge that the NAEP found an overall improvement in academic performance between 1976 and 1982 for both thirteen year olds and seventeen year olds. On ninety-eight items the thirteen year olds improved from an average number of correct responses of 61.1 percent in 1976 to 64 percent in 1982, a positive change of 2.9 percentage points; while on ninety items the seventeen year olds increased from an average of 67.7 percent correct answers to 69.8 percent, a positive change of 2.1 percentage points. These improvements may not sound startling, but they reflect the first upward movement of any kind for seventeen year olds in more than a decade of NAEP testing.[32]

One final point about the 1982 assessment. It reveals that concentration on civic values is even more necessary than is improvement in knowledge. In the section of the test on the United States, the NAEP indicated that gains for both thirteen and seventeen year olds were concentrated in the items having to do with factual knowledge of the structure and function of government, while attitudes regarding respect for the rights of others and constitutional rights tended to remain constant over the six-year period from 1976 to 1982. One possibly hopeful sign for the younger age group was that awareness of and support for constitutional rights climbed sharply among thirteen year olds but did not change among seventeen year olds. But there was still much to do, especially in the realm of civic values.

The Gathering Momentum for Civic Education

In the late 1970s the signs of a revival of interest in citizenship education began appearing in a number of important places. Key professional and academic associations, private foundations, an increasing number of state school officers and school administrators, politicians, voluntary organizations, and an outpouring of articles, books, surveys, and working papers began to attack the problem from a variety of approaches. Individual schools, whole school systems, and special projects run by universities and independent agencies began trying to improve citizenship education. This section discusses some of the major groups that have been involved and some useful surveys undertaken.[33]

Professional Organizations and Foundations

Among professional and academic organizations to be discussed here, the first is the American Political Science Association (APSA). This group reversed its fairly long-standing ignoring of the lower schools by appointing its Pre-Collegiate Committee in 1970 and conducted a useful though discouraging survey of civic and government programs in the elementary and secondary schools. Supported by a grant from the National Science Foundation, the committee began a Political Science Course Content Improvement Project. It sponsored investigations of the political learning process of elementary-school children and the development of curriculum and teaching materials on the decision-making process. This was done at the Mershon Center at Ohio State University under the direction of Richard C. Remy. Similarly, the APSA sponsored the research and writing of a new textbook aimed at the high school government course. This was carried out at the Social Studies Development Center at Indiana University, which had produced in 1971 a textbook by Howard Mehlinger and John Patrick entitled *American Political Behavior*. The newer project, also aided by Mehlinger and Patrick, was written by Judith Gillespie and Stuart Lazarus and entitled *Comparing Political Experiences*.

These projects represent a significant approach to reforming citizenship education: bringing up-to-date, scholarly knowledge, concepts, and evidence from the disciplines of political and social sciences into existing elementary and secondary school civics courses. Those behind these projects assume correctly that most teachers still rely heavily on textbooks as the staple of their teaching. Through these projects the APSA has been trying to remedy some glaring inadequacies of courses that its survey of 1971 revealed. Then, as the bicentennial years of the Constitution approached, the APSA joined with the American Historical Association to promote scholarly research leading to better teaching about basic constitutional principles and values through Project 87, whose scholarly and professional publications are enormously useful.

The second professional organization that renewed its interest in citizenship education in the 1970s and 1980s was the National Council for the Social Studies (NCSS), which had published yearbooks on the subject in 1951, 1960, and 1967. In 1975 the National Council's governing board made a commitment to put citizenship education at the top of its priorities for discussion and action for the following three years. The presidents during this period were James P. Shaver of Utah State University, Howard Mehlinger, and Anna Ochoa, both of Indiana University. The NCSS gave a great deal of attention to citizenship education from 1975 to 1978 at its national and regional meetings, where papers were read, speeches given, and actual workshops conducted on a variety of special civic-education projects for teachers ready to undertake new approaches to the old task of citizenship education. These meetings became valuable gathering places for those who wished to bring together a fragmented series of separate projects into something like a coherent constituency. The council published in 1977 a bulletin entitled *Building Rationales for Citizenship Education,* edited by Shaver.

Despite many meetings, committee reports, and innumerable articles and proposals, the NCSS could not reach a decision on the role of civic education in social studies. From 1980 to 1983, the NCSS looked as if it might succeed. As NCSS president, Todd Clark of the Constitutional Rights Foundation pushed hard for the development of a scope and sequence that would command wide consensus. On behalf of the board of directors, he appointed an ad hoc committee on essentials, scope, and sequence whose efforts were passed to another board-appointed group, the Task Force on Scope and Sequence, headed by John Jarolimek of the University of Washington. In 1983 this report urged forthright affirmation of democratic values and beliefs, along with knowledge and skills, as key elements in the goals of social studies:

Democratic processes include the practice of due process, equal protection, and civic participation, and are rooted in such values as:

Justice	Freedom
Equality	Diversity
Responsibility	Privacy
Rule of Law	International Human Rights

My reaction to the report was quite positive

because it takes seriously the oft proclaimed social studies goal of education for citizenship. It thus reaffirms a long-held traditional purpose of social studies, but does so by explicit and persuasive attention to the common core of civic values and citizenship in a democratic society. It does more than pay lip service to the citizenship goal; it spells out in very useful detail what is so often proclaimed in curriculum guidelines but then skirted or muffled when content, scope, or sequence are described.[34]

For reasons that I do not fully understand, the NCSS board did not specifically endorse the Jarolimek report, merely accepting it as a preliminary statement and asking for further reactions. Apparently the vast majority of social studies teachers approved, but, according to Donald H. Bragaw, NCSS president, a "smaller, but highly articulate, group, primarily from the college and university membership, believed that the report represented at best, a reinforcement of the status quo, if, indeed, it were not a step backward." So the board called for continuing discussion, which resulted in the publication in 1986 of yet another five "alternatives for social studies."

All five paid their respects in one way or another to the citizenship goal of social studies, but none could give top priority to the sustained scholarly study of the basic concepts underlying citizenship in a democratic constitutional order. Mathew Downey of the University of Colorado explicitly rejected the emphasis on civic values, claiming that social studies should promote private, as well as public, values, with special emphasis on history. Michael Hartoonian of the Wisconsin Department of Public Instruction and Margaret Loughlin of the University of Wisconsin-Green Bay argued that equal weight should be given to citizenship, the cultural heritage, academic knowledge, and "learning how to learn." Shirley Engle and Anna Ochoa of Indiana University opted for open-ended and problem-centered treatment dealing critically with important social issues, anticipating their new book of practical suggestions for curriculum making. Sounding very much like latter-day social reconstructionists, William. B. Stanley of Louisiana State University and Jack Nelson of San Jose State University concentrated on justice and equality as the core values of a democratic civic culture, with a view to social transformation and progressive social change through critical thinking and ethical decision making. And William M. Kniep of Arizona State University emphasized the necessity for American citizenship to include global perspectives.[35]

While thus delaying approval of a national scope of its own, the NCSS meanwhile moved to join several other learned societies and professional organizations in forming the new blue-ribbon National Commission on Social Studies. The aim of this group is to design an effective social studies program for the twenty-first century. This latest effort to improve the teaching of social studies enlisted as co-chairs Arthur S. Link, former president of the American Historical Association, professor of history at Princeton, and editor of the *Woodrow Wilson Papers;* Ernest L. Boyer, president of the Carnegie Foundation for the Advancement of Teaching; and Donald H. Bragaw, chief of the Bureau of Social Studies in the New York State Department of Education. Professor Link devoted his presidential address of December 1984 to reminding his fellow historians of the active role that the AHA had played in influencing the teaching of history in secondary schools in the late nineteenth and early twentieth centuries. He announced that the AHA Council had unanimously approved the appointment of a new National Commission on the Social Studies, whose purpose would be "to survey, as did the Committee of Seven, the current situation regarding history in our high schools and proper standards for the training of high school history teachers."[36]

As it turned out, the membership of the new commission was not confined to historians nor was its charter limited to history teaching, but encompassed the broader field of social studies as a whole. Sparked by the joint initiatives of the NCSS, the AHA, the Organization of American Historians, and the Carnegie Foundation for the Advancement of Teaching, the new commission attracted the endorsement of several score social science and other educational organizations dedicated to reforming social studies in the elementary and secondary schools, an aspect of the excellence movement that received only late attention, as we have seen.

The commission consists of prominent leaders in history and the social sciences, in the social studies profession at school and university levels, and in the public spheres of education and government. With a prominent social studies professional, Fay D. Metcalf, serving as executive director, the National Commission on Social Studies began its official work in October 1987.

The third set of professional associations that had a major impact on civic education was the American Bar Association and several state bar associations. In 1971, while Leon Jaworski was president, the ABA established its Special Committee on Youth Education for Citizenship. The Special Committee consisted of nine or ten lawyers who are ABA members along with an Advisory Commission consisting of a dozen educators especially concerned with citizenship education. The committee injected into current usage the term "law-related education," by which it means the effort to improve the citizenship knowledge, skills, and attitudes of American youth by promoting an understanding of law, the legal process, the legal system, and the fundamental principles and values upon which they are based.

The committee's staff has been active in promoting conferences, holding meetings, and publishing working papers, directories, and guidelines to stimulate projects, school systems, and individual schools and teachers to try some form of law-related education.[37] It does not have a particular approach, curriculum, or methodology to promote but tries to act as a facilitating and catalytic agency for innovation in law-related education. The number of projects, ranging from a few teachers in a single school to statewide programs, has mushroomed from around one hundred in 1971 to something between four hundred and five hundred in the 1980s; and statewide programs have expanded from five or six states in 1971 to thirty-five or more. Several organizations that began with statewide clienteles soon took on national proportions, notably Law in a Free Society/Center for Civic Education and the Constitutional Rights Foundation.

At the Federal Level

The later 1970s also saw an awakened interest in citizenship education by key people in the federal government, following on the heels of Richard Nixon's resignation in 1974 and Gerald Ford's accession to the presidency. Largely through the initiative of Frank Brown, director of the Kettering Foundation's Institute for Development of Educational Activities, President Ford's staff assistant for the Domestic Council was persuaded that a prospective White House Conference on Education should focus on education for citizenship, a subject thought highly appropriate in the wake of the Watergate scandal and the impeachment proceedings in the House of Representatives. But during the summer of 1975, the Secretary of Health, Education, and Welfare, Caspar Weinberger, vetoed the idea of a White House Conference on Education, largely on the grounds that it would probably call for new and larger amounts of federal spending and that this was contrary to President Ford's approach to government then.

Soon afterward, a new secretary of HEW was appointed, David Mathews, on leave from the presidency of the University of Alabama. Through the initiative of Geraldine Bagby of the Danforth Foundation, several people met with Mathews in October 1975 to talk about his concern to give high priority to increased citizen participation in governmental affairs in general as well as in education. The group from Danforth and Kettering included Stephen K. Bailey, then vice president of the American Council on Education, along with Terrel Bell, commissioner of education, and invited members of their staffs and consultants. At the meeting, Secretary Mathews asked Commissioner Bell to take steps to see what the Office of Education could do to promote citizen participation and citizen education. Bell quickly responded by appointing a citizen education staff to advise him and by calling a meeting of some forty-five to fifty key people to discuss what the federal government's policy should be.

Subsequently, a major national conference on education and citizenship was held in Kansas City in September 1976, sponsored jointly by the U.S. Office of Education (USOE) and the Council of Chief State School Officers. Though it was large, diffuse, and confusing to many, the Kansas City conference tried to bring together representatives of business, labor, community groups, and a wide range of voluntary agencies along with representatives of schooling, and it did focus considerable national attention on the problem. It may have done more good than a White House Conference, whose topics would have been dispersed even more widely over the whole range of problems of education and work.

The Citizen Education staff in the USOE kept at work, first under the leadership of Logan Sallada and then of Elizabeth Farquhar. The emphasis shifted somewhat away from a special interest in civic education in the schools and toward what came to be called "citizen education." This term highlighted the idea that all kinds of voluntary agencies have a role in the education of citizens along with the schools. Several conferences and several publications addressed the topics of just what these roles are and might be with regard, for example, to citizen education through the workplace, the mass media, and through all sorts of participation in voluntary and governmental agencies.[38]

While the USOE's Citizen Education staff worked on citizen participation, another governmental working group was established to make recommendations on what the federal government should do in the field of law-related education. This group, chaired by Steven Y. Winnick of the HEW General Counsel's Office, included members from the National Endowment for the Humanities, the National Institute of Education, and the Office of Juvenile Justice and Delinquency Prevention of the Justice Department as well as the Office of Education. Its final report was submitted to Commissioner Ernest L. Boyer on September 1, 1978. The study group consulted intensively with a wide range of people from the academic and professional world.

In its final report, the study group defined law-related education as "education to give people an adequate base of knowledge, understanding, and training about the law, the legal process, and the legal system that, as part of their general education, enables them to be more informed and effective citizens."[39]

Law-related education was thus defined so broadly that it could include school instruction in the basic political, philosophical, and moral values of American democratic citizenship. The study group also referred to the "fundamental legal principles and values" upon which the legal system is based. This embraces the definition of the moral goals of law-related education as given by Paul Freund, University Professor of Law at Harvard. He designated three goals, the second and third of which are understanding the functions of law and acquiring information about the law. But he declared that his first goal is the most important:

> First of all, there is the goal of learning moral reasoning or ethical analysis by continued practice in reaching decisions and having to justify them. I put this goal first because if I am right in thinking that some facility in moral reasoning is a product of the introduction of law into the schools, then the result is not limited to the knowledge of the law. It can pervade the entire educational process for the student who has learned the art. It carries over, in other words, throughout his active life.[40]

In 1978 Congress approved an amendment as Title III, Part F, of the Elementary and Secondary Education Act. It authorized the Commissioner of Education "to carry out a program of grants and contracts to encourage State and local educational agencies and other public and private nonprofit agencies, organizations, and institutions to provide law-related education programs." Although no funds were recommended by the Carter administration, and no funds were appropriated by this Law-Related Education Act of 1978, the first major legislative step had been taken along the general lines recommended by the study group. Section 347 of Title III of the Education Amendments of 1978 defined law-related education as "education to equip non-lawyers with knowledge and skills pertaining to the law, the legal process, and the legal system, and the *fundamental principles and values* on which these are based." (Emphasis added.)

Thus, through the efforts of the Study Group on Law-Related Education and the Citizen Education staff of the Office of Education, some excellent groundwork had been laid that could provide the basis for a federal role in promoting civic education in the schools. A $1 million appropriation was made for the fiscal year 1979–1980, and proposed regulations for administering the act were drawn up.[41] The regulations followed the law, which followed the study group's report in defining law-related education. This was a major development in federal policy for law-related education. Meanwhile, Congress had authorized the new Department of Education, and its first secretary had been appointed.

Despite the Reagan administration's failed efforts to abolish the Department of Education and to reduce federal funding for education, Congress continued to support law-related education in many ways. Central to this achievement were the efforts of the Coalition for Law-Related Education, spearheaded by the Center for Civic Education, the ABA Special Committee, the Constitutional Rights Foundation, and the National Institute for Citizen Education in the Law.

By 1987 Congress was allocating over $9 million a year to law-related education through the Department of Education, Department of Justice, and the Bicentennial Commission. This was not much compared to federal funding for other purposes, but it surely had something to do with the facts shown by a survey of the status of social studies reported by Carole Hahn in 1985.[42] In the decade following Richard Gross's study, law-related education had been added to social-studies programs in over half the states and ranked fourth in priority among nine goals of social studies. The fact that citizenship education ranked as first priority in the views of the forty-eight members of the Council of State Social Studies Specialists shows there is widespread consensus on the importance of civic values in American education.

The Role of the States

Meanwhile, the states were responding with considerable alacrity to the political demands that something ought to be done. Most states already had on their books a considerable body of mandates that, one way or another, related to citizenship education in the schools. A comprehensive study of such mandates made by the ABA Special Committee on Youth Education for Citizenship summarized the situation as of 1974–1975:

- Statutes in 45 states prescribe the study of constitutions (41 of both federal and state constitutions and 4 of the federal Constitution only).
- Statutes in 43 states require the study of American history (33 of both state and nation and 10 of nation only).
- Statutes in 38 states require the study of civics and government in some form.
- Every state has one or more of the above statutes on its books.
- 41 states prohibit graduation from high school of any students who have not taken the required courses on constitution or history or government.

• Statutes in 38 states require inculcation of various kinds of values or attitudes. These range from morality, piety, truth, benevolence, sobriety, frugality, moderation, and temperance to civic virtues, loyalty, and patriotism.[43]

The Special Committee's study found that enforcement or implementation of such laws and of the regulations following upon them varied greatly. Many social-studies teachers were not even aware of such mandates, while others assumed that suggested state curriculum guidelines were compulsory and were to be followed explicitly. In general, most educators thought that some kind of mandate was desirable, so long as it did not prescribe the details of curriculum or methods too closely and did not require political indoctrination of students or political advocacy by teachers.

Since the data for the Special Committee's study were gathered, several new trends in state legislation and regulations have taken place, as reported by LeAnn Meyer in her 1979 analysis for the Education Commission of the States. She reported that since 1973, about one-half of the states have taken action to require that students take a course related to citizenship education. As many as eleven states have moved to require the study of "free enterprise," sometimes in connection with "government" or "Americanism." (The chances are that the use of this phrase implies that positive and favorable teaching about private economic effort and the free market was expected by the legislators.) A second trend Meyer reported is the well-known legislative stampede to require tests of minimum competency in the basic skills for high-school graduation. Of the thirty-six states that initiated such programs, a study by Chris Pipho at the Education Commission of the States indicates that ten states included citizenship as one of the subjects to be tested.[44]

A third trend in the state initiatives that may be related to civic education is what is often referred to as "values education," "moral education," or "ethical-citizenship education." A well-publicized Gallup poll in 1976 revealed that two-thirds of those polled believe that schools should be more active in shaping desirable moral behavior of school children. Pursuing this theme, Mark Blum of the University of Louisville surveyed state departments of education to learn what they were doing or planning to do in this field. Blum reported that all forty-six states that responded were planning to integrate into any new civic education effort the concrete values and principles identified with the history of American democratic institutions and that thirty-one states had begun major revisions in their citizenship-education programs since 1970.[45]

The vast majority of responses of state departments of education agreed that ethical and moral values should somehow be related to civic education, whether in the curriculum or skills development, in regular courses or special projects, in curriculum guides or teacher-training activities, in the humanities or the behavioral sciences. Blum then classified the major efforts of the states into nine categories or types of programs of ethical-citizenship education and tabulated the number of states involved:

1. Values education
   a. Values clarification (38 states)
   b. Concrete values necessary for every citizen (e.g., liberty, equality) (39 states)
2. Moral reasoning (14 states)
3. Personal development (8 states)
   a. Deliberate psychological education
   b. Family therapy
   c. Self-enhancing education
   d. Life-skills education
4. Prosocial behavioral training (4 states)
   Behavioral modification, especially for delinquents
5. Law-related education (30 states)
6. Community education (7 states)
7. School-community education (25 states)
8. Economic-political practicum education (5 states)
9. Consumer education (21 states)

It is not easy to sort out the bases of classification and the statistical totals of states in this analysis. It is also troublesome to see included within the rubric of citizenship education such activities as values clarification, personal development, prosocial behavior modification, school community education, work-study plans, or consumer education. Such an all-inclusive approach to civic education is likely to lead to yet another laundry list of competencies, values, or behaviors, each of which may have some intrinsic usefulness for some educational purpose, but which provides no coherent or consistent intellectual framework by which to judge what civic education is or ought to be.

Major Approaches to Reform

A much more useful analysis is that by Fred Newmann of the University of Wisconsin, Madison, as published in the 1976 report of the National Task Force on Citizenship Education.[46] He listed eight identifiable but often overlapping approaches to citizenship education. They constitute a benchmark for evaluation. I have paraphrased his list and added some comments of my own regarding their importance during the past decade:

1. *Academic disciplines.* The courses in history, civics, and government have remained the staples of citizenship education in middle and high schools through much of our history. They have been expected to teach not only the facts and concepts from history and the social science disciplines but also to instill loyalty and patriotism among successive generations. The excellence movement since 1983 has tended to re-emphasize chronological history as portraying the common core of American values as they sprang from Western civilization. This has sometimes been associated with a call to de-emphasize social studies, which are characterized as a grab bag of bits and pieces from the social sciences.

In any case, it is clear that the average time devoted to history/social studies in high school graduation requirements across the country continues to be greater than to any subject except English/language arts. Statistics from the U.S. Department of Education for the school year 1984–85 showed the following:

English/language arts	3.8 credits
Social studies/history	2.8 credits
Mathematics	1.9 credits
Science	1.8 credits[47]

The prediction was that requirements in all subjects would increase by 1987–88, with greater gains being made by math and science. This proved to be the case. Between 1980 and 1987 math requirements were increased in 42 states, science in 36 states, and social studies in 29 states. In 1987 twenty-seven states required three or more years of social studies for high school graduation. Average requirements in history/social studies were highest in the North Atlantic Region (3.1 credits) and lowest in the Southeast (2.5 credits). This could help account for the fact that NAEP test scores in citizenship/social studies were lowest in the Southeast. Still, there was considerable room for explicit civic education in history, social studies, English, and language arts if decisions were made to do so.

2. *Law-related education*. This has been one of the fastest growing and most effective examples of renewed civic eduction, as just defined in the Law-Related Education Act of 1979. Excellent materials have been developed for use in existing courses or in separate courses in the schools. They range from "practical law" regarding the civil and criminal justice systems to underlying principles and concepts embedded in the Constitution and the Bill of Rights.

3. *Social problems and public issues*. This approach concentrates on particular policy issues or problems of predicted importance in the lives of students, such as war and peace, crime and drugs, poverty and environment, discrimination and segregation. This has long been a staple of "Problems of Democracy" courses, now given a new infusion of life by the cooperative project undertaken by the National Council for the Social Studies and the Domestic Policy Association's National Issues Forums.

4. *Critical thinking and decision making*. This is a long-established process approach derived from logic and philosophy to enable students to identify problems, marshal significant evidence, test the consequences of alternative solutions by inference, and make value judgments. Critical thinking has had a new birth of professional interest in recent years from both the radical and conservative poles of the political spectrum.

5. *Value clarification*. This approach enjoyed considerable popularity in the 1960s and early 1970s. It was viewed as an aid to students to become aware of the feelings and ideas that underlie their value choices and their actions. It was thus thought to enable students to become more autonomous and thoughtful about their personal and social life. Under sharp attack, particularly from conservative voices, for being value neutral or promoting moral relativism, values clarification has sharply declined as an approach to citizenship education.

6. *Moral development*. In the 1970s the psychological and philosophical views of cognitive moral development associated with Lawrence Kohlberg of Harvard elicited a great deal of attention in both academic circles and in school projects designed to help students face moral dilemmas in a constructive fashion. Kohlberg posited a theory of near universal progression of moral thinking and actions from early stages in which self and small groups are

the prime sources of conduct toward later stages in which principles of justice and freedom associated with a democratic constitutional order are uppermost. Although the Kohlberg approach to
stages of moral development declined in academic and school
circles, the clamor for reasserting traditional moral values in school
has been increasing in the 1980s. This has often centered on
reinforcing commonly accepted character values as the foundation
for good citizenship.

7. *Student participation and community involvement.* This approach stresses concrete experiences and firsthand contact with the
real world of politics, community service, and participation in
social agencies, political campaigns, or volunteer services of many
kinds. The learning by doing may reach beyond the local community to include contact with state and federal governments
through visits, seminars, or internships as well as competitions,
mock trials, or moot courts that hone the skills of citizen participation.

8. *Institutional school reform.* Many educators recognize that the
structure, governance, general quality of the school environment,
and the hidden curriculum of school life may have more influence
on citizenship education than does the official curriculum. Special
projects have embraced experiments with a "school within a
school," "a just community school," and the like as ways to
demonstrate civic skills in school life itself. The "effective schools"
movement of recent decades has re-emphasized the local school
site as the key to educational reform, but there has not been a
special concern for civic education in this movement. Rather, it
has emphasized the importance of the role of teachers in achieving
the autonomy worthy of a genuine profession.

These eight approaches by no means exhaust the roll of efforts to
inject new life and vitality into the social studies curriculum. One could
mention economic education (usually with an emphasis on the values of
free enterprise), global perspectives in education, multi-ethnic and multicultural education, or greater attention to the role of religion in
civilization. Seldom do such approaches claim citizenship as their central
or explicit goal. Whether the approach is through history or civics, law-
related education, public issues, or student participation, there is more
hope for civic education in the programs that stress the political concepts
underlying our democratic constitutional order. The test to use is
whether the program deals primarily with helping students and teachers
understand such concepts and thus to make rational and humane judgments concerning issues of public policy.

In the decade since Newmann drew up the list of eight approaches, he has continued to be an articulate spokesman and leader in the social studies. His general leaning toward stressing the skills of student partic-ipation in community involvement was apparent in his writings of the late 1970s.[48] But in the 1980s he made it clear that the members of the social-studies profession were not likely to agree on a single type of curriculum, no matter how much they might agree on the general rationale that citizenship was a major goal.[49] And even that priority was not clear from a survey that Robert Rutter conducted in the mid-1980s. In that survey, citizenship was ranked fifth by social-studies teachers in a list of eight goals, lagging behind basic literacy, good work habits and discipline, academic excellence, and personal growth.[50] Thus, in 1986 Newmann argued that the social studies profession should at least agree on ways to stress depth of study rather than coverage of masses of material, get students engaged, and increase the role and collegiality of teachers in designing the curriculum and governing the school. He even referred to "responsible citizenship" as little more than a slogan, for which James Shaver took him to task.[51]

Newmann's general pessimism concerning the possibility of consen-sus on matters of curriculum is substantiated by the range and variety of the literature on the social studies produced in the decade since 1976. The "Professional Library" drawn up by John D. Haas of the University of Colorado, Boulder, was eloquent testimony.[52] The writers of the many volumes cited by Haas might well agree with Newmann that social studies professionals will not reach consensus on a single specific curriculum or approach.

Still there is hope that social-studies professionals will reach suffi-cient consensus on the priority of the civic mission of education to be able to agree on the concepts and values that should be studied in their various approaches to the curriculum. Civic education should concen-trate on the principles and concepts of our democratic political system rather than trying to encompass a laundry list of valuable personal or social goals. Most educators would agree that civic education should include knowledge, skills, and values. Considerable gains have been made during the past decade in the first two: civic knowledge has been enhanced by updated scholarship in history, political science, other social sciences, and the humanities; civic skills have been sharpened through action learning and community participation. Civic values have been honored mostly in the breach.

There is little point in trying to stretch the scope of civic education or to dilute it with an array of efforts designed to include such private or personal activities as values clarification, family-related education, or personal development and social skills. Again, these may be perfectly useful, interesting, and personally or educationally rewarding activities, but civic education should concentrate on the prime, political purposes of education for citizenship.

To be sure, the Gallup polls have often reported that a large proportion of the adult public favors teaching "moral values" in the schools. But they usually mean stricter discipline or a return to the "traditional basic values" summed up as truthfulness, honesty, integrity, and good moral behavior. In the mid-1970s there was a wave of interest in values education among professional groups as well as among the public. Some states, including Maryland, Hawaii, and Michigan, adopted moral education as a state program.[53]

These proposals and others like them refer to obviously desirable traits of decent and humane relationships among people, but they are seldom founded on a well-formulated framework or conception of the meaning of citizenship. They mix up personal values with civic values. Although personal and social values are interrelated, moral or ethical values as often defined in school curriculums trail off into diffuse, naive, unsophisticated terms that carry little guidance beyond the obvious or the trite.

Simply translating the public's genuine concern over the decline of personal character or morals among youths into programs of moral education devoid of a sound scholarly basis weakens the revival of citizenship education. An instance along this line was reported in the February 1980 issue of *Basic Education*. It described a seminar on moral education at the National Humanities Center in December 1979. The learned professors of philosophy and history gave abstruse papers; but the upshot was that most of the attention was given to personal moral development, and there was general consensus against programmed moral education and against a course of moral indoctrination.

Not only is there momentum for civic education in the federal and state governments and in professional organizations, but there are also significant signs of revived interest among many voluntary and community organizations. One of the most significant of these was the formation in 1980 of a coalition of national organizations to promote citizenship and citizenship education, the Council for the Advancement of Citizenship. Its principal purposes are to:

- encourage citizens to learn about and exercise their democratic rights and responsibilities
- increase public awareness of the importance of citizenship and citizenship education as fundamental concerns in American life.
- improve citizenship education for children, youth, and adults in

schools, universities, communities, neighborhoods, societies, government, and the media

- foster the sharing of citizenship information among diverse groups across the spectrum of American society.

Under the dynamic leadership of Diane Eisenberg as executive director and a board of directors widely representative of professional, academic, voluntary, and public-interest organizations, the council has rapidly grown to a membership totaling more than 60 organizations.[54] In addition to publication of *Citizenship Education News,* a quarterly newsletter that carries articles about the civic activities of its member organizations, publications, and events, the council has held annual national forums since 1982 named for Senator Jennings Randolph, one of the council's principal founders. The subjects have focused on contemporary national issues with their implications for American citizenship: the new federalism, civic values in a technological age, the election of 1984, the First Amendment, the new immigration, and the Constitution. The Bicentennial Leadership Project, conducted jointly with the Center for Civic Education and funded by the J. Howard Pew Freedom Trust, conducted workshops to train hundreds of community leaders to develop programs on a grass-roots basis and designed to commemorate the Constitution's bicentennial.

The council has become a significant national venture. The early discussions leading to its formation deliberately ruled out the task of trying to define the meaning of citizenship at the outset or as a limitation on membership. The ideal of inclusivity was pretty well agreed to—at least until the formal organization was completed. Although the council has made its mark, it has not achieved adequately its purpose to "promote scholarly study of citizenship." Despite the success of the council's several ventures, there is still the need for the kind of formulation or conceptualization of the meaning of citizenship that I urged upon it from the beginning. Perhaps a consortium is not likely to produce such an intellectual framework, but it could be enormously influential in disseminating and promoting national discussion of the ideas forming a common core of civic values that hold the American polity together and give us a clearer vision of ourselves as a people. The weakest link in the citizenship chain so far has to do with civic values, but the time is ripe to deal explicitly and fundamentally with them at the highest level of objective scholarship.

A critical next step is to build upon the gains being made during the bicentennial years. We urgently need to capitalize on the public's concern for educational reform and for the Constitution. One or more philanthropic foundations could make an enormous contribution by sponsoring a series of seminars on civic values in American education, the goal of which would be to formulate a defensible conception of American citizenship in a modern American Republic. We have had successful seminars conducted by faculty members for other faculty members, by university scholars for school teachers, and by professional educators for each other. But what we need most is a series of continuing seminars, meeting periodically and long enough, to enable leading scholars from the major disciplines, influential professional educators, and leaders from the public and private sectors to see if it is possible to formulate a coherent conceptual framework regarding the meaning of citizenship in American life. Such formulations could be couched in terms that would appeal to education professionals as well as to concerned citizens and policymakers at large. These formulations would not be the abstruse colloquies of the ivory tower academics nor the hands on or how to guidelines of the classroom practitioner.

The next step would be for colleges and universities in cooperation with public and private schools to institute pilot programs of teacher education to test the framework of citizenship ideals in a variety of programs of pre-service and in-service training for teachers. As the Carnegie-sponsored National Board for Professional Teaching Standards materializes, civic learning for teachers through their liberal and professional preparation should play an appropriate role.

The time may be more ripe for a national approach to curriculum guidelines than at any time during the past thirty years. In 1957 and 1958 Paul Hanna of Stanford's School of Education startled the academic and professional communities by proposing that we move promptly to design a national curriculum:

> In a world as troubled as ours, do we not have to agree on a curriculum design that will at least expose all children in our nation to a common set of values and to a common fund of knowledge?
>
> Can our precious liberties and the right of the individual to be different be protected by a people whose education may not have prepared them to hold in common a belief in such ideals?
>
> Can a curriculum conceived primarily by a state board and the local school district and administered typically by the individual teacher provide adequate foundations for the nation's strength and welfare?
>
> Can we hope to survive as a free people unless our enculturation includes the most significant generalizations from the frontiers of knowledge?[55]

Hanna went on to propose the establishment of a national center or laboratory in which a number of fellows from the several academic disciplines, professional education, and the public would study alternatives and draw up a document "presenting a comprehensive design for the entire nation."

Its purpose would be "to establish a permanent, nonfederal National Curriculum Center or several such Centers whose goal should be the continuous examination of the exploding frontiers of human thought and achievement and to identify generalizations that must be incorporated into the national curriculum design."[56]

Hanna's proposals set off a rousing national debate. He had once again raised significant and controversial questions of lasting importance. Obviously, there was immediate response that American education is a local and state function, not federal. There may have been suspicion that such terms as "permanent" or "must" would transform any national effort into a propaganda tool for engaging in the emerging Cold War. Or it may simply have been that the idea of including all subjects for all grades into a comprehensive scheme was too all-encompassing for research-oriented academicians and professional specialists to accept.

Whatever the reasons for rejection of Hanna's specific proposal of a single all-embracing curriculum center, and his subsequent modifications to meet criticism, Hanna had remarkable success when he narrowed his efforts to the social studies curriculum. There, his proposals that the social studies be based upon a conceptual framework of "expanding environments"—beginning with the family and moving outward through school, neighborhood, and local communities to state, national, and international communities—met with enormous success. So successful did this idea become in influencing curriculum and textbooks that it is now under frontal attack by many present-day reformers who would restore chronological history to the central role in the social studies.[57] (For a full discussion of this movement, especially in California, see Chapter 1 of my *The Morality of Democratic Citizenship*.)

As we face the issues raised again by the educational-reform movements of the 1980s, it is useful to have available Hanna's proposals of the 1950s and 1960s to add to our perspectives. The concern for citizenship was present throughout his efforts.

It is also useful to note that educational scholars from vastly different political, economic, and social outlooks are now beginning to face the questions of civic education in a direct and explicit way. I have dealt with some examples in *The Morality of Democratic Citizenship*. In addition, the renaissance of civic learning is reflected in the efforts of several leading professionals in social studies to infuse new life into citizenship education. Shirley H. Engle and Anna S. Ochoa of Indiana University recently published a book on *Education for Democratic Citizenship* to bridge the gap between the goals of democratic citizenship and classroom practice.[58] And Donald Oliver of Harvard and Fred M. Newmann of Wisconsin are revising and reissuing their widely used Harvard *Public Issues Series,* first issued in 1967.[59]

These are heartening developments, but still more interesting is the growing concern for civic education among those faculty members in schools of education who are not primarily in the field of the social studies. A recent example is the volume of nine essays edited by Susan Douglas Franzosa of the University of New Hampshire, *Civic Education: Its Limits and Conditions.*[60] Although the title expresses skepticism about much that goes under the heading of civic education, at least civic education is being considered worthy of serious discussion by professors in the foundations of education, the history and philosophy of education, comparative education, and curriculum and instruction.

Some writers come to the subject from a professedly radical position that sees American schooling as historically reproducing an exploitative capitalist social system designed to exert and maintain the hegemony of the upper classes. Their general solution is to make civic education a means of emancipation and empowerment for the lower classes. Others couch their views in less extreme terms and view critical thinking as a tool of a more moderate resistance theory appropriate as a rationale for civic education in American public schools. The schools do have a role in social change.

Civic learning, even the term *civism,* is now being taken as an important subject of study, analysis, and criticism; civic learning is no longer something to be ignored or bowed to politely before passing on to something more important or enticing.

The authors of the essays in *Civic Education* make important points about privatism, elitism, and intellectual fragmentation (Donald R. Warren of Maryland); civic courage (George H. Wood of Ohio University); African-American contributions to civic theory (Beverly M. Gordon of Ohio State); the role of social-class differentiation (Andrew R. Trusz and Sandra L. Parks-Trusz of Tri-State Social Research Associates); multidimensional civism (Richard Pratte of Ohio State); highlighting the role of women in the history and theory of citizenship (Susan Douglas Franzosa of New Hampshire); the role of philosophy (James M. Giarelli of Rutgers); progressivism and comparativism in civic education (Ronald K. Goodenow of Boston University); and the role of symbolic systems (Betty A. Sichel of Long Island University).

Although several authors are obviously writing from a social-class orientation, they are not as shrill or contemptuous of their predecessors as were some of the radical revisionists of the 1960s or 1970s and as some of the conservatives and reactionaries of the 1980s are now. With improved civility, I hope that the study of civism and civic education may now go forward to see what commonality as well as what clear disagreements there may be among radicals, liberals, and conservatives. The aim is not to paper over differences or to seek a bland consensus harking back to the 1950s but, as the editor Franzosa said, to try to reconceptualize civic education by making "citizenship a central problematic within the curriculum."[61] Despite my disagreement with the major points of view of some of the authors, this book illustrates how useful the citizenship theme could become in the liberal and professional education of all teachers as well as in the social-studies curriculum of the schools.

Former senator Howard Baker coined a useful phrase when he spoke of the need for "recivilizing politics." I am asking for the "recivilizing of education," remembering that the term *civilizing* is rooted in the idea of *civis* (the citizen), *civitas* (the body of citizens or polity), and *civilitas* (the behavior and demeanor of a citizen). We need to put citizenship values at the heart of American education. That would indeed be the "recivilizing of American education."

CHAPTER 6

Capstone for Educational Reform: Civic Learning in the Education of Teachers

Almost everyone agrees that teachers and educational administrators need two major elements in their preparation: a sound liberal or general education and an appropriate professional education. Some argue that prospective teachers do not need the poor stuff they allege is taught in courses in pedagogy or "education." But if the excellence movement of the 1980s has done anything, it has begun to concentrate on the central role of the teachers in educational reform, and this has finally begun to point to needed reform in both elements of their preparation: the liberal education and the teacher education. How fares the civic mission in each of these?

In 1986 the call for educational reform for excellence reached a high point following the issuance in May of the report by the Carnegie Forum's Task Force on Teaching as a Profession. In July, the two major teachers' unions gave their approval, with some reservations. In August, the report of the National Governors' Association rallied around the major points of the Carnegie report. And in September, the president of the Carnegie Corporation, David A. Hamburg, made it clear that the corporation would continue to reinforce the momentum for educational reform, with financial aid for a decade if necessary.

State legislatures and state task forces quickly took note of the proposals, mainly to reinforce them, and the National Association of State Boards of Education began to mobilize to make sure that reforms were implemented in long-range state programs and not left solely to governors, legislatures, or unions. In addition, a Harris poll revealed that two-thirds to three-fourths of the public and of corporate business leaders approved the report's major proposals—even to the extent of being willing to pay higher taxes to bring them about.[1]

Backed by the prestige of the Carnegie Forum, the reputation of the task force members, the long record and the acknowledged leadership of the Carnegie Corporation in education, it was clear that the major ideas for reform promised to have a significant effect on the preparation, selection, and status of the teaching profession, the school curriculum, the textbooks, and the tests required of students and teachers alike. This effort to elevate the education of teachers was being likened to the role the Carnegie Corporation played in backing Abraham Flexner's studies that led to revolutionizing medical schools and the medical profession in the early twentieth century.

There isn't room here to deal with the report's many proposals aimed at restructuring the schools, the professional environment, incentives, or salaries of teachers. Instead, this chapter focuses on those aspects of teacher preparation that have direct bearing on the schools' civic mission. The task force called for sweeping changes in education that would do the following:

- create a National Board for Professional Teaching Standards, organized with a regional and state membership structure, to establish high standards for what teachers need to know and be able to do, and to certify teachers who meet that standard.
- require a bachelor's degree in the arts and sciences as a prerequisite for the professional study of teaching.
- develop a new professional curriculum in graduate schools of education leading to a Master in Teaching degree, based on systematic knowledge of teaching and including internships and residencies in the schools.
- mobilize the nation's resources to prepare minority youngsters for teaching careers.[2]

The Carnegie report rightly focuses on teachers as the keys to educational improvement and repeatedly refers to "what teachers need to know and be able to do." This is well enough, but in the long run it is the education of teachers in institutions of higher education that will make or break this bold plan for transforming teaching into the kind of profession that sets its own standards of excellence, as medicine and law now do.

But are the colleges and universities listening? If so, what are they learning from the Carnegie report, its predecessors, and its successors? Mostly, they hear that teachers need a "broad liberal education and thorough grounding in the subjects to be taught" and that the rigorous undergraduate curriculum should embrace "a common core of history, government, science, literature, and the arts." Fine, many of the higher education leaders will say, that's just what we are doing now. So what's new?

What should be new is a clear affirmation that the fundamental purpose of both liberal education and teacher education is ultimately the same as the purpose of universal schooling itself—namely, preparation for citizenship in a democratic political community. There should also be a spelling out of what that means for the substance and content of "what teachers need to know and be able to do" in the decades ahead.

This report is only one part of the program of the Carnegie Forum on Education and the Economy and thus is candidly aimed primarily at the *economic* role of American education. However, it does recognize the civic role of education:

> [W]e reject the view that preparation for work should be the only, or even the most important, goal of education. From the first days of the Republic, education has been recognized as the foundation of a democratic society for the nation and the individual alike. A passive electorate that derives much of its knowledge from television is too easily manipulated. School must provide a deeper understanding necessary for a self-governing citizenry. It must provide access to a shared cultural and intellectual heritage if it is to bind its citizens together in a commonwealth. It certainly must enable citizens of this country to make informed judgments about the complex issues and events that characterize life in advanced economies at the end of the 20th century. The cost of not doing so may well be the gradual erosion of our democratic birthright.[3]

So there is a fine statement of the most important goal of American education, but the report never seems to come back explicitly to that point. If schools are to perform their fundamental civic mission, then the teachers must be prepared to carry it out. What teachers need to know must include an understanding of the basic ideas and ideals that undergird a free and democratic society and the education that nourishes it. The substance of this knowledge is not to be decided primarily by state legislatures, Congress, or the U.S. Department of Education, but principally by the academic and professional communities, relying upon the best scholarly knowledge available. Will a national board try to assess such knowledge? We may need yet another commission or series of seminars to tackle this problem.

Meanwhile, all colleges and universities professing to prepare teachers should be mobilizing the resources of their several faculties of liberal arts and sciences, of professional education, and of other professional schools to plan and initiate effective programs of liberal education and of teacher education in which the civic purpose is prominent. They should also be taking account of those aspects of the history of higher education that may shed light on the seemingly intractable problems involved. Perhaps we could learn something from past efforts to focus on the civic purposes of liberal and teacher education. It is just as necessary to re-examine the content of the liberal education that prospective teachers undergo as it is to re-examine the content of their professional teacher education. It will not do to assume that any kind of liberal education must somehow be superior to any kind of teacher education. Both need to be reformed if we are to realize the goals envisioned in the reports of the Carnegie Task Force, its predecessors, and its successors.

This chapter discusses some of the traditions of liberal and teacher education that should be reckoned with in such reforms.

The Liberal Arts as the Civic Arts

In one of his last articles published before his tragic death in 1979, Charles Frankel, noted humanities scholar at Columbia University, made two important points relevant to this review of liberal education. One has to do with the endemic divisiveness among university faculties and disciplines and the consequent need to establish common, shared purposes in institutions of higher education. The other point underlines the civic function of liberal education as the common core of that shared purpose:

> University faculties are divided across generations, across the disciplines, often within the disciplines. Nothing was more conspicuous in the disturbances of the sixties than the irresolution and factionalism of faculties—their inability, except in rare circumstances, to stand together in defense of common principles or even to say what they were doing on the same campus . . . One of the most critical reasons is their weakened sense of shared educational and professional purposes . . .
>
> In every generation in which the humanities have shown vitality,

they . . . have performed an essential public, civic, educational func-
tion: the criticism and reintegration of the ideas and values of cultures
dislocated from their traditions and needing a new sense of meaning.
This is what humanistic scholars did in fifth- and fourth-century
Athens, in the thirteenth century—miscalled an age of unity—in the
Renaissance, and in the nineteenth century.[4]

The faculties of the liberal arts and sciences could strengthen their
sense of educational and professional purpose if they would revitalize
their joint efforts to perform their "essential public, civic function." It
is useful to recall that the very idea of a liberal education originated not
only with the humanities but with the idea of citizenship itself—in the
polis of democratic Athens and in the *civitas* of republican Rome. Since
those days and for nearly twenty-five hundred years, proponents of a
liberal education have periodically proclaimed that its primary purpose
has been civic: to prepare citizens for their roles in a political community
governed by man-made laws rather than by kinship, religion, or social
status.

In the hands of a Plato or an Aristotle, the idea of citizenship was
heavily freighted with aristocratic assumptions concerning the nature of
the desirable state. In the visions of a Pericles, Isocrates, Cicero, and
Quintilian, somewhat more democratic or republican goals were likely
to be stressed. But there was a strong and persistent current in Western
thought that said the civic and broadly political purpose of a liberal
education was paramount. After all, the term *liberal education* meant the
education of a free man. And this was likely to be reasserted and
reaffirmed during especially creative or critical periods of history, as in
the writings of the *humanista* in the city-states of Renaissance Italy, or of
the *philosophes* heralding the republican or democratic revolutions of the
nation-states in seventeenth and eighteenth century Europe and America.[5]

It seems clear that when the idea of political citizenship was strong,
the preferred content of liberal education was likely to be history, moral
philosophy, and law on top of grammar, rhetoric, and logic. But when
the ideas of leisure, contemplation, or salvation became the dominant
goals of education for the free man, the liberal studies of mathematics,
natural philosophy, metaphysics, and theology were viewed as the
proper topping off for grammar, rhetoric, and logic.

In any case, for the thousand years of the decline of the idea of
political citizenship during the medieval period, the liberal arts were
largely viewed as serving religious, intellectual, and theoretical purposes
rather than civic purposes. When the modern idea of citizenship in a

democratic or republican nation-state began to replace the medieval reliance on kinship, church, class, guild, monastery, manor, or court to maintain political order, the role of the liberal arts as civic arts re-emerged. Liberal education once again took on the mantle of preparation of free citizens for their essential public, civic function.

The belief that civism, or self-sacrifice for the public good, was the prime goal for higher education was the view of some of the more discerning founders of the American Republic. They argued that since the welfare of the new nation rested on an educated citizenry, liberal education must have a positive civic or political purpose; that is, it must develop the virtues, attitudes, and affections of republican civism. Liberal education was not primarily to perpetuate the English meaning of *civility*, which had taken on the connotation of aristocratic courtesy, polite learning, good breeding, and cultured refinement associated with a ruling class; nor was it primarily to prepare for a job or to improve one's economic status, nor primarily for the intellectual values of a disciplined mind per se; nor for individual self-fulfillment; not even for instilling the beliefs or faiths of a particular religious denomination, although most Americans of the day did believe that morality must rest upon their Protestant Christian versions of religion. The modern meaning of *citizen* thus came into English through the American Revolution. The English continued for some time to use the term to refer to the "inhabitant of a city."

Even before the adoption of the U.S. Constitution, some leaders of colonial college education had begun to stress the civic goal of higher education over a narrowly religious, denominational, or theological goal. In the 1750s, William Livingston argued for such reforms in the founding of King's College (he lost), as did Benjamin Franklin and William Smith at the College of Philadelphia (they won). Above all, however, it was Thomas Jefferson in his proposals for the reform of the College of William and Mary in 1779 who symbolized the call for the civic arts as embodied in the study of government, history, law, and public ethics. This view later found voice in Washington's proposals for a national university and in Jefferson's own plans for the University of Virginia.

In his final message to Congress in 1796, Washington said:

> The common education of a portion of our youth from every quarter, well deserves attention. The more homogeneous our Citizens can be made in these particulars, the greater will be our prospect of permanent union; and a primary object of such a National Institution [a National University] should be the education of our Youth in the science of

Government. In a Republic, what species of knowledge can be equally important? And what duty, more pressing on its Legislature, than to patronize a plan for communicating it to those, who are to be the future guardians of the liberties of the Country?[6]

The spirit of republican civism that should infuse higher education has perhaps nowhere been better expressed than by Jefferson's statement of the aims he held out for the University of Virginia in 1818. The first two purposes were:

To form the statesmen, legislators and judges, on whom public prosperity and individual happiness are so much to depend . . .
To expound the principles and structure of government, the laws which regulate the intercourse of nations, those formed municipally for our own government, and a sound spirit of legislation, which, banishing all arbitrary and unnecessary restraint on individual action, shall leave us free to do whatever does not violate the equal rights of another.[7]

Interestingly, just a few months before he died, Jefferson was proposing that the Board of Visitors of the University make clear its opinion that certain texts should be required for study in the school of law in pursuance of republican civism:

On the distinctive principles of government of our States, and of that of the United States, the best guides are to be found in, 1. The Declaration of Independence, as the fundamental act of union of these States. 2. The book known by the title of "The Federalist," being an authority to which appeal is habitually made by all, and rarely declined or denied by any as evidence of the general opinion of those who framed, and of those who accepted the Constitution of the United States, on questions as to its genuine meaning. 3. The Resolutions of the General Assembly of Virginia in 1799 on the subject of the alien and sedition laws, which appeared to accord with the predominant sense of the people of the United States. 4. The valedictory address of President Washington, as conveying political lessons of particular value.[8]

Some historians have found it incongruous that Jefferson, the great proclaimer of intellectual and religious freedom, was willing to prescribe the texts for the study of the civil polity in his beloved university. Still, it is an interesting list of prescribed texts, which in the hands of scholarly and critical teachers could raise many of those basic issues of federalist and republican government that are still being debated with great vigor. But the fact remains that political diversities or indifferences in the nation's early years held back realization of those civic purposes, which some Federalists and Republicans alike had argued should be at the core of a liberal education. Although every president from Washington through John Quincy Adams favored the establishment of a national university to promote a common preparation for citizenship, the idea never passed Congress, and in the several states the liberal arts were soon bent to different purposes.

The Decline of the Essential Civic Function

Although the civic purpose echoes throughout the nineteenth century, it did so ever more faintly. The civic purpose received due obeisance on proper occasions like commencements, but it gradually was crowded out by other purposes for higher education: denominational fealty, mental discipline, practical utility, or other aims.

In the early nineteenth century the religious revivals and denominational rivalries dominated the founding and operation of many liberal arts colleges. The civic purposes proclaimed by a Robert Livingston or a Thomas Jefferson ran up against demands to meet the commercial and industrial needs of a modernizing America by introducing studies of a more modern, practical, or scientific nature. But still more resistant was the view typified by the Yale Faculty Report of 1828, which stoutly maintained that a coherent and prescribed liberal arts curriculum must remain firmly grounded in the Greek and Latin classics and other humanistic studies of the Reformation tradition. Of these studies, the closest approach to an explicit civic purpose was probably achieved in the moral philosophy course usually required of all seniors and taught by the minister-president of the college. Although it certainly addressed civic virtues, it was likely to stress even more the personal, moral, and religious character required of a Protestant Christian citizen. Francis Wayland at Brown and James McCosh at Princeton were outstanding exemplars of this approach.

The secular civic purpose of liberal education was all but muted in the face of the religious/moral resurgence in the early nineteenth century as well as the aggressive economic and industrial enterprise of the late nineteenth century. Finally, by the early twentieth century, liberal education all but succumbed to the scholarly intellectualism of the new research-oriented academic disciplines, especially of the sciences flowing in from the German universities, or to the narrow specialization increasingly required for professional or graduate study. By the mid-twentieth century, advocacy of liberal education in any meaning was almost drowned out by the overwhelming emphasis on disciplinary specialization leading to graduate study, or on professional, vocational, or career training. And even when general education movements became popular, they were likely to stress simply *breadth* of knowledge, typically ranging across the humanities, social sciences, physical sciences, and arts.

Powerful voices were raised against this diminished role of liberal education in the face of departmental specialization, vocational and professional preparation, and the scholarly advancement of knowledge through research in the graduate schools. Early in the twentieth century, Woodrow Wilson at Princeton and Alexander Meiklejohn at Amherst called for reforms to strengthen the civic/moral purpose of liberal education. And in the 1920s and 1930s the New Humanists stressed religious/moral goals, and Robert M. Hutchins and Mortimer Adler argued for the intellectual virtues. The great debates of the interwar years were accompanied by a resurgence of new programs and new colleges to try to bring some coherence and unity into the college academic experience to avoid the "excessive smattering" or "suicidal specialization" of a runaway elective system.[9]

An important effort to put into practice a well-defined conception of the civic purposes of liberal education was made in the Experimental College at the University of Wisconsin beginning in 1927 under the leadership of Alexander Meiklejohn.[10] It was one of the several major innovations of the late 1920s and early 1930s. The Wisconsin experiment is especially significant for the present and future of American higher education because it took place at a state university, was no more selective in its admissions policy than the university itself, concentrated on the first two years of postsecondary education, stressed a two-year prescribed curriculum of common content centered upon the civilization of ancient Athens in the first year and modern America in the second year, and put great emphasis on the skills of reading and the art of writing as well as small-group discussion.

Above all, the Experimental College is relevant to the present because of its stress upon the necessity for students and faculty to study together and to confront the most fundamental civic/moral values of human civilization and to think critically and persistently about ways to improve the quality of life and the human condition. The emphasis on values permeated the required program. This was done not only to engage students in those activities of immediate value (literature, art, recreation) but above all to try to get them to understand basic human institutions as instrumentalities for furthering civic values (property, rulers and ruled, war and peace, status, education) and to engage in those activities of thinking and understanding by which the world of nature and humankind can be enhanced on behalf of human values (religion, science, philosophy, history).

The prescribed curriculum was interdisciplinary, but the purpose was not simply to acquire knowledge; it was primarily civic and moral: to prepare students to take their places as free and responsible citizens of the American political community, to think about important and significant problems required for creating a just and free civilization, and to build a sense of civic community in a segmented society and fragmented world. These goals were not to be achieved by the teacher asking the student "Do you find this interesting?" or "How do you feel about this?" but by saying "Don't you see that this is important and significant to think about and act upon as a responsible citizen and human being?"

Despite its short span of formal existence, the Experimental College continues to draw the attention of historians. In a remarkably prescient essay on "Stability and Experiment in the American Undergraduate Curriculum," Lawrence Veysey, professor of history at the University of California, Santa Cruz, had this to say in 1973:

> The great virtue of Meiklejohn's approach was that it combined respect for intellectual seriousness, the role of tradition, and contemporary relevance. . . Meiklejohn held in careful balance the theoretical and the practical, the critical and the affirmative . . . The college set out to create an atmosphere of critical, open-ended dialogue, buttressed by a constant effort to teach skill of expression that involved tutorial methods and occasional lectures . . . On the whole, the chances for such programs appear to have improved during recent years; they would certainly seem to offer the best alternative to elective freedom.[11]

In his *Handbook on Undergraduate Curriculum,* Arthur Levine lists the Wisconsin Experimental College as one of the twelve curriculum highlights of the period between 1900 and 1964; and he lists Joseph Tussman's Experimental Program at Berkeley (avowedly based on Wisconsin's Experimental College) as one of the thirteen curriculum highlights from 1965 to 1977.[12]

As Ernest Boyer and Arthur Levine have pointed out, there was a second revival of interest in general education in the 1940s and 1950s, which held out hopes that common shared values could become the basis of a core curriculum required of all students in the undergraduate years of particular colleges.[13] In this period, there was less talk of liberal education and more of general education. One reason for this can be attributed to James B. Conant who, as president of Harvard, appointed the committee that produced in 1945 the influential report *General*

Education in a Free Society. When asked why the Harvard committee talked about general education rather than liberal education, Conant replied that he did it deliberately because he saw no difference between the two. An earlier faculty committee had argued endlessly that *any* subject, properly taught, could be liberal. So he let that committee die and appointed a new one, which he hoped would come out with something new and which he himself called a Committee on the Objectives of General Education in a Free Society.[14]

Boyer and Levine report that they found a strong set of themes expressed in the stated purposes of the general-education movements of this period that point to a common set of values: "the preservation of democracy, the sharing of citizen responsibility, the commitment to ethical and moral behavior, the enhancement of global perspectives, and the integration of diverse groups into the larger society . . . The emphasis appeared consistently to be on shared values, shared heritages, shared responsibilities, shared governance, and a shared world vision."[15]

The question is, To what degree have the large number of new general-education programs actually achieved these goals? My guess is that the *stated* civic/moral purposes of preparing citizens often got lost in programs that tried to cover vast amounts of material in survey courses designed to range across broad fields of knowledge.

One thing seems clear. The idea of a common core of required study of either a "general" or a "liberal" sort almost disappeared during the 1960s and 1970s. Those requirements that remained usually consisted of a list of courses offered by disparate faculty members in different disciplines or departments from which students could select one or more. Relatively few colleges retained or developed interdisciplinary courses that were required of all students to meet their general-education requirements.[16]

In the mid-1960s there were indeed a few brave educators whose institutions were willing to let them try once again to swim against the tide of alternatives, free electives, nontraditional programs, individualized instruction, student-designed programs, encounter groups, and the like—what Riesman and Grant called the "popular reforms" of the late 1960s.[17] Interestingly enough, two of these took their inspiration directly from Alexander Meiklejohn and the Wisconsin Experimental College of thirty years earlier. From 1965 to 1969 Joseph Tussman at Berkeley and Mervyn Cadwallader at San Jose State University instituted two-year programs frankly modeled upon the civic assumptions and the prescribed curriculum of the Meiklejohn program.

There were some differences in content, but both agreed that the curriculum should be formulated jointly by faculty members drawn from several disciplines and prescribed in common for all students; and the goal was indeed civic/moral. Tussman, then professor of philosophy at Berkeley, put it this way: "The curriculum must be concerned with central moral, political, or social problems . . . it must be concerned with initiation into the great political vocation."[18] Cadwallader, now at the Union of Experimenting Colleges and Universities, recalled:

> My intention was to offer an experimental liberal curriculum . . . an education in political morality, very broadly defined. It was to be the kind of education that a citizen of a democracy must have if he is to participate critically, creatively, and responsibly in the political process of self-government. . . Both the Experimental Program at Berkeley and my program at San Jose were designed to teach young people to become intelligent, reasonable, and wise citizens. It was my assumption that the primary responsibility of a public college should be the liberal education of the public.[19]
>
> Somewhere, it seemed to me, all young Americans must learn the political morality of democracy and the deliberative arts of the political forum. It was, then, to provide a coherent and relevant political education that I hoped to revive Alexander Meiklejohn's Experimental College at San Jose State.[20]

As it turned out, only relatively few students or faculty members were predisposed to respond positively to this kind of relevance during the campus unrest of the late 1960s. So the experiments at Berkeley and San Jose lasted only four years (1965–1969), much as the Wisconsin experiment lasted only five years (1927–1932). The short life spans of these efforts have led to their being called failures. But if the Meiklejohn experiment can be an inspiration for two major efforts thirty years later, there is no reason why they in turn cannot be sources of renewed commitment yet another twenty years later. It is entirely possible that the 1980s could turn out to be more hospitable to a prescribed civic curriculum than were the depression years of the 1930s or the traumatic years of the early 1970s.

Indeed, for the past few years there has been a remarkable resurgence of interest in requiring some core elements of a liberal education that all students should acquire in common. After years of debate, Harvard reinstituted in 1979 a kind of requirement whereby students were expected to select six or eight courses from a list of eighty to one hundred core courses distributed over five academic areas: history; literature and the arts; science and mathematics; foreign languages and cultures; and social and philosophical analysis. Beginning in 1980, Stanford required a year course in Western culture and also at least one course from seven broad subject areas—which sounded much like Harvard's five, with the addition of human development and technology and applied sciences.

This is one kind of response to the general disarray that hit general education in the 1960s and 1970s. Another response was what Riesman and Grant called "models of telic reform" in their survey of more than four hundred college innovations of the period. They found three major models that attempted in different ways to reorient the whole character of undergraduate education by designing certain distinctive purposes and grounding them on certain authorities:

> 1. The neoclassical reform, stressing the intellectual virtues, grounded in the authority of the Great Books of the Western world (St. John's College).
> 2. The communal-expressive model, emphasizing the importance of the affective life in gaining acceptance, expressing feelings, achieving loving group support through encounter groups, grounded in the authority of the humanistic psychology of Carl Rogers, Abe Maslow, and Norman Brown (Kresge College of the University of California at Santa Cruz).
> 3. The activist-radical model, aiming at political power for social change and social reform whether of a revolutionary, socialist, or democratic ideology (College of Human Services in New York).[21]

The establishment institutions like Harvard and Stanford or the telic models described by Grant and Riesman do not pay much attention to the civic learning associated with maintaining and improving the fundamental civic ideas and values of the democratic political community.

Relatively little attention was given to civic learning in the voluminous products of the Carnegie Commission on Higher Education. Indeed, the commission seemed to recognize this fact when, in its final document, it set forth five purposes of American higher education and evaluated higher education's performance in achieving each purpose up to 1973:

1. The education of individual students, promoting their intellectual, aesthetic, ethical, and skill development. The commission rated the performance of this goal as generally adequate [B to B+]. Their recommendation: more attention to general education.
2. Advancement of human capability in society at large (stressing manpower and economic development and service to society).

Rating: superior [A]. Recommendation: better federal funding for basic and applied research; build up health care manpower; and life-long learning.

3. The enlargement of educational justice for the postsecondary age group. This goal stresses equality of opportunity for minority and low-income groups. Rating: unsatisfactory, but improving [Incomplete]. Recommendation: more financial aid.

4. Transmission and advancement of pure learning. The stress here is on intellectual and artistic creativity and research. Rating: superior [A]. Recommendation: more funds for research in humanities, social sciences, and creative arts.

5. Critical evaluation of society—through individual thought and persuasion—for the sake of society's self-renewal. Rating: uneven in the past and uncertain for the future [C −]. Recommendation: better rules to govern the institutional exercise of the critique of society. Carl Kaysen, a member of this commission, called this goal "general education for citizenship" and rated it poor [D].[22]

The commission conceded that the performance of higher education having to do with the fifth purpose has been the "most uneven, most controversial, and most in need of clarification." It is past time that we should take the commission seriously and concentrate upon clarifying the civic role of liberal education.

The Carnegie Council on Policy Studies in Higher Education, the commission's successor, gave a good deal more attention to liberal and general education. It commissioned Frederick Rudolph to do a rerun of his earlier history of higher education with emphasis on the college curriculum.[23] It commissioned Arthur Levine to compile a useful *Handbook on Undergraduate Curriculum* (noted earlier). And it published in 1977 a commentary on the *Missions of the College Curriculum,* issued by the Carnegie Foundation for the Advancement of Teaching, which called general education "an idea in distress" or a disaster area:

> No curricular concept is as central to the endeavors of the American college as general education and none is so exasperatingly beyond the reach of general consensus and understanding . . . it is poorly defined and is so diluted with options that it has no recognizable substance of its own . . . we would hope that the colleges could make greater efforts to define it and set limits on the extent to which further erosion will be permitted.[24]

As soon as Ernest L. Boyer became president of the foundation, it was clear that he began taking seriously this commentary on general education. He had already begun to elaborate on the theme of a core curriculum in the book that he wrote (with Martin Kaplan) while he was U.S. Commissioner of Education. In *Educating for Survival*, Boyer and Kaplan wrote: "Our own social and cultural condition calls out for a new core curriculum . . . The central focus of our quest is community . . . The new common core curriculum is built on the proposition that students should be encouraged to investigate how we are one as well as many; the core curriculum must give meaning, in a democratic context, to *e pluribus unum*."[25]

Then in the first report he wrote as president of the foundation, Boyer (with Arthur Levine) stressed the timeliness of a renewed stress on core requirements in general education. They proposed six broad subject areas to be the proper concern of general education: "Through general education, we would suggest, all students should come to understand that they share with others the use of symbols, membership in groups and institutions, the activities of production and consumption, a relationship with nature, a sense of time, and commonly held values and beliefs."[26]

It is important that the Carnegie Foundation is exerting leadership on behalf of a prescribed core curriculum in general education. At first I wished for a more explicit priority for the civic/moral values as exemplified in the Meiklejohn-Tussman-Cadwallader vein, but it appeared in a later statement by Boyer and Fred Hechinger. The book by Boyer and Levine specifically renounced the "resurrection of the traditional civics course." But a year or so later Boyer and Hechinger spoke forcefully and repeatedly of the importance of the "advancement of civic learning" as one of the essential goals of general education. They even sounded as though civics could indeed be resurrected to combat civic illiteracy:

> Specifically, we believe that tired old academic work-horse "civics" must be updated and restored in the curriculum to what was once an honored place.[27]
>
> . . . the nation's schools, colleges, and universities have a special obligation to combat growing illiteracy about public issues. Without any dilution of academic rigor, we believe civic understanding can be increased through courses ranging from literature and art to nuclear physics and industrial engineering. A better grounding in rhetoric and logic, and in the techniques of discussion and debate would also help prepare responsible citizens. Students should critically encounter the classic political thinkers from Plato, Hobbes, Locke, and Montesquieu to John Adams, James Madison, and John C. Calhoun. But, equally important, they should study government today, not just by examining its theory and machinery, but by exploring current public issues.[28]

This forthright emphasis on the civic purposes of general education deserves applause, as does the Boyer/Hechinger suggestion for new bachelor's or master's degrees in civic education aimed particularly at adults. A similar stress on the civic values of the humanities ran throughout the report of the Rockefeller Foundation Commission on the Humanities. This report came back to the term *liberal education* and underlined "humanism as a civic ideal," connecting "learning with civic duty" and resting democracy on the "principle of enlightened self-rule by the entire citizenry." The report said: "Our republic stands on a belief that educated citizens will participate effectively in decisions concerning the whole community. Humanistic education helps prepare individuals for this civic activity. The humanities lead beyond 'functional' literacy and basic skills to critical judgment and discrimination, enabling citizens to view political issues from an informed perspective."[29]

The notion of "informed perspective" is more fundamental than simply acquiring information about current issues, important as that is. As Meiklejohn put it, it is the effort to "understand what we know." Whether we speak of general education or liberal education, we cannot hope to cover all fields of knowledge, all past or contemporary social issues, or all the interests that students bring to college. Each college or program that professes liberal or general education should set about the task of defining the informed perspective or intellectual framework that will best enable students to make judgments about current issues and that will guide the building of a prescribed core curriculum that explicitly takes to heart the idea that civic learning is the highest priority.

In their canvass of the content of courses in the general education programs of more than three hundred colleges (as of 1980), Boyer and Levine identified three types of requirements: rather narrow disciplinary courses offered by regular academic departments or divisions; broad interdisciplinary courses; and programs based on themes. Boyer and Levine seem to prefer the thematic approach, which stresses ideas or issues that go beyond or across the traditional academic structures, but they also express doubts about that approach:

> What troubles us is that the vast majority of thematic programs seem so casually conceived. The topics often appear almost randomly selected. They touch only a fraction of the significant relationships that are widely shared. No guiding principle determines which themes are widely shared. No guiding principle determines which themes are selected for study and which are passed over. One year they move in one direction, the next in another. The result is a grab bag of unrelated

topics, often novel, occasionally significant, but almost always discon-
nected.[30]

In a recent book I attempted to spell out some of those themes and
concepts that are connected and that could provide a framework of
guiding principles that is both coherent and significant for civic learning
through a variety of prescribed curriculums.[31] The theme of democratic
citizenship represents a set of ideas that are peculiarly appropriate
subjects for interdisciplinary efforts and that would bring to bear the
resources of history, moral and political philosophy, literature and the
other humanities as well as political science, law, and the other social
sciences. The set of civic ideas could provide a principle for selecting
materials from the several disciplines rather than the purely informa-
tional effort to cover material.

In the final chapter of this book I propose a set of twelve civic ideas
or value-oriented claims that could be used as an intellectual framework
for designing the common civic core of liberal education.

Resurgence in the Early 1980s

Civic education also received a boost from David Mathews and his
associates at the Kettering Foundation. Mathews's special concern for
citizen education became apparent in the mid-1970s when he was
secretary of health, education, and welfare, and Terrel Bell was his
Commissioner of Education. Upon his return to the presidency of the
University of Alabama in 1977 and especially after his appointment as
president of the Charles F. Kettering Foundation, Mathews instigated a
broad-scale program aimed at reviving in colleges and universities a
lively concern for civic education.

Mathews stimulated and led more than a decade of remarkable
momentum, but there is room to mention only two points here. One is
the enthusiasm he engendered with the Association of American Colleges when Mark Curtis was president. A special issue of the association's quarterly, *Liberal Education,* was devoted to the topic "The Civic
Purposes of Liberal Learning," with sponsorship by the Kettering
Foundation,[32] and this became the theme of the association's annual
conference in 1983. It was in this volume that the phrase "the liberal arts
as civic arts" gained wide currency. The fourteen articles remain an
exceptionally useful resource for faculty and public discussion.

Discussion became the forte of a second development led on behalf
of Kettering by Larry McGehee, vice president for development and
professor of religion at Wofford College. The aim of Mathews and

McGehee and their associates was to promote grass-roots "conversations on the civic arts" among faculty members from a large number of colleges. As of March 1986 four rounds of such conversations had involved four hundred to five hundred people in meetings at Wofford, Dartmouth, Barnard, and Davidson colleges. The aim was to expand and formalize a major network of people and institutions to continue the gatherine momentum. The result was the formation of a coalition of seventeen colleges and universities, with support from the Exxon Education Foundation, to develop various models for education in the skills of citizenship.[33]

A third impetus promoted by Kettering tried to broaden the attention of the civic-arts movement to include specifically the education of those college students who were being prepared for a career of teaching in the schools. This took two major forms. One was designed to parallel the special issue of *Liberal Education,* whose audience is primarily the faculties of arts and sciences in liberal arts colleges, with a special issue of *The Journal of Teacher Education,* whose primary audience is the schools and departments of education in colleges and universities.

With special support from the Kettering Foundation and the cooperation of the American Association of Colleges for Teacher Education, a special issue of *The Journal of Teacher Education* was devoted to "The Civic Education of the American Teacher."[34] Some articles were written by the same academic leaders who wrote for *Liberal Education,* others by leaders from schools of education, all addressing from their various points of view the common civic theme for teachers. These included perspectives from history, political science, philosophy, sociology, law, public administration, psychology, minorities, and women, as well as from schools of education.[35]

The other Kettering initiative designed to bring together representatives from the academic disciplines and from professional education was a major invitational seminar held at the Hoover Institution of Stanford University on the theme "Civic Learning in the Education of the Teaching Profession." This was held in November 1984 with the co-sponsorship of twelve major associations and foundations. Its program and recommendations will be discussed at the end of this chapter.

1985 was a banner year for re-emphasizing the civic mission of liberal education. Reports from the Association of American Colleges and the Carnegie Foundation for the Advancement of Teaching set the pace, now joined by the Education Commission of the States, principally through Frank Newman, its new president.

In February 1985 the Association of American Colleges issued its report on *Integrity in the College Curriculum,* criticizing the bachelor's degree as largely meaningless and calling for a coherent course of study to be required of all students.[36] In almost all of its best generalizations, it refers to the goal of responsible citizenship. Under Mark Curtis's chairmanship (and probable authorship) the report was guided by an advisory committee for the association's Project on Redefining the Meaning and Purpose of Baccalaureate Degrees. Among the members were Ernest Boyer, Harold Enarson, Arthur Levine, Charles Muscatine, and Frederick Rudolph. The report could not be more explicit when it said that college graduates "must embody the values of a democratic society in order to fulfill the responsibilities of citizenship."

Nothing quite so explicit about civic values appeared in two other reports criticizing liberal education that had been issued just a few months earlier. In October 1984 a panel established by the National Institute of Education called for greater involvement of students as well as faculty in improving the excellence of undergraduate education.[37] It did speak of all citizens needing to "learn how to learn" and referred to "social responsibility." One of its twenty-seven recommendations urged college presidents to see that their institutions give evidence of loyalty to such ideas as "honesty, justice, freedom, equality, generosity, and respect for others—the necessary values of community." However, the report under the direction of Kenneth P. Mortimer, executive assistant to the president of Pennsylvania State University, made much less splash than did one that appeared a month later.

In November 1984 William J. Bennett, then director of the National Endowment for the Humanities, issued a report specifically on ways to improve the teaching of the humanities. The study group that advised him included Mark Curtis, Chester Finn, Hanna Gray, Paul Kristeller, Diane Ravitch, David Riesman, and John Silber. The basic theme was to reinstate the major ideas and values of Western civilization as the coherent core of the humanities for the bachelor's degree. The "educated person" was the goal. Little was said about citizenship, though it was clearly implied in the conclusion:

> We are part and a product of Western civilization. That our society was founded upon such principles as justice, liberty, government with the consent of the governed, and equality under the law is the result of ideas descended directly from great epochs of Western Civilization— Enlightenment England and France, Renaissance Florence, and Periclean Athens. These ideas . . . are the glue that binds together our pluralistic nation.[38]

But the biggest splash came a few years later in the aftermath of Allan Bloom's *The Closing of the American Mind*. From his vantage point on the Committee on Social Thought at the University of Chicago, Bloom attacked professors, administrators, and students alike for their neglect of the solid study of the classics of Western thought. They all had swallowed uncritically the moral and cultural relativism of modern social science and social history. Classical philosophy and natural rights have given way to empirical studies in nearly all the other disciplines, which express their fealty to relativism in truth and culture, equality, freedom, liberalism, minority identities, in sum, to openness. The remedy for liberal education is a restoration of the study of the core values to be found in the mainstream of Western philosophic thought and literary tradition.

Bloom's book became an instant hit and remained on the best-seller list for months. It became the darling of conservative columnists George F. Will, James J. Kilpatrick, and many others, but it was ferociously attacked from within the academy as well as from without. Ellen Goodman referred to Bloom as "Chicago's cranky curmudgeon," and the lead article in the *New York Times Magazine,* including the cover, was headed "Chicago's Grumpy Guru." Not since the 1930s and 1940s had liberal education so engrossed the media, when magazines as diverse as *Time, Christian Century, New Republic,* and *Fortune* devoted many articles to debates among Robert M. Hutchins, Alexander Meiklejohn, and John Dewey. Curiously, though Bloom advocates the Great Books program as the core of a liberal education, an idea originated by Hutchins at Chicago, he does not mention Hutchins or Meiklejohn. He does mention Dewey, only to excoriate him as the father of progressive education, the evil genius of openness in education.

Far from advancing the cause of civic learning in liberal education, the angry and sometimes uncivil debate over Bloom's irascible judgments on his students and his peers diverted attention from civism as well as civility. The benediction on the Bloom tirade could not be better put than by Bernard Murchland, professor of philosophy at Ohio Wesleyan, in his short piece in *The Antaeus Report,* "Higher Education after Bloom."

> Looking back we can discern three reasons for the success of that book. To begin with, it appealed to a large conservative audience which is predisposed to be critical of higher education. Secondly, it played to a strong sense of elitism that runs through the educational establishment . . . Thirdly, and most importantly, Bloom told the truth about the curriculum which not only lacks coherence and purpose but has abandoned all pretense to an integrated education.
>
> The covert message of Bloom's book is that the grand design for education in a democratic society as conceived by John Dewey and

others has failed. The (perhaps unintended) signal it sends to educators is that we have to rethink the democratic purposes of education, that the underlying assumptions of our educational practices are at logger-heads with desirable civic outcomes . . .

A better model can be found in the tradition of civic humanism that began with Socrates, was elaborated by Aristotle and important Ren-aissance thinkers, and found resonance in the thinking of the Founders of the American Republic . . .

Aristotle . . . concentrat[ed] on the meaning of citizenship and on how citizens relate to the polis, or what we would call the larger public. He thought of the public as a community of values which we share together and which we work together to realize . . . The highest human activity is value laden, all value laden activity is social in nature (that is, pursued by citizens in association with one another), therefore the highest human activity is what citizens do together. We may describe it as mind-opening activity.

An important task in educational reform is to incorporate the model of civic humanism into the curriculum.[39]

Exactly so. And "the curriculum" should be read to embrace the years from kindergarten through high school, college, and professional education. Meanwhile, before the Bloom phenomenon distracted the attention of the higher education community, the civic mission of liberal education was given a solid endorsement in a report sponsored by the Carnegie Foundation for the Advancement of Teaching. The author was Frank Newman, the newly appointed president of the Education Com-mission of the States. Bringing together two powerful proponents of civic learning in higher education, Newman gave uncommon national visibility to this theme in his report entitled *Higher Education and the American Resurgence*. In a forthright prologue, Newman argues that economic progress, important as that is, is not the most urgent issue facing American higher education:

The most critical demand is to restore to higher education its original purpose of preparing graduates for a life of involved and committed citizenship . . . The need to resolve complex problems intelligently places an even greater demand on higher education—a demand for graduates who have a profound understanding of what it means to be a citizen; graduates capable of helping this country to be not simply a strong competitor but a responsible and effective leader in a compli-cated world.

The college experience should . . . develop within each student a sense of country and community service and a desire to help others. Patriotism in the best sense means a willingness to believe in and work

for improvements in the country. This must not be a welcome byprod-
uct of a college education, but a central, urgent, and conscious purpose.[40]

Newman then spelled out in considerable detail his recommendations for achieving this central goal under such headings as "The New
Politics: Civic Involvement in an Age of Self-Interest," "Education for
Civic Responsibility," and "American Youth and the Ideal of Service."
He gave major prominence to the establishment of programs that
provide financial aid to college students in return for their engaging in
public and community service, somewhat on the model of ROTC and
the GI Bill. A key example is a Public Service Fellows Program for
teaching in which specified grants would be made to those selected in
return for their "social contract" agreement to serve for a stipulated
period of time as teachers in critical areas of need.

Newman's report was a persuasive rationale for the civic mission of
liberal education, and the Education Commission of the States gained
support for a network of several college presidents who had been urging
college students to implement their commitment to public service by
active participation during their college years. Led by Presidents Donald
Kennedy of Stanford, Howard Swearer of Brown, and Timothy Healy
of Georgetown, the network had become by July 1986 a coalition of
more than 120 college and university presidents. The group, now called
Campus Compact: The Project for Public and Community Service, has
its headquarters at Brown. Thus was rationale combined with action.

These action programs were another sign of the resurgence of civic
learning to be added to the variety of specific courses, seminars, and
study groups that several colleges were beginning to institute. A 1985
newsletter of the Association of American Colleges, edited by President
Arthur Levine and his assistant at Bradford College, described new
programs at Ohio Wesleyan, Syracuse, Wofford, Humphrey Institute at
Minnesota, Washington College, and a number of others and included
a bibliography. By 1988 these beginnings had been formalized into the
Public Leadership Education Project funded by the Exxon Education
Foundation and coordinated by the Kettering Foundation. Embracing
seventeen colleges and universities, it is designed to integrate theory,
practice, and service into a more unified academic experience and
ultimately to create a radically new model for civic education to prepare
civically competent citizens.[41]

In 1986 the reports on higher education continued to come from
various sectors of the academic community. In July a committee of the
Education Commission of the States urged state government officials to

press harder for the improvement of undergraduate education in their states, but among the twenty-two recommendations there was disappointingly little explicit attention to civic purposes.[42] In November the views of the state colleges were aired by a panel initiated by the American Association of State Colleges and Universities, chaired by former Secretary of Education Terrel Bell. Their concern was heavily weighted on the task of preparing the million new school teachers who would be needed in the next decade, and they were staking out their claim to that task, knowing that it could not be done alone by the small liberal arts colleges or by the leading research universities. They were thus joining the chorus asking for improvement in the undergraduate college experience.[43] The report was sharply critical of the Reagan administration's efforts to cut federal aid to public higher education and, instead, called for a "Marshall Plan" to help public higher education fulfill its public responsibilities. The report, however, did not go into details of a curriculum devoted to the civic mission. It remained to be seen whether a new Alliance for Undergraduate Education of twelve state universities would confront this issue directly.

This was, in effect, left to Ernest Boyer's report for the Carnegie Foundation, which announced the results of his study of 29 colleges and universities and surveys of 5,000 faculty members, 5,000 college students, and 1,000 college-bound high-school students. Boyer found eight points of tension that resound and expand the divisiveness lamented by Charles Frankel nearly a decade earlier. The first three are particularly pertinent to the civic theme: the discontinuity between schools and higher education, confusion over goals and loss of sense of mission, and divided loyalties among faculty members.

In his recommendations Boyer refined his long-standing proposals for an integrated core curriculum in general education and an "enriched major" that provides students with substantive knowledge and also expects students to examine that major's history and traditions, its social and economic implications, and its ethical and moral commitments. Thus, the general education, the major, and the entire culture of the institution should contribute to a sense of wholeness:

> Above all, we need educated men and women who not only pursue their own personal interests but are also prepared to fulfill their social and civic obligations . . . We emphasize this commitment to community not out of a sentimental attachment to tradition, but because our democratic way of life and perhaps our survival as a people rest on whether we can move beyond self interest and begin better to understand the realities of our dependence on each other.[44]

The two major reports issued in November 1986 before Boyer's exemplify the problem discussed in this chapter. Both reports called for the reform of liberal education and for higher education to do better at preparing college students for public service. But neither dealt specifically with the particular role of such education in the professional preparation of teachers for their civic mission. One cannot expect reports to do what they are not intended to do.

But those who are concerned with the education of teachers cannot simply assume that more of an unreformed liberal education will produce better teachers. The reform of liberal education and the reform of teacher education must not simply proceed on parallel or separate tracks. They must be planned and implemented jointly if education is to move, in Boyer's words, from "competence to commitment." That is the theme in the next pages.

The difficulty of the task is underlined by two other reports made public in November 1986. Edward Fiske of the *New York Times* indicated that the liberal arts were reviving as professional and business fields began to require more general education.[45]

But at the same time, a study of the changes in attitudes of college freshmen between 1966 and 1985 showed that freshmen were now more interested in high-paying careers that do not require more than a bachelor's degree. This was viewed as a threat to the liberal arts. Most troubling of all for the future of schooling was the decline of interest by college freshmen in becoming teachers in elementary or secondary schools. Whereas 25 percent of freshmen indicated teaching as a career in 1966, only 6 percent so indicated in 1985. This comes at a time when a million new teachers are needed in a decade, and the major reports on teacher education are proposing one or two years of graduate work for beginning teachers. Fortunately the trend began to turn upward. More than 8 percent of freshmen in 1987 indicated an interest in teaching in elementary or secondary school; and applications for admission to schools of education began to move sharply upward in the spring of 1988.[46]

In the last chapter of their book on reform and experiment in the American college during the 1960s and 1970s, Grant and Riesman remarked on the cyclical nature of reform, pointing to the reaction in the early twentieth century against the "overoptioned" nature of the elective system championed so aggressively by Charles W. Eliot at Harvard. They spoke warmly of A. Lawrence Lowell's arguments for a system of concentration and distribution of courses to achieve a greater sense of community, and they even expressed the hope that the academic world of the 1980s is "ripe for a new generation of Lowells."[47]

But they also pointed to the fact that Lowell's reforms actually strengthened the departmental structures, which foster the faculty divisiveness about which Charles Frankel wrote. And they agreed that departments did not provide the best form of academic community for undergraduate education. Their proposals thus embraced the idea of a pluralism of core programs or subcolleges to achieve greater coherence and community. They mentioned the Wisconsin Meiklejohn college and the Berkeley Tussman program as examples of desirable integrating experiences and common curriculums—but they pointed out that those programs failed and therefore probably cannot or should not be replicated.

Simply because those programs closed after four or five years does not mean they failed in the long run. If, indeed, there is a cycle to reform movements, it is entirely possible that the idea of a pluralism of subcolleges based on a variety of coherent and informed perspectives and prescribed curriculums designed by their interdisciplinary faculty members could become widespread in coming decades. This in fact was Meiklejohn's basic recommendation of 1932.[48]

There should not be a reincarnation of the exact curriculum of the Meiklejohn college of fifty years ago or of any other. The present faculty of each college or subcollege will inevitably design its own curriculum. After all, Meiklejohn himself announced to the assembled alumni in Annapolis, Maryland, twenty-five years after the closing of the Experimental College (and thirty years before the Constitution's Bicentennial) that he deeply regretted that the Experimental College's sophomore year curriculum had not concentrated on the "best reading material available for the study of American freedom," namely, the United States Constitution and the judicial opinions by which it has been interpreted. He expressed the hope in 1957 that "if any one of you or any number of you should someday share in starting another experimental college, or in making more experimental one which is now conventionalized, I hope you will consider the suggestion I am now making."[49]

The goal is not to try to return to some past curriculum model but to design new programs that will help secure the future of a free and democratic political community. Nothing less will do than requiring all college students to undertake the scholarly and critical study of those underlying civic principles and civic values necessary for generating an informed and effective citizenry.

"College students" should be interpreted to include those who attend the collegiate institutions that enroll the largest number, and the most rapidly increasing number, of students: the community colleges. Most often characterized as places for part-time study to develop a person's skills or personal interests, the community colleges have largely been overlooked as crucial agencies for civic education. One of the few advocates of teaching civic values in community colleges is Leonard P. Oliver, a staff associate of the Kettering Foundation:

> As interstitial institutions between secondary schools that offer pap as "civics" and four-year colleges and universities that assume it is the student's personal responsibility to gain the skills necessary for effective participation in civic and public life, the community colleges may be our only educational institution with the mission, resources, and interest to systematically and effectively infuse concepts of civic values and the civic arts into their educational programs.[50]

Oliver makes a persuasive case for rejecting a purely academic approach to the humanities and social sciences in community colleges, whose students are often properly concerned with career objectives. He argues for a cooperative multidisciplinary approach in which the instructors in humanities, social science, and career programs work together to deal with the social problems and public-issue dilemmas faced in the real world by their students:

> This does not mean an isolated course in civic education or a sequence of courses on government and politics. It means the encouragement of the kind of critical, analytical thinking that enables a student to build the capacity to exercise informed public judgment, to become a more responsible citizen. This is the core of teaching civic values and the civic arts—citizens bringing informed judgments to the decision-making process.[51]

There is, however, an ongoing debate in hundreds of colleges and universities about what should be required of undergraduates that would entitle them to be regarded as liberally educated, and there are similar debates about what prospective teachers should know. One of the most widely publicized debates was culminated at Stanford in March 1988.

As noted earlier, Stanford instituted in 1980 a required course in Western Culture, which all freshmen were to take by enrolling in one of eight "tracks." Each track varied somewhat according to the instructor's judgment and scholarship, but all required a common core of readings from such classics of the Western tradition as Homer, Plato, the Bible,

Virgil, Augustine, Aquinas, Machiavelli, Dante, Galileo, Rousseau, Darwin, Marx, Freud, and Mill. The eight tracks were identified as Great Works; History; Humanities; Philosophy; Literature and the Arts; Conflict and Change; Structured Liberal Education; and Values, Technology, Science and Society. The variety of tracks gave some flexibility for differing student interests, but the goal and the commonly required readings were to assure a common intellectual experience for all Stanford undergraduates.

When begun, the Western Culture course was hailed as one of the most innovative of the returns to a core curriculum following the fragmentation and diminished common requirements of the 1970s. Nevertheless, the course began to come under increasing criticism for not giving enough attention to non-Western cultures or to authors who were women or ethnic minorities. For the past two years the Stanford faculty and student body have been racked by charges that the course reflected ethnocentrism and racism, while the countercharges warned that the intellectual heritage of the West and America would be diluted or diminished if basic changes were made.

Finally, in March 1988, after many protracted debates, the Faculty Senate overwhelmingly approved a solution by a vote of thirty-nine to four, with five abstentions. The year-long requirement would remain, but the title was changed to "Cultures, Ideas, and Values" (CIV). The required texts would come from "at least one of the European cluster of cultures and from at least one of the non-European cultures that have become components of our diverse American society." In addition, each track was to include the study of some works written by women, minorities, and persons of color. One of the most controversial of the new instructional objectives was to give "substantial attention to the issues of *race, gender,* and *class* during each academic quarter, with at least one of these issues to be addressed explicitly in at least one major reading in each quarter."

Each year, beginning in 1989–90, the CIV faculty was to decide what the "common intellectual experience" should be for the coming year. This agreement need not be confined to a single list of core books but would be a series of syllabuses that agree on "those common elements—texts, authors, themes, or issues—that will be taught by all the tracks." It was agreed, however, that for the year 1988–89 all tracks would include study of Plato, the Bible, Augustine, Machiavelli, Rousseau, and Marx.

The Faculty Senate's decision attracted widespread attention in the national news media. This was dramatized when Secretary Bennett went to the Stanford campus to deliver a lecture in which he charged that the university's decision was "not a product of enlightened debate, but rather an unfortunate capitulation to a campaign of pressure politics and intimidation." These charges were immediately refuted by President Kennedy, the vice provost for academic planning and development, and the immediate past chairman and present chairman of the Faculty Senate.[52]

Now that Stanford has opted for CIV and has opened the way for innovative tracks to be developed, I have a suggestion in tune with the idea just discussed that the liberal arts should be viewed as civic arts. Why not enlist Stanford's school of education to work with the arts and humanities faculties in developing an experimental track for CIV? It might be dubbed CIVICS to stand for Cultures, Ideas, and Values in Communities and Schools. It would thus bring together and put into actual practice proposals for civic learning stemming from Meicklejohn to Boyer and Hechinger, to Newman and Campus Compact, and to Mathews and Oliver. And it would look forward to the application of CIV to the central theme of civism in the education of the teaching profession, as recommended in the succeeding pages of this book. The goal is a healthy balance between the values of cultural diversity and political cohesion in a democratic society.

Colleges and universities are being urged by their presidents to help improve the schools. Prospective teachers are being urged to acquire a strong liberal arts education. More intellectually able students are desperately needed to go into teaching rather than crowding into law, business, medicine, or engineering. Ways are being sought to enlist more minorities into teaching. What better way to attract excellent students to teaching in their early years of college than to announce that citizenship and civic education are themes or issues that can stand along with science, technology, social change, or cultural diversity as subjects worthy of rigorous liberal study? Aristotle's *Politics* could go along with Plato's *Republic*. What does citizenship in the secular world mean as defined in the Bible and in Augustine? As compared with Hobbes, Locke, and Montesquieu? How did Machiavelli, Rousseau, and Marx look upon citizenship? What role did or could civic education play in diverse ancient and modern cultures? In first, second, and third worlds?

If we are serious about improving the teaching profession—attracting to it higher-caliber college students, minority as well as majority, women as well as men—we should begin in the first year of college to make it clear that teaching is as legitimate an eventual goal of liberal study as any other profession. And we should begin that process in the early undergraduate years of the high-prestige universities and private colleges as well as in the state colleges and community colleges.

Civic Learning in Teacher Education

As happened so often in the past, teacher education was slow to appear
on the agenda for educational reform in the 1980s. When it did arrive,
the civic role of teacher education was relatively subdued compared
with attention to it in the reports on liberal education reform. Civic
learning was almost entirely lacking in the agendas of state governors,
state legislatures, and in all but a few of the pronouncements of the
federal government. Even then, it was more likely to come from
Congress, the National Endowment for the Humanities, or the Office
of Juvenile Justice and Deliquency Prevention than from the U.S.
Department of Education.

Reports of the 1980s that concentrated on improving the teaching
profession were of two general types: the commissions that included in
their membership a mix of business, political, and professional leaders;
and the pronouncements of those who were largely insiders immersed
in the task of teacher education in schools or departments of education
in institutions of higher education.

General reports of the former type poured forth in 1985 and 1986.
One that set the pattern was the California Commission on the Teaching
Profession, appointed jointly by the chairs of the state legislature's
Assembly and Senate Education Committees and by Bill Honig, the
state superintendent of public instruction. The commission itself was
chaired by Dorman L. Commons, a business executive, and supported
by a grant from the Hewlett Foundation. The commission report offered
useful suggestions concerning restructuring the levels in the teaching
career and establishing rigorous professional standards for selecting,
certifying, and paying teachers; redesigning the school as a more productive workplace for teachers and students; and recruiting able men
and women to a career of teaching.[53]

These major themes led to twenty-seven recommendations to the
governor, the legislature, local school districts, and the state school
superintendent. The report made excellent suggestions from a management and budget point of view, but it obviously did not get into
substantive matters of the curriculum or goals of public education.
Aside from some pertinent comments regarding education and citizenship, the report settled for recommending that teachers "acquire a
rigorous and broad liberal education in the humanities, natural and
social sciences, mathematics and language" and that there be a postgrad-
uate program that emphasizes "knowledge of the subject matter to be

taught, of learning and teaching methods, and skill in classroom management."

It is clear that this California report was echoed in the Carnegie Forum Task Force on the Teaching Profession, which, however, produced more far-reaching proposals and deliberately sought to embrace the whole nation. The Carnegie report also received strong support and reaffirmation by the National Governors' Association in its report and by resolution at its annual meeting in August 1986.[54] The governors resolved to push their state institutions of higher education to require a liberal arts education of prospective teachers, define more precisely the body of professional knowledge and practice that teachers must have, create a national board of certification, end undergraduate majors in education, and increase the clinical and practical experience of would-be teachers. In the governors' report, there is only one sentence in the section on teaching that mentions a civic purpose for education. In referring to the many reports already issued, the governors say: "The leaders in business, labor, education, the scholarly community, and politics who produced these reports assert a basic argument: modern times are forcing Americans to become much better educated, for economic, civic, and personal reasons."[55]

In their task force on parental involvement and choice, the governors came out strongly for more choice among schools, but they managed to confine their choice to public schools and thus avoided what could have been a volatile and controversial issue. Their prime concern was candidly expressed by Governor Lamar Johnson, president of the association, who was asked what had most captured the governors' attention. He replied: "Jobs. More than anything, it is the threat to jobs of the people who elect us."[56]

The good news was that business, labor, and political leaders were giving enormous attention to improving the status and quality of public school teachers. If the momentum could be translated into policies and institutional procedures, the 1980s might be able to nail down many desirable changes. But the bad news is that the institutions that prepare teachers may not be as alert to the possibilities of improving civic education as they are to the possibilities for raising academic standards and embracing a too narrow conception of preparation for teaching careers. In this respect, the most influential voices inside teacher education seemed to be going along with the Carnegie Task Force, the National Governors' Association, the California Commission, and other mixed groups.

In fact, those influential in teacher education seem to have had strong impact on the one report of the mixed business and political commission that dealt specifically with teacher education. Initiated by the American Association of Colleges for Teacher Education, the National Commission for Excellence in Teacher Education was chaired by C. Peter Magrath, now president of the University of Missouri at Columbia.[57] Aside from an early reference to Thomas Jefferson on the role of education in the nourishment of an educated citizenry in 1779 and to John Dewey's *Democracy and Education* (1916), the report lacks any further reference to the civic mission of education.

The report calls for intellectual rigor; special attention to attracting minority candidates for teaching; "a genuine liberal education" that includes courses in sociology, anthropology, psychology, literature, history, language, and the arts; and a professional education strongly oriented to classroom skill and management. Aside from a reference to the study of the history of public education, the final "Call for Change" says it all:

> To secure the future of the nation's children, a new generation of teachers is needed, teachers who are:
> - competent in their subjects,
> - skilled in teaching,
> - informed about children and their development,
> - knowledgeable about cognitive psychology,
> - schooled in technology,
> - informed about the latest, most relevant research,
> - able to work with peers and others in diverse environments,
> - confident of their roles and contributions.[58]

What happened to Jefferson? The same question could be put to one of the most influential collections of insiders within teacher education. A number of deans of schools of education in leading research universities, calling themselves the Holmes Group, began meeting in 1983 to consider how best to reform teacher education. The group finally issued a report in April 1986 and invited about 120 other such institutions to join in a coalition to promote an agreed-upon agenda.[59] By the end of November 1986 more than 90 institutions had joined the Holmes Group, whose chair was Judith E. Lanier, dean of the school of education at Michigan State University.[60] Without mentioning any civic purpose of education, the Holmes Group proclaimed five goals:

1. Make the education of teachers intellectually more solid. This includes a sharp criticism of the typical liberal arts education that undergraduate colleges now provide for prospective teachers.

2. Establish a ladder of professional career positions from novice to exceptional competence.

3. Create standards of entry to the profession by examinations and courses of study that are professionally relevant and intellectually defensible. This includes eliminating undergraduate majors in education and requiring a master's degree in teaching. The curriculum for this degree includes continued study of the candidate's major or minor academic field, studies of pedagogy and human learning, work in classrooms with children who are at-risk, and a full year of supervised teaching.

4. Connect their institutions closer to the schools.

5. Make schools better places for teachers to work and learn.[61]

The report forcefully attacked those who have suggested that courses in education should be abolished as requirements for teaching, but argued that those courses should be offered at the graduate level and based above all on recent research on human learning and the practice of pedagogy. In one sentence on the content of examinations to be required of professional teachers, the undefined term "foundations of education" is added to "reading, writing, academic subjects, and pedagogy." In another place, the report says competent teachers must have a "broad and deep understanding of children, the subjects they teach, the nature of learning and schooling, and the world around them." That final phrase is not explained or elaborated. Toward the end of the report, calling their colleagues to a collective commitment to action, the Holmes Group says it all succinctly: "Competent teaching is a compound of three elements: subject matter knowledge, systematic knowledge of teaching, and reflective practical experience."[62]

The deans and their faculties have certainly laid out goals that would go far toward improving the education of teachers, but something vital is missing. On the face of what the report says, it seems that a bright young person could achieve brilliantly all that the deans in the Holmes Group propose and still come out thoroughly naive, even ignorant, of the civic values of democracy, the continuing policy issues facing education in a political world, and the civic mission that public education ought to be playing. Perhaps the new collectivity should have at hand a little more history, something beyond the fact that Henry W.

Holmes, as dean of the Harvard Graduate School of Education, was trying to improve the education of teachers in the 1920s but with little success, in the view of Harvard President A. Lawrence Lowell, who is said to have remarked that the school of education is "a kitten that ought to be drowned."[63] William R. Johnson of the University of Maryland, Baltimore County, points to the irony that Dean Holmes himself worked assiduously to elevate the clinical aspects of teacher training in schools of education rather than the research elements, while the Holmes Group seeks to elevate the research agendas of schools of education.[64]

Lengthening Shadows of Past Reforms

This is not the place to recite the litany of blame that has so often attributed the low quality of education students to the low quality of the education faculty and education courses, or to the low prestige, working conditions, and salaries of practicing teachers. Nor is this the place to describe the range of prescriptions for improvement that in the 1970s came under such headings as "Teacher Competency Assessment" or "Competency-Based Teacher Education." In his DeGarmo Lecture of 1980, B. Othanel Smith, formerly of the University of Illinois, argued for making pedagogy a clinical study and putting it at the heart of teacher education.[65] That view is countered, though, by the questions that Harry Broudy, also of Illinois, raised in his 1979 DeGarmo Lecture to the Society of Professors of Education. After probing the reasons for the anomalous status of the college of education and its professors, Broudy arued that the special quality of a professional school of education is:

> competence to understand the social, historical, and philosophical contexts of schooling. There is no other way for educators and professors of education to regain credibility and leadership.
>
> Who if not professors of education and the professionals they instruct will think systematically and seriously about such questions as the following: Is there a unifying mission that could enable us to speak meaningfully of a public school? In what sense can the public school serve *in loco parentis,* as the surrogate of the community, and the cultural tradition? What is a creative pluralism in our culture and in our schools, and what sort of pluralism is destructive of culture itself?[66]

In the present political and intellectual climate of reform, it is important for the curriculum of teacher education to address such questions as these.

In November 1981 President Donald Kennedy of Stanford spoke about the role of universities in encouraging research in the social sciences and marshaling the results effectively in the public interest, notably through the school of education: "There can be no more important entry in the public policy agenda of the United States than the quality of our primary and secondary educational systems . . . it seems important to me to declare a strong institutional commitment to these issues, especially at a time when other research universities are raising questions about the continued existence of their schools of education."[67]

This is exactly the way that presidents of research universities, teaching universities, and of multitudes of liberal arts colleges ought to be thinking, speaking, and acting with regard to their schools and departments of education. President Derek Bok of Harvard struck a similar note in his annual report for 1985–86, urging schools of education to combine excellence in practice rather than trying to ape the other research faculties of the university. Although Bok agreed that schooling was the obvious centerpiece for study in a school of education and that it was as important as the study of law, medicine, or business, he made no mention of the civic purpose of schooling.[68] But it is doubtful whether other university presidents or their faculties of arts and sciences will respond positively to the pleas of a Kennedy or a Bok unless the deans and faculties of the schools and departments of education themselves can answer forcefully and persuasively Harry Broudy's questions about the "unifying mission" in relation to the viability and improvement of public schools and their civic mission.

So far, the Holmes Group and the Carnegie Forum Task Force are not doing this. The fortunes of public education and of schools of education are closely, if not inextricably, linked. Both will survive and prosper only if they take seriously their public purpose and put as their highest priority what I have been calling the revival of civic learning. An increasing number of school systems are beginning to reawaken to their fundamental civic goals, and a movement to reaffirm the civic purposes of liberal learning among colleges of liberal arts is under way. Those involved in teacher education should take heed.

The urgency of this task is underlined by the fact that the idea of public education and its civic role are being questioned more directly than at any time since public education was first acclaimed as an essential foundation of a democratic republic. Of concern have been the controversial efforts to reduce federal funding for public education; to slow desegregation and affirmative action in public education; to elevate religion and prayer in public schools; to achieve vouchers, tax credits,

or tax exemptions for private schools; to remove the authority of the
state in setting the qualifications of teachers and curriculum requirements for private schools; and to extend the monitoring and censorship
of texts and teaching materials regarding family life, sex, creationism,
and traditional values in general. But there are also the sober political
and intellectual views that regard the public and governmental role in
education as basically inimical to the public welfare when compared
with private and voluntary efforts. A good example is a paper by Denis
P. Doyle and Marsha Levine issued by the American Enterprise Institute
in 1981. It points to three major developments in the private sector:

> First is the steady and sustained growth of private elementary and
> secondary schooling just as American public education is entering a
> period of unprecedented decline. Second is an examination of the
> growth in labor, business and corporate education and training pro-
> grams, conservatively estimated to total thirty billion dollars a year.
> Third is an examination of private sector relationships with education
> institutions, public and private, higher and lower.
>
> The authors suggest that these phenomena are linked; that they
> reflect significant demand for high quality, non-traditional education
> arrangements, and that they imply the development of long-term
> trends that may permanently alter American education.[69]

Thus it is time for those in the field of teacher education to look
carefully again at where they have been and where they should be going.
What follows are some historical generalizations. First, specialized
courses for training teachers originated in this country as a means of
making possible and of improving a system of free, universal, common
schooling in the nation's early decades. Many school reformers in the
early nineteenth century who promoted the idea of public education
believed that such education must rest upon *public* institutions of teacher
education. So they set about to establish state normal schools and state
teachers colleges. But why state institutions? Because they believed that
the state would come closer to serving the public interest than would
private academies or colleges, or local pluralistic communities devoted
to religious, linguistic, or ethnic considerations.

Here is just one example. In 1826, James G. Carter—teacher, teacher
of teachers, Massachusetts legislator, and the first of an extraordinary
generation of school reformers—condemned the influence of private
academies as "hungry corporate beings" who had benefited only the
rich and prompted the middle classes to withdraw their children from
the public schools and secede from support of them. His remedies

included greater state authority for the education of primary school teachers:

> If the States continue to relieve themselves of the trouble of providing for the instruction of the whole people, and to shift the responsibilities upon the town, and the towns upon the districts, and the districts upon individuals, each will take care of himself and his own family if he is able, and as he appreciates the blessing of a good education. The rich will, as a class, have much better instruction than they now have, while the poor will have much worse or none at all. The academies and private schools will be carried to much greater perfection than they have been, while the public free schools will become stationary or retrograde; till at length, they will be thrown for support upon the gratuitous, and of course capricious and uncertain efforts of individuals . . .
>
> An institution for the education of teachers . . . would form a part, and a very important part, of the free school system . . . [W]e should thus secure at once a uniform, intelligent and independent tribunal for decisions on the qualifications of teachers . . . An institution for this purpose would become by its influence on society, and particularly on the young, an engine to sway the public sentiment, the public morals, and the public religion, more powerful than any other in the possession of government . . . It should be emphatically the State's institution . . . If it be not undertaken by the public and for public purposes, it will be undertaken by individuals for private purposes.[70]

In its origin, then, public teacher education was justified on the grounds that it would promote the original purposes of public education: to prepare citizens for the new nation. Public education had a public political purpose—not primarily a private purpose to promote self-fulfillment for individual life-styles or preparation for a job or for getting into college—but rather to transmit the knowledge and values necessary to preserve and promote the democratic polity.

Now, let's look at a different view that began to be expressed some half century later. By the 1880s, the growth of secondary schools focused attention on the need for special training for high school teachers. As the colleges became interested in this level of schooling, the question earlier posed by the public versus the private purposes of teacher education for primary school teachers began to recede in favor of the complex questions surrounding the relation of liberal and general education to professional and technical training in the preparation of secondary school teachers.

With some notable exceptions, teacher education has been preoccupied ever since with debates over liberal versus technical, or general versus professional, issues. For example, notice the difference in focus and in tone from that of James Carter when Charles Kendall Adams, historian and president of Cornell, spoke to the New England Association of Colleges and Preparatory Schools in 1888. He was arguing that colleges and universities ought to take up the systematic teaching of pedagogy to prepare young men to be educational leaders as well as proficient teachers. How was this to be done in addition to their collegiate liberal education? By four courses:

1. The History of Education; ancient, medieval and modern . . .
2. The Philosophy of Education . . . [T]he successful study and teaching of pedagogy, as a science, must rest very largely upon a psychological basis . . .
3. Methods in the Schoolroom. This is the practical side of the work, and should embrace a discussion of such questions as the art of teaching and governing; methods of most successfully imparting instruction; general schoolroom practice; general school management; the art of grading and arranging courses of study . . .
4. The Teachers' Seminary. Here should be freely examined and discussed the most obscure and difficult problems that confront the teacher. Then, in addition to these courses, there may well be given by professors in the leading departments of the college or university courses designed exclusively to instruct how to teach young pupils the subject in hand.[71]

Well, what have we here? Let's apply some modern terms to these courses and see what we have. Let's call history of education a "humanistic study." Note that President Adams's "philosophy of education" was primarily psychology; so let's call that a "behavioral study." Let's call methods in the schoolroom "teaching and learning theory with laboratory and clinical experience." Let's call the teachers' seminary a "practicum." And let's call courses in other departments of the college designed to teach the subject in hand "content of the teaching specialty."

What do we have? We have the 1975 *Standards of Accreditation of Teacher Education* issued by the National Council for the Accreditation of Teacher Education (NCATE). Of course, there are great differences in the "knowledge base" between the proposals of 1888 and the standards of 1975. But the point is that the framework for discussion had changed between the 1820s and the 1890s. The question was not so much, How can we train teachers to conduct schools that will primarily serve a public purpose? The question became and largely remains today, How can we train teachers most effectively to impart instruction in the classroom? The public purpose of teacher education goes largely unattended even in the reform documents of the late 1980s.

There have been minority voices raised periodically to try to refocus the problem on the public purposes of public education in the education of teachers. There have been at least two kinds of protest against the domination of teacher education by the academic concerns of colleges and universities or the pedagogical concerns of normal schools. One was a socially and politically conservative view that sought a highly professionalized and narrow approach to overcome the vagaries and incompetencies of local schools as well as the indifference or hostility of the collegiate academic disciplines. This approach was typified by the Carnegie Foundation study of the teacher education institutions of Missouri in 1920, a study associated with William S. Learned of the foundation and William C. Bagley and George D. Strayer of Teachers College, among others.

The interesting point here is that the authors blamed the inadequacy of the normal schools of Missouri on two factors: the normal schools had tried to become liberal arts colleges and thus neglected their primary purpose to train teachers for the public schools; and they had responded too easily to local pressures to become vocationally beneficial for individuals or for industry and business. The remedy? Stress their single purpose to train teachers for the public schools and give priority to state institutions to promote the primarily public and professional purpose:

> The efficient teacher training school of any grade is not to be measured by college, university, law, medical, or other liberal or professional institutions. These operate indirectly for the general good, but their direct aim is rather the intellectual or vocational benefit of the individual. The school for teachers, on the other hand, is the immediate instrument of the state for providing a given number and quality of public servants to discharge the main collective obligation of society to the next generation . . . First and last it serves the state and not individuals.[72]

This view of the value of a single-purpose normal school was destined to disappear. Normal schools became teachers colleges; teachers colleges became state colleges; state colleges became state universities. As this happened, however, state credentialing did not disappear with the single-purpose teacher education institutions. Rather, state credentialing adopted more of the academic discipline approach to the education of teachers; and in so doing the public purposes became ever more muted as the academic content on one side and the narrow pedagogical purposes of classroom management were elevated on the other side.

A second minority view toward a disciplinary dominance of teacher education stemmed from a socially reformist and politically liberal strand of thought that was attuned to the New Deal. This thinking initially found expression in John Dewey and flourished in the Department of Social and Philosophical Foundations of Education at Teachers College from the 1930s to the 1950s. These views were widely publicized by William H. Kilpatrick, George S. Counts, John L. Childs, Jesse Newlon, Lyman Bryson, Edmund deS. Brunner, Harold Rugg, Goodwin Watson, Bruce Raup, F. Ernest Johnson, Harold Clark, Edward H. Reisner, and Isaac Kandel, among others.

Under the dynamic instigation of this department and impelled by the domestic crises of the Depression and the impending worldwide conflicts between totalitarianism and democracy, the faculty of Teachers College instituted an academic requirement in the "foundations of education" for all master's degree candidates at the college. This amounted to one-fourth (eight out of thirty-two points) of a minimum total for a master's degree. For a time, the requirement even amounted to taking a single "integrated, core" course, taught by a number of panels of three to six faculty members (team teaching) and drawn from several disciplines and departments of the college (interdisciplinary). Many of the syllabuses, books of readings, notes, and materials developed for the course—known simply as Foundations of Education, or Education 200F—are deposited in the Hanna Collection of the archives of the Hoover Institution at Stanford University as well as the archives of Teachers College.

Once World War II was over, a resurgent Teachers College was blessed with the enrollment booms of the late 1940s and a rapidly expanding faculty, guided by the strong leadership of Dean Hollis L. Caswell, whose major concerns were the fields of curriculum and teaching. A movement to dilute the eight-point requirement in the foundations fields for the Master's degree accelerated until the foundations requirements—designed to achieve a common core of social, political, philosophical, psychological, and educational discourse for all Teachers College students—was on the way to becoming simply a nonmajor requirement. The assumption came to be whatever a student might take in general courses outside one's own department would be satisfactory. This creeping dilution and ultimately virtual defeat of the foundation's requirement paralleled what was happening to the core of liberal arts requirements for the baccalaureate degree during the 1950s and 1960s.

To reaffirm the role of educational foundations as a core requirement in the preparation of the teaching profession, the department drew up a statement of rationale developed over the academic year 1949–1950. The civic purpose was paramount:

> Educational foundations undertakes to bring together three types of resources to help educators study the central question, "What is the educational task in our culture?" To approach this question with scholarship, thoroughness, and creativeness, on one hand, and with awareness of practical realities in school and society on the other, the educational foundations draws upon three resources: the university disciplines, community and citizen activities, and the institutions of education. It is the special task of foundations to keep these routes open and to cultivate the resources to the highest possible levels in the attainment of educational direction and power . . .
>
> The foundations process . . . (1) deals with questions of educational direction, policy, and action in areas of unresolved problems in the culture, in such way (2) that every available, pertinent, and scholarly resource is brought authentically into the effort, (3) with a definite view to attain the greatest possible personal commitment to democratic beliefs, purposes, and goals, and (4) to extending the effort to gain the maximum possible community of understanding, purpose, and commitment. It need hardly be said that this is an effort to make a discipline of the democratic process, particularly as this becomes the concern of educators in a democracy.[73]

Far more influential, however, during the past fifty years have been two majority voices in teacher education. One was that of the Commission on Teacher Education of the American Council on Education (1938–46) headed by two other faculty members of Teachers College: E. S. Evenden as chairman and Karl W. Bigelow as director. A key member of the staff was Earl Armstrong, who became the executive officer of the National Council for Accreditation of Teacher Education (NCATE). The commission's stress on general education, subject matter preparation, child growth and development, direct experience, and student teaching have largely been carried over into the NCATE standards. They sound surprisingly similar to those of the Holmes Group and the Carnegie Task Force.

What the commission rather blandly called "social and community understanding" was included in the commission's general guidelines. But this was largely a formal bow to the social purposes of education, whereas the real concern focused on child development and teaching practice:

A teacher's behavior should be guided not only by a grasp of the needs and capacities for response of his pupils, but also by an informed awareness of the needs and expectations of the culture of which the school is an expression. Knowledge of the community is important. This will increase the teacher's understanding of the children and their opportunities, will sensitize him to local problems and resources, will help him to perform his professional role effectively.[74]

Although "skill in community analysis" and "skill in discerning community resources" are useful and worthy goals, there was little in the commission's documents of the need for commitment to democratic goals on behalf of freedom, equality, or justice that animated the foundations idea in Teachers College. It was present, however, in the short-lived Cooperative Program for the Pre-Service Education of Teachers set up for undergraduates in Columbia University and Barnard College and taught at Teachers College under the commission's auspices.

Under this program both Columbia and Barnard accepted 12 credits in education courses at Teachers College toward the total of 120 credits required of their students for the bachelor arts degree. One of the four three-credit seminars was devoted to the history and philosophy of liberal education as related to teaching in the elementary and secondary schools—a mini-foundations course representing one-fourth of the requirement in education.[75] The special master's program for Columbia and Barnard graduates also devoted one-fourth of the graduate year to educational foundations along with subject matter preparation in the Columbia Graduate Faculties and student teaching through Teachers College. A retrospective view of this and other such programs might be of use to the Holmes and Carnegie groups.

The lack of a motivating civic sense proved to be true of a second influential voice—that of former Harvard President James B. Conant in the early 1960s—that powerfully shaped present-day teacher education. Dr. Conant's goal was to achieve a truce in the war between the liberal arts professors and the professional educators of the late 1940s and 1950s. Remember that Arthur Bestor, James Koerner, Admiral Hyman Rickover, Albert Lynd, Mortimer Smith, and others were mercilessly attacking "soft pedagogy" in the schools and attributing the blame to the muddle-headed and progressive "educationists" in the colleges of education, a favorite target being John Dewey and Teachers College. Greater rigor of intellectual discipline was their key to reform. So when Conant moved from his study of the high school to the study of teacher education, the professional education establishment gave a huge sigh of relief to hear a more gentle and conciliatory voice than those mentioned above.

On balance, however, Conant threw his weight on the side of the academic disciplines in the general education of teachers and on classroom practice and pedagogy in the professional sequence, much as the Holmes Group now seems to be doing. He set forth four components of the intellectual equipment that should be prerequisite to the development of teaching skill: the "democratic social component"; interest in the way behavior develops in groups of children; a sympathetic knowledge of the growth of children; and the principles of teaching. He described the "democratic social component" as follows:

> Many of us have spoken of the task of our public schools in educating for citizenship in a free society; more recently the phrase "social responsibility" has gained currency . . . One hears much less in the 1960s than one heard in the 1920s about the need for social change . . . Many today may repudiate the progressive plea for social change, but no one thinks of repudiating the premises on which this plea was based . . . Liberals and reactionaries alike must agree that we need to develop future citizens whose actions will assure the survival of our free society. Call it education for citizenship or developing loyalty to the American way of life, twist it to the right or the left—within wide limits the postulate remains.[76]

With these reassuring words, written in 1963—just a few years before the free-speech movement began at Berkeley and the campus disturbances at Columbia, Wisconsin, and elsewhere—Conant turned virtually all of his detailed attention to his other three components of the theory and practice of teaching. Little more is said in his book, *The Education of American Teachers,* about the "democratic social component." In fact, he proceeded to belittle the social foundations courses, expressly advised their elimination, and argued that educational philosophy should go to professors of philosophy, educational history to professors of history, and educational sociology to professors of sociology. But he did reserve a strong place for professors of educational psychology in the schools of education, where indeed they predominate today.

In general, the educational establishment was grateful to Conant for his blessing upon most of their works in teacher education. The way was thus paved for a succeeding stress upon accountability and Competency-Based Teacher Education. CBTE swept the country, was adopted by the American Association of Colleges for Teacher Education and the National Council for Accreditation of Teacher Education, and was quickly mandated by many state legislatures and state departments of education. The social foundations idea and the democratic social com-

ponent receded in the face of the academic disciplines and psychology
on the one hand, and, on the other hand, a preoccupation with alternatives, student self-centeredness, reality therapy, individual learning
styles, behavioral objectives, and the multifaceted enticements of a
curriculum smorgasbord. It's not that these fragmented efforts to make
the school curriculum flexible and innovative are unimportant. But
those in teacher education, no less than those in liberal arts, must take
seriously the historic claim that we are preparing citizens. This may not
exhaust all of what we try to do in the schools, but it should be restored
and reshaped as the highest priority throughout the years of schooling.
Too often the democratic values are treated with passing references, all
but hidden, in a long list of general goals, purposes, behavioral objectives, or process skills, that typically make up the bulk of curriculum
guides and the scope and sequence frameworks drawn up by state or
local curriculum committees.

The fundamental ideas and values upon which our constitutional
order is built should become the core of sustained and explicit study,
based upon scholarly knowledge and searching criticism carried on
throughout the school years from kindergarten through high school
and the years of liberal education in college. Thus all teachers and
administrators should be prepared for this task in their liberal and
professional teacher education. It is clear that there will not be universal
agreement on the precise meaning of these key ideas and values, and it
is clear that there will not be a single curriculum design that should be
imposed upon all schools in the nation. But the public and the educational profession should be trying to become more knowledgeable and
explicit about the substantive concepts and ideas that form the common
core of American citizenship. Serious and sustained work on such ideas
and concepts could well be the heart of a joint enterprise like that
initiated by Stanford President Kennedy and supported by thirty-seven
university presidents under the auspices of the American Association of
Higher Education and the American Council on Education. In an open
letter of September 1987 to thirty-three hundred college and university
presidents, the Kennedy group urged colleagues to recognize the national emergency in education and to mobilize their institutions to
improve the quality of schooling and the education of teachers.[77]

Signs of a New Start

In the 1980s a few voices inside teacher education began to be heard
beneath the prevailing din for excellence and competence in the teaching
profession. The Society of Professors of Education sponsored the

Seventh Annual DeGarmo Lecture, held in conjunction with the annual convention of the American Association of Colleges for Teacher Education (AACTE) in February 1982 on the subject "Teacher Education and the Revival of Civic Learning."[78] A follow-up session that included responses from nine leaders in teacher education on the same subject was held the next year.[79]

The AACTE's *Journal of Teacher Education* devoted its entire issue of November–December 1983 to the same subject. That fall the American Educational Studies Association asked three of its leaders to deal with the role of the foundations of education in the education of teachers; and their statement dealt directly with the need to put civic values front and center in the preparation of teachers.[80]

With this modest momentum gaining some headway with the foundations scholars in teacher education, the time seemed ripe to broaden the discussion on the civic theme to include like-minded scholars from the liberal arts and related professional fields. This took the form of a national invitational seminar on the theme "Civic Learning in the Education of the Teaching Profession." With initial encouragement and support from the Kettering Foundation and also major support from the Hoover Institution and the National Endowment for the Humanities, the seminar was held at the Hoover Institution, November 11–13, 1984.[81]

I had hopes that this remarkable, and possibly historic, gathering would take steps that might place a fitting capstone on the present educational-reform movement in the United States. It is a capstone that could reinforce, not weaken, fragment, or overload, the foundational purpose for which universal education in American democracy was envisioned and created: namely, to develop civic intelligence and civic virtue among all citizens.

This gathering consisted of some sixty educators from a dozen academic organizations and thirty-two colleges and universities, large and small, public and private, from all parts of the country. Despite their disparate academic disciplines and professional expertise, they were united in wishing to improve the civic education of the American people by strengthening the liberal and professional preparation of those who teach and administer America's massive educational enterprise. They were almost equally divided between those who work in the liberal arts and sciences outside of schools or departments of education and those who work inside. They met to explore better ways by which they might collaborate within their own institutions and among a variety of institutions of higher education to mobilize the academic community on behalf of the civic purposes of public education.

It may not immediately be clear to the public why such a gathering could be historic. But to those in the academic world who have studied the successive waves of educational reform of the past one hundred years, or who have lived through "reforms" of the past fifty years, the significance may be more apparent. I have indicated briefly how in the 1880s the officials of the burgeoning common schools pleaded with the colleges and universities to undertake the professional training of teachers, a movement in which the universities had taken little or no part and had contributed almost nothing for the preceding fifty years. Thereupon, some major universities began to respond, typified by the inauguration of Teachers College in 1894, when the presidents of Columbia (Seth Low), Harvard (Charles W. Eliot), and Johns Hopkins (Daniel Coit Gilman) gave their academic blessings to the new venture, soon to be affiliated with Columbia.

But what happened? The new departments and schools of education became so aggressive, so popular, and, in the view of many of their liberal arts colleagues, so inferior academically that by November 1944—when Teachers College celebrated its fiftieth anniversary by inviting the current presidents of those three leading universities to speak—Harvard's President James Bryant Conant felt compelled to call for "a truce among educators." The "academic warfare," the "sniping," the "enemy fire" had become so intense that Conant urged a cease-fire in the criticism leveled at the "educationists" and an armistice between the warring educational factions, between the academics and the professional educators.[82]

President Conant's prestige and his studies in the early 1960s sponsored by the Carnegie Corporation helped in many ways, for a time. But it is all too apparent that the hostilities are still present in some of the current movements for reform, characterized by unfriendly proposals to eliminate undergraduate programs in teacher education, to reduce the influence of schools of education in the preparation of teachers, to bypass those schools in certification or credentialing, or to reduce their number.

The Hoover seminar was not convened simply to praise the schools of education—or to bury them. Rather, it was intended to see what could emerge from a gathering cosponsored by five pre-eminent organizations devoted broadly to the promotion of the scholarly arts and sciences and five significant organizations devoted to the professional education of teachers and administrators. The first group consisted of the Kettering Foundation, the National Endowment for the Humanities, the Carnegie Foundation for the Advancement of Teaching, the Association of American Colleges, and Project '87 (jointly sponsored by the

American Historical Association and the American Political Science Association). The latter group consisted of the American Association of Colleges for Teacher Education, the American Educational Studies Association, the Society of Professors of Education, the National Council for the Social Studies, and the Stanford University School of Education.

Each of these organizations nominated several individuals to be invited. The sixty individuals did not come just to speak for their organizations or simply to sign another cease-fire or concordat defining separate spheres of influence. They came to find out if genuine collaboration could be achieved by focusing their efforts not on college education in general but on a theme common to their purposes as scholars and educators of the American citizenry. They heard and discussed seventeen scholarly papers concerning the ways that the civic learning of the educational profession could be advanced by faculty members in departments of the humanities, social sciences, schools of education, and schools of law and of public administration or public affairs.[83]

Although there was not total agreement on all points, there was a remarkable unanimity on the importance of the civic mission of education and a clear consensus on a series of recommendations, summarized in the following pages, for innovation, research, and action. No manifesto was drawn up ahead of time to be signed and endorsed; there was no hidden agenda, no political or educational party line. The seminar reflected a wide spectrum of political, social, and economic views, but these were never in the foreground of debate. It also represented a wide spectrum of scholarly views and educational philosophies, and these were in the foreground to reveal the range of prevailing and historically persistent ideas that need to be examined and dealt with more thoroughly in both the short term and long term. Quick fixes by legislative bodies were not viewed as necessarily the way to move educational institutions in fundamental ways. But it was agreed that some kind of mechanism is necessary if desirable changes are to be accomplished in an unwieldy institution like American education.

The seminar recognized that many kinds of institutions and agencies affect citizenship attitudes and behavior, but the focus was deliberately trained on colleges and universities as key ingredients in the reform of the schools and of the teaching profession. We noted that it is not only the lower schools and the schools of education that are the subjects of criticism and reform today. Medical schools, law schools, business schools, journalism schools, graduate schools, and the undergraduate liberal colleges themselves are all targets of criticism and scrutiny, and most often because they are not pursuing diligently enough their ethical, social, and public responsibilities. As a headline in the *New York Times* put it some time later, "Increasingly, Pro Cash Beats Pro Bono."[84]

The seminar urged that leading university presidents, individually and in consort, redouble their efforts to mobilize their several faculties of arts, science, and education to work together on the civic ingredients of teacher education. In speaking to the group, Stanford President Kennedy stressed the necessary link between public service and teacher education in a particularly persuasive way, a message central to the theme of the seminar.

Finally, the need to develop a new and coherent conceptual framework on the meaning of citizenship in American life and education was emphasized as especially fitting because of the bicentennial of the Constitution and Bill of Rights. We need to develop a new conception of the civic mission of American education, one that Jefferson, Madison, Washington, and Adams would find congenial and yet that would be efficacious in coming decades. For those philanthropic foundations, professional organizations, public agencies, and independent groups genuinely seeking to raise the quality of public life in America, no more important investment could be made than to join in this effort.

The seminar concluded with reports from seven discussion groups that had been charged with formulating recommendations for steps to improve the civic learning of American teachers. The specifics of the various groups' recommendations are contained in the published *Proceedings*. They are summarized by Alan Jones, the editor, as follows:

> *Need for collaborative arrangements.* Innovative arrangements must be established on as many campuses as possible through which faculty members in the humanities, social sciences, education, and such other professional schools as law and public administration, can work together in creating a coherent conceptual framework for the teaching of civic learning as a major focus of the education of the teaching profession. Such specific notions as cross-campus seminars, campus-wide policy statements, and interdisciplinary teaching and research teams were proposed, and in several instances such activities on certain campuses were noted as examples or models to be emulated.
>
> It was also stressed that such arrangements should not be restricted to the college and university setting. Rather, higher education faculty should engage in similar dialogue with their counterparts in the public schools, as well as with a wide range of community groups. The quest for enhanced civic education of the education profession should involve all interested citizens, and should be responsive to local public concerns as well as to the contributions of the many scholarly disciplines involved.

Pilot teacher education programs. Pilot programs in teacher education should be established by colleges and universities which seek specifically to incorporate components designed to enhance the civic learning of teachers. Such programs will effectively involve faculty from many relevant disciplines, will work closely with the public schools, and will involve the many pluralistic groups within the community which profoundly affect citizenship values, attitudes, and behaviors.

Specific suggestions included a greater focus on problem solving and action learning, building grass roots support for civic education that addresses controversial issues, sabbatical leaves for teachers to work with political and social organizations in the community as well as in other nations and cultures, experimentation with alternative curriculum models for civic learning, development of community education programs, and other initiatives which stress direct involvement with the civic life of the communities in which teachers will work. As such pilot programs prove successful, such direct features of enhanced civic learning should be incorporated into all professional preparation programs for teachers and other educational personnel.

Increased research. Additional research on the meaning and nature of civic learning should be encouraged, supported, and utilized. Such research should involve scholarship from the humanities, social sciences, education, law, public administration, and other interested disciplines, and should include historical and normative as well as empirical and behavioral analysis. The focus of such research should be on the idea and practice of citizenship, on modes of effective civic education, and on the continuing search for a widely agreed-upon definition of citizenship and civic learning.

Specific calls were issued for usable summaries of past research on civic education, for case studies of the new pilot programs, for evaluation of effective methodology in civic learning, for study of the influences of television and other mass media with respect to civic education, for a better understanding of the importance of racial integration of schools as a part of civic education, for examination of the impact of various legislative requirements on civic learning, and for further research on the potential role of public service as a part of civic education. Once again, coalition efforts among scholars in the various disciplines is needed, and the establishment of an interdisciplinary journal to promote such research on citizenship and civic education was suggested.

Revitalization and reform. A coordinated national effort must be launched to revitalize civic education and to secure for it a high priority within the already ongoing spirit of reform of American education. To sustain the momentum of the seminar, a working committee should be established to maintain and expand the existing commitments for action, with a charge to publish and publicize results of the seminar, and to refine goals and objectives.

Specific opportunities for continuation of the work of the seminar exist in the upcoming bicentennial of the Constitution and the Bill of Rights, in the importance of enhanced civic learning in light of the increasing diversity of our nation, in proposals for a national service corps, in the development of model credential requirements for all teachers which would focus on civic learning, in the revision of national accreditation standards for teacher education to give greater importance to civic learning, in the development of policy statements outlining the responsibilities of institutions of higher education with respect to the civic learning of teachers, and in influencing the reform movement which has emanated from several national reports on public education and on higher education released in the last few years.

While the discussion and direction of the seminar followed a highly optimistic course . . . the discussion took note of many dire societal problems, ranging from the increasing disconnectedness of American society, to the widening gulf between rich and poor, to the danger that many of our public schools will become schools only for the poor and minorities, to the cloud of gloom under which we all live given the realization that humankind possesses the ability of nuclear self-destruction. It is in response to these very problems that the seminar concluded that we must embark immediately upon a pervasive effort to permeate all of our educational, public, and private institutions with initiatives aimed at increased and effective civic education. The four categories of recommendations noted above represent only a first step in that direction.[85]

The seminar prompted the president of the American Association of Colleges for Teacher Education—Robert L. Saunders, dean of education at Memphis State University—as well as the AACTE's board of directors to establish a task force on civic learning. The task force began its work in 1985, but by September 1986 had found that less than half its member institutions had even replied to a questionnaire on their offerings in civic learning. But nearly two hundred institutions would be interested in further discussion leading to development of model programs, and only a score already had such models.[86]

It may be that the ideas about teacher education promulgated at the 1984 Hoover Seminar appeared before their time in the educational-reform movement. Still, in late 1985 the Rand Corporation established the Center for the Study of the Teaching Profession to conduct research on teacher testing and certification, teacher selection and evaluation, and other ways to improve professional accountability.[87] Specific attention to teacher education was speeded up when the Carnegie Forum's Task

Force gave it national visibility in 1986. Another hopeful sign came from the Education Commission of the States (ECS). Whatever may have been the immediate initiative behind its concern, the ECS launched a series of regional forums that extended from the fall of 1986 to the end of 1987 on the theme "Teacher Education Programs: A Commitment for Cooperation."

> In each region, teacher training institutions, both public and private, were asked to participate, in addition to representatives from classroom teachers, state boards of education, state education superintendents, state departments of education, governors' offices, teacher training candidates and state legislators. State higher education governing and coordinating boards were also asked to send representatives, along with the American Association of Colleges for Teacher Education, the American Association of State Colleges and Universities, United Negro Fund, Inc. and the Rand Corporation.[88]

The goals were to raise the visibility of teacher education as the natural bridge between the institutions of higher education, the local school district, and the state department of education. Whether the ECS Teacher Education Project could become a vehicle for implementing proposals for enhancing civic learning in teacher education remained a question as of this writing.

Meanwhile, still other sectors were heard from on the theme of reforming professional education. On one side, a Consortium for Excellence in Teacher Education argued that their undergraduates in 114 selective liberal arts colleges would be discouraged from going into teaching if the Holmes and Carnegie proposals for required graduate study in education were followed for beginning teachers. Their statement on "Teacher Education and the Liberal Arts" argues that they must maintain certification options for students desiring to teach directly upon graduation with bachelor's degrees.[89] Another statement came at the same time from the seventeen-member National Commission on Excellence in Educational Administration, established by the University Council for Educational Administration, a consortium of fifty leading research universities offering doctoral degrees in educational leadership. Once again, neither the report nor its critics said much about the liberal arts or civic learning that should be required of school administrators.[90]

How could faculties of arts and sciences and faculties of education arrive at any common understandings in the midst of the clamorous and diverse views described in this book's preceding chapters? Even the most widely heralded and prestigious of the reform proposals were being criticized in many quarters. Prime examples are a series of articles in a special issue of *Social Education* devoted to criticism of the Holmes and Carnegie Forum reports by six social-studies professionals. Thomas S. Popkewitz of the University of Wisconsin, Madison, summarizes some of their conclusions as follows:

> 1. The documents are ahistorical and lack sustained philosophical, social, or political discussion of the current situation, yielding proposals that may only serve to conserve what the rhetoric suggests should be changed.
> 2. The reports maintain the conservative political climate of the 1980s, but must also be viewed in relation to the discourse about reform and change introduced into school affairs over the past three decades.
> 3. The reform of teaching and teacher education needs to consider the social character of education in modern industrial states.
> 4. The conception of knowledge in the reports is technical and procedural [rather than focusing on purpose and value].
> 5. The Holmes Report omits a role for minority teachers and minority perspectives.[91]

However, by the end of 1987 it appeared that major proposals for reforming teacher education were likely to emanate from the National Board for Professional Teaching Standards, as recommended by the Carnegie Forum's Task Force on Teaching as a Profession. The board had been established with James B. Hunt, Jr., former governor of North Carolina, as chairman and James A. Kelly, a former professor at Teachers College and officer of the Ford Foundation, as president. Two-thirds of the 63 board members must be teaching professionals, and a majority of the full board must be drawn from teachers in the elementary and secondary schools. The university members represented a variety of academic disciplines. Only five or six of the total could be identified as faculty members in schools of education and none in the social, historical, or philosophical foundations of education.[92]

It was not yet clear exactly what direction the board would take, but it was clear that important suggestions would come from a project funded by the Carnegie Forum and headed by Lee Shulman at Standord's School of Education. At the beginning of their search for an evaluation process suitable for the new national board, Shulman and Gary Sykes drew up a list of categories that might provide the knowledge base of teaching upon which the assessment of candidates for certification could eventually be based. They strongly emphasized in May 1986 that this list was a starting point for deliberation, and not final. But they also acknowledged that some of the sources of their thinking were the writings of B. O. Smith (as developed in Florida and Tennessee), the Holmes Group, and the California Commission on the Teaching Profession. Both had been involved in the reports of the latter two groups.

Their list of categories for assessment of what highly competent professional teachers need to know is as follows:

1. General/liberal education, including basic skills of reading, math, writing, and reasoning.
2. Content knowledge in the domains in which teaching will occur.
3. Content-specific pedagogical knowledge.
4. General knowledge of pedagogical principles and practice.
5. Curricular knowledge.
6. Understanding of student diversity and individual differences.
7. Performance skills (including voice, manner, poise).
8. Foundations of professional understanding (including history and policy; philosophy and psychology; cultural and cross-cultural factors; professional ethics).[93]

This is an important and useful, as well as familiar, list of essential knowledge and skills for teachers, but I hope that in the end the "foundations of professional understanding" will not become least in priority as well as last in listing. In a September 1987 progress report, the qualifications to be expected of board-certified teachers were stated in terms quite similar to those listed above, except that "the foundations of professional understanding" had become simply "the ethical imperatives of teaching."[94] This seemed to be a considerable narrowing of the meaning of foundations of education and thus perhaps a loss of opportunity to assess civic understanding among the best-qualified teachers of the nation.

One of the four prototypes being developed for assessment by the "wisdom of practice" of experienced and excellent teachers centers upon the teaching of a unit in secondary school social studies dealing with the "American Revolution and formation of government." Such a unit is universally taught in U.S. history classes and gives scope for the new social and ethnic history. The other models have to do with elementary school arithmetic, literacy (reading and writing), and secondary school biology. Each assessment prototype includes between ten and fifteen distinct exercises requiring from 45 minutes to three hours to administer:

Some of these exercises may be generalizable to other teaching areas; others will be quite domain-specific. Some exercises will deal with fairly generic teaching skills and understandings; others will focus on a particular subject. Thus a prototype is far more than a single instrument; it is a set of about a dozen exercises designed to assess the content of knowledge and pedogogical understandings and skills of candidates as these relate to the teaching of particular topics within particular subject areas.[95]

Shulman makes it clear that the project's prototypes are only starting points for the broader development that will be required by the national board and the full-scale assessment to come. Questions arise about the larger assessment: Will the "foundations of professional understanding" be included in the assessment of all teachers of all subjects? And will such understanding include the concepts and values not only of the ethics of the teaching profession but also of the morality of democratic citizenship as a common medium of discourse and commitment for all members of the teaching profession? Whatever the final results of the Stanford project may be, the newly constituted National Board for Professional Teaching Standards should take seriously both the history and the importance of civic learning in the education of teachers.

Civic understanding is equally important for school administrators and all members of the teaching profession, not simply social studies teachers. At the annual meeting of the Social Science Education Consortium at the Hoover Institution in June 1986, Jan Tucker of the University of Florida International University reported a survey in which he found that only a small percent of elementary school principals in Dade County, Florida, considered citizenship education to be a high priority and furthermore that they believed extracurricular activities were more important in achieving this goal than was the teaching of social studies.[96] The complaint is often made that school administrators are trained in "theories of organization which fail to account for the fact that the dominant purposes of schools are moral."[97] Surely, if we are to have national standards for the teaching profession, we must have a national vision of the civic mission of American education.

In their intriguing study of the schools of education in a number of leading universities, Geraldine Joncich Clifford and James W. Guthrie of Berkeley document how schools of education have tried to ape the schools of arts and sciences and neglected the needs of practitioners. They persuasively argue that schools of education should take the profession of practicing educators, not academia, as their main point of reference. In their proposals for reform, however, they say little about the place of civic learning in the liberal or technical preparation of the profession.[98]

Unless those influential in teacher education are determined to accelerate the momentum for civic learning, this present reform movement will become just one more episode for the future historian of teacher education. Or, worse, it will indeed become a major turning point, and the American teaching profession will have lost the heart of its fundamental public purpose in the course of its frantic search for brilliant, competent technical expertise. The United States desperately needs both civic purpose and technical expertise in its teaching profession if it is to compete economically and to exert democratic leadership in the world. The political sophistication of America's leaders and the citizenry who choose them may be an even more important goal for education than sharpened economic competitiveness.

_____

CHAPTER 7

What the Schools Should Teach:
The Twelve Tables of Civism

I have been arguing in this book that the best approach to "moral values" for the public schools to take is substantive teaching of the civic values underlying the ideals and practices of democratic citizenship. I do not couch these values in terms of imperatives that seem to imply only one correct answer or set of beliefs. Instead, I have tried to phrase them in the commonly used words and ideas that students and teachers should study and try to understand if they are to fulfill their obligations and rights as American citizens.

How are citizens to be prepared to judge the merits of public policies in domestic and foreign affairs as conducted by officials in office or as proposed by candidates for office? How are citizens to be enabled to judge the tangled web of one kind of morality in public talk and another kind of ethics in personal practice, whether found in government, the stock market, or corporate, labor, or religious enterprises? Surely not by any simple formulas of moral preachments or role modeling. In the long run, this can best be achieved only by careful judgments informed by a reasoned historical perspective and by a meaningful conception of the basic values underlying our constitutional order.

_____

An earlier version of this chapter appeared as "The Moral Imperative for American Schools: '. . . inflame the civic temper . . .' " in *American Journal of Education*, February 1988, pp. 162–194.

The time is ripe for American education to pay more attention to how much agreement there may be about the civic values that schools and colleges should transmit through serious study and debate. No one expects full agreement or uniform acceptance of beliefs. I would hope, however, that there might be some agreement about what is worth studying and learning. To this end, I offer a possible agenda in The Twelve Tables of Civism, with apologies to the decemvirs of the Roman Republic, who presumably drew up the original Laws of the Twelve Tables for the early Roman Republic, and to Aristotle's paradigm of the later Greek republics.[1] The Twelve Tables were the earliest codification of customary Roman civil and criminal law in the fifth century B.C. Aristotle posited that the true forms of government (monarchy, aristocracy, and republic), which served the public good, became corruptions when the rulers served their own interests and the king became a tyrant, the aristocracy an oligarchy, and the republic a democracy or mobocracy.

Why *twelve?* Because that is a parsimonious number of concepts with which to summarize the underlying principles and values of American citizenship that should be studied in school and college. Besides, they are fewer than the Maryland Values Education Commission's eighteen character and citizenship values or Edward Wynne's list of twenty-one values; and they are only slightly more than Chester Finn's ten values of cultural conservatism, but well under the 4,500 items of knowledge that E. D. Hirsch, Jr., proposes for cultural literacy.[2]

Why *tables?* Because a *table* may be defined as a schema or arrangement of words (or numbers) to exhibit a set of facts or ideas in a definite, compact, or comprehensive form. The tabular form should enhance the teaching effectiveness of the concepts by emphasizing the counterpoints between *unum* and *pluribus,* between the obligations of citizenship that bind us together as a political community and the rights of citizenship that betoken a democratic polity.

Why *civism?* As explained in Chapter 4, *civism* means simply "the principles of good citizenship." The term is a shorthand way of referring to the principles, sentiments, and virtues of good citizenship in a democratic republic.

I have no intention of urging a return to the Roman Twelve Tables, but if study of those tables helped maintain the Roman Republic long after the demise of the Greek republics, it was no mean achievement. For a republic celebrating its two hundredth anniversary, four hundred years does not look so bad. And if civic education can help stave off some of the "corruptions" suggested by Aristotle's paradigm, the

TWELVE TABLES OF CIVISM
FOR THE MODERN AMERICAN REPUBLIC

(with apologies to the "Laws of the Twelve Tables" of the early Roman Republic and to Aristotle's paradigm of the later Greek republics)

UNUM THE OBLIGATIONS OF CITIZENSHIP		PLURIBUS THE RIGHTS OF CITIZENSHIP	
Corrupted Forms of Unum	True Forms of Unum	True Forms of Pluribus	Corrupted Forms of Pluribus
"Law and order"	**Justice**	**Freedom**	Anarchy
Enforced sameness; conformity	**Equality**	**Diversity**	"Unstable pluralism"
Authoritarianism; totalitarianism	**Authority**	**Privacy**	Privatism; privatization
"Majoritarianism"	**Participation**	**Due process**	"Soft on criminals"
"Beguiling half-truth; plausible flasehood"	**Truth**	**Property**	"Property rights superior to human rights"
Chauvinism; xenophobia	**Patriotism**	**Human rights**	"Cultural imperialism"

DEMOCRATIC CIVISM

NOTE: Adapted from the "Decalogue of Democratic Civic Values" in R. Freeman Butts, *The Revival of Civic Learning* (Bloomington, Ind.: Phi Delta Kappa Educational Foundation, 1980), p. 128.

United States might have a better chance of celebrating a tricentennial or even a quatrocentennial. I offer the concepts suggested by the table as an agenda for revitalizing civic education in American schools and colleges, a common core of civic values fundamental to the theory and practice of democratic citizenship in the United States. Whatever religious sanctions or ethical principles may give them support, they are the moral imperatives for American schools.

Justice

The basic idea of justice (that which is fair) is pervasive in most social contacts and at most ages. But there is also a timely educational reason for starting with the concept of justice. The past two decades have witnessed a remarkable shift of interest in political philosophy to questions of morality, equality, authority, and the obligations of citizenship along with matters of freedom and rights of citizenship. It is a subject where several disciplines intersect: political science, philosophy, law, and religion. The idea of justice or fairness is thus a good starting point for study and discussion in school and college.[3]

It is useful to think of justice as the moral basis of a democratic society, what John Rawls calls the "first virtue of social institutions." It is what must govern the conduct of people in their relations to one another. Rawls speaks of a public sense of justice that produces a well-ordered society in which everyone accepts, and knows that others accept, the same principles of justice. This means that the members of a well-ordered society must develop strong moral sentiments and effective desires to act as the principles of justice require.

The public sense of justice establishes the claims of what is *right* above the claims of what is *good*, since what is good is defined differently by individuals and groups according to their particular life-styles and personal desires. The principles of what is right and what is just thus put limits on what may be reasonable conceptions of one's own good. A just social system defines the boundaries within which individuals and pluralistic communities may develop their aims and actions. Rawls's first principle of justice is the citizen principle: "Each person is to have an equal right to the most extensive total system of equal basic liberties compatible with a similar system of liberty for all."[4]

What are the "equal . . . liberties" of citizenship? They bear close resemblance to the American constitutional order guaranteed by the Bill of Rights:

The basic liberties of citizens are, roughly speaking, political liberty (the right to vote and to be eligible for public office) together with freedom of speech and assembly; liberty of conscience and freedom of thought; freedom of the person along with the right to hold (personal) property; and freedom from arbitrary arrest and seizure as defined by the concept of the rule of law. These liberties are all required to be equal by the first principle, since citizens of a just society are to have the same basic rights.[5]

Rawls's position cannot be covered thoroughly here, and it has been severely criticized by some philosophers and social scientists.[6] But his thinking points unmistakably to the priority of achieving a common civic community based on the citizen principle of justice, which I regard as the prime authority for the purposes of public education. Rawls has not elaborated a full-scale philosophy of education based on his underlying political and moral philosophy, as John Dewey did. But he has paved the way for philosophers and practitioners of education to restore a profound civic, moral, and political basis to public education.

One task is to try to find out if there are common agreements on civic education among academic specialists who differ among themselves on fine or major points of political philosophy. For example, Michael Walzer attacks many aspects of Rawls's position, but he also says that inclusive schools are better than separate schools and that teachers committed to the basic discipline necessary for democratic politics will try to establish a shared knowledge among their students. Walzer says: "The aim is not to repress differences but rather to postpone them, so that children learn to be citizens first—workers, managers, merchants, and professionals only afterward. Everyone studies the subjects that citizens need to know."[7]

Walzer goes on to say that equal citizenship requires a common schooling. He argues against vouchers and tuition tax credits for private schools but favors the state setting common curricular requirements for private schools—arguments that sound as though they coincide with Rawls's citizen principle of justice.

Freedom

What is most illuminating about Rawls's theory of justice is his assignment of first priority to the idea of *equal basic liberties*. The just political community will then be committed to the idea of freedom as well as equality. I view freedom as having at least three elements relevant to civic education.[8] Freedom involves:

(a) the right, the opportunity, and the ability of every human being to live his or her own life in dignity and security and to seek self-fulfillment or self-realization as a person or as a member of a chosen group without arbitrary constraint by others. This is the freedom of the person and of private action.

(b) the right, the opportunity, and the ability of every human being to speak, to read, to inquire, to think, to believe, to express, to learn, and to teach without arbitrary constraint or coercion by others, especially as a means for making deliberate choices among real alternatives on the basis of reason and valid and reliable knowledge. This is the freedom of the mind and of intellectual inquiry.

(c) the right, the opportunity, and the ability of every citizen to take active part in shaping the institutions and laws under which he or she lives in common with others and to do this by making uncoerced choices and by participating through active consent in cooperation with one's fellow citizens; and to do so in such a way as to promote justice, freedom, and equality for others. This is the freedom of the citizen and of public action.

Just as we need a public conception of justice as the basis for a well-ordered society, so do we need a public conception of freedom that is held sufficiently in common to assure the vitality of a free and democratic political community.

If these constitutional principles are to be taken seriously as fundamental to the well-being of a democratic political community, and if the prime responsibility of public education is to prepare citizens for their civic freedom and their civic obligations, then what of the rights and freedoms of parents and families to control the learning of their children and to control the teaching of their teachers?

Public-interest groups and community organizations should be as much concerned to demand freedom of thought for teachers and learners as they are concerned to demand parental and familial rights over the teaching and learning process. There is much evidence that community demands for censorship of books and teachers have increased again in the past twenty years.[9] They range from efforts to ban materials offensive to conservative-minded parents on matters of sex, religion, or politics to materials offensive to liberal-minded parents on matters of biased minority stereotypes or sex-role images of women and homosexuals. "Freedom from whom" thus poses one of the most difficult, sensitive, and inflammatory issues facing the interrelationships of school-community-home, as the bitter struggles over racial and ethnic inequality in segregated schools have illustrated. Without some guidelines, the cherished freedoms can lead to the corruptions of anarchy, license, and unbridled libertarian individualism, as Aristotle and subsequent advocates of a high ideal of citizenship so often feared.

Equality

Along with justice and freedom, the idea of equality runs throughout the American creed of value claims for a democratic political community. "All men are created equal" is the first of the self-evident truths of the Declaration of Independence. It even comes before the inalienable rights of life, liberty, and the pursuit of happiness. The idea of equality was a counterpoise in the eighteenth-century struggle for democracy against the tyrannies of privilege and the closed orders of aristocracy and hierarchy. But it is also true that ever since, there has been an almost constant discord between the claims of freedom and the claims of equality.

There have been two deep conflicts over the meaning of equality. Basically, does the phrase "all men are created equal" mean that in fact they *are* equal, or that they should be *treated* as though they are equal? Americans have generally put their emphasis on equal rights and equal opportunity rather than on enforcing an equality of condition or income, which has been the stated goal of some extreme egalitarian communities and socialist parties in this and other countries. Enforced conformity or uniformity imposed by totalitarian governments becomes a corruption of the democratic ideal of equality.

The Fourteenth Amendment puts the idea in terms of the "equal protection of the laws," but it was not until the civil rights movements of the 1950s and 1960s that positive government action was taken to wipe out longstanding legal restrictions on equality of opportunity in education, housing, voting, employment, and in a wide range of civil rights on behalf of disadvantaged and minority groups.[10] The 1954 *Brown* decision was a landmark in stressing equality of educational opportunity, followed a decade later by the Civil Rights Act, the Voting Rights Act of 1965, and much else.[11]

As the First Amendment was the charter for freedom, so the Fourteenth Amendment became the charter for equality. It was soon clear to the civil rights movement that a stronger, not weaker, government would be required to achieve equal protection of the laws to overcome the historic discriminations that had resulted when states and local communities practiced "freedom of choice" by allowing dominant local groups to impose their views on their institutions and their schools.

The Supreme Court said in *Brown* v. *Board of Education* that the constitutional command of the *national* political community on behalf of equality must override the freedom of lesser political communities to institute segregational practices. This was a historic moment in the relationships of school, community, and family. Its repercussions are still very much with us, but its meaning will vary drastically, depending on what community or group is appealed to as the most legitimate source of educational opportunity: one's family, neighborhood, race, religion, ethnic affiliation, or local, state, regional, or national community.

The philosophical contrast between equality and freedom has been sharply drawn in recent years by Rawls on one side and Robert Nozick, also professor of philosophy at Harvard, on the other side.[12] While Rawls argues that only those inequalities are justified that adhere to the benefit of the least advantaged through the action of the state, Nozick argues that justice requires that each individual has full entitlement to what he or she acquires justly, and thus can dispose of it with no interference whatsoever from the state. Limited government and a minimal state are required for full freedom of individual rights. This is bound to result in certain inequalities, because people indeed are unequal in talents, skills, and efforts; but *they,* not someone else, are entitled to what those talents, skills, and efforts produce. According to a minimalist view, any equality imposed by government is unjust. And, according to advocates of a welfare liberal state, the enforced conformity of a totalitarian state of the Left is as much a corruption of the principle of equality as is the enforced inequality of a totalitarian state of the Right.

If indeed, "all men are created equal" and are entitled to the "equal protection of the laws," a society that permits persecution, segregation, or discrimination on the basis of race, religion, ethnicity, national origin, or gender is to that extent an unjust society. Gender injustice is the latest to receive scholarly attention.[13] This persistent tension between equality and freedom should be faced in civic education programs as directly and as honesty in all its manifestations as possible. In recent years the tension has become especially strained with regard to the values of diversity.

Diversity

Respect for diversity and encouragement of a plurality of communities have been among the best elements of the American political system.

Millions of immigrants have been, and still are, attracted to the United States because of their hope for life in a society that provides greater justice, freedom, and equality than they knew in their homelands—and of course they hoped for greater economic advantage as well. And millions found their hopes at least partially realized in a country of enormously diverse geography, ethnicity, language, religion, race, and culture.

So diversity or plurality is one of the major values to be studied, analyzed, and honored in any program of civic education for American schools. This becomes all the more important as the arrival of large numbers of people from Latin America, South Asia, and other countries leads to heightened discussions of bilingual education and to efforts to make English the official language. Like all the other values, diversity has its problems and costs as well as its advantages and benefits. The problem is often simply referred to as the tension between unity and diversity, order and liberty, or the public and the private.[14]

There is merit in views that attempt to arrive at a balanced tension between the values of cultural plurality and political cohesion. For example, John Higham speaks of "pluralistic integration" and distinguishes between ethnic *boundaries* that keep people in or out of groups and ethnic *nuclei* that give identity and sustenance to different groups. In this sense, boundaries are permeable, but nuclei are respected:

> In contrast to the integrationist model, it [the pluralistic integration model] will not eliminate ethnic boundaries. But neither will it maintain them intact. It will uphold the validity of a common culture, to which all individuals have access, while sustaining the efforts of minorities to preserve and enhance their own integrity . . .
>
> No ethnic group under these terms can have the support of the general community in strengthening its boundaries. All boundaries are understood to be permeable. Ethnic nuclei, on the other hand, are respected as enduring centers of social action . . .[15]

The major point of my stress upon civism is to rediscover what political values we have in common as well as redefining the values of plurality. Another view with merit is a distinction posed by Michael Kammen, Cornell historian and winner of the Pulitzer prize for his *People of Paradox*. In his analysis of a plural society, Kammen distinguishes between "stable pluralism" and "unstable pluralism." An unstable pluralism occurs when the cleavages in society threaten the authority of the polity because of the conflict among racial, ethnic, religious, or regional groups, each of which forms its own political party and has its "own faction, each sect its own school, and each dogmatist his own ideology." On the other hand:

> Stable pluralism requires a strong *underpinning* of legitimacy. A plural society is best insured by the rule of law—law made within the framework of an explicit constitution by elected representatives, executed by a partially autonomous administrative staff, and adjudicated by an independent judiciary. Insofar as all of these were created in 1787 and achieved in 1789, those dates do distinguish a genuine watershed in American history.
>
> But stable pluralism in a democracy also requires a strong and lasting inventory of psychological legitimacy: understanding, acceptance, and pervasive confidence in the composite system necessary to make it run smoothly rather than by fits and starts.[16]

The building of a "strong and lasting inventory of psychological legitimacy" is one perceptive way to define the purpose of civic education for the schools of a democracy, in which a plurality of racial, ethnic, and religious communities is acknowledged and even welcomed. One need only note the stark contrast between the United States, with all its pluralist problems, and countries where unstable pluralism either prevents a psychological legitimacy toward government at all (as in Lebanon) or periodically threatens the stability of the polity (as in India, Sri Lanka, Malaysia, Nigeria, Ghana, Uganda, Northern Ireland, or Spain).[17]

Authority

The role of authority can usefully be illustrated for students at all age levels, ranging from the need for rules on taking turns in the kindergarten to the need for laws on stealing, assault, murder, and treason. At the heart of political authority is the difference between sheer power and legitimate, or rightful, authority. Power is usually considered to be the ability to exercise control over people or conditions so as to direct their conduct or influence the outcome of an event desired by those in positions of power. The most common examples of sheer power to control events are military force and money.

On the other hand, power becomes legitimate authority when recognized as such and sanctioned by custom, institutions, law, constitution, or morality. Authority in a democratic polity is thus the exercise of influence and command by those in positions of power when done so within the confines of rules made by the consent of the governed and considered over a period of time as legitimate.

The right of an official to make decisions, determine policies, and maintain order derives not from the official's private capacity but by virtue of a right conferred by the society. So the exercise of democratic political authority ideally should be under the constraint of the values of fundamental justice and fairness as well as functioning to ensure the greatest amount of freedom and equal opportunity for the individual under rules of due process and with a fair distribution of privileges and resources in the society. Failing these constraints, authority is corrupted into authoritarianism and totalitarianism. Without authority, freedom degenerates into license or anarchy, pluralism becomes unstable, and individuals can be assured of little privacy or due process.

Leonard Krieger, university professor of history at Chicago, points out that the idea of authority "as a consciously constituted or legitimate power to command or secure obedience," emerging during the sixteenth and seventeenth centuries, led historians to mark the period as the origin of the modern idea of citizenship in a nation-state. But he also indicates that there was another meaning of authority that originated in Rome, a meaning not so much associated with sheer power as with an uncoercive authority associated with people or knowledge whose trustworthiness and responsibility are a warrant or guarantee that their deliberate judgments, convictions, and decisions are worth following as models or examples.[18] An *auctor* in Latin is a trustworthy writer, a responsible person, a teacher, a guarantor, a model whose ideas and judgments are worth following.

It is this latter sense of authority as trustworthiness that has been so eroded in recent years. Students have revolted against the authority of schools and colleges, against the authority of government officials, against the authority of parents, churches, business, and other institutions that in the past have claimed the right to guide the conduct and behavior of the young. Much criticism has been levied at a narrow and self-serving conception of professionalism in education as in law, medicine, and business. To re-establish its authority as trustworthy, the educational profession may well learn some of the lessons of leadership being developed anew by John Gardner in his Leadership Studies Program, sponsored by Independent Sector. Gardner distinguishes leadership from coercion on one side and from authority as legitimized power of office on the other side. A leader is an active *auctor* who thinks in the longer term, looks beyond the immediate constituency, puts heavy emphasis on the intangibles of vision, values, and motivation, *and* political skill.[19]

These are large orders, but it is noteworthy that the concept of authority both as legitimate power and as trustworthy leadership has become a matter for serious scholarly study in recent years. I think especially of Richard Flathman's analysis of authority and citizenship, along with that of many other scholars.[20] The concept has also had a revival of interest among those in teacher education.[21] Kenneth Benne's seminal doctoral study of 1943 has been republished and evoked considerable discussion and critical comment. David Nyberg's more recent approach to power and authority is another useful example. Critical study of academic fare on authority, which is fundamental and necessary but too often is not applied to the theory or practice of civic education, would enable the profession to think of authority as more than orderliness and obedience in the "effective" classroom.

Privacy

Privacy is one of the basic pluralist values of a democratic political community, along with freedom, diversity, and due process. I distinguish it from the privatism or excessive privatization of public services (including education), which I view as a corruption of privacy. Just as freedom includes the right to live one's life in dignity and to seek one's self-development and self-fulfillment, so privacy is the right of individuals and groups to be left alone and to determine for themselves what information about themselves or their actions is communicated to others.[22]

Infringement of this right was one of the most irritating of the eighteenth-century practices that led to the Third Amendment's guarantees against the quartering of troops in private households and to the Fourth Amendment's guarantees that the people shall be secure in their persons, houses, papers, and effects against unreasonable searches and seizures. The revelations of the spying activities of the CIA and FBI on American citizens during the Vietnam War and the campus unrest, the Watergate tapes, and much else have led to new concerns about the protection of privacy. The development of electronic devices (such as computers that keep credit ratings on millions of consumers) has added a *1984* quality to all kinds of business activities as well as those of government agencies. The rapid development of technological surveillance led to some of the early scholarly studies of the idea of privacy.[23]

But the right of privacy has moved much beyond matters of information about a person that should be kept private from government or outside surveillance. It has been applied increasingly to matters of intimate associations that have been deemed beyond the criminal investigation and punishment by law. Although the word *privacy* does not appear in the Constitution or Bill of Rights (just as *education* does not), the right of privacy has been brought by the Supreme Court under the heading of freedom in the First Amendment, of liberty in the Fifth and Fourteenth Amendments as well as under the Fourth Amendment's protection of the person against search and seizure. The most controversial of these issues in the public eye have had to do with sexual relations, abortion, and homosexuality.

Although questions of the rights of privacy of students in elementary and secondary schools may once have seemed far removed from such constitutional questions, the demands for teaching values and morality have proliferated with the rise in juvenile pregnancy and drug abuse among teenagers. And inevitably, the issues of privacy versus authority and moral values versus academic excellence have spilled over into the schools. More than one federal judge has had to decide whether a student with a high academic record should be denied admission to the National Honor Society on the grounds that she was pregnant and thus morally unfit for the intellectual honor.[24]

Still more to the point of student privacy from search and seizure was the celebrated case of *New Jersey* v. *T.L.O.* in January 1985.[25] The case arose when a vice principal in Piscataway High School searched a student's handbag, suspecting that she had been smoking in the girls' lavatory, but found evidence of possible use and sale of marijuana. Were her rights to privacy under the Fourth Amendment's protection against search and seizure superior to the authority of school officials to uphold school rules and laws against use and sale of drugs? In a 6–3 decision, the court affirmed a middle course. It denied that school officials are acting in place of parents *(in loco parentis)* and thus they do not have all the rights that parents have to control and discipline their children. But it also affirmed that school officials must have "reasonable grounds" for believing that their search of lockers and handbags or persons would provide evidence of breaking the rules or the law. Students thus do have some, but not complete, constitutional rights to privacy, while teachers, not being parents, do have the obligation to apply the Fourth Amendment's protection of privacy to students and thus are in effect "officers of the Constitution." Starting with such cases that apply directly to students and teachers in school, the theme of good citizenship could surely come alive and then lead to serious study in school, college, and teacher education.

Due Process

While privacy concentrates on a citizen's being left alone, due process has to do with the rights of persons who have been accused of wrongs or injuries they have allegedly committed. Due process values center on the Fifth, Sixth, Seventh, and Eighth Amendments, with their presumption of innocence and their provisions for protection of individual rights in criminal cases and civil suits.[26] In addition to the useful articles on due process in the *Encyclopedia of the American Constitution* many new materials designed especially for use in secondary schools have been developed on the subjects of criminal justice and civil justice.[27] Of special interest to educators has been the development in recent years of the concepts of due process as applied specifically to teachers, students, and parents, Again, excellent materials are available.[28]

The drive to achieve more protection of due process for children's private rights in the juvenile justice system was directed at students in schools as well as those out of school. The key case here is *Goss* v. *Lopez,* which involved nine high school students in Columbus, Ohio, who were suspended during racial demonstrations in 1971 for up to ten days without a hearing, as permitted under Ohio law. The students charged that the law was unconstitutional under the Fourteenth Amendment because it deprived them without due process of their property (their right to attend school) and of their liberty (by injuring their reputation without a hearing). In January 1975 the court in a 5–4 decision declared the law unconstitutional and ruled that high-school students were to be granted due process in suspensions. This must include oral or written notice of the charges of misconduct, an explanation of the charges and the evidence against them, and an opportunity to give their side of the story before suspension from school.[29]

I have stressed the due process rights of children and students in this section principally becuase it is a subject that could quickly enlist the interest of students. There is a vast literature on due process for adults, illustrated by the *Encyclopedia of the American Constitution,* articles listed in Note 26. Teachers and officials of public schools have now been put on notice that they must be concerned for the due process rights of children as well as their own. They need to be as clear as possible about the relative allocation of power and responsibility among the parents, the child, and the state, whose officers they are. It is now clear that children, as well as adults, have constitutional rights and that the state may not be too intrusive into the parent-child relationship. But the state also has the obligation to protect children, when necessary for the child's welfare, even against the parents if they neglect or abuse the child. Children do not have all the due process rights that adults have, but they do have more than they did before *Goss*.

Property

The purpose of including property rights in a table of civism is not to suggest that students or teachers must take law courses in property or contracts, but to recognize the concept of property and private ownership as a basic element in the forming of the American Republic and to know some of the fundamental changes that have taken place during the past two hundred years. The emphasis here is not on a course in economics, free enterprise, or comparative economic systems. Some excellent materials for school use have been developed along these lines, and California and New York now require an economics course for graduation from high school.[30] Twenty-seven states now require some form of economics instruction, and fifteen states require a separate course.

Instead, the emphasis is the rights and responsibilities of ownership of property in a democratic society: the relationships to ownership of individuals, groups, and the state with regard to matters of justice, freedom, equality, authority, privacy, and due process. Rudimentary concepts of "what's mine," "what's yours," and rules about acquiring, using, transferring, and disposing of tangible properties can be developed in early years of schooling, as the materials developed by Law in a Free Society have shown.[31] Rules against stealing, damaging, or destroying the property of others and how arguments should be settled, equity achieved, and by whose authority play a large part in early schooling. The inclusion of intangible property (such as ideas, benefits, entitlements, or labor) along with tangible property then leads to further consideration of the rights and responsibilities regarding property, the scope and limits of ownership, and other major subjects of legislative and judicial concern.[32] It is clear that most of the founders believed that property and liberty went hand in hand. The federal Constitution was designed at least in part to free people and property from intrusion by the state governments.[33]

Charles A. Lofgren emphasizes how the commercial problems among the states under the Articles of Confederation led to granting of powers to Congress in Article I, Section 8 of the Constitution "to regulate Commerce with foreign nations, and among the several States, and with the Indian tribes." The twist of his argument, not often realized, is that the commerce clause was used by Congress in the Civil Rights Act of 1964 (and subsequently approved by the Supreme Court) to justify the federal government's role in protecting the civil rights of interstate travelers regarding segregated accommodations and restaurants.[34]

Kenneth M. Holland, political scientist at the University of Vermont, carries the argument to the new meanings of property increasingly defined under the welfare state to include social benefits and entitlements (including education). He refers to a formative article in 1964 by Charles Reich, who argued that welfare benefits were no longer a charity or government largess, but a new kind of property embracing rights that cannot be withdrawn or withheld without due process of law.[35] There is, of course, much controversy and debate over such broadening of the conception of property rights, whether justified on grounds of due process, privacy, equality, civil liberties, or justice. All the more reason for students and teachers to study these issues along with the other tables of civism. All the better to judge how far we have come from the compromise of the Constitution that regarded slaves as three-fifths of a person and *Dred Scott,* where slaves were viewed as nonpersons and as tangible, exchangeable property belonging to another, the ultimate corruption of property rights.

Participation

The idea of participation has undergone a great deal of modification since the Declaration of Independence asserted that the just powers of government derive from "the consent of the governed" and since the preamble of the Constitution made it clear that "We, the People" are sovereign. Much of the original notion of popular consent and of sovereignty of the people rested on the idea that the citizens would participate directly in the making of the laws and in the making of the fundamental contract known as the Constitution. But the idea of citizen participation had to change from the days of a Greek polis, with its few thousand citizens, or a New England town meeting, with its few hundred citizens. Debates over the meaning of *democracy* as direct participation by the entire body of citizens, contrasted to a *republic,* meaning participation through selected representatives, has continued from the Constitutional Convention and the *Federalist Papers* to the present.

The *idea* of participation as a key value in a democratic political community should be studied and debated by students and teachers along with the *practice* of participatory experience as illustrated in the citizen-participation movement in general and its counterpart in community-action programs for students in schools. In addition to political campaigning, voting, and lobbying, participation of a more direct and active sort has become increasingly important since the 1960s. After all, sit-ins, marches, freedom rides, and civil disobedience were a critical part of the practice of participation in the civil-rights movement. Draft-card burnings, demonstrations, and disruptions on college campuses highlighted "participatory democracy" when it became a by-word of the New Left movements of the 1960s and 1970s. The justification, costs, and benefits of these forms of a more direct participation movement along with those being advanced by thoughtful political scholars should be the subject of careful study and analysis in school and college.

But there is another model of participation that its advocates argue is more appropriate for the conditions of a modern technological society, where the issues are so complicated that direct decisions by the masses of citizens cannot be the rule. Rather, a representative model of participation should be revitalized to take better account of the expertise of professionals who, along with elected officials, are held accountable by the public. In the mid-1970s, a good example of this model, along with criticism of direct participation reforms was given by the late Stephen K. Bailey, political scientist in education and social policy at Harvard.[36]

It is heartening to see a revitalizing of the movement to increase direct involvement of citizens and to increase the effectiveness of direct participation. A growing body of scholarly underpinning for this trend has begun to replace Bailey's undisguised contempt for the "romantic half-truths" of the starry-eyed reformers of the 1960s and early 1970s.[37] One of the most persuasive of the more recent reformers is Benjamin R. Barber, political scientist at Rutgers, whose *Strong Democracy* has received wide attention. He argues that representative democracy is scarcely democracy at all and that a strong form of participatory democracy of genuine self-government is not only compatible with the Constitution but with the conditions of modern technological society.[38]

Some heartening evidences of making democracy work along the lines of public participation are the National Issues Forums sponsored by the Domestic Policy Association (DPA) under the stimulus and leadership of David Mathews, president of the Kettering Foundation. The network of several hundred organizations in DPA includes colleges, universities, and schools; libraries, museums, and historical associations;

churches, synagogues, and theological centers; community television stations; civic and professional organizations; student groups and senior-citizen centers. Especially pertinent here is the cooperative program with the National Council for the Social Studies to bring public policy issues into social studies classrooms.

To that end, Mathews and his associates at DPA and the Kettering Foundation drew up an interesting publication on the principles and practices of democracy, one used in training teachers and forum leaders. It contains a significant collection of extended quotations from historical sources like Pericles, Aristotle, Hobbes, Locke, Jefferson, Mill, Rousseau, and Tocqueville as well as from the new scholarship on citizenship, including Hannah Arendt, Benjamin Barber, Ronald Beiner, Bernard Murchland, Parker Palmer, Kenneth Prewitt, Michael Sandel, and Michael Walzer. Also important are the citations in the bibliography of Mathews's own writings on civic intelligence.[39] And not least in the lexicon of "public talk" is the necessity of being able to have access to and discern reliable and valid knowledge.

Truth

If we accept freedom of access to knowledge as the basis of a democratic society, then the reliability and the validity of public knowledge become of primary importance. The search for truth becomes one of the major goals of democracy. Therefore, respect for truth should begin with the young child, the parent, and the teacher as they try to distinguish the small fib and the white lie, which, while doing little harm to others, may become the big lie that may do irreparable harm to others. Then we come to the distinction between a falsification that arises from ignorance, partial knowledge, or mistake and a falsification deliberately undertaken with the intention to cover up one's own actions, to control the actions or beliefs of others, or to do actual harm to others. Thus the laws against perjury and libel incorporate into the polity the moral sense that truth is better than lying and that deliberate untruths are punishable for the sake of the common good and public welfare. The study and practice of truth telling become mandates for civic learning at every stage of education for citizenship.

In this complex and confusing arena of where, how, and why the truth should be told or not told, I can only hint at those aspects deserving careful study. One has to do with the rights and responsibili-

ties of citizens in seeking or telling the truth about one another, but
even more important is the role of government in revealing or hiding
the truth from its citizens.[40] A vast literature has accumulated, especially
since World War II, documenting the ways in which totalitarian nations,
both Communist and Fascist, and military dictatorships of virtually
every hue, have enforced controls over the flow of information and use
of falsification and lying when it served the purposes of those in control.
Deliberately deceiving the public is the essence of a closed society; every
coup is immediately accompanied by a closing down of newspapers and
taking over of radio and television stations. We have learned to expect
the strangling of truth by dictatorships of the Left and the Right.

Even more troublesome and alarming is the mounting concern
about lack of truth telling by the governments of democratic and free
societies. Major examples in the United States stem from deceptions
about Vietnam emanating from the government under Lyndon Johnson,
the attempted cover-ups of Watergate under Richard Nixon, and the
investigations about Nicaragua and Iran in 1986 and 1987 under the
Reagan administration. When trust in the veracity of the presidency and
of major government officials declines, the foundations of a free society
are at risk. Citizens who cannot distinguish between significant truth
and plausible falsehoods, beguiling half-truths, or outright lies cannot
retain their freedom. Nor can a government that lies to its citizens
continue to serve justice and equality, maintain its legitimate authority,
or even expect loyalty from its citizens.

Patriotism

This is one of the most difficult of the cohesive values to make clear and
persuasive to American students and teachers in the light of the traumatic events of the past two decades. Our predecessors from the time of
the American Revolution spoke of the individual's obligation for the
public good in terms of civic virtue, of patriotism and loyalty to the
new emerging nation as well as duty, discipline, and obedience to moral
and religious commandments. These were powerful sanctions for civic
education programs for generations, but they have been weakened in
the past fifty years. The military defense of the nation as a reason for
civic education probably reached its peak in World War II, when a vast
majority of the American people genuinely believed that defense against
the Nazi and Fascist aggression and the inhuman persecution of minorities justified a moral war. But the Korean War seemed less immediately

critical to the safety and security of the United States; and the Vietnam experience convinced large numbers that it was an immoral war and thus not justified as a reasonable cause for patriotism or military service.

A sense of obligation and responsibility manifested by loyalty, patriotism, discipline, and duty is still needed as a social and political glue if the structure of the democratic polity is to persist, let alone thrive. The schools alone cannot instill values of personal obligation and responsibility if other major social institutions are preaching and practicing advancement of self and private interests, an argument so persuasively advanced by Robert Bellah and his colleagues.[41] But this is no reason for the schools not to try, by reassessing what they can do and by seeking the aid of all community and public groups committed to the value claims of the democratic polity.

Loyalty, patriotism, discipline, and duty should be defined in terms of the richest fulfillment of the total set of democratic values in the Twelve Tables of Civism. Fortunately, there are signs of a growing effort on the part of some elements in the academic world to bring patriotism into the daylight of scholarly analysis and public discussion.

This is the major contribution of *The Reconstruction of Patriotism* by the University of Chicago's Morris Janowitz.[42] Some in the educational profession will view the book with suspicion simply because they assume automatically that anyone who believes in patriotism as a political value must be coming from a conservative or reactionary ideology. Some historians of education, including myself, will find fault with part of his history of citizenship education. Some social scientists will reject his arguments that behavioral and empirical opinion research has damaged education for citizenship, and many will think, "Here we go for indoctrination again."

But this book should be carefully read, critically analyzed, and used as a springboard for forthright discussion and research to improve our present understanding of patriotism, what role schools should play in promoting civic knowledge and commitment to democratic values, and what appropriate responsibility rests with those who prepare teachers in colleges and universities.

The theme of "restoring a meaningful balance" between rights and obligations runs throughout the book. It is a theme that is readily applauded by conservative sources, whether organized on a large scale by politicians in Washington, business, or religion, or whether rising from myriad localities, schools, and families in the call for more discipline, responsibility, hard work, and moral values. But it is a theme that deserves better than knee-jerk rejection by liberals or mindless acceptance by conservatives. Fortunately, liberals as well as conservatives are seeking valid normative formulations of obligation in the meaning of citizenship.[43]

In the bulk of this book Janowitz deals with the major institutions for civic education: military service as civic education, civic education in school and college, and national or community service as agencies of civic education. Janowitz argues that with the decline of universal, obligatory military service through conscription and the rise of an all-volunteer (or mercenary) force, the contribution of the armed forces to civic education has also declined. With regard to the idea of national service, he speaks wistfully of the Civilian Conservation Corps and the failure to update the CCC as well as the Job Corps, VISTA, the Teacher Corps, and the Peace Corps.

Perhaps Janowitz was more prophetic than he knew. There are signs today of a revival of enthusiasm for public and community service on college campuses. Witness "Campus Compact," sponsored by the Education Commission of the States (as noted in Chapter 6). New interest in youth service is illustrated in a research study completed in 1986 for the Ford Foundation by Richard Danzig and Peter Szantos in which four models are outlined: mandatory school-based programs; a national draft, including an option for military or civilian service; federally supported all-voluntary youth service; and universal service that could be completed at any age.[44]

Representative Leon Panetta of California has repeatedly introduced bills for volunteer national service; and Representative Constance Morella of Maryland introduced in the 100th Congress a bill to establish a Peace Corps training program on college campuses modeled on the ROTC. And in May 1988, the Democratic Leadership Council offered a plan for national youth service to be called a Citizen Corps in which young people could serve for a year or two in military or public-service jobs with subsistence wages. For each year of service the member would receive a voucher worth $10,000, which could be used for further education, job training, or as a down payment on a home.

The long-term test, however, will be whether American education can strengthen the sense of community and cohesion among succeeding generations through stress upon civic virtue and personal obligation for the public good without weakening the struggle for freedom, diversity, due process, and human rights. The closet door may be opening a bit in the academic world and in the public press. But reconstructing the idea of patriotism and citizenship is formidable, and the designing and carrying out of appropriate educational programs dedicated to civic consciousness, civic intelligence, or civic learning is even more monumental.

Human Rights

Today, the obvious interdependence of the world requires that civic virtue or obligation for the public good encompass a wider and more positive moral element than solely the need to defend the American public order when it is threatened from within or without. It reminds us that the superjingoistic patriotism, which in the past has often been narrowly conceived as loyalty or obligation to one's own nation, must now be imbued with a broader international outlook that honors the world's diversity of peoples but also seeks a new and larger cohesion based upon the concepts of common human rights.

So I come, finally, to a value for American civic education that requires a basic change in our historical views and values of citizenship. The idea of national citizenship must now take account of the vast changes in the world that have occurred since the end of World War II. Increasingly popular terms to define the set of phenomena that began with the term "One World" in the 1940s are now "global interdependence," "global perspectives," or simply "global education."[45]

The term "global education" has been attacked by political and religious conservatives on the grounds that it seeks to elevate socialist values and denigrate true American values, or that it sees no superior values in the American way of life and thus preaches a kind of moral relativism or moral neutrality.[46] I hope that no one could read and understand the first eleven of my tables of civism and still think that I see no superior values in the ideals of American citizenship. But instead of "global education," I advocate the term "international human rights," or simply "human rights," as a device to broaden civic education for Americans and yet not get overwhelmed by studying all aspects of all the world's peoples and cultures.

In fact, I come very close to the definition of global education in the report by the Study Commission on Global Perspectives in Education, chaired by Clark Kerr, which outlines what students need to know to function as citizens of the United States in an increasingly interdependent world.[47] The most extensive courses of study along these lines are contained in the two-year program in global studies required in grades 9 and 10 by the New York State Board of Regents for graduation from high school.[48] The object of such study is partly to understand why some nations and peoples have chosen a different way from that of the United States. But if the world is truly interdependent and if U.S. citizenship is genuinely devoted to democratic values, then global study should be searching for and preferring democratic answers to global issues as well as simply understanding the reasons for diverse views.

The idea and practice of citizenship itself as conceived in various nations could be a major theme for this study. What does citizenship mean for Christians and Moslems in Lebanon, for blacks in South Africa, for Jews and dissidents in the Soviet Union, for ethnic and language groups in India, Sri Lanka, China, or Nigeria, and for new immigrants to the United States? A greater attention to human rights would give opportunities to address the positive aspects of democratic values and the obstacles or threats to such rights in various national approaches to citizenship. There is the danger of trying to do too much in too scattered and superficial fashion, as well as the danger of competition in the school curriculum between civic education, global education, and multicultural education. These three efforts to redirect the school curriculum are often carried out independently of one another. There has been too little effort to interweave the three and too little recognition of their natural affinity. Indeed, they are often disparate, and sometimes even antagonistic, in their pressures on the schools.[49]

My principal argument is that these three major drives in American education are rightly interdependent; that keeping these movements separate is essentially artificial and constitutes a distortion of the logic that binds them together; that reasoned awareness of and respect for disparate cultures is increasingly necessary in a world of international conflict; that international security for the United States is inseparably tied to the maintenance of an intelligent, informed citizenry; and that an intelligent citizenry is necessary to keeping a society free of intolerance, racism, sexism, and ethnocentric behavior. These several impulses should be unified if the nation's interests in freedom, equality, justice, and the public good are to be served. Teaching and learning in the social studies have historically had a large part to play in these sets of values, but they have seldom been brought together in a coherent program of studies.

We should try to select from the almost infinite mass of information those elements of world studies that focus on international human rights and that illuminate the other eleven concepts in my table of civic values. Study of international human rights should be linked to questions of justice, freedom, equality, diversity, authority, privacy, due process, truth telling, property rights, and participation, stressing how these values are honored or violated in various nations and in the relations among nations.

Examples of the interplay between cohesive civic values and diversifying pluralist values are especially pertinent in the realm of human rights. They can come from the worst examples of genocide, culminating in the Holocaust of Hitler's Germany, the devastation resulting from arbitrary rule in Amin's Uganda, or outbreaks of terrorism all over the world. They can come from positive gains for human rights in Argentina, Poland, and elsewhere. They can come from study of dissidents seeking and being denied freedom and due process in Iran, China, Cuba, or the Soviet Union, or in military dictatorships in Chile, Haiti, or Panama.

And closer to home, they can be illustrated by the problems for human rights arising from the influx of Cubans to Florida or Mexicans, Vietnamese, and Koreans to California. Historic problems of immigration, nativism, segregation, and integration are all revived in contemporary confrontations over international as well as domestic human rights. In accordance with a law passed by the California Assembly in 1985, the state department of education drew up a model curriculum on human rights and genocide to be incorporated in existing courses in history/social science for grades 7 to 12, inclusive.[50]

As we commemorate the period between the bicentennial of the U.S. Constitution in 1787 and the adoption of the Bill of Rights in 1791, civic educators are being urged to re-examine the basic ideas and values of the American democratic civic community. As anyone who has read this far would know, I heartily approve of this move. And I would urge that a complementary study of some of the basic documents that set forth contemporary statements of international human rights should be undertaken for the sake of comparison and contrast.[51]

The twofold aim of such a study is to consider how to improve the American political system as well as to consider how the United States could play a more constructive and humanitarian role in the world. Of particular interest and importance would be a study of the Helsinki Final Act of 1975, in which the Soviet Union and its East European allies agreed with the North Atlantic Treaty Organization nations to promote human rights. A comparison of the Final Act with the earlier UN formal documents and with later practices—as revealed and discussed at general meetings in succeeding years at Belgrade, Madrid, and Vienna and at a special meeting in Ottawa in 1985—would reveal how far short the Communist nations have fallen from the agreement. Yet the release of Anatoly Shcharansky, Yuri Orlov, Andrei Sakharov, and other dissidents under Mikhail Gorbachev might also reveal that steadfast promotion of the ideals of human rights by the United States and by the West is having an effect. But there is one innovative and national approach readily at hand that could invigorate the civic life of those schools that take part.

The National Competition on the Constitution and Bill of Rights, officially cosponsored by the U.S. Bicentennial Commission, is being conducted between 1987 and 1991 by the Center for Civic Education. The competition is between school classes and groups of students rather than between individual students. The competition is being held in every congressional district and culminates in regional, state, and national awards. Classes prepare for the competition through the use of specially prepared study units on the historical ideas and political concepts underlying the Constitution's framing, adoption, and amendment, with special attention to the Bill of Rights and the changes in constitutional thought that followed ratification.

After completing their study, the classes compete as teams in demonstrating their knowledge and understanding of constitutional principles. Each class will complete a qualifying multiple-choice test whose score will represent an average of the scores of all students in the whole class and then participate in a mock congressional hearing on a series of selected fundamental constitutional issues. As judged by a panel of experts from the community, the combined score on the quality of their presentations at the hearing decides which class will continue in the competition. In both the test and the hearing the entire class contributes to the preparation for the competition through individual study, group discussion, and other group activities in the school and in the community.

Not many will expect such competitions to elicit the emotional fervor of a championship football or basketball game, but they certainly can and do create increased enthusiasm for studying, learning, and contributing to the school's common effort to understand what democracy is all about, which, after all, is a higher priority for universal schooling than athletic contests alone. Those who have watched or read about real congressional hearings, such as the Iran/Contra hearings in 1987, surely know the importance of reading, writing, speaking, and critical thinking in the effort to understand ideas basic to the conduct of political and moral affairs in a democratic society.

The competition could well motivate students and teachers alike to become much more aware of the need to clarify their own school's practices of authority and due process, freedom and diversity, equality and justice, patriotism and truth-telling as public goods. A Roper survey of youth attitudes shows clearly that high school students are aware of social issues involved in school discipline, privacy, sex education, alcohol and drug abuse, prayers, and busing.[52]

The schools have an unparalleled opportunity to influence an entire generation of high-school youth during the next few years. The combination of the Constitution's bicentennial, the appointment of one or more Supreme Court justices, and the election of 1990 could give unprecedented vitality to close study of basic constitutional issues and principles. Each school jurisdiction will decide for itself how to approach such an agenda.

It may surprise some would-be reformers that students in general like their schools and that they rank the study of current events, social studies, and history just below math, English, and computer skills in importance to them. And the thing that makes youth "feel good" above all others is "being an American." Feeling good is good. But now the moral task of the school is to help students seek to understand what, in the worthiest sense, that means for their moral conduct in school as students and as citizens. The ingredients to energize the civic temper of youth are at hand, if we can only find the necessary sparks.

Such sparks were clearly visible during a three-day period late in April 1988 in Washington, D.C., but they were overshadowed by a much-heralded event taking place at the White House. One might say these were two Janus-like faces of educational reform.

Recall that Janus was the Roman deity of new beginnings and new openings, usually represented symbolically as a head with two faces back-to-back, as if one were looking backward and one forward in time or space.

The most obvious of these faces received extensive press coverage as Education Secretary Bennett issued his latest report on the condition of American education. Although Bennett found some improvement during the past five years, he felt this progress was neither good enough nor fast enough in strengthening the academic curriculum or in promoting the discipline of achievement and hard work.

Almost predictably, his report provoked critical responses by highly involved and responsible leaders in the teaching profession and at universities nationwide, who argued publicly that Bennett's generalizations were too hasty, superficial, and premature and that Bennett expected instant improvement, despite limited federal support. All this commotion took place even before Bennett formally presented his report to President Reagan in a ceremony at the White House. To the reading and viewing public this was by far the more familiar face of educational reform.

Meanwhile, during those same days in Washington, a second face of "quiet reform" was occurring in an unprecedented event taking place across town in the National Defense University at Fort McNair and later in the Federal District Court of Appeals. The occasion was the final round in the National Bicentennial Competition on the Constitution and the Bill of Rights.

Although this may sound uneventful to an outsider, it was the experience of a lifetime for the one thousand high-school students and their teachers who had won state championships in forty-three states and had come to Washington for the national finals. Champions in what? In knowledge of the thought and practices of constitutional government that led to the Declaration of Independence, the Constitution, and the Bill of Rights, the formation of the state and federal governments, and the gains and losses attending the rights and responsibilities of American citizens since that time.

With the guidance of their teachers, these students from classes in history, government, civics, and the problems of democracy had been hard at work studying the specially prepared text on these matters for several weeks. They had passed a group qualifying test of knowledge as measured by the average score of all twenty to thirty members of the class. And they had competed successfully with teams from other schools in their congressional district and finally in their state. They did this by displaying their knowledge and understanding before a panel of judges in the form of a mock congressional hearing.

In the Washington finals a panel of three to six members of each team took turns presenting their views orally on a series of important constitutional questions put to them by the judges. The students then engaged in a lively give-and-take by answering follow-up questions from the panel of experts, which consisted of attorneys, judges, academic scholars in law, political science, and history, school administrators, social-studies teachers, state legislators, law enforcement officials, and education correspondents for press and radio.

This was no stilted classroom exercise learned by rote to be recited from memory from a boring textbook. These high-school students, on the verge of becoming voting citizens, discussed key constitutional questions with knowledge, insight, and maturity. Some of the issues discussed included the justice of capital punishment, the consequences of civil disobedience, equality of opportunity, freedom of speech and religion or prayer in public schools, the separation of powers and checks and balances in matters of domestic and foreign policy from Watergate to Nicaragua, judicial activism versus judicial restraint, and the role of due process in matters of life, liberty, and property. They not only knew about *Marbury* v. *Madison* but also about *Brown* v. *Board of Education, Roe* v. *Wade, Engel* v. *Vitale,* and on and on.

Indeed, the issues addressed were not remote, pedantic, or useless matters of little relevance to the lives of the students. These students were vigorously and enthusiastically forming judgments, taking positions, and often disagreeing about what these issues meant to them as individuals and as prospective voting citizens. They were doing all this as members of a class team, trying to excel as a group for the sake of their class, their teacher, their school, their community and state. While decorum and attentiveness appropriate to a congressional hearing were maintained throughout the alloted time for each session, the resounding applause at the conclusion of the sessions signaled the students' approval of their teammates' accomplishments and served as encouragement for those yet to compete.

After two days of such rigorous sessions, the ten highest-rated teams competed in a third and final round of hearings held in the austere judicial setting of the Federal District Court of Appeals. And later that evening at the Grand Hyatt Hotel the entire thousand attended the awards banquet to receive scrolls and pendants of honor from former Chief Justice Warren E. Burger. When the three highest-ranking state teams were finally announced, the bursts of applause, squeals and screams, hugging and tears rivaled the emotional release and enthusiasm, if not the raucous behavior, at the winning of a championship basketball or football game. Best of all, the expressions of appreciation students bestowed upon their teachers were observably sincere and affectionate. No winning athletic coach could have been more touched or gratified. Some, of course, had to murmur, "Wait till next year."

Still more important to remember is that these events were the culmination of weeks of hard work that had involved some 500,000 students and 6,000 teachers in 423 congressional districts from Maine to Hawaii. All had engaged in weeks or months of studying, discussing, coaching—and, above all, thinking. The enterprise was supported by federal funds under an act of Congress, supplemented by states, school districts, and contributions from hundreds of professional, business, labor, and voluntary agencies, which helped to pay expenses for students and teachers to travel to state capitals and to Washington. Eighty U.S. senators and 380 U.S. representatives signed on as sponsors, making the effort wholly bipartisan.

The size and success of this first year of a five-year project was convincing evidence for the success of the "second face" of educational reform, which has opened the door to a better civic education for all American youth. It behooves would-be "education presidents," "education governors," and "education legislators" to consider carefully what this and like projects could mean for the future of America. It is a long-term investment in the kind of educational reform that seeks to prepare coming generations for informed, responsible, and committed American citizenship. Whichever political party is elected in November 1988, this long-term investment in civism is vital.

To this end, a second major national effort was launched in the summer of 1988 to draw up and disseminate an exemplary curriculum framework for instruction in civic education at all levels in elementary and secondary schools. Funded for two years by the Pew Charitable Trusts, the project Civitas will be conducted by the Center for Civic Education and the Council for the Advancement of Citizenship. The framework will (1) delineate the "fundamental civic principles and values of our constitutional republic," (2) formulate a defensible conception of citizenship embodying the best of our historical traditions but also looking to the future, and (3) indicate examples of democratic values that are especially appropriate for study at various age and grade levels. I applaud the purposes of project Civitas and wish it well. It could also help to redirect the educational reform movement of the 1980s.

To that goal this book is dedicated along with its companion piece, *The Morality of Democratic Citizenship*. I close both books with the same words:

> As the United States embarks upon its third century, the role of education is fortunately regarded as a high priority in our national life. There are clamorous demands that education must sharpen the competitive edge of the United States in the world economy. Others argue that the schools should return to the safe harbors of traditional moral and religious values as embodied in the Judeo-Christian heritage and Western civilization. Still others call for piloting the schools through the uncharted shoals of moral choice by means of cultural literacy, intellectual excellence, or critical thinking. These views have their many persuasive advocates, but I believe there is a still more cogent priority.
>
> This book argues for revitalizing the historic civic mission of American education. This means explicit and continuing study of the basic concepts and values underlying our democratic political community and constitutional order. The common core of the curriculum throughout school and college years should be the morality of citizenship. For this goal to be realized, scholarly study of civic morality should be the first priority in the liberal and professional education of the teaching profession. In the long run, the intellectual, moral, and political agenda for American education, its curriculum, its common life, and its governance must rest upon the study and practice of the obligations as well as the rights of democratic citizenship.[53]

If the "first face" of the educational-reform movement overlooks, or looks away from, an improved civic education, American democracy itself is indeed at risk, at home as well as abroad.

Notes

Chapter 1

1. Donald M. Stewart, "Back to the Future Won't Work for Education," *Education Week,* June 17, 1987.
2. The National Commission on Excellence in Education, *A Nation at Risk: The Imperative for Educational Reform* (Washington, D.C.: Government Printing Office, April 1983), p. 7.
3. Report of Third Anniversary Conference of the National Commission on Excellence, Salt Lake City, April 25–26, 1986, pp. 24–29.
4. Report of The Twentieth Century Fund Task Force on Federal Elementary and Secondary Education Policy, *Making the Grade* (New York: The Twentieth Century Fund, 1983), p. 4.
5. Ibid., p. 20.
6. Ernest L. Boyer, *High School: A Report on Secondary Education in America* (New York: Harper and Row, 1983), pp. 1 and 6.
7. Committee on Economic Development, *Children in Need: Investment Strategies for the Educationally Disadvantaged* (New York: Committee on Economic Development, 1987).
8. Twentieth Century Fund Task Force, *Making The Grade,* p. 11.
9. Mortimer Adler, *The Paideia Proposal: An Educational Manifesto* (New York: Macmillan, 1982), chs. 1–4. See also Rockefeller Commission on the Humanities, *The Humanities in American Life* (Berkeley: University of California Press, 1980), chs. 1–2.
10. John I. Goodlad, *A Place Called School* (New York: McGraw-Hill, 1983). For brief summaries, see *The Phi Delta Kappan* issues for November and December 1979; January and February 1980; and March and April 1983.

11. Theodore R. Sizer, *Horace's Compromise: The Dilemma of the American High School.* (Boston: Houghton Mifflin, 1984), p. 86. A later study, in the mode of Goodlad and Sizer, recognized the value of core studies in history and social science but concentrated on elevating the autonomy of the individual school and the responsibility of the local teaching staff as means to strengthen the moral authority and ethos of the school on behalf of democratic ideals. See Gerald Grant, *The World We Created at Hamilton High* (Cambridge, Mass.: Harvard University Press, 1988).

12. Ibid., p. 133.

13. Theodore R. Sizer, *High School Reform and the Reform of Teacher Education* (Minneapolis, Minn.: Society of Professors of Education, 1984), p. 6. For an interesting contrast, see my own 1982 DeGarmo Lecture, *Teacher Education and the Revival of Civic Learning* (Minneapolis, Minn.: Society of Professors of Education, 1982).

14. Arthur G. Powell, Eleanor Farrar, and David K. Cohen, *The Shopping Mall High School: Winners and Losers in the Educational Marketplace* (Boston: Houghton Mifflin, 1985); and Robert L. Hampel, *The Last Little Citadel* (Boston: Houghton Mifflin, 1986).

15. *Academic Preparation for College: What Students Need to Know and Be Able to Do* (New York: College Entrance Examination Board, 1983); *Academic Preparation in Social Studies* (New York: College Entrance Examination Board, 1986).

16. For the monthly *Newsletter,* see Educational Excellence Network, now moved to the Washington office of Vanderbilt University, with Chester E. Finn as director.

17. Chester E. Finn, Jr., Diane Ravitch, and Robert T. Fancher, eds., *Against Mediocrity: The Humanities in America's High Schools* (New York: Holmes and Meier, 1984), p. 260. The call to re-emphasize history as the central core of the social studies was further promoted in 1984 by the formation of the Clio Project at the University of California at Berkeley with support from the California State Department of Education; see Bernard R. Gifford, ed., *History in the Schools: What Shall We Teach?* (New York: Macmillan, 1988). See also Chapter 1 of R. Freeman Butts, *The Morality of Democratic Citizenship* (Calabasas, Calif.: Center for Civic Education, 1988).

18. *Education for Democracy: A Statement of Principles; Guidelines for Strengthening the Teaching of Democratic Values* (Washington, D.C.: American Federation of Teachers, 1987), p. 8.

19. Ibid., p. 16.

20. E. D. Hirsch, Jr., *Cultural Literacy: What Every American Needs to Know* (Boston: Houghton Mifflin, 1987), p. xvii. One exasperated classroom teacher called Hirsch's items a "loony list" of disjointed facts: Susan Ohanian, "Finding a 'Loony List' While Searching for Literacy," *Education Week,* May 6, 1987.

21. Hirsch, *Cultural Literacy,* p. 145.

22. See *Chronicle of Higher Education,* August 5, 1987.
23. See *Education Week,* March 4, 1987, and February 4, 1987.
24. James D. Carroll, et al., *We The People: A Review of U.S. Government and Civics Textbooks* (Washington, D.C.: People for the American Way, 1987).
25. Report of the Study Commission on Global Education, *The United States Prepares for Its Future: Global Perspectives in Education* (New York: Global Perspectives in Education, 1987).
26. Beatrice Gross and Ronald Gross, eds., *The Great School Debate: Which Way for American Education?* (New York: Simon and Schuster, 1985).
27. John H. Bunzel, ed., *Challenge to American Schools: The Case for Standards and Values* (New York: Oxford University Press, 1985).
28. Bill Honig, *Last Chance for Our Children: How You Can Help Save Our Schools* (Menlo Park, Calif.: Addison-Wesley, 1985).
29. Marvin Lazerson, et al., *An Education of Value: The Purposes and Practices of Schools* (New York: Cambridge University Press, 1985).
30. Letter to me, dated December 2, 1980.
31. *The Nation's Report Card: Improving the Assessment of Student Achievement* (Cambridge, Mass.: National Academy of Education, Harvard Graduate School of Education, 1987), p. 24.
32. Ibid., p. 46.
33. Ibid., pp. 51–52.
34. National Commission for Excellence in Teacher Education, *A Call for Change in Teacher Education* (Washington, D.C.: American Association of Colleges for Teacher Education, 1985).
35. California Commission on the Teaching Profession, *Who Will Teach Our Children: A Strategy for Improving California Schools* (Sacramento, Calif: The Commission, 1985).
36. Holmes Group, *Goals for Educating Teachers as Professionals* (New York: Random House, 1986).
37. Task Force on Teaching as a Profession, *A Nation Prepared: Teachers for the 21st Century* (New York: Carnegie Forum on Education and the Economy, 1986), p. 14.
38. William James, "The Moral Equivalent of War," document no. 27 (New York: American Association for International Conciliation, February 1910), p. 6.
39. Ibid., p. 17.
40. Ibid., p. 16.
41. Ibid., pp. 18–19.
42. Ethics and Public Policy Center, *Newsletter* (Washington, D.C., January 1987), p. 1. For an excellent collection of readings concerning the role of ethics in politics, drawn from both Democratic and Republican administrations since 1960, see Amy Gutmann and Dennis Thompson, eds., *Ethics and Politics: Cases and Comments* (Chicago: Nelson-Hall, 1984). For a fundamental analysis of political ethics by the Whitehead Professor of Political Philosophy at Harvard and director of the universitywide Program in

Ethics and the Professions, see Dennis F. Thompson, *Political Ethics and Public Office* (Cambridge, Mass.: Harvard University Press, 1987).

43. R. Freeman Butts, "Education for Citizenship: The Oldest, Newest Innovation in the Schools," *Vital Issues,* vol. 26, no. 8, April 1977 (Washington, Conn.: Center for Information on America), pp. 1–2.

44. Lewis J. Perelman, *Technology and the Transformation of Schools* (Alexandria, Va.: National School Boards Association, 1987).

45. See *Redesigning America's Schools: The Public Speaks* (New York: Carnegie Forum on Education and the Economy, 1986).

46. Felix G. Rohatyn, "Ethics in America's Money Culture," *New York Times,* June 3, 1987.

47. See, for example, Elmer U. Clawson, *Our Economy: How It Works* (Menlo Park, Calif.: Addison-Wesley, 1984). See also Steven L. Miller, *Economic Education for Citizenship* (Bloomington: Social Studies Development Center, Indiana University, 1988).

48. See text in *Education Week,* November 28, 1984.

49. *The Forgotten Half: Non-College-Bound Youth* (Washington, D.C.: William T. Grant Foundation Commission on Youth and America's Future, 1988); summary in the *Phi Delta Kappan,* February 1988, pp. 409–14.

50. See *Education Week,* April 11, 1984. Sharp "exploitative and deceitful practices" by some for-profit schools led Secretary Bennett to ask Congress to curb their abuse of federal financial aid; *Education Week,* February 17, 1988.

51. *The National Review,* August 5, 1983.

52. Robert Nisbet, "The Conservative Renaissance in Perspective," Twentieth Anniversary Issue, *The Public Interest,* no. 81, Fall 1985, pp. 128–41.

53. Ibid., p. 141.

54. *Youth Policy,* June 1986 (Washington, D.C.: Youth Policy Institute).

55. William J. Bennett, *First Lessons: A Report on Elementary Education in America* (Washington, D.C.: U.S. Department of Education, September 1986), pp. 15–16.

56. Gene V. Glass, "What Works: Politics and Research," *Educational Researcher,* April 15, 1987.

57. *Education Week,* April 15, 1987.

58. William Lowe Boyd, "Rhetoric and Symbolic Politics: President Reagan's School-Reform Agenda," *Education Week,* March 18, 1987.

59. *Education Week,* June 10, 1987.

60. Joe Nathan, "The Rhetoric and the Reality of Expanding Educational Choices," *Phi Delta Kappan,* March 1985, pp. 476–81. See also my reply in *Kappan,* September 1985, pp. 86–92.

61. *Time for Results* (Washington, D.C.: National Governors' Association, 1986); see also articles in *Phi Delta Kappan,* November 1986, pp. 197–227.

62. Mel Gabler and Norma Gabler, "Mind Control Through Textbooks," *Phi Delta Kappan,* October 1982, p. 86.

63. Special Issue, "Religion in the Public Schools," *Educational Leadership,* May

1987. See especially: J. Charles Park, "The Religious Right and Public Education," pp. 5–10; Donna Hulsizer, "Public Education on Trial," pp. 12–16; C. Glennon Rowell, "Implications of the Tennessee Textbook Controversy for Public Education," pp. 14–15; Charles C. Haynes, "Religious Freedom: Teach It or Lose It," pp. 18–20; R. Freeman Butts, "A History and Civics Lesson for All of Us," pp. 21–25; and Robert L. Cord, "Church-State Separation and the Public Schools: A Re-evaluation," pp. 26–32.

64. For a summary of the studies, see John W. McDermott, Jr., "The Treatment of Religion in School Textbooks: A Political Analysis and a Modest Proposal," *Religion and Public Education,* Fall 1986, pp. 62–77.

65. Paul C. Vitz, *Religion and Traditional Values in Public School Textbooks* (Washington, D.C.: National Institute of Education, 1986.)

66. Charles C. Haynes, *Religious Freedom in America* (Silver Spring, Md.: Americans United Research Foundation, 1986); O. L. Davis, Jr., et al., *Looking at History: A Review of Major U.S. History Textbooks* (Washington, D.C.: People for the American Way, 1986); and James D. Carroll et al., *We The People: A Review of U.S. Government and Civics Textbooks* (Washington, D.C.: People for the American Way, 1987).

67. Richard John Neuhaus and Michael Cromartie, eds., *Piety and Politics: Evangelicals and Fundamentalists Confront the World* (Washington, D.C.: Ethics and Public Policy Center, 1987).

68. Robert Nisbet, "The Conservative Renaissance in Perspective," *The Public Interest,* Fall 1985, p. 139.

69. Quoted in the *New York Times,* July 15, 1986.

70. Beverly LeHaye, "Whose Ethics in the Government Schools?" *Kappa Delta Pi Record,* Spring 1987, pp. 72–75.

71. See, e.g., Michael Hudson, "Censorship Threatens Education," *Kappa Delta Pi Record,* Spring 1987, pp. 67–71; and Christy Macy and Ricki Seidman, "Attacks on 'Secular Humanism': The Real Threat to Public Education," *Kappa Delta Pi Record,* pp. 76–80.

72. Quoted in the *New York Times,* August 23, 1980.

73. Quoted in the *New York Times,* August 24, 1984.

74. *Mozert* v. *Hawkins County Public Schools,* U.S. District Court for the Eastern District of Tennessee, Northeastern Division, No. CIV-2-83-401, 1986. Quoted from the court's decision in *Education Week,* November 5, 1986.

75. Ibid.

76. *Smith* v. *Board of School Commissioners of Mobile County,* U.S. District Court for the Southern District of Alabama, Southern Division, No. CIV-82-0544-BH, March 4, 1987.

77. Ibid., U.S. Court of Appeals, Eleventh Circuit, No. 87-7216, August 26, 1987.

78. *Edwards* v. *Aguillard,* No. 85-1513 (1987).

79. See, e.g., the series of articles in the *Phi Delta Kappan,* February 1988, pp. 415–31.

80. James E. Wood, Jr., *Secular Humanism and the Public Schools* (New York: United Ministries in Education and the National Council of Churches of

Christ in the U.S.A., 1986), p. 26, note 9. The U.M.E. consists of various agencies of seven denominations: American Baptist Churches, Christian Church (Disciples of Christ), Church of the Brethren, The Episcopal Church, Moravian Church, Presbyterian Church (USA), and the United Church of Christ.

81. Ibid., p. 3.
82. Ibid., p. 19.
83. Marc Lilla, "What is the Civic Interest? *The Public Interest,* Fall 1985, p. 75.
84. Ibid., pp. 75–76.
85. See, e.g., the list of my publications in Part I, note 2, beginning with R. Freeman Butts, "The Public School: Assaults on A Great Idea," *The Nation,* April 10, 1973, pp. 553–60.
86. National Assessment of Educational Progress, "Citizenship and Social Studies Achievement of Young Americans: 1981–82; Performance and Change Between 1976 and 1982" (Denver: Education Commission of the States, October 1983).
87. Research on political socialization expanded enormously in the mid-1970s and then waned in the late 1970s. For summaries of research on political socialization, see the following studies: Robert Coles, *The Political Life of Children* (Boston: Atlantic Monthly Press, 1985); Jack Dennis, ed., *Socialization to Politics: A Reader* (New York: Wiley, 1973); Lee H. Ehman, "The American School in the Political Socialization Process," *Review of Educational Research,* Spring 1980, pp. 99–119; Mary A. Hepburn, "What Is Our Youth Thinking? Social-Political Attitudes of the 1980s," *Social Education,* November/December 1985, pp. 671–77; M. Kent Jennings and Richard G. Niemi, *The Political Character of Adolescence: The Influence of Families and Schools* (Princeton, N.J.: Princeton University Press, 1974); Lynell Johnson and Robert D. Hess, "Kids and Citizenship: A National Survey," *Social Education,* November/December 1984, pp. 502–505; Byron G. Massialas, ed., *Political Youth, Traditional Schools* (Englewood Cliffs, N.J.: Prentice-Hall, 1972); Byron G. Massialas, "Political Socialization and Citizen Competencies: A Review of Research Findings"; Judith V. Torney, "The Definition of Citizen Capacities and Related Psychological Research," *Citizen Education Behavior Variables: Final Report* (Philadelphia: Research for Better Schools, July 31, 1978); and Judith Torney-Purta and John Schwille, "The Values Learned in School: Policy and Practice in Industrialized Countries," a paper prepared for the National Commission on Excellence in Education, August 1982.
88. *Milwaukee Journal,* July 11, 1983.
89. George Orwell, *1984* (New York: New American Library, 1961), pp. 246–47 and 251.
90. Amy Gutmann, *Democratic Education* (Princeton, N.J.: Princeton University Press, 1987), pp. 287–88.

Part I

1. For text, see *Chronicle of Higher Education,* May 4, 1988; for critics, see *Education Week,* May 4, 1988.
2. My publications, relating to the civic role of the school in American society and published between 1973 and 1980 include the following: "The Public School: Assaults on a Great Idea," *The Nation,* April 30, 1973; "The Public Purpose of the Public School," *Teachers College Record,* December 1973; "Public Education and Political Community," *History of Education Quarterly,* Summer 1974; "Foundations of Education and the New Civism," *Educational Studies,* Fall/Winter 1975; "The Search for Purpose in American Education," *College Board Review,* Winter 1975/1976; "Compulsory Education: History, Current Status, Trends," U.S. Office of Education, Region VII, Kansas City, Mo., regional conference on "Compulsory Education: Responsibilities and Alternatives," Overland Park, Kansas, December 3–4, 1975; "Once Again the Question for Liberal Public Educators: Whose Twilight?" *Phi Delta Kappan,* September 1976; "The Public School as Moral Authority," in Association for Supervision and Curriculum Development, *The School's Role as Moral Authority* (Washington, D.C.: ASCD, 1977); "Historical Perspective on Civic Education in the United States," in National Task Force on Citizenship Education, *Education for Responsible Citizenship* (New York: McGraw-Hill, 1977); "Education for Citizenship: The Oldest, Newest Innovation in the Schools," *Vital Issues,* April 1977; "Educational Vouchers: The Private Pursuit of the Public Purse," *Phi Delta Kappan,* September 1979; *Public Education in the United States: From Revolution to Reform* (New York: Holt, Rinehart, and Winston, 1978; and *The Revival of Civic Learning: A Rationale for Citizenship Education in American Schools* (Bloomington, Ind.; Phi Delta Kappa Educational Foundation, 1980).

   Chapters 2, 3, and 4 are adapted and updated from a hitherto unpublished research study submitted at the request of the Community Education Program of the U.S. Office of Education, pursuant to Order No. P00780606, dated August 30, 1978, and entitled "Historical Perspective on the Role of the School in American Society: Changing Interrelationships of Schools, Communities, and Homes," August 1979. Several research papers by other scholars were prepared for a major National Forum on School-Community-Home Relationships held at the Shoreham Hotel, Washington, D.C., March 10–11, 1980.
3. J. W. Getzels, "The Communities of Education," *Teachers College Record,* May 1978, p. 681.
4. For early summaries of the literature on the history of the family and education, see the entire issues of the *Teachers College Record,* December 1974 and May 1978, especially the historiographical articles by Lawrence A. Cremin.

   One of the most useful collections of original documents on the family and education from 1600 to 1973 is contained in three large volumes edited by Robert H. Bremner, *Children and Youth in America: A Documentary History* (Cambridge, Mass.: Harvard University Press, 1970, 1971, and 1974).

For a variety of publications summarizing recent historical scholarship on the family, see *The Journal of Interdisciplinary History,* Autumn 1971 and April 1975; Peter Laslett, ed., *Household and Family in Past Times* (New York: Cambridge University Press, 1972); Michael Gordon, ed., *The American Family in Social-Historical Perspective,* 3rd ed. (New York: St. Martin's Press, 1983); Carl N. Degler, *At Odds: Women and the Family in America from the Revolution to the Present* (New York: Oxford University Press, 1980); Donald M. Scott and Bernard Wishy, *America's Families: A Documentary History* (New York: Harper and Row, 1982); W. Norton Grubb and Marvin Lazerson, *Broken Promises: How Americans Fail Their Children* (New York: Basic Books, 1982); Barbara Finkelstein, "Literature Review: Incorporating Children into the History of Education," *The Journal of Educational Thought,* April 1984, pp. 21–41; N. Ray Hiner and Joseph M. Hawes, eds., *Growing Up in America: Children in Historical Perspective* (Urbana and Chicago: University of Illinois Press, 1985); Steven Mintz and Susan Kellogg, *Domestic Revolutions: A Social History of American Family Life* (New York: Free Press, 1988).

5. See, e.g., Mary Jo Bane, *Here to Stay* (New York: Basic Books, 1976); Christopher Lasch, *Haven in a Heartless World: The Family Besieged* (New York: Basic Books, 1977); Arlene Skolnick, "The Family Revisited: Themes in Recent Social Science Research," *Journal of Interdisciplinary History,* Spring 1975, pp. 703–19; Urie Bronfenbrenner, "American Family in Decline," *Current,* January 1977; Kenneth Keniston, *All Our Children* (New York: Harcourt, Brace, Jovanovich, 1977); Robert Coles, "American Family: A Haven Invaded," *Horizon,* April 1978; Amitai Etzioni, "Family: Is It Obsolete?" *Current,* Spring 1977; Nathan Glazer, "Rediscovery of the Family," *Commentary,* March 1978; Joseph Featherstone, "Family Matters," *Harvard Educational Review,* February 1979; Barbara Finkelstein, "Family Studies," *Encyclopedia of Educational Research,* 5th edition (New York: Macmillan, The Free Press, 1982), vol. 2, pp. 656–70; Eleanor D. Macklin and Roger H. Rubin, eds., *Contemporary Families and Alternative Lifestyles: Handbook on Research and Theory* (Beverly Hills, Calif.: Sage Publications, 1983); Rosalie G. Genovese, ed., *Families and Change: Social Needs and Public Policies* (New York: Praeger Special Studies—Praeger Scientific, 1984); Paul Bohannan, *All the Happy Families: Exploring the Varieties of Family Life* (New York: McGraw-Hill, 1985); Daniel Patrick Moynihan, *Family and Nation* (New York: Harcourt, Brace, Jovanovich, 1986); and Shirley Bryce Heath and Milbrey Wallin McLaughlin, "A Child Resource Policy: Moving Beyond Dependence on School and Family," *Phi Delta Kappan,* April 1987, pp. 574–80.

6. David L. Angus, "Families Against the System: 50 Years of Survival, 1880–

1930," paper presented at American Educational Studies Association, Washington, D.C., November 3, 1978.

7. For an overview of the varieties of nontraditional families and the child-rearing practices associated with them, see Michael E. Lamb, ed., *Nontraditional Families: Parenting and Child Development* (Hillsdale, N.J.: Laurence Erlbaum Associates, 1982).

8. Bohannan, *All the Happy Families,* p. 1.

Chapter 2

1. Lawrence A. Cremin, *American Education: The Colonial Experience, 1607–1783* (New York: Harper and Row, 1970); *American Education: The National Experience, 1783–1876* (New York: Harper and Row, 1980); and *American Education: The Metropolitan Experience* (New York: Harper and Row, 1988). Intimations of the contents of Cremin's three volumes are given in his *Traditions of American Education* (New York: Basic Books, 1977). Our book, written together, was a pioneer in relating American education to intellectual, political, economic, and cultural history: R. Freeman Butts and Lawrence A. Cremin, *A History of Education in American Culture* (New York: Holt, 1953).

2. For the colonial period and its background in Europe, see R. Freeman Butts, *The Education of the West* (New York: McGraw-Hill, 1973), especially chs. 8 and 12. For the period from the Revolution onward, see R. Freeman Butts, *Public Education in the United States* (New York: Holt, Rinehart, and Winston, 1978).

3. For revisionist studies of the family and community during the colonial period, see John Demos, *A Little Commonwealth: Family Life in Plymouth Colony* (New York: Oxford University Press, 1970); Philip J. Greven, Jr., *Four Generations: Population, Land, and Family in Colonial Andover, Massachusetts* (Ithaca, N.Y.: Cornell University Press, 1970); Kenneth A. Lockridge, *A New England Town, The First Hundred Years: Dedham, Massachusetts, 1636–1736* (New York: Norton, 1870); and Michael Zuckerman, *Peaceable Kingdome: New England Towns in the Eighteenth Century* (New York: Knopf, 1970).

4. Ross Beales, "In Search of the Historical Child," in Ray Hiner and Joseph M. Hawes, eds., *Growing Up in America: Children in Historical Perspective* (Urbana and Chicago; University of Illinois Press, 1985), pp. 22–23.

5. Cremin, *American Education: The Colonial Experience,* p. 549.

6. For details, see R. Freeman Butts, *The American Tradition in Religion and Education* (Boston: Beacon Press, 1950).

7. Cremin, *American Education: The Colonial Experience,* p. 538.

8. See especially Frederick Rudolph, ed., *Essays on Education in the Early Republic* (Cambridge, Mass.: Harvard University Press, 1965); and Wilson

Smith, ed., *Theories of Education in Early America 1655–1819* (New York: Bobbs-Merrill, 1973).

9. Gordon S. Wood, *The Creation of the American Republic, 1776–1787* (Chapel Hill: University of North Carolina Press, 1969).

10. Edgar W. Knight and Clifton L. Hall, eds., *Readings in American Educational History* (New York: Appleton-Century-Crofts, 1951), p. 113.

11. Ibid., pp. 299–300.

12. Ibid., p. 115.

13. *The People Shall Judge: Readings in the Formation of American Policy* (Chicago: University of Chicago Press, 1949), vol. I, p. 253.

14. Julian P. Boyd, ed., *The Papers of Thomas Jefferson,* vol. 9 (Princeton, N.J.: Princeton University Press, 1954), p. 151.

15. David Tyack and Thomas James, "Education for a Republic: Federal Influence on Public Schooling in the Nation's First Century," *this Constitution,* Winter 1985, pp. 17–24.

16. Benjamin Rush, "Thoughts Upon the Mode of Education Proper in a Republic" in Frederick Rudolph, ed., *Essays on Education in the Early Republic,* pp. 13, 15, and 17.

17. Noah Webster, "On the Education of Youth in America," in Frederick Rudolph, ed., *Essays on Education in the Early Republic,* p. 45.

18. Robert Coram, "Political Inquiries: To Which Is Added, a Plan for the General Establishment of Schools throughout the United States" in Rudolph, *Essays,* p. 113.

19. John C. Fitzpatrick, ed., *The Writings of George Washington* (Washington, D.C.: Government Printing office, 1940), vol. 30, p. 493.

20. Samuel Harrison Smith, "Remarks on Education: Illustrating the Close Connection between Virtue and Wisdom," in Rudolph, *Essays,* p. 210.

21. Samuel Knox, "An Essay on the Best System of Liberal Education, Adapted to the Genius of the Government of the United States," in Rudolph, *Essays,* p. 315.

22. Ibid., p. 368.

23. See the somewhat conflicting views of this development by Carl F. Kaestle, *The Evolution of an Urban School System, New York City, 1750–1850* (Cambridge, Mass.: Harvard University Press, 1973); and Diane Ravitch, *The Great School Wars: New York City, 1805–1973* (New York: Basic Books, 1974).

24. See Eugene D. Genovese, *Roll, Jordan, Roll: The World the Slaves Made* (New York: Pantheon, 1972); Winthrop D. Jordan, *White over Black: American Attitudes Toward the Negro, 1550–1812,* (Baltimore, Md.: Penguin, 1968); Ira Berlin, *Slaves Without Masters: The Free Negro in the Antebellum South* (New York: Pantheon, 1974); David Brion Davis, *The Problem of Slavery in the Age of the Revolution, 1720–1823* (Ithaca, N.Y.: Cornell University Press, 1975); and Herbert G. Gutman, *The Black Family in Slavery and Freedom, 1750–1925* (New York: Pantheon, 1976).

25. See Barbara Finkelstein, "Uncle Sam and the Children: A History of

Government Involvement in Child Rearing," in Hiner and Hawes, eds., *Growing Up in America,* pp. 255–66.

26. Mary Beth Norton, *Liberty's Daughters: The Revolutionary Experience of American Women, 1750–1800* (Boston: Little, Brown, 1980), p. 256.

27. Linda K. Kerber, *Women of the Republic: Intellect and Ideology in Revolutionary America* (Chapel Hill: University of North Carolina Press, 1980), p. 193. See also John Rury, "Education in the New Women's History," *Educational Studies,* Spring 1986, pp. 1–15.

28. Robert V. Wells, "Family History and Demographic Transition," in Hiner and Hawes, eds., *Growing Up in America,* pp. 61–85.

29. Robert H. Bremner, ed., *Children and Youth in America: A Documentary History* (Cambridge, Mass.: Harvard University Press, 1970), vol. I, p. 146.

30. Ibid., p. 148.

31. Ibid., p. 182.

32. David J. Rothman in a review of Bremner in *The Journal of Interdisciplinary History,* Autumn, 1971, pp. 367–77.

33. Jan Lewis, *The Pursuit of Happiness: Family and Values in Jefferson's Virginia* (New York: Cambridge University Press, 1983).

34. Daniel P. Jordan, *Political Leadership in Jefferson's Virginia* (Charlottesville: University Press of Virginia, 1983).

35. Joseph F. Kett, *Rites of Passage: Adolescence in America, 1790 to the Present* (New York: Basic Books, 1977), p. 85.

Chapter 3

1. For elaboration of the modernization theme in relation to Western education, its justification, and bibliographical references, see R. Freeman Butts, *The Education of the West* (New York: McGraw-Hill, 1973).

2. Michael Kammen, *People of Paradox: An Inquiry Concerning the Origins of American Civilization* (New York: Random House, Vintage, 1973), pp. 60–61.

3. Ibid., p. 85.

4. Robert H. Wiebe, *The Segmented Society: An Introduction to the Meaning of America* (New York: Oxford University Press, 1975), p. x.

5. Ibid., p. 19.

6. Anthony F. C. Wallace, *Rockdale: The Growth of an American Village in the Early Industrial Revolution* (New York: Knopf, 1978).

7. Paul Boyer, *Urban Masses and Moral Order in America, 1820–1920* (Cambridge, Mass.: Harvard University Press, 1978).

8. David B. Tyack, "The Spread of Public Schooling in Victorian America: In Search of a Reinterpretation," paper prepared for Social Science History Association, Nov. 3–5, 1978; and Daniel Walker Howe, ed., *Victorian America* (Philadelphia: University of Pennsylvania Press, 1976).

9. Robert Kelley, "Ideology and Political Culture from Jefferson to Nixon,"

American Historical Review, vol. 82, 1977, pp. 531–62; and *The Cultural Pattern in American Politics* (New York: Knopf, 1979).

10. For an excellent summary of this historical scholarship on a wide range of topics, see William H. Cartwright and Richard L. Watson, Jr., eds., *The Reinterpretation of American History and Culture* (New York: National Council for the Social Studies, 1973). Especially useful here are the chapters on race and nationality in Part II and chapters on "The Jacksonian Era, 1824–1848" by Frank Otto Gatell; or "Politics from Reconstruction to 1900" by Walter T. K. Nugent; and "The Progressive Years, 1900–1917" by Robert H. Wiebe.

11. For the best overall study of schools and modernization in the cities, see David Tyack, *The One Best System: A History of American Urban Education* (Cambridge, Mass.: Harvard University Press, 1974). The subject of the modernization theme related to urban education has received much scholarly attention since the publication of an early revisionist study by Michael B. Katz, *The Irony of Early School Reform: Educational Innovation in Mid-Nineteenth Century Massachusetts* (Cambridge, Mass.: Harvard University Press, 1968). His "hard" class analysis has been multiplied in a number of successive studies, but also modified and moderated by several more recent studies. See e.g., Maris A. Vinovskis, *The Origins of Public High Schools: A Reexamination of the Beverly High School Controversy* (Madison: University of Wisconsin Press, 1985); David John Hogan, *Class and Reform: School and Society in Chicago, 1880–1930* (Philadelphia: University of Pennsylvania Press, 1985); and Ira Katznelson and Margaret Weir, *Schooling for All: Class, Race, and the Decline of the Democratic Ideal* (New York: Basic Books, 1985). These latter studies, among others, have revealed the complexity, subtlety, and interrelations of social class, labor, ethnicity, and race in American education.

12. Robert H. Wiebe, *The Search for Order, 1877–1920* (New York: Hill and Wang, 1967).

13. For extensive documentation of original sources on campaigns for reform of child labor, rights of parents and children, aid to dependent children, child welfare services, compulsory attendance, juvenile delinquency, and health care, see Robert H. Bremner, ed., *Children and Youth in America: A Documentary History, Vol. II, 1866–1932* (Cambridge, Mass.: Harvard University Press, 1971).

14. Barbara Finkelstein, "Uncle Sam and the Children," in N. Ray Hiner and Joseph M. Hawes, eds., *Growing Up in America: Children in Historical Perspective* (Urbana and Chicago: University of Illinois Press, 1985).

15. For details, see Walter Trattner, *Crusade for the Children: A History of the National Child Labor Committee and Child Labor Reform in America* (Chicago: Quadrangle Books, 1970).

16. Wiebe, *The Segmented Society,* p. 45.

17. Quoted in Michael B. Katz, ed., *School Reform: Past and Present* (Boston: Little, Brown, 1971), pp. 284–86.

18. Quoted in Bremner, *Children and Youth in America, Vol. I, 1600–1865,* pp. 455–57.

19. For engrossing details of the conflict between Catholics and the Protestant-oriented Public School Society in New York City, see Diane Ravitch, *The Great School Wars* (New York: Basic Books, 1974).

20. John Higham, *Strangers in the Land: Patterns of American Nativism, 1860–1925* (New York: Atheneum, 1974), chapter 2.

21. *Meyer v. Nebraska,* 262 U.S. 390 (1923).

22. *Pierce v. Society of Sisters,* 268 U.S. 510 (1925).

23. Horace M. Kallen, *Culture and Democracy in the United States* (New York: Boni and Liveright, 1924).

24. See, e.g., Robert A. Carlson, *The Quest for Conformity: Americanization Through Education* (New York: Wiley, 1975).

25. In addition to Higham, *Strangers in the Land,* see, e.g., Milton M. Gordon, *Assimilation in American Life: The Role of Race, Religion, and National Origins* (New York: Oxford University Press, 1964); and Leonard Dinnerstein and David M. Reimers, *Ethnic Americans: A History of Immigration and Assimilation* (New York: Dodd, Mead, 1975).

26. Timothy Smith, "Immigrant Social Aspirations and American Education, 1880–1930," *American Quarterly,* Fall 1969, p. 542.

27. David K. Cohen, "Immigrants and the Schools," *Review of Educational Research,* February 1970, p. 24.

28. Michael R. Olneck and Marvin Lazerson, "The School Achievement of Immigrant Children," *History of Education Quarterly,* Winter 1974, pp. 453–82.

29. Stephan Thernstrom, *The Other Bostonians: Poverty and Progress in the American Metropolis, 1880–1970* (Cambridge, Mass.: Harvard University Press, 1973); see also Thomas Kessner, *The Golden Door: Italian and Jewish Immigrant Mobility in New York City, 1880–1915* (New York: Oxford University Press, 1977).

30. Quoted in Bremner, *Children and Youth in America,* vol. II, p. 1189.

31. *Plessy v. Ferguson,* 163 U.S. 537 (1896).

32. See, e.g., Guadalupe San Miguel, Jr., "Status of the Historiography of Chicano Education: A Preliminary Analysis," *History of Education Quarterly,* Winter 1986, pp. 523–36.

33. David Hogan, "Education and the Making of the Chicago Working Class, 1880–1930," *History of Education Quarterly,* Fall 1978.

34. Quoted in David Tyack, ed., *Turning Points in American Educational History* (Waltham, Mass.: Blaisdell, 1967), p. 236.

35. Ibid., p. 238.

36. Alan Wieder, "From Cheerleader to Skeptic: The Immigrant Family and American Schooling," paper delivered at American Educational Studies Association, Washington, D.C., Nov. 3, 1978. For general background, see Irving Howe, *World of Our Fathers* (New York: Harcourt, Brace, Jovanovich, 1976).

37. David Angus, "Families Against the System: 50 Years of Survival, 1880–

1930," paper delivered at American Educational Studies Association, Washington, D.C., Nov. 3, 1978, p. 8.

38. See notes 4 and 5 of the introduction to Part I. For the period dealt with in this chapter, see Tamara K. Harevan, *Family Time and Educational Time* (New York: Cambridge University Press, 1982); Ronald D. Goodenow and Diane Ravitch, eds., *Schools in Cities: Consensus and Conflict in American Educational History* (New York: Holmes and Meier, 1983); and the critical essay review of Goodenow and Ravitch by David J. Hogan, "Whither the History of Urban Education," *History of Education Quarterly,* Winter 1985, pp. 527–41.

39. See Tamara K. Harevan and Maris Vinovskis, eds., *Family and Population in Nineteenth Century America* (Princeton, N.J.: Princeton University Press, 1978).

40. Daniel Patrick Moynihan, *The Negro Family* (Washington, D.C.: U.S. Department of Labor, 1965); also see Lee Rainwater and William L. Yancey, eds., *The Moynihan Report and the Politics of Controversy* (Cambridge, Mass.: Massachusetts Institute of Technology, 1967).

41. For a useful listing of monograph studies on black families, see Lawrence A. Cremin, "The Family as Educator: Some Comments on the Recent Historiography," *Teachers College Record,* December 1974, pp. 256 and 263. See particularly Elizabeth H. Pleck, "The Two-Parent Household: Black Family Structure in Late Nineteenth-Century Boston," *Journal of Social History,* vol. 6, 1973; and William Harris, "Work and the Family in Black Atlanta, 1880," *Journal of Social History,* vol. 9, Spring 1976.

42. Herbert G. Gutman, *The Black Family in Slavery and Freedom, 1750–1925* (New York: Pantheon, 1976). See also John W. Blassingame, *The Slave Community: Plantation Life in the Antebellum South* (New York: Oxford University Press, 1972); and Eugene J. Genovese, *Roll, Jordan, Roll: The World the Slaves Made* (New York: Pantheon, 1975).

43. Angus, "Families Against the System," p. 2.

44. Ibid., pp. 21–22.

45. Joseph F. Kett, "History of Age Grouping in America," in Report of the Panel on Youth of the President's Science Advisory Committee, *Youth: Transition to Adulthood* (Chicago: University of Chicago Press, 1974).

46. Joseph F. Kett, *Rites of Passage: Adolescence in America 1790 to the Present* (New York: Basic Books, 1977).

47. See, e.g., Arthur G. Wirth, *Education in the Technological Society: The Vocational-Liberal Studies Controversy in the Early Twentieth Century* (Scranton, Pa: Intext, 1971); and Marvin Lazerson and Norton W. Grubb, eds., *American Education and Vocationalism: A Documentary History, 1870–1970* (New York: Teachers College Press, 1974).

48. For the range of community pressures upon the schools, see David Tyack, "The History of Secondary Schools in Delivering Social Services," manuscript for National Institute of Education, June 1978.

49. See, for example, Paul C. Violas, *The Training of the Urban Working Class:*

A History of Twentieth Century American Education (Chicago: Rand McNally, 1978).

50. Ruth Miller Elson, *Guardians of Tradition: American Schoolbooks of the Nineteenth Century* (Lincoln, Nebr.: University of Nebraska Press, 1964), p. 338.
51. Ibid., p. 285.
52. Ibid., p. 340.
53. Lawrence A. Cremin, *The Republic and the School: Horace Mann on the Education of Free Men* (New York: Bureau of Publications, Teachers College, Columbia University, 1957), p. 93.
54. Ibid., p. 95.
55. Ibid., p. 97.
56. See, e.g., Diane Ravitch, "Decline and Fall of Teaching History," in *New York Times Magazine,* November 17, 1985; and Paul Gagnon, *Democracy's Untold Story: What World History Textbooks Neglect* (Washington, D.C.: American Federation of Teachers, 1987). For a full discussion of the role of history in social studies, see R. Freeman Butts, *The Morality of Democratic Citizenship* (Calabasas, Calif.: Center for Civic Education, 1988), ch. 1.
57. Quoted in Daniel Calhoun, ed., *The Education of Americans: A Documentary History* (Boston: Houghton Mifflin, 1969), p. 495.
58. Hazel W. Hertzberg, *Historic Parallels for the Sixties and Seventies: Primary Sources and Core Curriculum Revisited* (Boulder, Colo.: Social Science Education Consortium, Publication 135, 1971), pp. 11–12.
59. National Education Association, Commission on the Reorganization of Secondary Education, *Cardinal Principles of Secondary Education,* U.S. Bureau of Education, Bulletin 35 (Washington, D.C.: Government Printing Office, 1918), p. 14.
60. Ibid.

Chapter 4

1. Robert H. Wiebe, *The Segmented Society* (New York: Oxford University Press, 1975), pp. 8–9 and pp. 108–205.
2. Nathan Glazer, *Affirmative Discrimination* (New York: Basic Books, 1975), pp. 12–20.
3. John Higham, "Another American Dilemma," *The Center Magazine,* vol. 7, no. 4, July/August 1974, pp. 67–74.
4. See; e.g., Michael Novak, *The Rise of the Unmeltable Ethnics* (New York: Macmillan, 1972); Nathan Glazer and Daniel Patrick Moynihan, *Beyond the Melting Pot* (Cambridge, Mass.: Massachusetts Institute of Technology Press, 1963); Lawrence H. Fuchs, ed., *American Ethnic Politics* (New York: Harper and Row, 1968); Edgar Litt, *Ethnic Politics in America* (Glenview, Ill.: Scott Foresman, 1970); Andrew M. Greeley, *Why Can't They Be Like Us?* (New York: American Jewish Committee, 1968); Andrew M. Greeley, *The American Catholic: A Social Portrait* (New York: Basic Books, 1977);

Peter Schrag, *The Decline of the WASP* (New York: Simon and Schuster, 1971); William M. Newmann, *American Pluralism: A Study of Minority Groups and Social Theory* (New York: Harper and Row, 1973).

5. Michael Novak, "The New Ethnicity." *The Center Magazine,* July/August 1974, pp. 18–19.
6. Ibid., p. 25.
7. Andrew M. Greeley, "The Ethnic Miracle," *The Public Interest,* no. 45, Fall 1976, p. 29.
8. Robert Nisbet, *Twilight of Authority* (New York: Oxford University Press, 1975), p. 278.
9. Milton Friedman, *Capitalism and Freedom* (Chicago: University of Chicago Press, 1962); and Milton Friedman and Rose Friedman, *Free to Choose* (New York: Harcourt, Brace, Jovanovich, 1979).
10. Nisbet, *Twilight,* p. 278.
11. Ibid., p. 286.
12. See, e.g., Henry J. Perkinson, *Two Hundred Years of American Educational Thought* (New York: McKay, 1976), pp. 282–352.
13. Clarence Karier, Paul Violas, and Joel Spring, *Roots of Crisis: American Education in the Twentieth Century* (Chicago: Rand McNally, 1973), p. 5. See also Michael B. Katz, *Class, Bureaucracy, and Schools* (New York: Praeger, 1971), ch. 3; and Joel Spring, *A Primer of Libertarian Education* (New York: Free Life Editions, 1975); and Samuel Bowles and Herbert Gintis, *Schooling in Capitalist America: Educational Reform and the Contradictions of Economic Life* (New York: Basic Books, 1976). For revisions of revisionists, see Ira Katznelson and Margaret Weir, *Schooling for All: Class, Race and the Decline of the Democratic School* (New York: Basic Books, 1985).
14. *History of Citizen Education Colloquium Papers* (Philadelphia: Research for Better Schools, April 19–20, 1978; see also Final Report submitted to National Institute of Education, July 31, 1978).
15. Robert Nozick, *Anarchy, State, and Utopia* (New York: Basic Books, 1974), p. ix.
16. Ibid., pp. 320–21.
17. Ibid., p. 322.
18. Theodore R. Sizer, "Education and Assimilation: A Fresh Plea for Pluralism," *Phi Delta Kappan,* September 1976, p. 34.
19. Ibid.
20. Ibid., p. 35.
21. Arthur G. Powell, Eleanor Farrar, and David K. Cohen, *The Shopping Mall High School: Winners and Losers in the Educational Marketplace* (Boston: Houghton Mifflin, 1985).
22. See, for example, the special issue of *Harvard Educational Review,* August 1972; and Vernon Smith, Robert Barr, and Daniel Burke, *Alternatives in Education* (Bloomington, Ind.: Phi Delta Kappa, 1976).
23. See, e.g., Williams Snider, "The Call for Choice: Competition in the Educational Marketplace," a special 24-page section of *Education Week,* June 24, 1987; Joe Nathan, "Results and Future Prospects Of State Efforts to

Increase Choice Among Schools," *Phi Delta Kappan,* June 1987, pp. 67–73; and Charles L. Glenn, "The New Common School," *Phi Delta Kappan,* December 1987, pp. 290–94, a preview of his book, *The Myth of the Common School* (Amherst: University of Massachusetts Press, 1988).

24. David B. Tyack, "The History of Secondary Schools in Delivering Social Services," unpublished paper prepared for the National Institute of Education, June 1978.
25. *Meyer* v. *Nebraska,* 262 U.S. 390 (1923).
26. *Pierce* v. *Society of Sisters,* 268 U.S. 510 (1925).
27. *Minersville* v. *Gobitis,* 310 U.S. 586 (1940).
28. Ibid.
29. *West Virginia* v. *Barnette,* 319 U.S. 624 (1943).
30. *Wisconsin* v. *Yoder,* 406 U.S. 213 (1972).
31. Ibid.
32. Robert M. Hutchins, "The Schools Must Stay," *The Center Magazine,* Jan./ Feb. 1973, vol. 6, p. 1.
33. R. Freeman Butts, "The Public School: Assaults on a Great Idea," *The Nation,* April 30, 1973; *Compulsory Education: Responsibilities and Alternatives,* Regional Conference, U.S. Office of Education, Overland Park, Kansas, December 3–4, 1975.
34. Stephen Arons, *Compelling Belief: The Culture of American Schooling* (New York: McGraw-Hill, 1983). Arons continued these arguments on behalf of language-minority children, eliciting strong rebuttals; see, e.g., *Education Week,* October 1, 22, and 29, 1986.
35. See, for example, John E. Coons and Stephen D. Sugarman, *Education by Choice: The Case for Family Control* (Berkeley: University of California Press, 1978); and Thomas James and Henry M. Levin, *Public Dollars for Private Schools: The Case of Tuition Tax Credits* (Philadelphia: Temple University Press, 1983).
36. James C. Carper and Neal E. Devins, "The State and the Christian Day School," in James E. Wood, Jr., ed., *Religion and the State: Essays in Honor of Leo Pfeffer* (Waco, Texas: Baylor University Press, 1985), pp. 211–32. See also James C. Carper and Thomas C. Hunt, eds., *Religious Schooling in America* (Birmingham, Ala.: Religious Education Press, 1984). For revealing insights into the way sacred values shape civic values inside a fundamentalist school, carefully done by an outsider, see Alan Peshkin, *God's Choice: The Total World of a Fundamentalist Christian School* (Chicago: University of Chicago Press, 1986).
37. Stephen R. Graubard, "Confronting the Obvious: Social Class and its Devastating Effects on American Schooling," *Daedalus,* Summer 1983, pp. 208–09.
38. Coons and Sugarman, *Education by Choice;* for background arguments see John E. Coons, Stephen D. Sugarman, and William H. Clune, *Private Wealth and Public Education* (Cambridge, Mass.: Harvard University Press, 1970).
39. "An Initiative for Family Choice in Education," draft of March 5, 1979.

40. R. Freeman Butts, "Educational Vouchers: The Private Pursuit of the Public Purse," *Phi Delta Kappan*, September 1979, pp. 7–9.

41. Joe Nathan, "Results and Future Prospects of State Efforts to Increase Choice Among Schools," *Phi Delta Kappan*, June 1987, pp. 746–52.

42. Deborah Meier, "Central Park East: An Alternative Story," *Phi Delta Kappan*, June 1987, pp. 753–57.

43. Mary Anne Raywid, "Public Choice, Yes; Vouchers, No!" *Phi Delta Kappan*, June 1987, pp. 762–69.

44. John E. Chubb and Terry M. Moe, "No School Is An Island: Politics, Markets, and Education," *The Brookings Review*, Fall 1986. This article is based on a forthcoming book by Chubb and Moe, *Politics, Markets, and School Performance*. Their study is based on the longitudinal survey *High School and Beyond*, upon which the controversial and influential books by James S. Coleman and his colleagues were based: *High School Achievement: Public, Catholic and Private Schools Compared* (New York: Basic Books, 1982) and *Public and Private High Schools: The Impact of Communities* (New York: Basic Books, 1987). See also James S. Coleman, "Families and Schools," *Educational Researcher*, August/September 1987, pp. 32–38.

45. Lee M. Wolfle, "Enduring Cognitive Effects of Public and Private Schools," *Educational Researcher*, May 1987, p. 10.

46. Daniel Yankelovich, *The New Morality: A Profile of American Youth in the Seventies* (New York: McGraw-Hill, 1974).

47. Daniel Yankelovich, *New Rules: Searching for Self-Fulfillment in a World Turned Upside Down* (New York: Random House, 1981).

48. Daniel Patrick Moynihan, *Family and Nation* (San Diego: Harcourt, Brace, Jovanovich, 1986).

49. Current Population Reports, Population Characteristics, *Marital Status and Living Arrangements: March, 1984* (Washington, D.C.: U.S. Bureau of Census, July 1985). See also 1987 publications of the Children's Defense Fund and the House Select Committee on Children, Youth, and Families.

50. For contrasting views of the role of government and schools in relation to family life, see Kenneth Keniston, *All Our Children: The American Family Under Pressure.* (New York: Harcourt, Brace, Jovanovich, 1977).

51. Presidential Panel on the Family, *New York Times,* November 14, 1986. Critical of both conservatives and liberals, University of Chicago sociologist William Julius Wilson counters conservative claims that the welfare state causes poor family life; see his *The Truly Disadvantaged: The Inner City, the Underclass, and Public Policy* (Chicago: University of Chicago Press, 1987).

52. J. R. Reingold and Associates, *Current Federal Policies and Programs for Youth* (Washington, D.C.: William T. Grant Foundation Commission on Youth and America's Future, June 1987); James Wetzel, *America's Youth: A Statistical Snapshot* (Washington, D.C.: William T. Grant Foundation Commission on Youth and America's Future, July 1987); and *The Forgotten Half: Non-College-Bound Youth* (Washington, D.C.: William T. Grant Foundation Commission on Youth and America's Future, 1988).

53. Anne C. Lewis, "Who Will Mind the Children?" *Phi Delta Kappan,* December 1987, pp. 252–53.
54. Forum of Educational Organization Leaders, *Education Week,* June 10, 1987.
55. Perry London, "Character Education and Clinical Intervention: A Paradigm Shift for U.S. Schools," *Phi Delta Kappan,* May 1987, p. 668.
56. Ibid., pp. 671–72.
57. George J. McKenna III, "Why 'Demanding Black Families' Are Not the Solution," *Education Week,* December 3, 1986. McKenna was also at odds with another black principal, Joe Clark, of Eastside High School of Paterson, N.J., who gained notoriety and the cover of *Time* for his bullhorn and baseball bat tactics in enforcing discipline in his inner-city school; see "Getting Tough," *Time,* February 1, 1988, pp. 52–58.
58. *The New York Times Book Review,* December 11, 1977.
59. See, for example, Carole E. Jaffe, *Friendly Introducers: Childcare Professionals and Family Life* (Berkeley: University of California Press, 1977); and Sally Provence, Audrey Naylor, and June Patterson, *The Challenge of Daycare* (New Haven, Conn.: Yale University Press, 1977).
60. Beatrice Paolucci and Stanley P. Wronski, "The American Family and Social Education," *Social Education,* October 1977, p. 470.
61. J. W. Getzels, "Socialization and Education: A Note on Discontinuities," *Teachers College Record,* December 1974, pp. 218–25.
62. For excellent historical documentation, see Robert H. Bremner, ed., *Children and Youth in America,* vol. III (Cambridge, Mass.: Harvard University Press, 1974).
63. *In Re Gault,* 387 U.S. 1 (1967).
64. Harold Howe II, "The Prospect for Children in the United States," *Phi Delta Kappan,* November 1986, pp. 191–96.
65. *Parham* v. *J.R.,* 442 U.S. 584 (1979).
66. Human Development Services, *Child Abuse and Neglect: State Reporting Laws* (Washington, D.C.: U.S. Department of Health and Human Services, May 1978). For a detailed look at child protective legislation and judicial decisions, see Robert H. Mnookin, *Child, Family, and State: Problems and Materials on Children and the Law* (Boston: Little, Brown 1978); Robert H. Mnookin, ed., *In the Interest of Children: Advocacy Law Reform and Public Policy* (New York: W. H. Freeman, 1985); and Linda Gordon, *Heroes of Their Own Lives; The Politics and History of Family Violence: Boston 1880–1960* (New York: Viking, 1988).
67. David L. Clark and Terry A. Astuto, "The Significance and Permanance of Changes in Federal Education Policy," *Educational Researcher,* October 1986, p. 13.
68. Robert Constable and Herbert J. Walberg, "The New Thrust Toward Partnership of Parents and Schools," *The Journal of Family and Culture,* Fall 1987.
69. Terrel H. Bell, interviewed in *The Chronicle of Higher Education,* March 18, 1987, p. 28, regarding his book, *The Thirteenth Man: A Reagan Cabinet Memoir* (New York: Free Press, 1987).

Part II

Chapter 5

1. See, for example, the summary volume: Charles E. Merriam, *The Making of Citizens: A Comparative Study of Methods of Civic Training* (Chicago: University of Chicago Press, 1931).
2. John Dewey, *The Public and Its Problems* (New York: Henry Holt, Swallow Press, 1954), p. 15.
3. Ibid., p. 63.
4. See, for example, Charles A. Beard, *A Charter for the Social Sciences* (New York: Scribner's, 1932); Bessie L. Pierce, *Citizens Organizations and the Civic Training of Youth* (New York: Scribner's, 1933); Charles E. Merriam, *Civic Education in the United States* (New York: Scribner's, 1934); Jesse H. Newlon, *Educational Administration as Social Policy* (New York: Scribner's, 1934); George S. Counts, *The Social Foundations of Education* (New York: Scribner's, 1934); Merle E. Curti, *The Social Ideas of American Educators* (New York: Scribner's, 1934); Rollo M. Tryon, *The Social Sciences as School Subjects* (New York: Scribner's, 1935); Howard K. Beale, *Are American Teachers Free?* (New York: Scribner's, 1936); Howard K. Beale, *A History of Freedom of Teaching in American Schools* (New York, Scribner's 1941); and *Conclusions and Recommendations of the Commission* (New York: Scribner's 1934).
5. Quoted from a letter to Charles Beard from Counts, Horn, and Newlon, dated April 19, 1930, on file in the Counts archives at Southern Illinois University, Carbondale; Courtesy of Lawrence Dennis.
6. See, for example, George S. Counts, *Dare the School Build a New Social Order?* (New York: John Day, 1932); William H. Kilpatrick, ed., *The Educational Frontier* (New York: Century, 1933); Harold Rugg, *Culture and Education in America* (New York: Harcourt, Brace, 1931); and John L. Childs, *Education and Morals* (New York: Appleton-Century-Crofts, 1950).
7. National Education Association, Educational Policies Commission, *The Unique Function of Education in American Democracy* (Washington, D.C.: National Education Association, 1937).
8. National Education Association, Educational Policies Commission, *The Purposes of Education in American Democracy* (Washington, D.C.: National Education Association, 1938), p. 108.
9. Quoted in Citizenship Education Project, *Building Better Programs in Citizenship Education* (New York: Teachers College, Columbia University, 1958), p. 273.
10. See, for example, *Improving Citizenship Education: Policies and Procedures of the Citizenship Education Project* (New York: Teachers College, Columbia University, 1952); *Resources for Citizenship: A Guide to the Selection of Teaching Materials* (New York: Teachers College, Columbia University, 1955); William S. Vincent, et al., *Building Better Programs in Citizenship: A Guide for Teachers, Administrators, and College Instructors* (New York: Teachers

College, Columbia University, 1958); *Laboratory Practices in Citizenship: Learning Experiences in the Community* (New York: Teachers College, Columbia University, 1958); and a text for secondary-school students, *When Men Are Free: Premises of American Liberty* (Boston: Houghton Mifflin, 1955).

11. For a well-rounded analysis of the project, see Richard W. Streb, "A History of the Citizenship Education Project: A Model Curriculum Study" (Ed. D. Diss., Teachers College, Columbia University, 1979).

12. American Association of School Administrators, *Educating for American Citizenship* (Washington, D.C.: AASA, 1954), p. 5.

13. Diana L. Reische, *Citizenship: Goal of Education* (Washington, D.C.: American Association of School Administrators, 1987).

14. Ryland W. Crary, ed., *Education for Democratic Citizenship* (Washington, D.C.: National Council for the Social Studies, 1951).

15. Erling M. Hunt, et al., *High School Social Studies: Perspectives* (Boston: Houghton Mifflin, 1962), pp. 99–100.

16. *Social Education,* vol. 36, no. 7, November 1972.

17. National Assessment of Educational Progress, *Changes in Political Knowledge and Attitudes, 1969–1976* (Denver: Education Commission of the States, March 1978).

18. Ibid., pp. 59–61. The consultants were Anna Ochoa of Indiana University and president-elect of the National Council for the Social Studies; Celeste Woodley, social-studies specialist for the Boulder Valley (Colorado) schools; and myself.

19. American Political Science Association, Committee on Pre-Collegiate Education, "Political Education in the Public Schools: The Challenge for Political Science," *PS,* Newsletter of the American Political Science Association, Summer 1971, vol. IV, no. 3, p. 7. The general findings are characteristic of other writings in political socialization and political science. See, for example, Frederick M. Wirt and Michael W. Kirst, *The Political Web of American Schools* (Boston: Little, Brown, 1972).

20. Richard E. Gross, "The Status of the Social Studies in the Public Schools of the United States: Facts and Impressions of a National Survey," *Social Education,* March 1977, pp. 194–200 and 205.

21. Ibid., p. 199.

22. John Jarolimek, "The Status of Social Studies Education: Six Case Studies," *Social Education,* November/December 1977, pp. 575–76.

23. James P. Shaver, O. L. Davis, Jr., and Suzanne W. Helburn, "An Interpretive Report on the Status of Pre-College Social Studies Education Based on Three NSF-Funded Studies" (Washington, D.C.: National Council for the Social Studies, 1978). See also *Social Education,* October 1979, pp. 515–18.

24. See especially, *Social Education,* January 1986, articles by Harriet Tyson-Bernstein and Arthur Woodward, "The Great Textbook Machine and Prospects for Reform," pp. 41–45; Raymond English, "Can Social Studies Textbooks Have Scholarly Integrity?" pp. 46–48; Carl E. Schomberg, "Texas and Social Studies Texts," pp. 58–60; and Kathy Postel Kretman

and Barbara Parker, "New U.S. History Texts: Good News and Bad," pp. 61–63.

25. Frances FitzGerald, *America Revised* (New York: Atlantic-Little Brown, 1979).

26. Michael Novak, Jeane Kirkpatrick, and Anne Crutcher, *Values in an American Government Textbook* (Washington, D.C.: Ethics and Public Policy Center, 1978). For similar disputes over the portrayal of ethnic minorities in American history textbooks, see Nathan Glazer and Reed Ueda, *Ethnic Groups in History Textbooks* (Washington, D.C.: Ethics and Public Policy Center, 1983).

27. Jean Anyon, "Ideology and United States History Textbooks," *Harvard Educational Review*, August 1979, pp. 361–86.

28. Paul C. Vitz, "Religion and Traditional Values in Public-School Textbooks: An Empirical Study," (Washington, D.C.: National Institute of Education, Final Report G84-0012; Project No. 2-0012; Equity in Values Education, 1986; O. L. Davis, Jr., et al., *Looking at History: A Review of Major U.S. History Textbooks* (Washington, D.C.: People for the American Way, 1986), and Charles C. Haynes, *Religious Freedom in America* (Silver Spring, Md.: Americans United Research Foundation, 1986).

29. Paul Gagnon, *Democracy's Untold Story: What World History Textbooks Neglect* (Washington, D.C.: American Federation of Teachers, 1987).

30. Arthur N. Applebee, Judith A. Langer, and Ina V. S. Mullis, *Literature & U.S. History: The Instructional Experience and Factual Knowledge of High School Juniors* (Princeton, N.J.: Educational Testing Service, 1987); and Diane Ravitch and Chester E. Finn, Jr., *What Do Our 17-Year-Olds Know?* (New York: Harper and Row, 1987).

31. National Assessment of Educational Progress, "Citizenship and Social Studies Achievement of Young Americans 1981–82; Performance and Changes Between 1976 and 1982" (Denver: Education Commission of the States, October 1983), p. 13.

32. Ibid., p. 24.

33. For the "state of the art" in the 1970s, see National Task Force on Citizenship Education, *Education for Responsible Citizenship* (New York: McGraw-Hill, 1977); Elizabeth Farquhar and Karen S. Dawson, *Citizen Education Today: Developing Civic Competencies* (Washington, D.C.: U.S. Office of Education, 1979); LeAnn Meyer, *Programs and Problems: The Citizenship Education Issue* (Denver: Education Commission of the States, 1979); Byron G. Massialas and Judith V. Torney, *Behavior Variables Related to Citizen Education Objectives* (Philadelphia: Research for Better Schools, 1978); Mary Jane Turner, *Who Teaches Citizenship? A Survey of Documents and Resources* (Boulder, Colo.: ERIC Clearinghouse and Social Science Education Consortium, 1977); and Byron G. Massialas, "Education and Political Development," *Comparative Education Review*, June/October 1977, pp. 274–95.

34. "In Search of a Scope and Sequence for Social Studies," *Social Education*, April 1984, pp. 249–63.

35. "Scope and Sequence: Alternatives for Social Studies," *Social Education,* November/December 1986, pp. 484–541.

36. Arthur S. Link, "The American Historical Association 1884–1984: Retrospect and Prospect," *American Historical Review,* February 1987, p. 16.

37. Useful publications include *Law-Related Education: Guidelines for the Future* (St. Paul, Minn.: West Publishing Co., 1975); *Teaching Teachers About Law* (Chicago: American Bar Association, 1976); *Directory of Law-Related Education Projects,* (Chicago: American Bar Association, periodically revised); *Update on Law-Related Education,* published three times a year; Lynda Carl Falkenstein and Charlotte C. Anderson, eds., *Daring to Dream: Law and the Humanities for Elementary Schools* (Chicago: American Bar Association, 1980); and Mary Jane Turner and Lynn Parisi, *Law in the Classroom* (Boulder, Colo.: Social Science Education Consortium, 1984).

38. The titles published by the U.S. Office of Education, Washington, D.C., in 1978 were: Ann Parker Maust and Lucy Knight, *An Analysis of the Role of the U.S. Office of Education and Other Selected Federal Agencies in Citizen Education;* Larry Rothstein, *New Directions in Mass Communications Policy: Implications for Citizen Education and Participation; Examining the Role of the Workplace in Citizen Education;* Nea Carroll Toner and Walter B. Toner, Jr., *Citizen Participation: Building a Constituency for Public Policy;* Robert H. Salisbury, *Key Concepts of Citizenship: Perspectives and Dilemmas;* and Willis W. Harman, *Citizen Education and the Future.*

39. *Final Report of the U.S. Office of Education Study Group on Law-Related Education* (Washington, D.C.: U.S. Government Printing Office, 1979), pp. 1–2.

40. Paul A. Freund, "Law in the Schools: Goals and Methods," *Social Education,* May 1973, p. 363.

41. *Federal Register,* Vol. 44, No. 127, Friday, June 29, 1979.

42. Carole L. Hahn, "The Status of the Social Studies in the Public Schools of the United States: Another Look," *Social Education,* March 1985.

43. American Bar Association, Special Committee on Youth Education for Citizenship, *Mandate for Change: The Impact of Law on Educational Innovation* (Chicago: American Bar Association, 1979). See especially chapter 3.

44. LeAnn Meyer, *Programs and Problems,* p. 33.

45. Mark Blum, *Ethical-Citizenship Education Policies and Programs: A National Survey of State Education Agencies* (Philadelphia: Research for Better Schools, Spring 1977).

46. Fred M. Newmann, "Alternative Approaches to Citizenship Education: A Search for Authenticity," National Task Force on Citizenship Education, *Education for Responsible Citizenship,* pp. 180–84.

47. Center for Statistics, Office of Educational Reseach and Improvement, *Bulletin,* Washington, D.C., U.S. Department of Education, September 1986, p. 9.

48. Fred M. Newmann, *Education for Citizen Action: Challenge for Secondary Curriculum* (Berkeley, Calif.: McCutchan, 1975) and Fred M. Newmann, Thomas A. Bertocci, and Ruthanne M. Landsness, *Skills in Citizen Action:*

An English-Social Studies Program for Secondary Schools (Madison: University of Wisconsin, 1977).

49. Fred M. Newmann, *Educational Reform and Social Studies: Implications of Six Reports* (Boulder, Colo.: Social Science Education Consortium, 1985).

50. Robert A. Rutter, "Profile of the Profession," *Social Education,* April–May 1986.

51. See Fred M. Newmann, "Priorities for the Future," *Social Education,* April–May 1986; and James Shaver's response to this article in *Social Education,* November–December 1986; and Newmann's response to him, *Social Education,* April–May 1987, pp. 232–33.

52. John D. Haas, "A Social Studies Professional Library," *Social Education,* January 1987, pp. 60–72.

53. See, for example, *Report of the State of Maryland Values Education Commission* (Baltimore: Maryland State Department of Education, 1983).

54. The Council for the Advancement of Citizenship. 1724 Massachusetts Avenue, N.W., Washington, D.C. 20036.

55. Paul R. Hanna, *Assuring Quality for the Social Studies in Our Schools* (Stanford, Calif.: Hoover Institution Press, 1987), p. 32.

56. Ibid., p. 38.

57. See, for example, Diane Ravitch, "Tot Sociology: Or What Happened to History in the Grade Schools, " *The American Scholar,* Summer 1987.

58. Shirley H. Engle and Anna S. Ochoa, *Education for Democratic Citizenship: Decision Making in the Social Studies* (New York: Teachers College Press, 1988).

59. Donald Oliver and Fred M. Newmann, *Taking a Stand* (Boulder, Colo.: Social Science Education Consortium, 1988).

60. Susan Douglas Franzosa, ed., *Civic Education: Its Limits and Conditions* (Ann Arbor, Mich.: Prakken Publications, 1988).

61. Ibid., p. 161.

Chapter 6

1. Report of a Survey by Louis Harris and Associates, *Redesigning America's Schools: The Public Speaks* (Washington, D.C.: Carnegie Forum on Education and the Economy, 1986).

2. Carnegie Forum on Education and the Economy, *A Nation Prepared: Teachers for the 21st Century; The Report of the Task Force on Teaching as a Profession* (Washington, D.C.: Carnegie Forum on Education and the Economy, 1986), p. 3.

3. Ibid., pp. 14–15.

4. Charles Frankel, "The Academy Enshrouded," *Change* December 1977, pp. 25 and 64.

5. For elaboration of these views, see R. Freeman Butts, *The College Charts Its Course* (New York: McGraw-Hill, 1939, reprint edition by Arno Press,

1971); *The Education of the West* (New York: McGraw-Hill, 1973); *The Revival of Civic Learning* (Bloomington, Ind.: Phi Delta Kappa Educational Foundation, 1980), ch. 2; and *The Morality of Democratic Citizenship: Goals For Civic Education in America's Third Century* (Calabasas, Calif.: Center for Civic Education, 1988). See also David W. Robson, *The College in the Age of the Revolution* (Westport, Conn.: Greenwood Press, 1985); Bruce A. Kimball, *Orators and Philosophers: A History of the Idea of Liberal Education* (New York: Teachers College Press, 1986); and Jack C. Lane, "The Yale Report of 1828 and Liberal Education," *History of Education Quarterly,* Fall 1987, pp. 325–38.

6. John C. Fitzpatrick, ed., *The Writings of George Washington* (Washington, D.C.: U.S. Government Printing Office, 1940), vol. 35, p. 317.

7. Saul K. Padover, ed., *The Complete Jefferson* (New York: Duell, Sloan and Pearce, 1943), p. 1098.

8. Gordon C. Lee, ed., *Crusade Against Ignorance: Thomas Jefferson on Education* (New York: Teachers College, Columbia University, 1961), pp. 136–37.

9. Butts, *The College Charts Its Course,* part IV.

10. See Alexander Meiklejohn, *The Experimental College* (New York: Harper, 1932); and Meiklejohn, *The Experimental College,* edited and abridged by John Walker Powell (Washington, D.C.: Seven Locks Press, 1981).

11. In Karl Kaysen, ed., *Content and Context: Essays on College Education,* a report prepared for the Carnegie Commission on Higher Education (New York: McGraw-Hill, 1973), pp. 54–57.

12. Arthur Levine, *Handbook on Undergraduate Curriculum,* a report prepared for the Carnegie Council on Policy Studies in Higher Education (San Francisco: Jossey-Bass, 1977), pp. 344–47 and 373–76.

13. Ernest L. Boyer and Arthur Levine, *A Quest for Common Learning: The Aims of General Education* (Washington, D.C.: Carnegie Foundation for the Advancement of Teaching, 1981), ch. 2.

14. A conversation with James B. Conant at the Columbia University Faculty Club, New York City, November 17, 1960, concerning *General Education in a Free Society,* Report of the Harvard Committee (Cambridge, Mass.: Harvard University Press, 1945). See especially Conant's introduction.

15. Boyer and Levine, *Quest for Common Learning,* p. 58.

16. Ibid., pp. 23–26.

17. Gerald Grant and David Riesman, *The Perpetual Dream: Reform and Experiment in the American College* (Chicago: University of Chicago Press, 1978), part II. They single out Evergreen College as something of a bellwether of the "overoptioned life" (p. 366). See Richard M. Jones, *Experiment at Evergreen* (Cambridge, Mass.: Schenkman, 1981). Jones makes it clear that Evergreen's coordinated programs followed the Meiklejohn-Tussman model of pedagogic processes and team teaching but did not follow the Meiklejohn-Tussman model of a prescribed curriculum and common reading. See chs. 1 and 2, especially pp. 21–24.

18. Joseph Tussman, *Experiment at Berkeley* (New York: Oxford University Press, 1969), p. 120.

19. Mervyn L. Cadwallader, "Experiment at San Jose," a paper presented to the 1981 Conference on Alternative Higher Education, Evergreen State College, Olympia, Washington, p. 6.
20. Ibid., p. 9.
21. Grant and Riesman, *The Perpetual Dream,* part I and appendix 1.
22. Carnegie Commission on Higher Education, *The Purposes and Performance of Higher Education in the United States: Approaching the Year 2000* (New York: McGraw-Hill, 1973), pp. 1–2, 54, and 92.
23. Frederick Rudolph, *The American College and University: A History* (New York: Knopf, 1962); and *Curriculum: A History of the American Undergraduate Course of Study Since 1936* (San Francisco: Jossey-Bass, 1977).
24. Carnegie Foundation for the Advancement of Teaching, *Missions of the College Curriculum: A Contemporary Review with Suggestions* (San Francisco: Jossey-Bass, 1977), pp. 164 and 184.
25. Ernest L. Boyer and Martin Kaplan, *Educating for Survival* (New Rochelle, N.Y.: Change Magazine Press, 1977), pp. 56 and 59.
26. Boyer and Levine, *Quest for Common Learning,* p. 35.
27. Ernest L. Boyer and Fred M. Hechinger, *Higher Learning in the Nation's Service* (Washington, D.C.: Carnegie Foundation for the Advancement of Teaching, 1981), p. 47.
28. Ibid., p. 48.
29. *The Humanities in American Life,* Report of the Rockefeller Foundation Commission on the Humanities (Berkeley and Los Angeles: University of California Press, 1980), p. 12.
30. Boyer and Levine, *Quest for Common Learning,* p. 25.
31. Butts, *Revival of Civic Learning,* ch. 5.
32. "The Civic Purposes of Liberal Learning," a special issue of *Liberal Education,* Winter 1982, cosponsored by the Kettering Foundation and the Association of American Colleges. See also a special issue of *National Forum* on "The Citizen and the Government," Spring 1981, especially articles by guest editor David Mathews ("Thinking About the Citizen and Government") and Mark H. Curtis ("Reflections on the Civic Purpose of Liberal Learning").
33. For a special report by Larry McGehee on "The Coming of the Civic Arts Network," see *The Antaeus Report,* issued by Bernard Murchland of Ohio Wesleyan University, Spring 1985, with a selected bibliography; and Suzanne Morse, "Partners in Public Leadership Education Project," *Connections,* Spring 1988 (Dayton, Ohio: Kettering Foundation).
34. "The Civic Education of the American Teacher," a special issue of *The Journal of Teacher Education,* November/December 1983.
35. R. Freeman Butts, *Teacher Education and the Revival of Civic Learning* (Minneapolis, Minn.: Society of Professors of Education, February 18, 1982); and R. Freeman Butts et al., Ayers Bagley, ed., *Civic Learning in Teacher Education* (Minneapolis, Minn.: Society of Professors of Education, 1983).
36. Association of American Colleges, *Integrity in the College Curriculum: A*

Report to the Academic Community (Washington, D.C.: The Association, 1985).

37. National Institute of Education, *Involvement in Learning: Realizing the Potential of American Higher Education* (Washington, D.C.: Government Printing Office, 1984).

38. William J. Bennett, *To Reclaim a Legacy: A Report on the Humanities in Higher Education* (Washington, D.C.: National Endowment for the Humanities, 1984).

39. Allan Bloom, *The Closing of the American Mind: How Higher Education Has Failed Democracy and Impoverished the Souls of Today's Students* (New York: Simon and Schuster, 1987). For an insightful view of Bloom and his critics, see James Atlas, "Chicago's Grumpy Guru," in *New York Times Magazine,* January 3, 1988. For Bernard Murchland's summation, see "Higher Education After Bloom," *The Antaeus Report,* The Center for the Study of Education and Society, Ohio Wesleyan University, Winter 1988, p. 1.

40. Frank Newman, *Higher Education and the American Resurgence* (Princeton, N.J.: Princeton University Press, 1985). Quotation from text in *Chronicle of Higher Education,* September 18, 1985, pp. 17 and 22.

41. Headquarters for Campus Compact is Box G, Brown University, Providence, RI 02912; see, e.g., *Chronicle of Higher Education,* October 23, 1985, and January 21, 1987. See also Association of American Colleges, "Promoting Civic Literacy," *The Forum for Liberal Education,* March 1985. For information about the Public Leadership Education Project, write Suzanne Morse, Kettering Foundation, 200 Commons Road, Dayton, OH 45459.

42. Education Commission of the States, *Transforming the State Role in Undergraduate Education: Time for a Different View* (Denver, Colo.: The Commission, 1986).

43. American Association of State Colleges and Universities, *To Secure the Blessings of Liberty,* a report of the National Commission on the Role and Future of State Colleges and Universities (Washington, D.C.: The Association, 1986).

44. Ernest L. Boyer, *College: The Undergraduate Experience in America* (New York: Harper and Row, 1987), pp. 7–8. For comments on the student union as a "laboratory of citizenship," a topic Boyer did not discuss, see Porter Butts, "The Union as Community Center," *Bulletin of the Association of College Unions—International,* November 1987, pp. 30–31; for historical background, see Porter Butts, *The College Union Idea* (Stanford, Calif.: Association of College Unions—International, 1971).

45. *New York Times,* November 9, 1986. Fiske dealt with teacher education in the special section of the *New York Times,* April 12, 1987.

46. Alexander W. Astin and Kenneth C. Green, *The American Freshman: Twenty Year Trends, 1960–1985* (Los Angeles: Higher Education Research Institute, Graduate School of Education, University of California, Los Angeles, 1986). Reported in *Chronicle of Higher Education,* November 5, 1986. Astin's data for 1987 are reported in *Education Week,* January 20, 1988. See "Allure

of Teaching Reviving; Education School Rolls Surge," *New York Times,* May 6, 1988.

47. Grant and Riesman, *The Perpetual Dream,* p. 387 onward.

48. Powell, *Meiklejohn's Experimental College,* pp. 110–11.

49. Alexander Meiklejohn, "The American College and American Freedom," an address delivered at the reunion of the Experimental College held at St. John's College, Annapolis, Md., on May 10, 1957, on the 25th anniversary of the closing of the college and Meiklejohn's 85th birthday. Quoted in Cynthia Stokes Brown, ed., *Alexander Meiklejohn: Teacher of Freedom* (Berkeley, Calif.: Meiklejohn Civil Liberties Institute, 1981), p. 107.

50. Leonard P. Oliver, "Teaching Civic Values and Political Judgment in the Community College," in Judith Eaton, ed., *Colleges of Choice* (New York: Macmillan, 1987), pp. 197–98.

51. Ibid., p. 211. For a strong affirmation that community colleges should require a core of common learning, see the report of a commission headed by Ernest L. Boyer, *Building Communities: A Vision for a New Century* (Alexandria, Va.: American Association of Community and Junior Colleges, 1988).

52. For the final debate and the complete text of CIV as adopted by the Faculty Senate on March 31, 1988, see Stanford University, *Campus Report,* April 6, 1988; for Secretary Bennett's lecture and replies to it by university officials, see ibid., April 20, 1988; for the text of the Bennett/Kennedy debate on the MacNeil/Lehrer Newshour on April 19, 1988, see ibid., April 27, 1988.

53. California Commission on the Teaching Profession, *Who Will Teach Our Children? A Strategy for Improving California's Schools* (Sacramento, Calif.: The Commission, November 1985).

54. National Governors' Association, *Time for Results: The Governors' 1991 Report on Education* (Washington, D.C.: The Association, 1986).

55. Quoted in *Chronicle of Higher Education,* September 3, 1986, p. 84.

56. Quoted in *Education Week,* September 10, 1986, p. 37.

57. National Commission for Excellence in Teacher Education, *A Call for Change in Teacher Education,* (Washington, D.C.: American Association of Colleges for Teacher Education, 1985).

58. Ibid., p. 31.

59. *Tomorrow's Teachers: A Report of the Holmes Group* (East Lansing, Mich.: 501 Erickson Hall, Michigan State University, 1986).

60. For the list of member institutions, see *Education Week,* November 26, 1986, p. 9.

61. Excerpted from *Chronicle of Higher Education,* April 9, 1986, p. 27.

62. Ibid., p. 36.

63. Derek Bok, "The Challenge to Schools of Education," *Harvard Magazine,* May–June 1987.

64. William R. Johnson, "Empowering Practitioners: Holmes, Carnegie, and the Lessons of History," *History of Education Quarterly,* Summer 1987, pp. 221–40.

65. B. Othanel Smith, "Now Is the Time to Advance Pedagogical Education," *Educational Theory,* Summer 1980, pp. 177–83; and the special issue of *The Kappan,* October 1980 on "Reform in Teacher Education," which Smith wrote for and edited.

66. Harry S. Broudy, *What Do Professors of Education Profess?* Fourth Annual De Garmo Lecture (Minneapolis, Minn.: Society of Professors of Education, February 28, 1979), p. 13.

67. Donald Kennedy, "Advancing Knowledge," Seventy-Fifth Anniversary Colloquium of the Carnegie Foundation for the Advancement of Teaching, November 23, 1981, quoted from the text published in the Stanford University *Campus Report,* November 25, 1981, p. 14.

68. Bok, "Challenge to Schools of Education," *Harvard Magazine,* May–June 1987.

69. Denis P. Doyle and Marsha Levine, "Myths and Shadows: Some Preliminary Observations on Education and the Private Sector in an Era of Limits," prepared for Public Policy Week, December 7–11, 1981 (Washington, D.C.: The American Enterprise Institute for Public Policy Research), abstract p. 1.

70. Quoted in Daniel Calhoun, *The Educating of Americans: A Documentary History* (Boston: Houghton Mifflin, 1969), pp. 182–83.

71. Quoted in Merle L. Borrowman, ed., *Teacher Education in America: A Documentary History* (New York: Teachers College Press, 1965), pp. 90–92.

72. Ibid., pp. 206–07.

73. R. Freeman Butts, "Reflections on Forty Years in the Foundations Department at Teachers College," delivered on the occasion of the William H. Kilpatrick Award in Philosophy of Education, April 11, 1975, pp. 25–28, unpublished. See Hanna Collection, Archives of the Hoover Institution, Stanford University, for primary sources on the teaching of social foundations at Teachers College, 1935–1955. Mark B. Ginsburg seriously underestimates our attention to class and gender in his article, "Teacher Education and Class and Gender Relations: A Critical Analysis of Historical Studies of Teacher Education," *Educational Foundations,* Spring 1987, pp. 4–36.

74. Borrowman, *Teacher Education,* pp. 236–37.

75. See E. S. Evenden and R. Freeman Butts, *Columbia University Cooperative Program for the Pre-Service Education of Teachers* (New York: Teachers College, Columbia University, 1942).

76. James B. Conant, *The Education of American Teachers* (New York: McGraw-Hill, 1963), p. 113–14.

77. For the text of the open letter and the signatories, see *Chronicle of Higher Education,* September 23, 1987.

78. R. Freeman Butts, *Teacher Education and the Revival of Civic Learning* (Minneapolis, Minn.: Society of Professors of Education, 1982).

79. R. Freeman Butts and others, *Civic Learning in Teacher Education,* SPE Monograph Series 1983, Ayers Bagley, ed. (Minneapolis, Minn.: Society of Professors of Education, 1983).

80. Mary Anne Raywid, Charles A. Tesconi, Jr., and Donald R. Warren, *Pride*

and Promise: Schools of Excellence for All the People (Westbury, N.Y.: Pride and Promise, AESA, 1984).

81. Alan H. Jones, ed., *Civic Learning for Teachers: Capstone for Educational Reform* (Ann Arbor, Mich.: Prakken Publications, 1985).

82. James B. Conant, "A Truce Among Educators," *Teachers College Record,* December 1944, pp. 162–63.

83. Jones, *Civic Learning,* pp. 12–147.

84. The *New York Times,* March 22, 1987.

85. Jones, *Civic Learning,* pp. 166–68.

86. Survey data compiled by Penelope Early, director of federal and state relations, American Association of Colleges for Teacher Education, One Dupont Circle, N.W., Washington, D.C., 20036.

87. Center for the Study of the Teaching Profession, *Annual Report,* October 1985 to September 1986 (Washington, D.C.: Rand, 1986).

88. *Education Week,* April 22, 1987, p. 25.

89. *Education Week,* March 18, 1987, p. 10. See also, "Liberal Arts Colleges Wary of Teacher-Training Shifts," *Education Week,* November 4, 1987.

90. *Education Week,* March 18, 1987, p. 1.

91. Thomas S. Popkewitz, "Improving Teaching and Teacher Education," *Social Education,* November/December 1987, p. 495. See also pp. 496–521.

92. For the membership of the National Board for Professional Teaching Standards, see *Education Week,* October 21, 1987, p. 7.

93. Lee Shulman and Gary Sykes, "A National Board for Teaching? In Search of a Bold Standard," Carnegie Forum on Education, May 1986.

94. Lee S. Shulman, "An Assessment for Teaching: An Initiative for the Profession," *Phi Delta Kappan,* September 1987, p. 41. See also Samuel S. Wineburg and Suzanne M. Wilson, "Models of Wisdom in the Teaching of History," *Phi Delta Kappan,* September 1988, pp. 50–58.

95. Ibid., p. 43.

96. Jan L. Tucker, "Citizenship Education Through the Eyes of Elementary School Principals," the Social Science Education Consortium, Hoover Institution, Stanford University, June 19, 1986.

97. Robert Stout, "Executive Action and Values," *Issues in Education,* Winter 1986, pp. 198–214.

98. Geraldine Joncich Clifford and James W. Guthrie, *Ed School: A Brief for Professional Education* (Chicago: University of Chicago Press, 1988).

Chapter 7

1. Quoted in Paul Monroe, ed., *Source Book of the History of Education for the Greek and Roman Period* (New York: Macmillan, 1901, 1908), p. 345. Benjamin Jowett and S. H. Butcher, eds. and trans., *Aristotle's Politics and Poetics* (New York: Heritage Press, 1964).

2. *Report of the State of Maryland Values Education Commission* (Baltimore, Md.:

Maryland State Department of Education, January 31, 1983); Edward Wynne, "A List of Values," *Character II* (September/October 1986); Chester E. Finn, Jr., "Giving Shape to Cultural Conservatism," *The American Spectator* (November 1986); and E. D. Hirsch, Jr., *Cultural Literacy: What Every American Needs to Know* (Boston: Houghton Mifflin, 1987).

3. See, e.g., John Rawls, *A Theory of Justice* (Cambridge, Mass.: Harvard University Press, 1971); Michael J. Sandel, *Liberalism and the Limits of Justice* (New York: Cambridge University Press, 1982); Michael Walzer, *Spheres of Justice: A Defense of Pluralism and Equality* (New York: Basic Books, 1983); Ronald Dworkin, *A Matter of Principle* (Cambridge, Mass.: Harvard University Press, 1985); Lawrence Friedman, *Total Justice* (New York: Basic Books, 1985); and Bruce A. Ackerman, *Social Justice in the Liberal State* (New Haven, Conn.: Yale University Press, 1980). For curriculum materials, kindergarten through twelfth grades, see Law in a Free Society, *Justice* (Calabasas, Calif.: Center for Civic Education, 1979); and *Update on Law-Related Education* (Chicago: American Bar Association, Spring 1987).

4. Rawls, *Theory of Justice*, p. 302.

5. Ibid., p. 61.

6. See, e.g., Robert Nozick, *Anarchy, State, and Utopia* (New York: Basic Books, 1974); and William R. Torbert, "Doing Rawls Justice," *Harvard Educational Review*, November 1974.

7. Michael Walzer, *Spheres of Justice: A Defense of Pluralism and Equality* (New York: Basic Books, 1983), p. 203.

8. For my views on freedom, see R. Freeman Butts, "Freedom and Responsibility in American Education," *Teachers College Record*, December 1952, pp. 117–24; and "The Free Man in the Free Society,' ch. 12 in *What Is the Nature of Man? Images of Man in Our American Culture* (Philadelphia: Christian Education Press, 1959), pp. 146–60.

9. See Robert O'Neil, *Classrooms in the Crossfire* (Bloomington, Ind.: University of Indiana Press, 1980). For an excellent high-school text on freedom, see Isidore Starr, *The Idea of Liberty: First Amendment Freedoms* (St. Paul, Minn.: West Publishing Co., 1978). For articles on freedom of teaching and censorship in schools, see *Update on Law-Related Education*, especially Spring and Fall 1985 and Winter 1986; and *Social Education*, October 1987. See also Leonard Levy, et al., *Encyclopedia of the American Constitution* (New York: Macmillan, 1986); articles entitled: Academic Freedom; *Adler v. Board of Education;* Bill of Rights; Civil Liberties; Establishment of Religion; Family and the Constitution; First Amendment; Freedom of Association; Freedom of Petition; Freedom of the Press; Freedom of Speech; Loyalty Oaths; Public Forum; Religion in Public Schools; Religious Liberty; Separation of Church and State; Virginia Statute of Religious Liberty.

10. See Levy, *Encyclopedia of the American Constitution*, articles entitled: Affirmative Action; *Brown v. Board of Education;* Children's Rights; Civil Rights; Civil Rights Act of 1964; Desegregation; Discrete and Insular Minorities; Equal Protection of the Laws; Fourteenth Amendment; Incorporation;

Racial Discrimination; Racial Quotas; Segregation; Separate But Equal Doctrine; Sex Discrimination.

11. *Brown* v. *Board of Education*, 347 U.S. 483 (1954). The excruciating tension between the majestic ruling of the Supreme Court and the tugs of home, church, tavern, and neighborhood is vividly portrayed in the lives of three families in Boston wrenched by the demands of desegregation in a book by J. Anthony Lukas, *Common Ground: A Turbulent Decade in the Lives of Three American Families* (New York: Knopf, 1985). See also Richard Kluger, *Simple Justice: The History of Brown v. Board of Education and Black America's Struggle for Equality* (New York: Knopf, 1976); and Gary Orfield, *Must We Bus? Segregated Schools and National Policy* (Washington, D.C.: Brookings Institution, 1978).

12. Nozick, *Anarchy, State, and Utopia.*

13. David K. Kirp, Mark G. Yudof, and Marlene Strong Franks, *Gender Justice* (Chicago: University of Chicago Press, 1986). Compare with Nathan Glazer, *Affirmative Discrimination: Ethnic Inequality and Public Policy* (New York: Basic Books, 1974).

14. See, e.g., Robert H. Wiebe, *The Segmented Society: An Historical Preface to the Meaning of America* (New York: Oxford University Press, 1975); Milton M . Gordon, *Assimilation in American Life: The Role of Race, Religion, and National Origins* (New York: Oxford University Press, 1964); and John Higham, "Integration vs. Pluralism: Another American Dilemma," *The Center Magazine*, July/August 1974, pp. 67–73. For debates over "English only" in several states, see articles by James Crawford in *Education Week*, June 17, 1987; and for special reports on bilingual education, see *Education Week*, March 18, March 25, and April 1, 1987.

15. Higham, "Integration vs. Pluralism," pp. 72–73.

16. Michael Kammen, *People of Paradox: An Inquiry Concerning the Origins of American Civilization* (New York: Vintage Books, 1973), p. 85.

17. See Donald L. Horowitz, *Ethnic Groups in Conflict* (Berkeley, Calif.: University of California Press, 1985); and Levy, *Encyclopedia of the American Constitution*, articles on American Indians and the Constitution; Chinese Exclusion Act; and *Lau* v. *Nichols*. For useful materials to aid teachers to teach about the "new immigration," see the articles and bibliographies in *Social Education*, March 1986.

18. Leonard Krieger, "The Idea of Authority in the West," *American Historical Review*, April 1977, pp. 249–70.

19. John W. Gardner, *The Nature of Leadership: Introductory Considerations* (Washington, D.C.: Independent Sector, 1986), p. 6.

20. Richard Flathman, "Citizenship and Authority: A Chastened View of Citizenship," *News for Teachers of Political Science*, Summer 1981, pp. 9–19.

21. Kenneth D. Benne, *A Conception of Authority* (New York: Teachers College, Columbia University, 1943; New York: Russell and Russell, 1971); David Nyberg, *Power Over Power* (Ithaca, N.Y.: Cornell University Press, 1981); Henry A. Giroux, "Authority, Intellectuals, and the Politics of Practical Learning," *Teachers College Record*, Fall 1986. See also articles by David

Nyberg and Paul Farber, Kenneth Benne, Dale Mann, and others. For excellent curricular materials for grades kindergarten through 12, see Law in a Free Society, *Authority* (Calabasas, Calif.: Center for Civic Education, 1977). For constitutional issues, see Levy, *Encyclopedia of the American Constitution*, articles on Compelling State Interest and Federalism.

22. See Levy, *Encyclopedia of the American Constitution;* see articles entitled Abortion and the Constitution, Fourth Amendment (Historical Origins), *Griswold* v. *Connecticut, New Jersey* v. *T.L.O.*, Privacy and the First Amendment, *Right of Privacy, Roe* v. *Wade*, Searches and Seizures, *Substantive Due Process*, and Unreasonable Search.

23. See, for example, Alan F. Westin, *Privacy and Freedom* (New York: Atheneum Press, 1970); Charles Fried, *An Anatomy of Values* (Cambridge, Mass.: Harvard University Press, 1970); and J. Roland Pennock and John W. Sherman, eds., *Privacy* (New York: Atherton Press, 1971). For curriculum materials, kindergarten through twelfth grade, see Law in a Free Society, *Privacy* (Calabasas, Calif.: Center for Civic Education, 1979).

24. *Wort* v. *Vierling*, U.S. District Court for the Central District of Illinois, September 1984.

25. *New Jersey* v. *T.L.O.*, 469 U.S. 325 (1985).

26. Levy, ed., *Encyclopedia of the American Constitution;* see articles entitled: Children's Rights; Double Jeopardy; Exclusionary Rule; Fair Trial; Fifth Amendment; Fourteenth Amendment; *In Re Gault; Goss* v. *Lopez;* Habeas Corpus; Juvenile Proceedings; Loyalty-Security Programs; Miranda Ruling; Procedural Due Process, Civil; Procedural Due Process, Criminal; Right Against Self-Incrimination; Trial by Jury.

27. Law in a Free Society, *Justice* (Calabasas, Calif.: Center for Civic Education, 1979); Constitutional Rights Foundation, *Living Law: Civil Justice* (New York: Scholastic Book Services, 1978); Constitutional Rights Foundation, *Living Law: Criminal Justice* (New York: Scholastic Book Services, 1978); National Street Law Institute, *Street Law: A Course in Practical Law* (St. Paul, Minn.: West Publishing Co., 1975; 3rd ed. 1986); and American Bar Association, *Update on Law-Related Education*, Spring 1987 and Fall 1983.

28. Isidore Starr, *Justice: Due Process of Law* (St. Paul, Minn.: West Publishing Co., 1981); and Louis Fischer and David Schimmel, *The Civil Rights of Teachers* (New York: Harper and Row, 1973); David Schimmel and Louis Fischer, *The Civil Rights of Students* (New York: Harper and Row, 1975); and David Schimmel and Louis Fischer, *The Rights of Parents in the Education of their Children* (Columbia, Md.: National Committee for Citizens in Education, 1977). See also, Alan Levine, et al., *The Rights of Students: The Basic ACLU Guide to a Student's Rights* (New York: Richard Baron, 1973); David Rubin, *The Rights of Teachers* (New York: Bantam Books, 1984); and Martin Guggenheim and Alan Sussman, *The Rights of Young People* (New York: Bantam, 1985).

29. *Goss* v. *Lopez*, 419 U.S. 565 (1975).

30. See, for example, Elmer U. Clawson, *Our Economy: How It Works* (Menlo Park, Calif.: Addison-Wesley, 1984); and *Model Curriculum Standards: Grades*

Nine Through Twelve (Sacramento, Calif.: California State Department of Education, 1985), pp. HS 51–59.

31. See Law in a Free Society, *On Property* (Calabasas, Calif.: Center for Civic Education, 1974); and American Bar Association, *Update on Law-Related Education,* Spring 1987.

32. See Levy, *Encyclopedia of the American Constitution,* articles entitled Affected with a Public Interest, Contract Clause, *Dartmouth College* v. *Woodward, Dred Scott* v. *Sandford,* Due Process of Law, Economic Liberties, Economic Regulation, Eminent Domain, Freedom of Contract, Natural Rights, Obligation of Contracts, Police Power, Public Purpose, Substantive Due Process, Social Compact, State Police Power, Taking of Property.

33. Betty Southard Murphy, "The Commercial Republic and the Dignity of Work," *National Forum,* Fall 1984, pp. 49–52; and Jack P. Greene, "The Pursuit of Happiness: The Private Realm, Commerce, and the Constitution," *this Constitution,* Fall 1985, p. 40.

34. Charles A. Lofgren, "To Regulate Commerce": Federal Power under the Constitution," *this Constitution,* Spring 1986, pp. 4–11.

35. Kenneth M. Holland, "The Constitution and the Welfare State," *this Constitution,* Summer 1986, pp. 18–23. See also Charles A. Reich, "The New Property," *The Yale Law Journal,* April 1964, esp. pp. 771–74 and 778–86.

36. Stephen K. Bailey, *The Purposes of Education* (Bloomington, Ind.: Phi Delta Kappa, 1976), pp. 84–94.

37. See Edward Schwartz, *The Institute Papers: Towards a Recovery of Civic Idealism* (Philadelphia: Institute for the Study of Civic Values, 1975) and the analysis in Robert N. Bellah, et al., *Habits of the Heart* (Berkeley: University of California Press, 1985), esp. pp. 214–18; see also Peter Berger, *To Empower People: The Role of Mediating Structures and Public Policy* (Washington, D.C.: American Enterprise Institute for Public Policy Research, 1977).

38. Benjamin R. Barber, *Strong Democracy: Participatory Politics for a New Age* (Berkeley: University of California Press, 1984); and Benjamin R. Barber, "Voting is Not Enough," *Atlantic Monthly,* June 1984, p. 52. Compare with Levy, *Encyclopedia of the American Constitution,* articles on Citizenship, Popular Sovereignty, and Voting Rights.

39. David Mathews, *Democracy: Principles and Practices* (Dayton, Ohio: Domestic Policy Association, September 1986).

40. Robert S. Peck and Mary Manemann, eds., *Speaking and Writing Truth: Community Forums on the First Amendment* (Chicago: American Bar Association, 1985). See also Levy, *Encyclopedia of the American Constitution,* articles on Libel and the First Amendment, Seditious Libel.

41. Robert N. Bellah, et al., *Habits of the Heart: Individualism and Commitment in American Life* (New York: Harper and Row, 1985). For curriculum materials stressing citizens' obligations, kindergarten through grade 12, see Law in a Free society, *Responsibility* (Calabasas, Calif.: Center for Civic Education, 1979).

42. Morris Janowitz, *The Reconstruction of Patriotism: Education for Civic Consciousness* (Chicago: University of Chicago Press, 1983).

43. See, e.g., Michael Walzer, *Obligations: Essays on Disobedience, War, and Citizenship* (Cambridge, Mass.: Harvard University Press, 1970); Duane E. Smith, "The Case for Patriotism," *Freedom at Issue,* May/June 1973, pp. 9–13; John W. Gardner, *Morale* (New York: W. W. Norton, 1978); People for the American Way, *Quarterly Report,* June 1981, p. 1; Jack Beatty, "The Patriotism of Values," *The New Republic,* July 4 and 11, 1981; R. W. Apple, Jr., "New Stirrings of Patriotism," *New York Times Magazine,* December 11, 1983; Orrin G. Hatch, "Civic Virtue: Wellspring of Liberty," *National Forum,* Fall 1984, pp. 34–38; Frank Newman, *Higher Education and the American Resurgence* (Princeton, N.J.: Princeton University Press, 1985); Neely D. McCarter "The Church and Patriotism," *Pacific School of Religion Bulletin.* Fall 1986; The Patriotic Majority, "Toward a Patriotic Rebirth: A Patriotic Agenda for the 100th Congress," adv., *New York Times,* January 25, 1987, p. 24.

44. Richard Danzig and Peter Szanton, *National Service: What Would It Mean?* (New York: Ford Foundation 1986).

45. For emphasis on global interdependence as it relates to education see, for example, Lee Anderson, *Schooling and Citizenship in a Global Age* (Bloomington, Ind.: Mid-America Program for Global Perspectives in Education, 1978); the Interdependence Series published by the Aspen Institute for Humanistic Studies, especially Ward Morehouse, *A New Civic Literacy: American Education and Global Interdependence* (Princeton, N.J.: Aspen Institute, October 1975). For more current studies, see the special issues on international human rights and global education in *Social Education,* September 1985, September 1986, and October 1986; the publications of Global Perspectives in Education, 45 John St., New York, N.Y. 10038; Social Science Education Consortium, Boulder, Colo.; Center for Teaching International Relations, University of Denver; Foreign Policy Association, New York City; Michigan Department of Education, Lansing; and New York State Education Department, Albany.

46. See, for example, Gregg L. Cunningham, "Blowing the Whistle on 'Global Education,' " (Denver: Regional Office, U.S. Department of Education, 1986). See the responses to Cunningham's study by Barry Simmons, director of the Center for Teaching International Relations at the University of Denver, and Andrew Smith, president of Global Perspectives in Education, in *The Social Studies Professional,* September/October 1986. In January 1987 the board of directors of the National Council for the Social Studies unanimously rejected Cunningham's argument, *Social Education,* April/May 1987, pp. 242–49.

47. Study Commission on Global Education, *The United States Prepares for its Future: Global Perspectives in Education* (New York: Global Perspectives in Education, 1987).

48. *Social Studies 9 and 10: Global Studies; Tentative Syllabus* (Albany: New York State Education Department, 1987).

49. See R. Freeman Butts, "International Human Rights and Civic Education," in Margaret Stimmann Branson and Judith Torney-Purta, eds., *International Human Rights, Society, and the Schools* (Washington, D.C.: National Council for the Social Studies, 1982), pp. 23–33.
50. *Model Curriculum for Human Rights and Genocide* (Sacramento: California State Department of Education, 1987).
51. For a useful compendium of the United Nations documents, see Thomas Burgenthal and Judith V. Torney, *International Human Rights and International Education* (Washington, D.C.: U.S. National Commission for UNESCO, 1976); see also Howard D. Mehlinger, ed., *UNESCO Handbook for the Teaching of Social Studies* (London: Croom Helm, 1981); Donald Vandenberg, *Human Rights in Education* (New York: Philosophical Library, 1983); and *The Teaching of Values and the Successor Generation* (Washington, D.C.: The Atlantic Council of the United States, 1983).
52. *The American Chicle Poll* (Morris Plains, N.J.: Warner-Lambert Company, 1987).
53. R. Freeman Butts, *The Morality of Democratic Citizenship: Goals for Civic Education in the Republic's Third Century* (Calabasas, Calif.: Center for Civic Education, 1988), pp. 183–84.

Index